500 MPRE
PRACTICE QUESTIONS FOR 2020

PROFESSIONAL RESPONSIBILITY
COURSE SUPPLEMENT
(REVISED AND UPDATED)

Professor Drury Stevenson

Cover photo: Stone frieze of law professor lecturing while his students sleep, from the main entrance of the Yale Law School. Photo © Rena Tobey, used by permission.

Note for law students:

These 500 sample questions have the same format and style as the questions on the current Multistate Professional Responsibility Exam (MPRE). The multiple-choice format also provides a useful way to test students' knowledge of each provision or clause in each of the Model Rules, as well as the drafters' official Comments (which the MPRE tests along with the Model Rules themselves). No other MPRE practice book currently on the market has as many sample questions, or as broad coverage, as this book.

The practice questions are also extremely useful in mastering the material covered in every Professional Responsibility/Legal Ethics course, which is a required course at every American law school.

The arrangement of topics in this book follows the order of how heavily the MPRE tests each Rule. The bar examiners publish useful information on their website, http://www.ncbex.org/exams/mpre, including a list of all topics tested, and how heavily the exam tests each separate topic: http://www.ncbex.org/pdfviewer/?file=%2Fdmsdocument%2F2. This book follows that order, but most Professional Responsibility courses do not, but these practice questions will still give students proficiency in the material covered throughout the course, in preparation for their final exam.

This compendium of questions is a supplement to the author's recently published Glannon Guide to Professional Responsibility (2nd ed.). The Glannon Guide provides detailed explanations for each of its questions (more than 220 questions), as well as a helpful introduction to each topic. This book provides only an answer key and a few citations to Model Rule subsections, the Restatement (Third) of the Law Governing Lawyers, ethics opinions, and court cases, but it has more questions. In addition, this book devotes special attention to topics covered less thoroughly in the Glannon Guide and law school courses materials generally, such as attorney-client privilege and legal malpractice. For best results, use the two books together.

"Rule" in the hints after the questions refers to the applicable provision of the ABA Model Rules of Professional Conduct (2018), the primary basis for the MPRE. "Restatement" in this book refers to the American Law Institute's RESTATEMENT OF THE LAW (THIRD) - THE LAW GOVERNING LAWYERS.

This is a revised and updated edition for 2020, and reflects the most recent amendments to the Model Rules.

Table of Contents

NOTE: "Lawyers' Duties to the Public and the Legal System" (2–4%, least tested subject on MPRE) subtopics are within prior sections

PART I:

HEAVILY TESTED SUBJECTS on the MPRE

[**NOTE:** In the author's law school courses on Professional Responsibility, PART I is material covered in the first half of the semester. If the class has a midterm exam, only the material in Part I is on the midterm.]

CONFLICTS OF INTEREST

RULE 1.7   CONFLICT OF INTEREST: CURRENT CLIENTS

1. Big Firm represents hundreds of corporate clients out of a dozen offices in different states. The firm has no formal procedures in place to check for conflicts at the outset of representation for new clients, but the managing partner of the firm has an incredible memory and has never failed to spot a potential conflict of interest in the past. An attorney agrees to represent a new corporate client that owns many subsidiaries, and checks with the managing partner, who assured Attorney there are no potential conflicts. After the new corporate client had disclosed a substantial amount of confidential information, it emerged that some of its subsidiaries were directly adverse to other clients of Big Firm. The attorney was completely unaware of the potential conflicts at the time he agreed to the representation, despite asking the corporate client a few questions about the opposing parties in pending litigation it might have. Will the attorney be subject to discipline for not declining representation in this case?

a)   Yes, because ignorance caused by a failure to institute reasonable procedures, appropriate for the size and type of firm and practice, will not excuse a lawyer's violation of the Rules regarding conflicts of interest.

b)   Yes, because there is a presumption that a company owning several subsidiaries will have at least one adverse interest to other clients of a Big Firm.

c)   No, as he was unaware of the conflict at the time, but now that the conflict is apparent, Attorney must withdraw from representation

d)   No, because the attorney at least partly relied upon the managing partner's prowess in identifying conflicts, given that the managing partner had never before made a mistake.

Rule 1.7 Cmt 3

2. An attorney sued Giant Company on behalf of a client in a personal injury matter. During the protracted litigation that ensued, Conglomerate bought Giant Company. The attorney was already representing Conglomerate in a regulatory compliance matter before a federal administrative agency. Assuming this development was unforeseeable at the outset of representing the client against Giant Company,

will the attorney have the option to withdraw from one of the representations to avoid the conflict?

a)   Yes, because one matter is in state court and the other matter is a completely unrelated federal administrative proceeding.

b)   Yes, but the attorney must seek court approval where necessary and take steps to minimize harm to the clients, and he must continue to protect the confidences of the client from whose representation the lawyer has withdrawn.

c)   No, if a conflict arises after representation is underway, the lawyer ordinarily must withdraw from the representation of both clients, unless the lawyer has obtained the informed consent of each client at the outset of the representation.

d)   No, because the federal administrative matter would preempt state tort law under the Supremacy Clause.

Rule 1.7 Cmt 25

3. A husband and wife decide to divorce and reach an agreement to share the same lawyer in hopes of saving money. They hire an attorney to represent each of them in Family Court for the dissolution of marriage. The attorney explains that there is an obvious conflict of interest here, but the husband and wife insist, and sign informed consent forms waiving the conflict and their rights to assert any future claims related to the conflict. The husband and wife have no children, and they have always kept separate bank accounts. Each purchased their own car from the money in their own bank account and each car's title is in only one name. They live in an apartment whose lease is expiring soon, so there is no real property to divide. Would it be proper for the attorney to represent both in the divorce?

a)   Yes, because it appears on these facts that there will be no assets in dispute at all, so the theoretical conflict of interest would have no bearing on their case.

b)   Yes, because both clients consented in writing, the dual representation does not violate law, and the attorney could have a reasonable belief that he will be able to provide competent and diligent representation to each affected client.

c)   No, because contingent fees are not permissible in divorce cases, and the husband and wife's sole motivation in sharing a lawyer was to save money.

d) No, because the representation involves the assertion of a claim by one client against another client represented by the lawyer in the same litigation or other proceeding before a tribunal

Rule 1.7(b)(3)

4. Three individuals plan to form a joint venture and ask an attorney to represent them in drafting the necessary documents and making the necessary filings with government agencies. They have already agreed that everyone will contribute exactly one-third of the startup funds for the venture, each will own a one-third share, each will have equal control over the Board, and each agrees to indemnify the others for a one-third share of any personal liability related to the joint venture. They have also agreed that they will have no non-compete agreements. The joint venture will hire managers, marketers, and other employees to operate the business. The three individuals are co-owners of a patent that could potentially be very lucrative when they bring it to market, and they have known each other and worked together for a long time. The attorney cannot find any current areas of conflict between them, though he knows that it is technically possible that some unforeseen conflict could arise in the future. The shared objectives and goals of the group lead the attorney to conclude that no conflicts of interest are present and that it would be counterproductive to try to convince each member of the group to sign an informed consent form acknowledging that conflicts of interest exist and that the attorney may still represent everyone at once. May the attorney trust his professional judgment and proceed without obtaining separate consent forms from each person in the joint venture?

a) Yes, if the attorney has a reasonable belief that he will be able to provide competent and diligent representation to each client, because the representation does not involve the assertion of a claim by one client against another client represented by the lawyer in the same litigation or other proceeding before a tribunal.

b) Yes, because the mere possibility of subsequent harm does not itself require disclosure and consent.

c) No, the situation is likely to limit materially the attorney's ability to recommend or advocate all potential positions that each might take because of his duty of loyalty to

the others; representing the group's overall interests in effect forecloses alternatives that would otherwise be available to the client.

d) No, because the fact that the individuals already decided to create a joint venture, and sought representation together from a single lawyer, constitutes implied consent to the common representation despite any potential conflicts of interest involved.

Rule 1.7 Cmt 8

5. A client owns a partnership share of a closely held business, and the other partners vote to impose an involuntary buy-out of the client to remove him from the firm. The client is clearly upset about this, but the partnership agreement clearly permits involuntary buyouts by a majority vote of the other shareholders. Then the client hires an attorney to represent him in the buyout transaction, to review the necessary documents and provide legal counsel about it. No litigation is under consideration yet. The attorney's sister is also a lawyer in that city, at another firm, and the sister represents the other shareholders in the partnership. Nevertheless, the attorney did not disclose that her sister represented the other partners, as she and her sister are not close and rarely speak, and the matter is unlikely to turn into litigation. Is the attorney, or the other lawyers in her firm, subject to disqualification in this matter?

a) No, because the attorney and her sister are not close enough for there to be a substantial risk that they will share confidential information, and the matter seemed unlikely to turn into litigation.

b) No, so long as both sisters give informed consent in writing, and each believes that she will be able to provide competent and diligent representation to her client

c) Both the attorney and her firm would be subject to disqualification, because the client did not give written informed consent.

d) The attorney would be subject to disqualification, but ordinarily the other lawyers in her firm would not be subject to disqualification.

6. An attorney has applied to make a lateral move from her firm to Big Firm, and she has already gone through the first two of three rounds of interviews for the position. Then the attorney agrees to represent a client in filing a breach of contract claim against Construction Company over a commercial development project. Big Firm is representing Construction

Company, and the firm's lawyers drafted the contract that forms the basis of the client's complaint. The client claims that Construction Company breached a certain provision of the contract that is ambiguous; Construction Company is confident that its conduct falls within the contractual language in that provision. Is it proper for the attorney to undertake representation of the client in this case?

a) Yes, assuming the client gives informed consent to the representation despite the conflict of interest here.

b) Yes, because there is no clear conflict of interest here, because the attorney has not yet started working at Big Firm and could not have participated at all in drafting the contract provision that is now in dispute.

c) No, as during the previous interviews, the attorney was likely to have gleaned some confidential information about Construction Company from Big Firm.

d) No, because when a lawyer has discussions concerning potential employment with an opponent of the lawyer's client, or with a law firm representing the opponent, such discussions could materially limit the lawyer's representation of the client.

Rule 1.7 Cmt 10

7. A group of several individuals seeking to form a joint venture asked an attorney to represent them in drafting the necessary documents and making the necessary filings with government agencies. Two of the individuals were to provide most of the initial funds for the startup; two others were experienced inventors who were to provide new product designs; two others had expertise in business management and were to serve as managers; and two had proven records in high-end sales and marketing. They have not yet resolved the allocation of ownership shares, bonuses for managers, whether to have anti-compete agreements for each participant, whether patents will belong solely to the joint venture or partly to the inventors themselves, and whether sales reps will work on salary or commissions. Everyone says that she wants whatever terms would be best for the joint venture overall, rather than what would be most beneficial for each one individually. The shared objectives and goals of the group lead the attorney to conclude that no conflicts of interest are present and that it would be counterproductive to try to convince each member of the group to sign an informed consent form acknowledging that conflicts of interest

exist, and that the attorney may still represent everyone at once. May the attorney trust his professional judgment and proceed without obtaining separate consent forms from each person in the joint venture?

a) Yes, because the mere possibility of subsequent harm does not itself require disclosure and consent.

b) Yes, assuming the attorney has a reasonable belief that he will be able to provide competent and diligent representation to each client, because the representation does not involve the assertion of a claim by one client against another client represented by the lawyer in the same litigation or other proceeding before a tribunal.

c) No, the situation is likely to limit materially the attorney's ability to recommend or advocate all potential positions that each might take because of his duty of loyalty to the others; representing the group's overall interests in effect forecloses alternatives that would otherwise be available to the client.

d) No, because the fact that the individuals already decided to create a joint venture, and sought representation together from a single lawyer, constitutes implied consent to the common representation despite any potential conflicts of interest involved.

Rule 1.7 Cmt 8

8. Three individuals hire an attorney to represent them as co-defendants in a tort action. At the outset, the attorney tells them that there could be a potential conflict of interest if he represents all three of them, and that they will need to sign informed consent forms, which they do. The three individuals have common goals and interests in the litigation, so they do not hesitate to sign the forms or inquire further about the implications of the potential conflicts. No further discussion occurs about the issue, and the attorney proceeds with the representation. Could the attorney end up having a duty to withdraw from representation later in the litigation, if the clients gave written consent to the shared representation at the outset?

a) Yes, when undertaking representation of multiple clients in a single matter, the information must include the implications of the common representation, including potential effects on loyalty, confidentiality and the attorney-client privilege and the advantages and risks involved.

b) Yes, if the liability insurers for the three co-defendants disagree on the terms of settlement and were unincluded in the original written consent.

c) No, because the attorney dutifully obtained written consent from each client, as required by the Rules of Professional Conduct.

d) No, assuming no situations arise where the lawyer obtains confidential information from one client that he could use to harm the interests of another client, and none of the clients file a crossclaim against another co-defendant.

Rule 1.7 Cmt 18

9. Husband and Wife wanted to hire a certain attorney to prepare their wills. Before the formalities of representation were final, husband spoke with the attorney privately by phone and disclosed that Husband had been having an affair, and that his lover might be pregnant. Husband forbids the attorney to tell Wife about this. Then the attorney realizes there could be potential conflicts of interest between husband and wife about the wills, distribution of assets, potential challenges to the will by offspring from outside the marriage, and potential claims for child support against Husband's estate. Would it be proper for the attorney to proceed with representing Husband and Wife in preparing their wills?

a) Yes, assuming each provides written consent after receiving warnings about the potential conflicts that often emerge in dual representation

b) Yes, because this is a transactional matter, not litigation in which adverse claims could arise.

c) No, because the attorney cannot violate the duty of confidentiality to Husband, which would be necessary to obtain informed consent from Wife.

d) No, because it would be improper to prepare a will for Husband under such circumstances.

10. Business Manager and Shift Supervisor, who worked at a customer service call-center, became co-defendants in a lawsuit by a disgruntled former employee. The plaintiff claimed to have been the victim of gender discrimination in the form of a hostile work environment, as well as intentional and negligent infliction of emotional distress related to the same factual allegations about her treatment at the workplace. Business Manager hired a certain attorney to represent both himself and the Shift Supervisor, who had been the plaintiff's direct superior. Based on Business Manager's initial investigation and review of the personnel files of the plaintiff and the Shift Manager, he believes the allegations are baseless and that the suit will end in a dismissal or summary judgment before trial. Shift Supervisor had a spotless work history, but the plaintiff had numerous interpersonal conflicts with her peers, was frequently late for work or missed work completely, and was the subject of several customer complaints. From his consultations with the defendants, the attorney understood that the complaints targeted the Business Manager and Shift Supervisor equally. Business Manager and Shift Supervisor both gave the attorney written informed consent to the potential conflicts of interest in having the attorney represent both. Business Manager obtained tentative permission to have the business cover the legal fees for the attorney. Near the end of the discovery phase, however, plaintiff produced numerous inappropriate love letters to her from Shift Supervisor, many with explicit sexual overtures, and a few that sounded threatening based on her lack of response to previous letters. In addition, several co-workers of plaintiff gave depositions explaining that they had witnessed Shift Supervisor engaging in inappropriate and unwanted touching of plaintiff on many occasions. Several also testified that Shift Supervisor would often accost her for ten or fifteen minutes outside, before she could reach her workstation, and that this was the cause of her tardiness for work. Business Manager had never heard about any of these problems before. Moreover, during depositions the plaintiff explained that she always had little contact with Business Manager and had no direct complaints about his treatment of her, and she acknowledged that she had never complained to Business Manager about Shift Supervisor's harassment of her. She disclosed that Business Manager was a co-defendant only because her attorney believed it was necessary to name someone from upper management in the lawsuit to trigger the legal protections of Title VII and other antidiscrimination laws. Business Manager then revoked his consent to the conflict of interest, explaining that he wanted separate representation from Shift Supervisor. Trial was due to begin two weeks later. Would it be proper for the attorney to continue representing either Shift Supervisor or Business Manager, but withdraw from representing the other?

a) Yes, the attorney can potentially continue to represent Business Manager but not Shift Supervisor, because Shift Supervisor engaged in misconduct that was unknown to Business Manager, and Business Manager is the one who arranged for the payment of the legal fees.

b) Yes, the attorney can potentially continue representing Shift Supervisor but not Business Manager, given the nature of the conflict, the fact that Business Manager revoked consent because of a material change in circumstances, the expectations of Shift Supervisor, and so on.

c) No, the attorney must petition the court to withdraw from representing both clients, as he has now obtained confidential information about each of them, and one is unwilling to consent to the continued common representation.

d) No, the attorney must continue to represent both clients, because it is the eve of trial and withdrawing would be prejudicial to them, and both consented in writing to the potential conflicts involved with using the same lawyer.

Rule 1.7 Cmt 21

11. An attorney has a private practice in a large rural township, and she specializes in commercial real estate transactions, such as the sale and lease of farmland, stables, granaries, and mills. As the only lawyer in the township with expertise in this area, she has represented most of the parties who buy and sell commercial real estate there. As a result, most of her clients pose potential conflicts of interest with other current, former, or future clients, so the attorney has a standard "waiver of future conflicts" form that explains conflicts of interest that typically arise in commercial real estate transactions, and she asks every client to sign it at the commencement of representation. The client is a major landholder in the township, who inherited extensive tracts of farmland from his family, who in previous generations were some of the original settlers in the area. Over the years, the client has sold off dozens of small parcels of farmland to neighboring farmers or small businesses such as honey processors, taxidermists, a hardware store, and a veterinarian. The client has also bought properties at times that were adjacent to his existing landholdings. The client has always used other lawyers for these transactions in the past, and in each previous instance, the other

party had separate counsel. The client now wants to hire the attorney to sell a parcel to a real estate developer. Buyer (the developer) is also a client of the attorney on unrelated matters, but the Buyer has hired another lawyer to handle this certain matter. The client and Buyer have had a good working relationship in the past and have consummated a few transactions that went smoothly. When the client meets with the attorney to review and sign a retainer for this representation, the attorney includes with the retainer her standard "waiver of future conflicts" form, without additional oral explanation except to mention that she represents Buyer in an unrelated matter. The client reads the form and signs it. As the negotiations for the sale to the developer proceed, a new conflict arises between the client's interests and the unrelated matters for which the attorney has represented the developer, as one will significantly affect the road traffic for the other. This was an unexpected development, though not unusual – such situations were familiar and routine for the attorney and the parties. Is the attorney's standardized "waiver of future conflicts," signed by the client, likely to be effective in this situation?

a) Yes, if the client agrees to consent to a specific type of conflict with which the client is already familiar, then the consent ordinarily will be effective regarding that type of conflict.

b) Yes, because the conflict of interest was unforeseeable at the time the representation began, and the client was aware that the attorney represented the Buyer.

c) No, because it violates the Rules of Professional Conduct for a lawyer to ask a client to waive future claims such as a conflict of interest, unless the client has representation by outside counsel in deciding whether to sign the waiver.

d) No, because it violates the Rules of Professional Conduct for a lawyer to use a standard, one-size-fits-all consent form without additional oral explanation.

Rule 1.7 Cmt 22

12. An attorney represented a client in a residential real estate transaction. At the same time, the attorney agreed to represent the defendant in a large class-action lawsuit, an alcoholic beverage maker that understated the alcohol content of its products on its labels, leading to numerous cases of inadvertent intoxication, liver damage from continuous

consumption, and a few deaths from overconsumption that led to alcohol poisoning. The client was an unnamed member of the plaintiff class in the class-action lawsuit against the alcohol producer. The attorney did not inform the client that he was representing the defendant in the class-action lawsuit or seek consent from the client or from the alcohol producer. Plaintiffs' counsel in the class action lawsuit discovered this situation, and he asked the court to disqualify the attorney from representing the defendant. Should the attorney be subject to disqualification under such circumstances?

a) Yes, because the attorney represents clients whose interests are directly adverse, and he did not seek or obtain written informed consent to the conflict of interest.

b) Yes, because the client will obviously feel betrayed when she learns that the attorney is representing the defendant in the class action lawsuit, and the attorney might have confidential information from representing a client in the real estate transaction that would be prejudicial in the class action lawsuit.

c) No, because a lawyer seeking to represent an opponent in a class action does not typically need the consent of an unnamed member of the class whom the lawyer represents in an unrelated matter.

d) No, because the interests of the client and the alcohol producer are not adverse, as the client merely hired the attorney to handle a residential real estate matter.

Rule 1.7 Cmt 25

13. Two separate clients hired the same attorney, signing their retainer agreements one week apart, on unrelated matters, though both involve property owners' rights under the state's common law doctrine of public trust for beaches, which guarantees public access to beaches up to the vegetation line on the shore. In one case, erosion has moved the boundary back on the property owner's lot to the point where his house is now clearly on the public access portion, and he seeks a declaratory judgment that erosion cannot jeopardize the private ownership of a building and its curtilage. Current public trust doctrine in the state would suggest that the property owner has lost all the value in his property, so he needs to seek a change or exception to the current law. The other case involves a property owner whose lots had always been separated from the beach by a small public

park, but erosion has eliminated the park and given him water access from his property, which has doubled the value of his land under current public trust doctrine. The state government, however, is seeking a declaratory judgment in his case, arguing for an exception or change to the current law that would rob the owner of the windfall he received due to the erosion. Does this situation present a conflict of interest that would require the attorney to obtain informed consent, in writing, from both clients, before proceeding with the representation?

a) No, the mere fact that advocating a legal position on behalf of one client might create precedent adverse to the interests of a client represented by the lawyer in an unrelated matter does not create a conflict of interest.

b) No, given that both are declaratory judgment actions, it is not possible that one client's interests could be adverse to the other's.

c) Yes, a conflict of interest exists if there is a significant risk that a lawyer's action on behalf of one client will materially limit the lawyer's effectiveness in representing another client in a different case, as when a decision favoring one client will create a precedent likely to seriously weaken the position taken on behalf of the other client.

d) Yes, but this type of conflict involves a question of law, so it is nonconsentable by the two clients.

Rule 1.7 Cmt 24

14. An experienced attorney handles claims against banks for many clients for issues regarding the failure of banks to investigate in a timely manner claims of fraud or unauthorized use of bankcards. Most of the attorney's work consists of sending demand letters, and most cases never actually result in the filing of a suit. Bank, a small local bank, retains the attorney to handle a certain claim against a customer for non-payment of a loan. The attorney has not represented any clients against Bank. Even so, the attorney includes in his contract for services a clause in which Bank waives any conflicts that may arise in the future - conflicts that involve the attorney representing clients against Bank for issues regarding failure to investigate claims of fraud or unauthorized use of bankcards. Is the attorney's conduct proper?

a) Yes, attorneys may include waivers of future conflicts assuming clients are aware of the waiver.

b) Yes, attorneys can include waiver clauses for specific future conflicts in their contracts, if the clients are aware of the waiver, and if the contract delineates the types of future representations that may arise.

c) No, attorneys cannot ever include waivers of future conflicts in contracts.

d) No, attorneys cannot include waivers of future conflicts in contracts specifically for financial claims.

Rule 1.7 Cmt 22

15. A certain attorney represents Conglomerate Corporation in a regulatory compliance matter, drafting documents for Conglomerate to file with the Securities and Exchange Commission and the Federal Trade Commission regarding executive salaries (for the SEC) and product market share (for the FTC's antitrust inquiry). Conglomerate Corporation owns or co-owns numerous subsidiaries and affiliates in unrelated industries. This attorney's retainer agreement limits his representation exclusively to the SEC and FTC regulatory matters. Victim hires the attorney to represent him in a personal injury suit against Subsidiary Corporation, partly owned by Conglomerate Corporation, over a slip and fall accident in Subsidiary's parking lot. Is it proper for the attorney to represent Victim in a tort action against an affiliate or subsidiary of his other client, Conglomerate Corporation?

a) Yes, a lawyer who represents a corporation or other organization does not, by virtue of that representation, necessarily represent any constituent or affiliated organization, such as a parent or subsidiary, and the lawyer for an organization may provide representation adverse to an affiliate in an unrelated matter.

b) Yes, so long as the attorney obtains written informed consent from both Victim and the legal representative of Conglomerate Corporation, after explaining the conflict of interest fully to each client.

c) No, unless the attorney obtains written informed consent from both Victim and the corporate director of Conglomerate.

d) No, because the parties are directly adverse in litigation, and therefore the conflict of interest described here is nonconsentable under the Rules of Professional Conduct.

Rule 1.7 Cmt.34

16. The Workers' Union at a manufacturing plant is having annual collective bargaining negotiations with the Management. Wages and benefits are not in dispute this year, as the parties reached an agreement in the previous year's collective bargaining about a five-year schedule for wages and benefits that was acceptable to both the Union and Management. The sole issue in dispute this year is about hiring. The Workers' Union wants the plant to hire five or six new assembly line workers so that there will be more efficiency and more flexibility for workers requesting days off or changes in their shifts. The Management wants to hire fewer new workers, potentially two at most, to keep payroll costs down and their stock share prices high. The Union and Management agree to hire a certain attorney, an experienced labor lawyer at an outside firm, to facilitate the collective bargaining negotiations. Neither side is currently expecting a breakdown in bargaining that would lead to litigation. Would it be proper for the attorney to have both the Union and the Management as clients while facilitating the negotiations?

a) Yes, assuming both clients provide written informed consent, common representation is permissible where the clients' interests mostly align, even though there is some difference in interest among them, so a lawyer may seek an agreement between them on an amicable and mutually advantageous basis

b) Yes, because conflicts of interest rules do not apply outside the litigation arena, and the parties here are not litigating and do not expect to litigate, but instead are merely hiring the attorney to facilitate negotiations of an issue where the two sides are not far apart.

c) No, because the parties' interests as directly adverse, and a lawyer may not seek to establish or adjust a relationship between clients on an amicable and mutually advantageous basis.

d) No, because conflicts of interest in a negotiation situation are nonconsentable, as no lawyer would be reasonable to believe that the conflict of interest would not materially limit his ability to represent both sides; this is especially true of collective bargaining in the employment context.

Rule 1.7 Cmt 28

17. Two brothers work together in a family landscaping business, and each is a named defendant in a lawsuit over a broken sewage pipe on a client's property where the brothers were digging holes to plant new trees. The two

brothers hire their family's attorney to represent them. Though the brothers get along reasonably well, there are several topics they avoid discussing, especially related to family matters and the inheritance, and who is to blame for some lost clients and damaged equipment in the recent past. Then the attorney explains the potential for conflicts of interest in the common representation and asks if they are willing to sign a waiver to the conflicts. One asks the lawyer privately about the issue of confidentiality and privileged information, because it is possible that litigation could emerge within the family later over various issues – the inheritance, control of the business, liability for business losses, and even a marital dispute. Does the common representation have implications for the attorney-client privilege?

a) Yes, regarding the attorney-client privilege, the prevailing rule is that, as between jointly represented clients, the privilege does not attach, and lawyers should assume that if litigation eventuates between the clients, the privilege will not protect any such communications.

b) Yes, regarding the attorney-client privilege, the prevailing rule is that, as between jointly represented clients, common representation provides extra protections for privileged information, and this is one of the main benefits of sharing the same lawyer.

c) No, regarding the attorney-client privilege, the prevailing rule is that, as between jointly represented clients, attorney-client privilege still applies to all communications between each client and the lawyer, so clients sharing a lawyer should know that the lawyer may not disclose to them confidential information from the other clients.

d) No, regarding the attorney-client privilege, the prevailing rule is that, as between jointly represented clients, the lawyer may not have ex parte communications with any of the clients, but all communications must occur when all clients are present, to safeguard the privilege.

Rule 1.7 Cmt 30

18. A producer of popular energy drinks and the owner of a popular chain of video-rental kiosks wanted to undertake a joint venture to distribute energy drinks and DVD rentals through the same kiosks. They approached a certain attorney to work out the details of the joint venture and draft the necessary legal documents. The attorney would provide common representation to both as clients in the matter. As part of obtaining informed consent from the clients regarding potential conflicts, the attorney explains that all information would be available to the other client, even information that otherwise would have been confidential information in a normal representation with a single client. Then the attorney explains he will have to withdraw if one client insists that the attorney keep certain information from the other, if the information was relevant and material to the representation. The energy drink maker, however, has a secret formula for the drinks, and the DVD kiosk owner has a trade-secret method of tracking the distribution and stocking of the DVDs in the kiosks minute-by-minute. Neither wanted the other to discover their trade secrets, but the attorney may eventually possess the secrets as part of his document review for the joint venture. Neither client clearly needs to know the trade secrets of the other, however, to proceed with the joint venture. Eventually, the attorney concludes that failure to disclose one client's trade secrets to another client would not adversely affect the representation in this case and agrees to keep that information confidential with the informed consent of both clients. Is the attorney's conduct proper?

a) Yes, in limited circumstances like this, it would be appropriate for the lawyer to proceed with the representation when the clients have agreed, after receiving adequate disclosures, that the lawyer will keep certain information confidential.

b) Yes, because no litigation is pending between the clients and the lawyer has not represented them before in other matters, and both are willing to provide written informed consent to the conflicts inherent in common representation.

c) No, continued common representation will certainly be inadequate if one client asks the lawyer not to disclose to the other client information relevant to the common representation.

d) No, because the lawyer has an equal duty of loyalty to each client, and each client has the right to know about anything bearing on the representation that might affect that client's interests and the right to expect that the lawyer will use that information to that client's benefit.

Rule 1.7 Cmt 31

19. A certain attorney agrees to represent a group of three individuals in the same matter, a

business transaction. Their interests are not directly adverse. This attorney has represented each of the clients in separate matters previously, and he is already working under a retainer to do legal work for each under the same hourly rates. Two of the clients are currently traveling overseas, but everyone agrees to the representation by conference call. The attorney explains potential conflicts of interest that could arise in common representation, and all clients consent orally to the common representation despite the potential conflicts. Then the attorney proceeds with working on their matter for three weeks until all the clients are back from traveling and can sign written consent forms. By that time, the attorney has completed 50 hours of work, and has acquired significant confidential information by and about each of the three clients. Would the attorney be subject to discipline for performing this legal work before obtaining written consent to the conflict by each conflict?

a) Yes, because common representation requires informed consent in writing from each client at the outset of representation.

b) Yes, because the fact that it was a transactional matter and not litigation means that the attorney could easily have waited three weeks until all clients could be present to sign written consent forms.

c) No, it was not feasible to obtain or transmit the writing at the time the client gives informed consent, so the lawyer could obtain or transmit it within a reasonable time thereafter.

d) No, because oral consent to a conflict of interest is enough when the parties are not directly adverse and each already has an established relationship with the attorney.

Rule 1.7 Cmt 20

20. An attorney serves as the lawyer for a corporation and is a member of its board of directors. Which of the following is true regarding this situation?

a) The attorney is subject to discipline, because the responsibilities of the two roles may conflict, as when Attorney must advise the corporation in matters involving actions of the directors, and there is always a material risk that the dual role will compromise the lawyer's independence of professional judgment

b) The attorney must limit his legal representation of the corporation to transactional and regulatory matters, and cannot represent the corporation in litigation against adverse parties, as there is always a material risk that the dual role will compromise the lawyer's independence of professional judgment

c) The attorney must have the final word on decisions of the board when he is present as a director, because Attorney bears responsibility for the decisions in the form of potential legal malpractice liability, which does not apply to the other directors who are not lawyers.

d) The attorney must advise the other board members that in some circumstances, matters they discuss at board meetings while the attorney is there as a fellow director would not be protected by the attorney-client privilege in later litigation; and that conflict of interest considerations might require the attorney's recusal as a director, or might require the attorney to decline representation of the corporation in a matter.

Rule 1.7 Cmt 35

21. A municipal election for a seat on the city council was remarkably close one year, resulting in a run-off election that was ever closer. Both candidates claimed victory, and each accused the opposing candidate of voter fraud and violations of various election rules. There is potential for litigation if the two cannot agree as to a winner in the election, with one or the other conceding. A certain attorney is a prominent lawyer in the community and has previously represented each candidate in various legal matters. Both candidates would like to hire the attorney to represent them in negotiating a resolution to the election. Each candidate fully understands their adverse interests and the potential conflicts of interest for the attorney, but each is willing to provide written informed consent to have the attorney represent them both in facilitating the negotiations. May the attorney represent both candidates in this negotiation?

a) Yes, common representation is permissible where the clients' interests align overall, even though there is some difference in interest among them, so the attorney may pursue an agreement on an amicable and mutually advantageous basis.

b) Yes, because conflicts of interest rules do not apply outside the litigation arena; the parties here are not litigating, and no litigation is pending, but instead are merely hiring the attorney to facilitate negotiations of an issue where the two sides are not far apart.

c) No, a lawyer may not represent multiple parties to a negotiation whose interests are fundamentally antagonistic to each other, even in a negotiation.

d) No, because the fact that the attorney has represented each of the parties in the past means that he would possess confidential information that would make mutual representation nonconsentable in this case.

Rule 1.7 Cmt 28

22. Two sisters are co-tenants of a house that they inherited from their father. They want to sell the house and hire an attorney to handle the real estate transaction. This attorney explains the potential for conflicts of interest in detail, and each sister readily agrees to provide written informed consent in the form of a waiver of future conflicts of interest. After a prolonged period, they finally find a buyer who is interested in the house, but the buyer wants to impose several onerous conditions on the purchase and engages in unreasonably protracted negotiations over the purchase price. The sisters themselves cannot agree on whether to accept any of the buyer's proposals, further dooming the negotiations. Eventually, one sister becomes frustrated with the attorney over the prolonged, hitherto unsuccessful negotiations, and fires the attorney. The other sister wants the attorney to continue the representation. Regarding the sister who seeks to discharge the attorney, may she do so?

a) Yes, but only if discharging the lawyer will not be prejudicial to the interests of the buyer, who has already invested a lot of time and energy in the negotiations to purchase the property.

b) Yes, each client in the common representation has the right to discharge the lawyer as stated in Rules of Professional Conduct and the accompanying Comments.

c) No, because she signed a waiver of future conflicts of interest, which is binding and safeguards the attorney against premature discharge.

d) No, because by agreeing to common representation with her sister, she implicitly agreed that discharging the attorney would require assent of both sisters, as they are both clients.

Rule 1.7 Cmt 33

23. Three co-owners of a successful startup business hire a certain attorney to help with working out the financial reorganization of their enterprise. The attorney seeks to resolve potentially adverse interests by developing the parties' mutual interests. In assenting to represent all the parties as clients simultaneously, the attorney agrees to adjust the relationship between clients on an amicable and mutually advantageous basis. The clients each provide written consent to the potential conflicts of interest. Is it proper for the attorney to represent three clients with potentially adverse interests in a negotiated transaction?

a) Yes, common representation is permissible where the clients' interests mostly align, even though there is some difference in interest among them, so the attorney may pursue an agreement on an amicable and mutually advantageous basis.

b) Yes, because conflicts of interest rules do not apply outside the litigation arena, and the parties here are not litigating and do not expect to litigate, but instead are merely hiring the attorney to facilitate negotiations of an issue where the two sides are not far apart.

c) No, because the parties' interests as directly adverse, and a lawyer may not seek to establish or adjust a relationship between clients on an amicable and mutually advantageous basis.

d) No, because conflicts of interest in a negotiation situation are nonconsentable, as no reasonable lawyer would believe that the conflict of interest would not materially limit his ability to represent both sides; this is especially true of collective bargaining in the employment context.

Rule 1.7 Cmt 28

24. An experienced attorney practiced at a small firm in a rural area. The attorney regularly represented the county school district in employment discrimination matters. One day, a group of citizens asked the attorney to represent them before the county planning commission to oppose the widening of a county road. The school district had separate budgetary funding, and it had an elected governing Board with its own authority to hire legal counsel. In contrast, the members of the county planning commission were appointees by the County Executive, and lawyers at the County Solicitor's office handled the legal work for the commission, though the

commission and the County Solicitor's office received their funding from separate line items in the county budget. Would it be proper, under these facts, for the attorney to agree to represent the citizens against the Commission, without informing them of her existing relationship with the School District, and without also securing the Board's consent?

a) The attorney must obtain informed consent, confirmed in writing, from the school district and the citizen group regarding the conflict of interest.
b) The attorney cannot represent the citizens group against the county, because that would constitute a nonconsentable conflict of interest.
c) The attorney would have no obligation under the ethical rules to inform the citizens group about her representation of the school district, or the school district about her representation of the citizens group against the county planning commission in the road-widening dispute.
d) The attorney cannot provide representation to the citizen group against the county planning commission in the road-widening dispute, but another lawyer in the attorney's firm could represent them.

ABA Formal Op. 97-405

25. Conglomerate Corporation owns a little more than half the stock of Giant Company. Conglomerate's stock, in turn, is public, available on the public stock exchange, as is the remainder of the stock in Giant Company. The president of Conglomerate Corporation has asked Attorney Stevenson to represent Giant Company in a deal by which Giant would make a proposed transfer of certain real property to Conglomerate Corporation. The property in question is unusual because it contains an underground particle collider used for scientific research, but also valuable farmland on the surface, as well as some valuable mineral rights in another part of the parcel. These factors make the property value difficult to assess by reference to the general real-estate market, which means it is difficult for anyone to determine the fairness of the transfer price in the proposed deal. Would it be proper for Attorney Stevenson to facilitate this property transfer at the behest of the president of Conglomerate, if Attorney Stevenson would be representing Giant as the client in this specific matter?

a) Yes, because Conglomerate Corporation owns more than half of Giant Company, so the two corporate entities are one client for purposes of the rules regarding conflicts of interest.
b) Yes, because the virtual impossibility of obtaining an appraisal of the fair market value of the property means that the lawyer does not have actual knowledge that the deal is unfair to either party.
c) No, because the attorney would be unable to inform either client fully about whether the proposed transfer price would be in their best interest.
d) No, not unless the attorney first obtains effective informed consent of the management of Giant Company, as well as that of Conglomerate, because the ownership of Conglomerate and Giant is not identical, and their interests materially differ in the proposed transaction.

RESTATEMENT § 131

26. Mr. Burns, the chief executive officer of Conglomerate Corporation, now faces criminal charges of discussing prices with the president of a competing firm. If found guilty, both Mr. Burns and Conglomerate Corporation will be subject to civil and criminal penalties under state and federal antitrust laws. An attorney has been representing Conglomerate Corporation. She has conducted a thorough investigation of the matter, and she has personally concluded that no such pricing discussions occurred. Both Conglomerate Corporation and Mr. Burns plan to defend on that ground. Mr. Burns has asked the attorney to represent him, as well as Conglomerate Corporation, in the proceedings. The legal and factual defenses of Conglomerate Corporation and Mr. Burns seem completely consistent at the outset of the matter. Would the attorney need to obtain informed consent to a conflict of interest from both Mr. Burns and a separate corporate officer at Conglomerate Corporation before proceeding with this dual representation?

a) Yes, the likelihood of conflicting positions in such matters as plea bargaining requires the attorney to obtain the informed consent of both clients before proceeding with the representation.
b) Yes, because it will always be in the best interest of a corporation to blame the

11

individual who acted in the situation, to avoid liability under a theory of respondeat superior.

c) No, because their legal and factual assertions appear identical in this case, so the risk of contradiction or adverse positions in the litigation is de minimis.

d) No, because no one else at Conglomerate Corporation would be able to provide effective consent to the potential conflict of interest on behalf of the organization, if the chief executive officer has required the dual representation to occur.

RESTATEMENT § 131

27. An attorney decides to purchase "litigation cost protection" insurance for matters she handles on a contingency fee basis. Plaintiffs' lawyers can buy this type of insurance on a case-by-case basis, for a one-time premium payment. The insurance is available for purchase up to three months after the filing of the initial complaint. Note that this policy is separate and distinct from malpractice liability insurance. The purpose of this type of insurance is to reimburse the attorney for litigation costs advanced by the attorney - only in the event of a trial loss. Do the Model Rules of Professional Conduct prohibit the attorney from purchasing litigation cost protection insurance for her contingency fee cases?

a) Yes, because the client and the attorney may have different cost-benefit calculations.

b) Yes, for an attorney may prefer that his client accept a low settlement offer to ensure that the attorney receives his fee, while the client wants to reject a settlement offer and take his chances at trial.

c) No, insurance coverage is categorically outside the scope of the Model Rules.

d) No, the attorney may purchase litigation cost protection insurance so long as she does not allow the terms of the coverage to adversely affect her independent professional judgment, the client-lawyer relationship, or the client's continuing best interests.

N.C Formal Ethics Op. 2018-6

28. An attorney purchased "litigation cost protection" insurance at the outset of representing a plaintiff in a personal injury case.

When the attorney recovered funds for the client through a settlement or favorable trial verdict, the attorney proposed to receive reimbursement for the insurance premium from the judgment or settlement funds. The attorney disclosed the cost of the insurance to the client as part of the representation agreement. Was it proper for the attorney to include in a client's fee agreement a provision allowing the attorney's purchase of litigation cost protection insurance and requiring reimbursement of the insurance premium from the client's funds in the event of a settlement or favorable trial verdict?

a) Yes, because the Model Rules do not purport to regulate insurance for lawyers, which is a matter of state statute.

b) Yes, if the amount charged to the client is fair and reasonable, and the lawyer fully explains to the client what litigation cost protection insurance is, why the lawyer believes a litigation cost protection policy will serve the client's best interests, that the client should get the advice of independent legal counsel regarding the arrangement, that other lawyers may advance the client's costs without charging the client the cost of a litigation cost protection policy; and the client gives informed consent in writing, while the lawyer maintains independent professional judgment.

c) No, because the client and the lawyer have different cost-benefit calculations in this scenario.

d) No, lawyer may not include in a client's fee agreement a provision allowing the lawyer's purchase of litigation cost protection insurance and requiring reimbursement of the insurance premium from the client's funds in the event of a settlement or favorable trial verdict

N.C Formal Ethics Op. 2018-6

29. The Board of Directors of Giant Corporation, acting pursuant to its articles and by-laws, votes not to declare a preferred stock dividend because of a perceived shortage of working capital. The Board takes this action contrary to the recommendation of the attorney for Giant Corporation. The attorney believes that there is a reasonable argument that the dividend can be omitted, but that a tribunal would most likely order the dividend declared. Thereafter, the

attorney implements the decision of the Board, memorializing its decision in a resolution. Several shareholders file suit to compel Giant Corporation to issue a dividend. Accordingly, which of the following is correct?

a) The attorney has a conflict of interest to which the Board cannot consent

b) The attorney has a conflict of interest due to the lawsuit, but the client could consent to the conflict and permit the representation.

c) An attorney-client relationship does not yet exist, so consent would be legally void.

d) Neither the attorney's earlier advice nor the lawsuit itself creates a conflict of interest that would prevent the attorney from defending against the suit.

RESTATEMENT § 131 Illus. 1

RULE 1.8 CURRENT CLIENTS: SPECIFIC RULES

30. An attorney agreed to represent a new client in a potential litigation matter, but the client had insufficient funds to pay the attorney's fees. Instead, the client asked the attorney to propose an amount that would be a reasonable fixed fee for the matter. The client then offered to sign over title to a small parcel of real estate worth about the same amount as the proposed fixed fee, and the attorney agreed. The value of the property, and the proposed fixed fee, were fair and reasonable, and the client agreed to these terms in writing. The attorney did not advise the client to seek the opinion of independent legal counsel for this transaction, and did not obtain signed, written consent from the client about the attorney's role in the transaction. Based on these facts, could the attorney be subject to discipline for violating the provisions Model Rule 1.8 that govern business transactions with clients?

a) Yes, because a lawyer must meet the written notice requirements of Model Rule 1.8 when the lawyer accepts an interest in the client's business or other nonmonetary property as payment of all or part of a fee.

b) Yes, because an attorney may not accept an ownership interest in the client's property as part of the fee for undertaking a representation in a litigation matter.

c) No, because Rule 1.8 does not apply to ordinary fee arrangements between client and lawyer.

d) No, because the fee was fair and reasonable, and the attorney provided the terms to the client in written form.

Rule 1.8(a) Cmt. 1

31. An attorney represented a client who was a stockbroker in a boundary dispute with the client's neighbor. Before the conclusion of the representation, the attorney also made some personal investments using the same client's brokerage services, receiving the same terms, services, and fee waivers that other customers of the brokerage firm received. The attorney did not advise the client to seek the opinion of independent legal counsel for this transaction, and did not obtain signed, written consent from the client about the attorney's role in the transaction. The terms of the brokerage services agreement were in writing, as usual. Based on these facts, were the attorney's actions proper in this transaction?

a) Yes, because the essential terms of the agreement were in writing, and it does not appear that the attorney charged the client any additional legal fees for this transaction.

b) Yes, this is a standard commercial transaction between the attorney and the client for a service that the client normally would market to others.

c) No, because the attorney did not advise the client in writing to seek the opinion of independent legal counsel for this transaction.

d) No, the client did not provide signed, written consent regarding about the attorney's role in the transaction.

Rule 1.8(a) Cmt. 1

32. An attorney, a venture capitalist, and a land developer agreed to form a corporation to develop a new shopping mall. Their agreement allocates ownership shares based on the appraised value of the venture capitalist's land, which he is contributing for this enterprise, the market value of the developer's design and construction work, and the attorney's regular fees for the hours contributed to the formation and ongoing representation as corporate counsel. The attorney was already representing both the venture capitalist and the developer as his clients

in unrelated matters. Which of the following is NOT a duty of the attorney in this situation, if the attorney performs the others?

a) The attorney must fully disclose in writing all the terms of the development corporation ownership agreement to the developer and the venture capitalist in language they understand, and the terms of the agreement are objectively fair and reasonable the two clients.

b) The attorney must advise the developer and the venture capitalist in writing that they should obtain the advice of independent legal counsel on the transaction, and give them time to do so;

c) The attorney must withdraw from representing the venture capitalist and the developer on the other matters, at least until the process of forming the corporation is complete, to avoid conflicts of interest.

d) The venture capitalist and the developer give informed consent, in writing, to the terms of the transaction and the attorney's role in the transaction, including whether the attorney is representing them in the transaction.

Rule 1.8(a); RESTATEMENT § 126

33. An attorney made an agreement to borrow money from a client who had received a large inheritance. The attorney agreed to pay the client the same interest rate that banks in that area were charging for unsecured business loans, and she gave the client a detailed written disclosure of the terms and conditions of the loan, with phrasing that a nonlawyer could understand. The client gave written, signed consent to the essential terms of the loan, including the fact that the attorney was not representing the client in the transaction. During one of their conversations about the loan, the attorney also advised the client in writing that it would be prudent to obtain the advice of another lawyer about the transaction, and she offered to give the client time to find another lawyer, but the client did not want to do this. Upon consummation of the agreement, the client transferred the loan amount to the attorney, who made regular payments according to the terms of the agreement, eventually repaying the full amount with interest. Based on these facts, were the attorney's actions proper in this transaction?

a) Yes, because the attorney repaid the loan with interest, so the client suffered no adverse consequences.

b) Yes, because the attorney complied with the requirements of the Model Rules for this type of transaction with a client.

c) No, based on the facts here, the client did not sign the written advisement to seek the opinion of independent legal counsel.

d) No, it was impermissible for the attorney to borrow money from a current client, even though the attorney fully repaid the loan.

Rule 1.8(a)

34. A transactional attorney agreed to represent a new client who already had representation by trial counsel on another matter. The client agreed to a complex fee arrangement, which included a fixed flat fee for the first phase of the transaction, a modest hourly rate for the remainder of the transaction, and a modest contingent fee in addition to these other fees, scaled to the outcome of the transaction – that is, a higher contingent fee for obtaining more favorable final terms in the transaction. The attorney did not advise the client to seek the opinion of independent legal counsel for this transaction, and did not obtain signed, written consent from the client about the attorney's role in the transaction. The client's other lawyer reviewed the terms of the fee agreement and advised the client to accept it. Based on these facts, could the attorney be subject to discipline for violating the provisions Model Rule 1.8 that govern business transactions with clients?

a) Yes, because the attorney did not advise the client in writing to seek the opinion of independent legal counsel for this transaction.

b) Yes, the client did not provide signed, written consent regarding about the attorney's role in the transaction.

c) No, because the client had representation by another lawyer in the transaction.

d) No, because Rule 1.8 does not apply to ordinary fee arrangements between client and lawyer.

Rule 1.8(a) Cmt. 1

35. A certain attorney represents a client in a civil suit. The client and the attorney often discuss their hunting trips and have gone hunting together on several occasions. The client tells

the attorney he is purchasing a piece of property for hunting with five other people and asks the attorney if he would like to go in on the purchase. The attorney tells the client he would like to join in the purchase and he provides the client with a check for his portion of the purchase price. Is the attorney subject to discipline?

a) Yes, attorneys shall not enter into transactions with clients that result in joint ownership of property.

b) Yes, attorneys shall not engage in social activities with current clients or enter into transactions that result in joint ownership of property.

c) No, attorneys may enter into transactions with clients assuming the transactions are not related to the current representation of the client and the client gives informed consent.

d) No, attorneys can enter into fair and reasonable business transactions with clients assuming the client receives an advisory in writing of the benefit of seeking advice from independent counsel and gives informed consent, in writing and signed by the client, of the transaction details.

Rule 1.8(a)

36. An attorney represented a client in a litigation matter, and while the matter was still pending, the attorney and the client also agreed to purchase an investment property together. The client had another lawyer who regularly represented the client in transactional matters, but not litigation. The litigation attorney and the client contributed equal amounts toward the purchase of the investment property, and each received an equal share. The attorney did not advise the client in writing of the desirability of obtaining the opinion of independent legal counsel in the transaction, but the client nevertheless asked his other lawyer, who handled the client's transactional matters, to review the terms and render an opinion. The other lawyer provided the client with a written disclosure of the terms and conditions of the agreement and recommended that the client proceed. Did the litigation attorney act properly in this transaction, purchasing an investment property with the client?

a) Yes, because the client had representation by another lawyer in the transaction.

b) Yes, because the joint investment did not relate to the attorney's representation of the client, which pertained to a litigation matter.

c) No, because the attorney did not advise the client in writing to seek the opinion of independent legal counsel for this transaction.

d) No, because the transaction was not fair and reasonable to the client.

Rule 1.8(a) Cmt. 4

37. A certain client needed to sell a parcel of real estate to pay off a large amount of credit card debt. He brought this situation to the attention of his attorney, who was representing him in his interactions with collection agencies and credit bureaus. The attorney offered to purchase the property immediately for the full amount of the client's outstanding credit card debt – just over a hundred thousand dollars – without delaying the matter by arranging a mortgage first, or having the property appraised. The client was disappointed, because he thought the property was worth more than that, but he agreed due to his dire financial circumstances. The attorney fully disclosed the terms of the purchase to the client, in understandable written form, and advised the client in writing that it would be prudent to consult with another lawyer about the transaction, which the client could not realistically afford to do. The client gave written, informed consent to the terms of the sale and the attorney's role in the transaction. Two months later, the attorney sold the property to a developer for three times the amount he had paid for it. Did the attorney act within the requirements of the Model Rules?

a) Yes, the lawyer complied with the Model Rules' notice requirements for business transactions with clients.

b) Yes, because the client felt disappointed after the transaction, and the attorney should have given more consideration to the client's feelings.

c) No, because the client could not realistically afford to obtain the advice of independent legal counsel regarding the transaction.

d) No, because the transaction was objectively unfair.

Committee on Prof. Ethics v. Baker, 269 N.W.2d 463 (Iowa 1978) Rule 1.8(a); RESTATEMENT § 126

38. An attorney has a successful blog about legal practice, and the blog generates substantial side income for the attorney. The attorney posts entertaining stories about his clients that attract the attention of his readers and make the blog successful and lucrative. He does not obtain client consent for these posts, but he is careful 1) not to post anything that would seriously injure the client's reputation or legal interests, and 2) not to post information about individuals that is truly confidential, that is not part of the public record. On the other hand, he does post about his personal observations and opinions of clients and their lifestyles, and often shares generalizations based on confidential information of former clients, such as: "On three occasions I've had clients who lived a double life, maintaining separate families in separate cities, and their families never knew." Another post recounted, "Last year I had a client who admitted after the case ended that he had been sleeping with one of the jurors." Apart from potential violations of Rule 1.6 (client confidentiality), which of the following is true?

a) The attorney may share non-confidential information and opinions about clients in a public forum that generates revenue for the lawyer.

b) The attorney can share confidential information about clients on social media after the representation has ended, if the client has refused to pay the legal fees owed to the attorney.

c) The attorney can share information on monetized social media about what transpired in the courtroom, except in cases with a sealed record, because normally courtroom proceedings are public.

d) The attorney has a common-law fiduciary duty not to profit from using client information even if the use complies with the lawyer's ethical obligations, without accounting to the client for any profits made.

ABA Formal Ethics Op. 18-480 (2018), fn. 16, citing RESTATEMENT § 60(2)

39. Asylum Now is a nonprofit organization that advocates for refugees and immigrants from poor countries. The Board of Directors for Asylum Now wants to bring a test case in federal court to challenge the constitutionality of detaining refugees who enter the country under duress without a visa. Asylum Now has offered to pay an attorney to seek the release of a certain refugee currently in federal detention, and to use this case to challenge current federal laws and regulations that mandate such detentions. The refugee consents to the representation, as well as the payment of legal fees by Asylum Now, and agrees to have his case be the test case that might benefit others. During the representation, the attorney meets several times with the directors of Asylum Now to discuss how to frame their argument in the case in a way that would shape public policy in the right direction. Is it permissible for the attorney to undertake the representation, given this arrangement?

a) Yes, the attorney may accept payment by Asylum Now and may agree to make contentions that Asylum Now wishes to have tested by the litigation.

b) Yes, if the attorney agrees to prioritize the interests of Asylum Now as the payor over the personal wishes of the refugee, who is merely a representative of the larger class of victims that will benefit from the litigation.

c) No, a lawyer may not accept compensation for representing a client from one other than the client

d) No, a lawyer may accept payment from a third party, but that party cannot ask the lawyer how the representation is progressing.

Rule 1.8(f); RESTATEMENT § 134

40. Conglomerate Corporation hired an attorney to represent one of its employees, a delivery truck driver, who is the defendant in a personal injury lawsuit. The incident that caused the plaintiff's injury was potentially within the scope of the employee's duties, and under Conglomerate's ultimate supervision. Conglomerate's directors asked the attorney what the truck driver intends to testify about the accident and its surrounding circumstances. The employee consented to having Conglomerate pay his legal fees, but the attorney did not ask the driver specifically about sharing this type of information with Conglomerate during the representation. Would it be improper for the attorney to give this requested information to Conglomerate's directors?

a) Yes, a lawyer shall not accept compensation for representing a client from one other than the client, especially an employer.
b) Yes, without specific authorization from the employee-client, the attorney may not disclose to Conglomerate how the employee intends to testify.
c) No, a lawyer may represent a client even when a third person will compensate the lawyer, if the client consents to the other party's payment.
d) No, if the employee authorized the attorney to accept payment from his employer, he impliedly authorized the attorney to disclose otherwise confidential information about the representation to the employer, so that the employer can protect its own legal interests.

Rule 1.8(f); RESTATEMENT § 134

41. An attorney was preparing a will for one of her wealthy elderly clients. The client had no surviving family members – her spouse had passed away years before, as had her siblings, and she had no children. The client asked the attorney for suggestions about potential beneficiaries of the estate, besides her favorite charities, and she offered to leave the attorney some items. The attorney replied, "Well, I've represented you on various matters over the years, and I have always looked out for your best interests, so I would not object if you included me in the will. I've always admired your collection of antique furniture and books." The client was delighted by the idea and instructed the attorney to include a provision in the will bequeathing all the antique furniture and books in her large home to the attorney. The attorney prepared the will as instructed and the client executed it. Was the attorney's conduct proper?
a) Yes, because the client asked her for suggestions about potential heirs and was excited about leaving something in the will to the attorney.
b) Yes, because the attorney was not depriving any other potential heirs of the specific items she requested, as the client had no surviving relatives.
c) No, because the way the attorney suggested a specific bequest was manipulative and the elderly client was vulnerable to coercion or exploitation.

d) No, because the attorney should not have prepared the will if the document made a significant bequest to the attorney.

Rule 1.8(c)

42. A certain attorney, a partner at a law firm, prepares a will for Sister. In the will, Sister directs the attorney to receive a substantial part of her estate. Then the attorney also recommends Sister appoint the attorney as the executor of the will because of his knowledge in this field. The attorney explains to Sister the role of the executor and the pay the executor of the estate will receive and discussed alternative executor choices with her. In addition, the attorney recommends Sister seek independent legal counsel regarding the issue of the executor. Sister does so, and then she asks the attorney to list him as executor in the will. Is the attorney subject to discipline?
a) Yes, attorneys cannot include substantial gifts to themselves in legal instruments such as wills prepared by the attorney for the client.
b) Yes, attorneys cannot recommend that a client appoint the attorney as the executor unless the client obtains the advice of independent legal counsel and gives informed consent confirmed in writing.
c) No, attorneys may permissibly include gifts to themselves in a will prepared by an attorney for a person related to the attorney, even if the gift is substantial.
d) No, an attorney may recommend the client appoint the attorney as executor assuming the client receives advice from independent legal counsel regarding the appointment of the attorney as executor prior to signing the will.

Rule 1.8(c)

43. A certain attorney obtained a successful outcome in a client's matter, and the client was grateful. The client sent the attorney a gift basket that year as a holiday gift, containing high-quality fresh fruit, sample-size jars of gourmet fruit preserves, and a few other delicacies. The gift basket cost the client $50. Is it proper for the attorney to accept this gift, or must the attorney refuse it?
a) Yes, because assuming a lawyer does not solicit the gift, there is no restriction on lawyers accepting unsolicited gifts from clients.

b) Yes, a lawyer may accept a simple gift such as a present given at a holiday or as a token of appreciation.

c) No, a lawyer shall not accept any substantial gift from a client, unless the lawyer or other recipient of the gift is a relative of the client.

d) No, because the lawyer's entire compensation for obtaining the favorable outcome should have been in the original retainer agreement and its schedule of fees, so any additional compensation or transfers from a client to a lawyer constitute an unwritten modification of the retainer agreement.

Rule 1.8(c) Cmt. 6

44. A client hires an attorney to represent her in business litigation. Another lawyer in the firm, unknown to the attorney, approaches the client with a proposal for an unrelated business transaction, the sale of a parcel of real estate adjacent to the lawyer's own land. The client agrees to sell the other lawyer in the firm the parcel of real estate for a reasonable price. The lawyer is not involved at all in the representation of the client and works exclusively in the estate-planning department of the firm, rather than in litigation. Must the lawyer nevertheless advise the client in writing of the desirability of seeking the advice of independent legal counsel, and obtain written informed consent from the client before proceeding with the purchase?

a) Yes, because the fact that the lawyer owns the adjacent real estate to the client's parcel of land means that he has a special conflict of interest with the client that would not necessarily apply to the other lawyers in the same firm.

b) Yes, because a prohibition on conduct by an individual lawyer under the conflicts of interest rules would automatically apply to all lawyers associated in a firm with the personally prohibited lawyer, even if the first lawyer is not personally involved in the representation of the client.

c) No, because the lawyer who is buying the real estate from the client is not involved in the representation of the client, and the Rules of Profession Conduct would not impute the attorney's potential conflicts of interest to the other lawyers in the firm.

d) No, because the lawyer is willing to pay a fair and reasonable price for the parcel of land, so there is no risk that the transaction will be to the disadvantage of the client.

45. An attorney had his own firm specializing in small business transactions. The clients were small business owners who did not have in-house counsel or other legal representation. His representation agreements with clients included all necessary disclosures, fee schedules and rates, and a clause stipulating that all potential legal malpractice claims would go through binding arbitration. The attorney would explain this term fully to each client, but he would decline representation for any potential client who would not agree to binding arbitration. The attorney did this in hopes of limiting his future malpractice liability to clients. Was it permissible for the attorney to do this?

a) Yes, because the clients gave informed consent, confirmed in writing.

b) Yes, a lawyer may make an agreement with the client to arbitrate legal malpractice claims, provided such agreements are enforceable and the lawyer fully informs the client of the scope and effect of the agreement.

c) No, a lawyer may not make an agreement prospectively limiting the lawyer's liability to a client for malpractice unless the client has independent legal representation in making the agreement.

d) No, a lawyer cannot make a binding arbitration agreement with a client if the lawyer's purpose in doing so is to limit the lawyer's liability for future malpractice claims by the client.

Rule 18(h) Cmt. 14

46. An attorney regularly represented clients in transactional matters. While she was representing a certain client in negotiating and drafting a contract, the client asked the attorney to represent her in a lawsuit as well. The attorney felt nervous because she rarely did litigation work, so she asked the client to sign a waiver of potential malpractice claims that could arise from the litigation work. She orally advised the client to talk to another lawyer about the waiver before signing it, but the client felt that she already had legal representation, as this attorney was handling her transactional matters. The client readily agreed to the waiver. The attorney competently handled the litigation matter, and the case settled before trial with a favorable result for the client. Could the attorney

be subject to discipline for obtaining a malpractice waiver from the client?

a) Yes, the attorney is making an agreement prospectively limiting the lawyer's liability to a client for malpractice, and the client does not have independent representation in making the agreement.

b) Yes, because she did not advise the client in writing about the desirability of seeking independent legal counsel about the waiver, but merely gave an oral recommendation.

c) No, the client already had legal representation from the attorney on another matter, so is was permissible for the attorney to make an agreement limiting future malpractice claims.

d) No, the waiver was moot because the attorney did not commit malpractice and the client obtained a favorable result.

Rule 1.8(h)

47. An attorney worked in the legal department of Conglomerate Corporation for a few years, then left there to start his own firm. His experience at Conglomerate proved useful, as he regularly represented some of Conglomerate's newer industry rivals in their transactional and pre-litigation work – small startup businesses that did not have in-house counsel. Whenever a new client needed legal representation in a matter that could potentially be adverse to the legal interests of one of his other clients, the attorney would obtain informed consent, confirmed in writing to the potential conflict of interest. In such cases, the attorney would also ask new clients to sign a waiver of liability for all potential legal malpractice by the attorney. Attached to the waiver was a cover sheet explaining what the waiver entailed, the downsides for the client in signing a waiver, and recommending the client seek the advice of independent legal counsel in connection therewith. As with the consent to conflicts of interest, the clients normally gave informed consent, confirmed in writing, to the waiver of malpractice claims against the attorney. Could the attorney be subject to discipline, based on these facts?

a) Yes, because the attorney is representing industry rivals or competitors of his former client and employer, Conglomerate Corporation, without obtaining Conglomerate's consent.

b) Yes, because the attorney is making an agreement prospectively limiting the

lawyer's liability to a client for malpractice, and the client does not have independent representation in making the agreement.

c) No, the clients gave informed consent, confirmed in writing, to both the conflict of interest and the waiver of malpractice claims.

d) No, the attorney advised the clients in writing of the desirability of seeking the advice of independent legal counsel in connection therewith.

Rule 1.8(h)

48. A plaintiff who had prevailed at trial needed representation for the appeal, because the defendant in the case appealed the verdict. Plaintiff's counsel did only trial work, not appellate work, and referred the client to an appellate attorney nearby. The trial lawyer even offered to accompany the plaintiff to the initial consultation with the appellate attorney to help facilitate the transition and to safeguard his client's interests in retaining new counsel. Instead, the plaintiff fired the trial lawyer, terminating the representation, and then went alone to the consultation with the appellate attorney. The appellate attorney asked the plaintiff to sign an agreement waiving potential malpractice claims against the appellate attorney, because the appellate attorney did not want to be responsible for the trial lawyer's mistakes. The appellate attorney did not inform the plaintiff fully about the risks or downsides of waiving malpractice future malpractice claims, nor did he advise the plaintiff of the desirability of seeking the advice of independent legal counsel in connection therewith. Could the attorney be subject to discipline, based on these facts?

a) Yes, because the plaintiff already had independent representation by counsel, so it was improper for the attorney to attempt to shift all potential liability onto another lawyer.

b) Yes, the attorney made an agreement with an otherwise unrepresented client that prospectively limited his liability for malpractice.

c) No, the plaintiff already had independent legal counsel in connection to the malpractice waiver.

d) No, when a lawyer brings another attorney into the matter to assist with an appeal, the lawyers and the client must agree in writing about how they will allocate responsibility and legal fees for the representation.

49. A plaintiff who had prevailed at trial needed representation for the appeal, because the defendant in the case appealed the verdict. Plaintiff's counsel did only trial work, not appellate work, and referred the client to an appellate attorney nearby. The trial lawyer even accompanied the plaintiff to the initial consultation with the appellate attorney to help facilitate the transition and to safeguard his client's interests in retaining new counsel. The appellate attorney asked the plaintiff to sign an agreement waiving potential malpractice claims against the appellate attorney, because the plaintiff had not yet terminated the representation with her trial lawyer, and the appellate attorney did not want to be responsible for the trial lawyer's mistakes. The appellate attorney did not inform the plaintiff fully about the risks or downsides of waiving malpractice future malpractice claims, nor did he advise the plaintiff of the desirability of seeking the advice of independent legal counsel in connection therewith. Could the attorney be subject to discipline, based on these facts?

a) Yes, because the plaintiff already had independent representation by counsel, so it was improper for the attorney to attempt to shift all potential liability onto another lawyer.

b) Yes, the attorney made an agreement prospectively limiting his liability to a client for malpractice.

c) No, when a lawyer brings another attorney into the matter to assist with an appeal, the lawyers and the client must agree in writing about how they will allocate responsibility and legal fees for the representation.

d) No, the plaintiff already had independent legal counsel in connection to the malpractice waiver.

50. An experienced attorney had his own solo law practice. The attorney agreed to provide representation to a certain client, which would entail researching and writing several legal opinions for the client pertaining to the client's anticipated litigation, and the attorney's usual hourly rate. The proposed research and writing would require a substantial amount of time, so their agreement stipulated that the attorney would bill the client every two months. The client paid the first bill and then stopped paying. After several months, the anticipated litigation

began, and the client requested copies of all the remaining legal opinions that the attorney had agreed to write. The attorney had followed state laws to secure a lien on his work product for the client after the client stopped paying. Could the attorney be subject to discipline if he were to retain the documents that the client has not yet paid for?

a) Yes, the attorney has now acquired an impermissible proprietary interest in the cause of action or subject matter of the client's litigation.

b) Yes, the Model Rules forbid a lawyer to acquire a lien merely to secure the lawyer's fee or expenses.

c) No, if a client refuses to pay the fees that a lawyer has already earned, the lawyer owes no ethical duties to the client, because the client has nullified the client-lawyer relationship.

d) No, a lawyer may acquire and act upon a lien authorized by law to secure the lawyer's fee or expenses.

Model Rule 1.8(i) Cmt. 16; RESTATEMENT § 43

RULE 1.9 DUTIES TO FORMER CLIENTS

51. Attorney Stevenson did not know anything about the construction industry, but he thought he knew how to draft contracts. Giant Equipment Corporation manufactures cranes, bulldozers, and large backhoes used for building construction. These machines are pricey. Twenty-seven months ago, the manufacturer hired Attorney Stevenson to help with drafting Purchase and Sale Contracts for the manufacturer to use for all these items of heavy equipment. Attorney Stevenson advised the company on what provisions to include and some of the exact wording they should use in the Purchase and Sale Agreements. Then the representation ended, and the company has not contacted an attorney since. Last week, Ashby Building Construction retained Attorney Stevenson to handle a dispute with a manufacturer of one of its construction cranes. It soon becomes apparent learns that the piece of equipment came from Giant Equipment Corporation, and that the procurement officer for Ashby consummated the purchase by signing one of the contacts on which Attorney Stevenson had advised Giant. Now Ashby wants to rescind

20

the contract and return the machine for a full or partial refund, because it used the crane for a week before it broke down. Would Attorney Stevenson be subject to disqualification in a such a latter, if litigation ensued?

a) Yes, because the items are so expensive, and Ashby used the machine for only a week before it became unusable.

b) Yes, Attorney Stevenson cannot seek to rescind on behalf of a new client a contract drafted on behalf of the former client.

c) No, because Ashby is not seeking any damages besides a refund in exchange for returning the faulty machine, and this merely puts the manufacturer back in the same place as if the sale had never occurred, so there is no potential harm to the manufacturer.

d) No, because representation of the manufacturer ended a while ago, so there is no conflict of interest or direct adversity between current clients.

Rule 1.9 Cmt. 1

52. Attorney Stevenson was willing to represent anyone, and rarely turned clients away. In fact, Attorney Stevenson would push the permissible limits under the conflicts of interest rules. At one point, Stevenson helped a construction company obtain the necessary permits from federal, state, and municipal agencies for constructing a new shopping center in an affluent suburban area. Obtaining the permits was not difficult – in fact, Attorney Stevenson found this kind of legal work boring. Before the construction was complete, another company acquired the property and the building project, and brought the construction to completion. Seventeen months after the building was open for tenants, one of the tenants missed to pay rent for his unit for three consecutive months, and the property manager started an eviction process. The tenant hired the same attorney to represent her in the eviction proceedings. The shopping center's owner filed a motion to have the attorney disqualified due to the substantial relationship between his previous work in securing construction permits for the building and the present eviction action against the tenant. Should Attorney Stevenson's previous work for the construction company disqualify him from representing tenant in the eviction proceedings?

a) Yes, because both matters involve the same commercial real estate property, so the matters have a substantial factual

relationship, creating a presumption that Attorney Stevenson has confidential information that would be prejudicial to the opposing party in the new matter.

b) Yes, because the lawyer now represents a party with directly adverse interests to his own former client.

c) No, because another company bought the property before the construction was complete, so there is no conflict of interest for the attorney at this time.

d) No, the matters are not related enough, because they do not involve the same transaction or legal dispute, and any confidential information learned while obtaining the construction permits prior would be unimportant for the nonpayment of rent by a tenant sometime later.

Rule 1.9 Cmt. 3

53. A doctor was facing criminal charges for an illegal kickback scheme – accepting bribes to refer patients to a certain hospital. The attorney representing the doctor in the criminal matter previously represented the hospital, and he had drafted one of the contractual agreements between the doctor and the hospital that federal prosecutor now allege to have been a sham agreement (payment for services never rendered). The attorney also provided some legal advice several years ago to another doctor, in one passing conversation, and that doctor now turns out to be part of the same kickback scheme. This other doctor, in fact, has turned state's witness in the case against the attorney's current client. The federal prosecutors have filed a motion to disqualify the attorney from the case because he is a potential witness about the agreement between the doctor. On the other hand, it has not yet listed him as a witness who will testify at trial, and it does not appear his testimony would be necessary to prove any of the elements in the case, given the number of other witnesses and documentary evidence available. How should the court rule on the motion to disqualify?

a) The court should grant it because the co-defendant in the case, the hospital, was a former client of the attorney.

b) The court should deny it because the government has not met its burden of showing that the attorney would be a necessary witness in the case, or that he possessed confidential information about the other doctor who will serve as a hostile witness in the case.

c) The court should deny it because disqualifying the attorney would be unduly prejudicial to the doctor who is the defendant.

d) The court should grant it because the lawyer is likely to be a necessary witness in the case, and because he will have to cross-examine a former client, the other doctor who is a hostile witness.

United States v. Beauchamp, 2017 WL 1684406 (N.D. Tex. May 2, 2017)

54. Media Company holds the exclusive right to license and distribute certain pay-per-view sporting events, which commercial establishments must license to broadcast at their facilities. It sued a sports bar, for broadcasting one of its major sporting events without a license. The Three Brothers Law Firm were involved before the Media Company filed suit, and Three Brothers Firm had managed to broker a tentative settlement agreement between the parties. Afterward, however, the parties reneged on the agreement and litigation ensued. Three Brothers Firm now represents the defendant sports bar in the matter, and it is counsel of record. Media Company has filed a motion to disqualify Three Brothers from the case, but the attorneys there claim that Media Company was never their client. There was no representation agreement between Media Company and Three Brothers, and Media Company never paid Three Brothers any legal fees. On the other hand, Media Company was otherwise unrepresented during the pre-trial attempt at negotiating a settlement, and its managers asked attorneys from Three Brothers for advice about whether to agree to the settlement instead of going to trial, and initially followed their legal advice on several points. Should the court now disqualify Three Brothers Firm from the case entirely?

a) Yes, because they obtained confidential information during the negotiations in the same matter, or a matter with significant overlap.

b) Yes, but only if the lawyers at Three Brothers Firm advised the sports bar to abandon the tentative settlement agreement.

c) No, because the attorneys are blood relatives working in the same firm.

d) No, because the firm was serving as a third-party neutral in the previous settlement negotiations, so neither party had a client-lawyer relationship with the firm.

Rule 1.9

55. A businessperson hired a certain attorney to represent her in a tax dispute with the government, in which the government accused her of hiding assets in overseas accounts and failing to report income from certain obscure investments. During this representation, the attorney learned extensive private financial information about client, but the representation ended at the resolution of the tax case. Several years later, after the termination had ended, the husband of the client filed for divorce. The attorney was the only lawyer the husband knew, so he retained the attorney to represent him in the divorce against the client. Her new lawyer moves to have the attorney disqualified from representing the husband, but the attorney claims that the matters did not relate to each other enough to merit disqualification. Is the attorney correct?

a) Yes, because resolving disputes with a government entity involves numerous procedural protections and administrative burdens of proof that are inapplicable in divorce proceedings in Family Court.

b) Yes, because the attorney's representation of Businesswoman terminated at the resolution of the tax matter, so there is no potential for betraying a current client by representing Businesswoman's husband.

c) No, matters are "substantially related" if there is a substantial risk that confidential information from the prior representation would materially advance the client's position in the subsequent matter, such as personal financial information.

d) No, because Businesswoman's troubles with the government over unpaid taxes are unlikely to be what led to the divorce from her husband, and the stress that the tax case put on the marriage is likely to be a major issue in the divorce proceeding.

Rule 1.9 Cmt. 3; Joe Hand Promotions, Inc. v.

22

56. An attorney worked at Big Firm, which a court disqualified from representing a client in a case because one of the other lawyers at the firm had a conflict of interest regarding a former client, and this conflict was imputable to the entire firm. The firm was not timely in implementing screening measures and became subject to disqualification. The attorney was at the firm during this time but was not involved in the matter and did not learn any confidential information about the client. Eventually, the attorney left that firm and went to work at another firm. It turned out that the attorney's new firm is representing the client instead – the client hired the new firm after the previous firm was subject to disqualification. The new firm has no measures in place to screen the attorney from participation in the matter, though the attorney is not in fact participating in the representation. Will the new firm be subject to disqualification now, because the attorney joined the firm from another firm that was subject to disqualification?

a) Yes, because the "taint" that the attorney brings from being part of a firm disqualified from the matter will now be imputable to the other lawyers in the new firm, without adequate screening measures in place.

b) Yes, unless the opposing party gives informed consent, confirmed in writing, to the new firm's representation of the client despite the attorney's presence at the firm.

c) No, assuming the attorney receives no part of the fees received for the representation.

d) No, there is no doctrine of double-imputation that would impute a purely imputed conflict from the attorney onto the other lawyers in the new firm.

Rule 1.9

57. An attorney practiced family law. One of her previous cases involved representing a man who wanted to remove his estranged wife as the beneficiary of his life insurance policy. The attorney was successful in this undertaking for the client. Two years later, the client died, never having divorced his estranged wife. The wife asked the same attorney to represent her and to convince the insurer to undo the change in

beneficiary so that the wife could receive the proceeds from her husband's life insurance policy. This representation would require extensive negotiation with the insurance company to convince the company that the previous change was invalid. Prior to his death, the husband, whom the attorney had represented, had sent the wife a letter saying that he made a mistake in removing her as the insurance beneficiary, and that he did not understand at the time the consequences of what he was doing. Would it be proper for the attorney to represent the wife in this matter?

a) Yes, because the husband is dead and cannot suffer any injury or adverse legal consequences from her representation of the wife.

b) Yes, because the husband expressed in writing that he regretted changing the beneficiary, so the attorney can assume that representing the wife would fulfill the wishes of the former client, that is, the husband.

c) No, because the subsequent representation would require the attorney to attack the same work the attorney performed for the former client.

d) No, because the husband did not inform the attorney in writing that he regretted his prior decision about changing the beneficiary.

RESTATEMENT § 132(d)(ii) Ill. 1

58. An attorney provided lobbying services as part of his practice. He represented Giant Gas Company for a few years lobbying on environmental issues related to fracking. During the representation on a certain matter, the attorney learned the basis for Giant's fracking decisions in terms of location, timing, and methodology. Conglomerate Corporation, a major purchaser of the natural gas produced from fracking, has now asked the same attorney to represent it in an antitrust lawsuit against Giant Gas, alleging a conspiracy to impose limits on production. Conglomerate's claims against Giant Gas are likely to include addressing the same production decisions that the attorney learned about in his representation of the latter. This confidential information would certainly advance Conglomerate's position in the

anticipated antitrust matter. The attorney no longer represents Giant Gas, because the company was not timely in paying the attorney's fees for the lobbying work. Would it be proper for the attorney to represent Conglomerate in this matter against Giant Gas?

a) Yes, because the attorney no longer represents Giant Gas, who forfeited the right to have any say in the matter when they refused to pay the attorney's fees on time.

b) Yes, because the matters are completely unrelated, given that the new representation would involve antitrust litigation and the former representation involved lobbying on environmental issues.

c) No, even if both parties give informed consent in writing to the attorney's representation of Conglomerate in the new matter, the fact that the attorney has confidential information relevant to the new representation makes the conflict nonconsentable.

d) No, there is a substantial relationship between the matters, so the attorney may not represent Conglomerate in the matter without effective consent from both Conglomerate and Giant Gas.

RESTATEMENT § 132(d)(iii). Ill. 2

59. An attorney worked as in-house counsel for Conglomerate Corporation for eight years, dealing with every aspect of management and corporate affairs, in addition to regulatory compliance. Conglomerate then hired a new CEO, who promptly fired the attorney and replaced him with another lawyer who was a nephew of the CEO. Giant Company has asked the attorney who formerly worked for Conglomerate to represent Giant in an antitrust matter against Conglomerate Corporation. The contemplated lawsuit focuses on specific incidents that took place after the attorney left Conglomerate, but the lawsuit involves sweeping charges of longstanding anti-competitive market strategy and pricing practices by Conglomerate, which would include the time when attorney worked there. Would it be improper for the attorney to represent Giant Company in this matter against Conglomerate?

a) Yes, the breadth of confidential client information of Conglomerate previously accessible to the attorney during the prior representation, and the breadth of issues open in Giant Company's contemplate lawsuit, creates a substantial risk that the information would materially prejudice Conglomerate in the upcoming litigation.

b) Yes, because Conglomerate fired the attorney and replaced him with the new CEO's nephew, there is a substantial risk that the attorney would have personal animosity toward Conglomerate and the CEO that would materially impair the attorney's ability to provide competent, zealous representation to Giant Company.

c) No, because the factual basis for the contemplated lawsuit involves decisions that transpired after the attorney left Conglomerate, and the sweeping charges of longstanding anti-competitive practices are too general to involve specific confidential information known to the attorney from his employment there.

d) No, by terminating the attorney who was in-house counsel, Conglomerate effectively waived any future conflicts of interested related to the attorney's work there, so the attorney would only need consent from Giant Company, who will certainly provide it.

RESTATEMENT § 132(d)(iii) Ill. 3

60. An attorney represented a home builder at the closings of the sales of a few homes that the builder had constructed in a new subdivision. It is not unusual for lawyers who conduct residential real estate closings to encounter issues related to marketability title. Recently, the home builder switched to using another law firm, so the attorney no longer represents the builder. A prospective new client has consulted with the attorney about providing representation. This prospective client is a landowner in an adjacent town, who wants to sue the same home builder, that the attorney formerly represented over a parcel of land on which the home builder plans to construct a few homes. The prospective client claims to have an ownership interest in the property. The contemplated lawsuit would involve whether the landowner or home builder have clear title to the property. Would it be

improper for the attorney to represent the new client against the home builder over the marketability of title for this new parcel of land?

a) Yes, the marketability of title in the same geographic area would necessarily involve too much relevant confidential information, so there is a substantial relationship between the two matters and the attorney should not undertake the new representation.

b) Yes, the home builder is likely to feel a sense of betrayal when his own former attorney represents an opposing party in a lawsuit against the builder, and such breaches of trust undermine confidence in the legal system.

c) No, but only if both the home builder and the new client provide informed consent, confirmed in writing, and the attorney believes that he can provide competent representation to the new client without a material impairment.

d) No, the attorney's knowledge of marketability of other tracts is not necessarily relevant to litigation involving the marketability of title to the new parcel, so the attorney may represent the new client without informed consent of the home builder.

RESTATEMENT § 132(d)(iii) Ill. 4

61. An attorney formerly represented Pharma Giant in obtaining FDA approval to market prescription drug Opticoton for treating diseases of the eye. Drug Conglomerate has now asked the attorney to help it obtain FDA approval for sale of prescription drug Dermicon for treating diseases of the skin. Drug Conglomerate is also interested eventually seeking FDA approval to market a variant form of Dermicon to treat diseases of the eye. If the FDA approved this application, Dermicon would significantly cut into the market share of Opticoton and Pharma Giant's profits from the drug. The attorney gleaned confidential information while representing Pharma Giant that relates extensively to work that the attorney would undertake in helping Drug Conglomerate obtain approval for Dermicon to be marketed as an eye salve, but none of the information would relate to Dermicon's use as a skin medicine. Drug Conglomerate and the attorney agree that the

attorney's work will relate only to FDA approval for use of Dermicon to treat diseases of the skin. With this limitation in place, would it be impermissible for the attorney to represent Drug Conglomerate in obtaining the initial approval for Dermicon as a skin medicine, without obtaining Pharma Giant's informed consent?

a) Yes, because it is foreseeable that after the FDA approves Dermicon as a skincare drug, it will be easier for Drug Conglomerate to obtain additional approval for its use as an eye salve, sold in a different form.

b) Yes, because Pharma Giant has a right to the attorney's unwavering loyalty and confidentiality, and the attorney has a fiduciary duty to protect a former client's profits or commercial interests in the future.

c) No, because the limitation on the representation removes any substantial relationship between the two matters or concerns about confidential information from a former client giving a strategic advantage to the new client.

d) No, because otherwise the attorney would have an unethical restrain on his right to practice law or represent future clients.

RESTATEMENT § 132(e) Ill. 5

RULE 1.10
IMPUTATION OF CONFLICTS

62. A thirty-lawyer firm in Chicago affiliated with Boutique Firm, three lawyers in a small city in New England. Each firm includes, on its masthead under the list of its own lawyers, the affiliation of the other firm (with its lawyers each named). Each firm also mentions the affiliation

with the other in its Martindale-Hubbell listing. Boutique Firm has represented Conglomerate Corporation in intellectual property matters for a few years, and has on file extensive information about Conglomerate's patents, patent applications, and prior patent litigation. Recently, Copycat Company has hired the thirty-lawyer firm in Chicago to seek a declaratory judgment that it is not infringing on certain patents owned by Conglomerate Corp., or in the alternative, that these specific patents are invalid. Conglomerate Corporation hired a new litigation firm to represent it in the matter, due to its concern about its regular firm having a conflict of interest. During the pleading and discovery phase, Conglomerate filed a motion to disqualify the Chicago firm from representing Copycat Company, due to its affiliation with Boutique Firm, even though Boutique Firm is not handling Conglomerate's litigation in this matter. Should the court grant the motion to disqualify the Chicago firm?

a) Yes, because it was misleading advertising for a firm in one state to identify a separate firm in another state as "affiliated," as this creates the impression for potential clients that the lawyers from one firm are also employees of the other.

b) Yes, because separate firms that publicly identify themselves as "affiliated," even if they are located several states away from each other, count as the same firm for purposes of imputed conflicts of interest under Rule 1.10.

c) No, because Boutique firm is not representing Conglomerate in the pending patent litigation, and the firm that does represent Conglomerate has no obvious connection to the Chicago firm.

d) No, because the Chicago firm and Boutique Firm (in New England) are separate firms, far away from each other geographically, and there is no reason to think that confidential information from a tiny firm in New England would pass over to a Chicago firm that merely has an "affiliation" for marketing purposes.

Mustang Enters., Inc. v. Plug-In Storage Sys., Inc., 874 F. Supp. 881 (N.D. Ill. 1995)

63. A jury convicted a defendant of murder, and they sentenced him to death. His lawyer at trial was unimpressive, and there were potential points to raise in an ineffective assistance of counsel appeal. For his appeal, the defendant used a different attorney from the same firm as his trial lawyer - one of the lawyers at the firm handled trials, and the other appeals. Can the appellate attorney from the same small firm as the trial lawyer handle this appeal?

a) Yes, if the client consents to the potential conflict of interest.

b) Yes, because there is no conflict of interest if the appellate attorney's own conduct is not in question.

c) No, because under the legal standard for ineffective assistance of counsel, the appeal would potentially require the attorney to disparage the representation of his own colleague as being unreasonably poor.

d) No, because a firm that loses a death penalty case at trial is not competent to handle the appeal, which is a matter of life and death for the client.

Cannon v. Mullin, 383 F.3d 1152 (10th Cir. 2004)

64. A potential client sought representation from an attorney in a legal dispute over the inheritance rights in an estate matter. The attorney was indecisive, because the estate was extremely complicated, so he met with the client several times over the next few months, trying to understand the intricacies of the will, the trusts involved, and the rival heirs. The potential client provided extensive confidential information about the estate to the attorney in meetings, phone calls, and emails. Eventually, however, the attorney declined the representation. During this time, the attorney had been in negotiations with another lawyer about forming a new law firm together. The other lawyer, unfortunately, was representing the rival heir, that is, the opposing party in the same estate matter. When the attorney and the other lawyer formed their new firm, the heir who had been the potential client then sought to have the attorney's new firm disqualified from the estate matter, arguing for imputation of the attorney's knowledge of confidential information to the other lawyer, who was the heir's opposing counsel in the case. The

other lawyer, who was now partners with the first attorney, argued that no client-lawyer relationship had existed between the heir and the attorney, because the attorney had declined the representation at the end. The heir who had been the prospective client insisted that the attorney had received confidential information from her, and that he had disclosed it to the other lawyer, who represented the rival heir in the matter. As a factual matter, the judge ruled that the prospective client-heir had introduced substantial evidence that she had provided extensive confidential information to the attorney in the process of seeking representation from him; conversely, the judge was surprised that the attorney had almost no evidence to show that he had not disclosed any confidential information to his new partner. How should the court rule on the motion to disqualify both lawyers?

a) The court should deny the motion, if no client-lawyer relationship formed between the attorney and the heir who is now requesting the disqualification.

b) The court should deny the motion, if the attorney who had the confidential information is not participating at all in the estate matter.

c) The court should grant the motion, because lawyers have some ongoing duties of confidentiality toward prospective clients, even after declining the representation, and the other lawyer has a conflict of interest by imputation.

d) The court should grant the motion, because the formation of a new firm or partnership between lawyers when a legal dispute is already pending creates an irrebuttable presumption that the lawyers disclosed confidential information to each other.

> In re Whitcomb, 575 B.R. 169 (S.D.Tex.-Houston Div. 2017).

65. An associate in a law firm consulted with a prospective client about providing legal representation. The prospective client wanted to file a lawsuit against a nightclub. A fistfight had erupted at the nightclub between two other patrons, and the potential client had intervened to try to break it up. One of the fighting patrons shoved him out of the way, and he sustained some bruising when he fell. Worse, the nightclub's security guard then arrived and misinterpreted the situation, and he thought the prospective client had started the fight. The security guard dragged him outside behind the nightclub, where the two had an angry exchange of words. The security guard became enraged and beat the prospective client badly, leaving him with a concussion, black eyes, some missing teeth, and broken ribs. The security guard had been since quit working there and was judgment-proof, but the nightclub had a long prior history of problems with this guard resorting to unnecessary violence against unruly patrons and the club. The associate attorney immediately agreed to represent the prospective client, and only later discovered that the managing partner at his firm owned a 50% share of the same nightclub as a side investment. Even so, the partner gave the associate permission to represent the victim, because he said the bar's liability insurer would cover the claim and settle quickly, and it would generate fees for the firm. Furthermore, the potential client, who ran a real estate business, might hire the firm for other lucrative legal matters. The nightclub's liability insurer, however, refused to settle the matter before the plaintiff had filed a claim in court, and as soon as the associate filed the claim, the insurer's lawyer filed a motion to disqualify the associate's entire firm from the case. Should the court disqualify the firm because one of the partners has invested money in the nightclub, even if that partner is not directly involved in the representation?

a) Yes, because the partner's conflict of interest would impute to all the other lawyers in the firm, especially if the managing partner has the conflict and associates are handling the representation with his permission.

b) Yes, because the motivation of the partner and the associate is to generate legal fees for the firm, in the short term from the nightclub's liability insurer, and in the long run from future legal work brought to the firm from this client.

c) No, because the partner with the ownership interest in the nightclub is not the one providing representation to the victim, and he expressly allowed the associate to take the case, saying it would be good for the firm and would not injure his commercial interests.

d) No, because the potential client deserves to have legal representation, and it would be prejudicial to him to disqualify his entire law firm after the filing of the claim.

Rule 1.10 Cmt.3; RESTATEMENT § 123

66. Alpha Firm and Beta Firm represent the two parties in a high-stakes commercial transaction – the sale of a subsidiary corporation from one large, international conglomerate to the other. An attorney at Alpha Firm is married to a lawyer at Beta firm, but the spouse at Beta Firm is not involved in the representation. If a problem arose, would a tribunal that follows the ABA Model Rules impute the marriage-based conflict of interest that Alpha Firm's attorney to all the other lawyers in the firm, if another lawyer at Alpha Firm handled the representation in this case?

a) Yes, because personal conflicts of interest automatically impute to the other lawyers at the same firm.
b) Yes, because conflicts based on marriage or family relationships receive special scrutiny from the courts and are the most frequent basis for disqualification.
c) No, because a conflict arising from a lawyer's marriage to another lawyer at an opposing law firm is not necessarily imputed to all other lawyers in the firm.
d) No, because the representation involves a transactional matter, and disqualification due to imputed conflicts of interest applies only in the litigation context.

Rule 1.10 Cmt. 3[1]

67. Xavier Firm is about to file a patent-infringement action on behalf of a new client

---

[1] TEXAS LAW STUDENTS note that Texas has a different (older) rule than the ABA Model Rules for this type of imputation scenario. According to Texas Ethics Opinion #666 (December 2016) https://www.legalethicstexas.com/Ethics-Resources/Opinions/Opinion-666.:

[Texas Disciplinary] Rule 1.06(f) requires imputation of personal interest conflicts under Rule 1.06(b)(2). Consequently, if a lawyer would be prohibited from undertaking representation on a matter because the representation 'reasonably appears to be or become adversely limited' by the lawyer's relationship with the lawyer's spouse, no other lawyer in the firm may undertake the representation without obtaining the client's informed consent under Rule 1.06(c).

against an alleged infringer (the opposing party). Xavier Firm has no patent lawyers in its office, so it affiliates with Yankee Firm, which specializes in patent and trademark law, to handle the representation. Yankee Firm has had no connection with the opposing party, but an attorney in Yankee Firm represents Bruce Wayne against Tony Stark, another of Xavier Firm's clients, in an unrelated matter. For purposes of analyzing the conflict of interest in the representation of the new client against the patent infringer, would a court or disciplinary authority impute the attorney's representation of Bruce Wayne to Xavier Firm, and Xavier Firm's relationship with Tony Stark to Yankee Firm?

a) Yes, because one lawyer's conflict of interest applies by imputation to all other lawyers at the firm, and an affiliated firm is functionally the same firm for purposes of conflicts analysis.
b) Yes, because obviously the representation of the new client and the patent infringer by the respective firms in the new matter will mean that they share confidential information with each other about all their other cases.
c) No, because a lawyer's individual conflict of interest would not apply by imputation to other lawyers in the same firm unless they are directly involved in the representation.
d) No, because the fact that Xavier Firm and Yankee firm represent opposing clients in a different, unrelated matter would not prevent their affiliation in the patent matter.

RESTATEMENT § 123

68. Attorney Ames and Attorney Adams work in the corporate legal office of Risk Company. A federal regulatory agency is investigating of the activities of Risk Company and is deciding whether to initiate criminal charges against Risk Company, some of its employees, or both. The regulatory agency has a long-established practice of not charging corporations for violations that corporate employees commit, where the corporation can show convincingly that it actively sought to discourage the offense in question. Showing this practice would, however, almost guarantee that an employee would face charges individually for the violation. Stevenson is a Risk Company employee upon whose

activities the agency has begun to focus. Before Attorney Adams' employment by Risk Company, she had been in private practice and had advised Stevenson with respect to the very conduct that is the subject of the agency investigation. Can Attorney Ames, who works with Attorney Adams, represent Risk Company in the matter before the regulatory agency, without obtaining informed consent from Stevenson?

a) Neither Attorney Ames nor any other member of Company's corporate legal office may represent Company without obtaining Stevenson' informed consent.

b) Attorney Adams can screen himself from the matter, and then Attorney Ames can represent Risk Company as in-house counsel in appearances before the agency officials.

c) Attorney Ames should not undertake the representation himself, but he can arrange for an supervise outside counsel in handling the matter for Risk Company.

d) Attorney Ames can represent Risk Company in the matter, because in-house counsel for corporations are exempt from the usual imputation of conflicts of interest from one lawyer to others in the same firm.

RESTATEMENT § 123

69. An Assistant District Attorney, who has recently joined a county prosecutor's office, represented a defendant at a preliminary hearing in a pending criminal case while in private practice. Now that this attorney has joined the prosecutor's office, how can the office proceed with the prosecution of the same defendant?

a) The new attorney, or any other lawyer in the prosecutor's office, could proceed with the prosecution, because there an exception in the conflict of interest rules for prosecutors.

b) The office must either hire a special prosecutor for the case, borrow a prosecutor from a neighboring jurisdiction, or implement effective screening measures to exclude the new attorney from the prosecution.

c) The prosecutor's office cannot prosecute the defendant for the same charge (it must drop the charges), but it could charge him for other crimes in the future.

d) The prosecutor's office must either drop the charges or refer the case to the federal prosecutors at the U.S. Attorney's office, who constitute another sovereign or jurisdiction for purposes of lawyers' conflicts of interest.

RESTATEMENT § 123 Imputation of a Conflict of Interest to an Affiliated Lawyer, sec. d(iii).

70. Attorney Stevenson is a partner in ABC law firm, and Lawyer Best formerly was a partner. A new client has sought to retain Attorney Stevenson to file suit on behalf of the client against Conglomerate Corporation. Before joining the ABC firm, Lawyer Best had represented Conglomerate Corporation at an earlier stage of the current dispute. Lawyer Best has now resigned from the ABC firm, disclosed no confidential information about Conglomerate Corporation relevant to the matter to other lawyers in ABC, left no files at ABC that relate to the proposed suit, and will not share in fees derived by the ABC firm from the representation of the new client. Given that Lawyer Best represented Conglomerate Corporation in the same matter, and then worked for ABC law firm in between (but has recently left the firm), is it proper for Attorney Stevenson to represent the new client in the matter against Conglomerate?

a) No, because Lawyer Best worked on the same matter, so his conflict of interest applies by imputation to all the lawyers who worked with him at ABC firm.

b) No, unless Conglomerate gives informed consent, in writing, to the potential conflict of interest that arose from having Lawyer Best at the firm until recently.

c) Yes, the firm could have represented the new client even if Best was still working there, because his work for Conglomerate occurred while he worked at another firm, at an earlier stage in the current dispute.

d) Yes, given Lawyer Best's departure and the fact that nobody else at the firm learned confidential information about Conglomerate Corporation, there is no remaining imputation of Best's conflict of interest.

RESTATEMENT § 124 sec. c(i).

71. An attorney was an associate at Big Firm. In his first year there, as a recent law school graduate, the attorney had a twenty-minute conversation with a more senior associate about research strategies involving a narrow issue of venue in federal court. The research was part of the representation of Big Bank, in the case of Developer v. Big Bank. The attorney's time sheets (billing records) from the time clearly document the length of the conversation and its subject matter. The entire conversation focused on the facts pleaded in the complaint and answer; the attorney learned no confidential information about the matter. Eventually, the attorney left Big Firm to become an associate at Boutique Firm. Eighteen month later, a partner assigned the attorney to represent the same Developer against Big Bank in a matter that overlapped on many points with the matter in which Big Firm had represented Big Bank. Lawyers at Big Firm still represent Big Bank, and they inform the bank's officials that the attorney who worked for them is now working at Boutique Firm, representing the Developer. Big Bank instructs the lawyers at Big Firm to seek the disqualification of the entire Boutique Firm from representing the Developer in the matter. How could Boutique firm avoid the imputation of a conflict of interest to its lawyers.

a) Boutique Firm cannot avoid imputation of the attorney's conflict of interest because it should have known about the attorney's prior work before it hired him, and the matter is, in substance, the same as the matter the attorney worked on a Big Firm.

b) If Boutique Firm immediately terminates the attorney and forbids the lawyers remaining there from having any contact with him, it can avoid disqualification in this matter.

c) At most, Boutique Firm would need to screen the attorney from the matter and have other lawyers represent the Developer, but even this may be unnecessary, because the attorney learned no confidential information about Big Bank at his previous firm.

d) At best, Boutique Firm could offer to serve as a third-party neutral between the Developer and Big Bank to resolve the matter, but it cannot provide representation in the form of advocacy due to the attorney's

prior work on the representation of Big Bank.

RESTATEMENT § 124, sec. d(i)

72. Big Bank hired Big Firm to represent it in a matter against Developer. Big Firm's partners explained to Big Bank before commencing the representation that they had hired an associate who previously worked for the firm that was representing Developer, and that he had worked on various matters for Developer while there. None of the associate's work was on the same case that was now pending, but it was unclear whether some of the matters had overlapping factual or legal issues with the present matter. Big Firm gives consent to the representation despite the conflict of interest, but it conditioned its consent on Big Firm implementing strict measures to screen the associate from any participation in the matter – including relocating the associate to another office at the firm, where he would not have day to day contact with lawyers representing Big Bank. The partners agreed, but it took a few months for them to free up office space to move the associate out of his current office, which was the office between the two lawyers serving as lead counsel in Big Bank's matter. Otherwise, the firm followed the standard screening procedures delineated in Model Rule 1.10. If a disciplinary action or legal malpractice action arose later regarding the representation of Big Bank, would the associate's conflict of interest be imputable to the other lawyers at Big Firm?

a) No, because Big Firm complied with the screening requirements of the Model Rules, and it was unreasonable for the bank to require more screening procedures than those delineated in the Model Rules.

b) No, because Big Bank consented to the conflict of interest, and it was not Big Firm's fault that it took a long time to find another office for the associate.

c) Yes, because the presence of an attorney who might have worked on closely related matters created an imputed conflict of interest, and the imputation was not removable in this case.

d) Yes, a client's informed consent to a conflict can be qualified or conditional, as here, and

Big Firm violated the client's condition, so it did not have valid consent to the conflict.

RESTATEMENT § 122

73. A prospective client met with an attorney at Boutique Firm for an initial consultation about a personal injury lawsuit over injuries the prospective client had sustained. The attorney declined the representation because he thought the client's case was unwinnable and would therefore generate no fees. During the consultation, the attorney asked some probing questions about the incident, and the client admitted facts indicating an unreasonable assumption of foreseeable risks beforehand, as well as the client's own intoxication at the time, which in the case would constitute contributory negligence. Furthermore, the client had failed to take obvious measures afterward to mitigate the damages. The attorney was certain that all these unfavorable facts would come out during discovery, and the client's claim would become laughable at trial. Two months later, another client came in for a consultation with another lawyer at Boutique Firm. This prospective client had was service of process in a new personal injury lawsuit, and he was the named defendant. The plaintiff in the lawsuit was the same individual who had met with the first attorney for a consultation a few weeks before. Boutique firm agreed to take the case and represent the defendant in the litigation. Which of the following is true, according to the MRPC?

a) Boutique Firm cannot represent the defendant in the case because an attorney there learned confidential information from the opposing party as a prospective client during an initial consultation two months ago, and it would be subject to disqualification if it handled the litigation.

b) The other lawyer at Boutique Firm can represent the defendant in the matter if the first attorney has not disclosed any confidential information to others in the firm, and the firm carefully screens the attorney completely from the matter and provides written notice to the other party.

c) Either the attorney or the other lawyer at Boutique Firm can represent the defendant, because the plaintiff was never a client of the firm, but merely came in for an initial

consultation, at the end of which the attorney immediately declined representation.

d) Either the attorney or the other lawyer at Boutique Firm can represent the defendant because the unfavorable information the client shared during the consultation, though confidential at the time, will inevitably come out during discovery no matter who represents the discovery.

Model Rule 1.18 (duties to prospective clients), Rule 1.10 (imputation of conflicts), and Rule 1.0(k)(definition of "screening")

74. A prospective client met with an attorney at Boutique Firm for an initial consultation about a personal injury lawsuit over injuries the prospective client had sustained. The attorney declined the representation because he thought the client's case was unwinnable and would therefore generate no fees. During the consultation, the attorney asked some probing questions about the incident, and the client admitted facts indicating an unreasonable assumption of foreseeable risks beforehand, as well as the client's own intoxication at the time, which in the case would constitute contributory negligence. Furthermore, the client had failed to take obvious measures afterward to mitigate the damages. The attorney was certain that all these unfavorable facts would come out during discovery, and the client's claim would become laughable at trial. Two months later, another client came in for a consultation with another lawyer at Boutique Firm. This prospective client had was service of process in a new personal injury lawsuit, and he was the named defendant. The plaintiff in the lawsuit was the same individual who had met with the first attorney for a consultation a few weeks before. Boutique firm agreed to take the case and represent the defendant in the litigation, and it has no measures in place to screen the attorney who consulted with the prospective client from participating in the matter. Which of the following is true, according to the MRPC?

a) The other lawyer at Boutique Firm can represent the defendant in the matter if the first attorney has not disclosed any confidential information to others in the firm, and he does not in fact disclose any confidential information the attorney learned during the consultation.

b) Boutique Firm cannot represent the defendant in the case because an attorney there learned confidential information from the opposing party as a prospective client during an initial consultation two months ago, unless Boutique Firm obtains informed consent in writing from both the defendant and the opposing party, who was a prospective client during a one-time consultation.

c) Either the attorney or the other lawyer at Boutique Firm can represent the defendant, because the plaintiff was never a client of the firm, but merely came in for an initial consultation, at the end of which the attorney immediately declined representation.

d) Either the attorney or the other lawyer at Boutique Firm can represent the defendant because the unfavorable information the client shared during the consultation, though confidential at the time, will inevitably come out during discovery no matter who represents the discovery.

Model Rule 1.18; Rule 1.10; Rule 1.0(k)(definition of "screening")

75. An attorney was an associate in Big Firm for eighteen months from early 2003 to late 2004. Another lawyer at Big Firm had been representing MindGames Inc., a creditor in the bankruptcy proceeding of Education Support International since 1999. The associate left Big Firm in 2004 to work for Regional Cancer Center as general counsel, where the medical director was Dr. House. There is a long, sad story here, but the bottom line is that Education Support International, which was still in bankruptcy, also owed money to Dr. House as a major shareholder of the failed company. In the summer of 2005, the bankruptcy court entered judgment in favor of MindGames Inc. and the shareholders, and MindGames immediately filed for sanctions against (compensation from) the shareholders, including Dr. House. At that point, Dr. House's lawyer withdrew from representation because the case had taken a complicated turn, and Dr. House asked the general counsel at his

medical center - the associate we met at the beginning of this story - to represent him going forward. MindGames filed a motion to disqualify the attorney from representing Dr. House in the proceeding and the appeal, because he had formerly worked at Big Firm, in an office a few doors down from their own lawyer there. The bankruptcy judge agreed, applying an irrebuttable presumption that the attorney learned confidential information about MindGames while working at Big Firm, but the attorney insists he never worked on any MindGames matters and has did not learn any confidential information. The attorney has appealed the disqualification to the Fifth Circuit. How should the circuit court rule?

a) It should reverse the disqualification order because the imputed conflict of interest disappeared when the attorney left Big Firm to work for Regional Cancer Center, given that the attorney knew no confidential information about MindGames.

b) It should reverse the disqualification because so much time has elapsed since the attorney worked at Big Firm, making any confidential information he learned presumptively outdated.

c) It should uphold the disqualification because the appellate court should defer to a trial court on matters of attorney conduct and conflicts of interest.

d) It should uphold the disqualification because of the irrebuttable presumption in the Model Rules that a lawyer who works at a firm has access to confidential information about all the clients of the firm.

In re ProEducation Intern., Inc., 587 F.3d 296 (5th Cir. 2009) (leading case on imputation/disqualification in the 5th Circuit, frequently cited by lower courts)

76. The plaintiffs' lawyers in a large class action suit against an insurer contacted an attorney at another firm seeking some advice. The attorney they called was a former commissioner with the state Insurance Commission, so he had vast insider knowledge of the regulation of the insurance industry in that state. The attorney talked to the plaintiffs' lawyers for thirty minutes on the phone, during which the plaintiffs' lawyers shared some confidential information

about the class action, including their theories of the case and litigation strategies. A year later, the attorney left his firm and went to work for Boutique Firm. Around the same time, the defense team representing the insurance company in the class action – three lawyers – also moved as a group to the same Boutique Firm, but to their office in another city. Boutique Firm because the counsel of record for the defendant insurer. The plaintiffs' lawyers learned of this convergence, and they *expressed concern that an attorney who had confidential information from their side of the case was now working with opposing counsel at the same firm. Boutique Firm immediately implemented strict screening procedures, and the managing partners made inquiries to confirm that the attorney had not already transmitted confidential information to the defense team for the matter, who were working in another office. The plaintiffs' lawyers were unsatisfied and filed a motion to disqualify all the lawyer in Boutique Firm from representing the insurer defendant in the class action. While the motion was pending, the attorney who had the confidential information left Boutique Firm to accept a government appointment. Should the court disqualify Boutique Firm, due to the imputed conflict of interest?

a)   Yes, because there is an irrebuttable presumption that an attorney from another firm with confidential information will share that information with other lawyers at his new firm.

b)   Yes, because the case involves a class action, where courts are particularly sensitive to the problems of confidential information passing between lawyers.

c)   No, because the firm avoided imputation of the conflict by implementing effective screening measures, and the fact that the lawyer was geographically in another office, and has already departed to work elsewhere, also support denying the motion.

d)   No, because it was a bizarre coincidence that the defense team would end up migrating laterally to the same firm that the attorney joined around the same time, so there was no bad faith on the part of the lawyers.

Kirk v. First American Title Ins. Co., 183 Cal.App.4th 776, Cal.App. 2 Dist (Cal. 2010)[2]

77. A large municipality has a labor dispute with its police union. The chairperson of the city council is a lawyer – she works for the city council part time, and she also has a law partnership with one other lawyer. As chairperson of the city council, she has the final word on which items will be on the council's agenda at each meeting. A few city council members who support the police union want their modest proposal for police pension reform to be on the agenda at an upcoming meeting. The police pension fund has not received its full contribution from the city for several years, and even though all current retired officers are receiving their full pension benefits on time, a wave of expected retirements over the next few years would create a crisis if the pension remains underfunded. The proposal would require the city to make a significant increase in its annual contributions to the fund, which would force cuts elsewhere in the city budget. The chairperson's law firm partner represents the police union in a variety of legal matters. The chairpersons has screened herself from the representation, will receive no share of any legal fees from her partner's representation of the union in the pension reform matter, and she will recuse herself from debating or voting on the proposal at the city council meeting. May the attorney who is the chairperson's partner continue to represent the police union?

a)   Yes, if the chairperson honors her promise to abstain from voting or even participating in the debate about the police union proposal.

b)   Yes, the police union is not the client of the chairperson of the city council.

c)   No, because some of the other city council members are already supporting the police union in the pension reform matter.

d)   No, due to imputation of the chairperson's conflict of interest to her law firm partner.

---

[2] The case is worth reading because the court decides to follow the 2009 amendments to ABA Model Rule 1.10, which California's state bar had already decided not to adopt. It provides a thorough explanation of the policy considerations for the pre-2009 rule and the post-2009 version of Rule 1.10.

78. A local abortion clinic hires the McCorvey Law Firm to represent it in an enforcement action brought by a state health agency. The action pertains to alleged health code violations at the clinic. The firm's principle partner, Norma McCorvey, has strong, outspoken political beliefs against abortion, and cannot set aside her personal convictions to provide representation to the clinic in the matter. An associate at the firm, however, supports the clinic's mission, and offers to represent the clinic instead of Attorney McCorvey. If McCorvey agrees to let the associate represent the clinic, would it be proper for the associate to do so, despite the partner's strong convictions that the clinic should be shut down?

a) No, because the named partner at the firm has a material limitation that creates a conflict of interest that would be imputed to the rest of the lawyers at the firm.

b) No, because the lawyers at the firm hold opposing political beliefs on a matter that is material to the representation, and this disagreement creates a conflict of interest for the firm as an entity.

c) Yes, because Attorney McCorvey's political beliefs are not relevant in the decision about whether to provide representation, given that the opposing party is a state health agency enforcing the health code, and the underlying constitutional issues surrounding abortion are unlikely to affect the case.

d) Yes, because even though Attorney McCorvey could not effectively represent the client due to her political beliefs, this would not materially limit the representation by the associate at the firm.

Rule 1.10 Cmt.3

RULE 1.11
CONFLICTS OF INTEREST FOR FORMER & CURRENT GOVERNMENT OFFICERS & EMPLOYEES

79. An attorney worked as a prosecutor in a local district attorney's office. A month before leaving there to go into private practice, she briefly worked on a case in which applied for the search warrants for the police to try to locate a fugitive suspect. When the police apprehended the fugitive a few weeks later, another prosecutor filed the charges and proceeded with the case.

Eventually, the attorney who had left to start her own practice received a referral client who turned out to be the same defendant. When she filed an appearance to represent the defendant, however, the prosecutor filed a motion to have her disqualified, because she had worked on the same case by applying for the warrants. The attorney responded that the defendant was not even in custody yet when she applied for the warrants, that the warrant application was a purely administrative chore, and that the filing of the charges did not occur until after she left her position there. How is the court likely to rule?

a) The court will disqualify the attorney from serving as defense counsel because she had participated in the matter personally and in a substantial way as a prosecutor.

b) The court will disqualify both her and the prosecutor from the case, as they were colleagues when she participated in the matter personally and in a substantial way.

c) The court will deny the motion to disqualify the attorney because she did not participate in a substantial way in the case while she was at the district attorney's office.

d) The court will first assess whether the attorney has confidential information that could be prejudicial to the opposing party in the case.

Registe v. State, 697 S.E.2d 804 (Ga. 2010)

80. Conglomerate Corporation spilled a large quantity of toxic sludge along the edge of its property, and spillage polluting two adjacent properties, one parcel owned by a private individual, and the adjoining parcel that was state-owned. The subdivision of the state that owned the polluted parcel agreed with the private landowner to be co-plaintiffs in a tort action against Conglomerate as the polluter, and to use the same attorney to represent both the state and the private landowner. The private landowner was mostly concerned about the loss to his property values, as this was an investment property. The state was concerned entirely with cleanup costs and the threat to public health. An authorized official at the state agency provided the attorney with written consent to the potential conflicts of interest inherent in the joint representation, as did the private landowner. Under such circumstances, would it be improper for the same attorney to represent both the government and a private party at the same time, in the same matter?

a) Yes, the Model Rules prohibit lawyers representing the government from simultaneously representing a private party in the same matter, even with consent from the would-be clients.

b) Yes, because the private party's interests are purely financial, while the state's interests involve a balancing of various competing interests of the public.

c) No, the fact that the state represents the public interest cancels out and potential conflict of interest on the part of the private party and makes the Rules of Professional Conduct inapplicable.

d) No, after obtaining the necessary written consent, the attorney may represent both the private party and a government agency.

Model Rule 1.11, Cmt. 9

81. After law school, an attorney worked for the local City Attorney's office in a mid-sized municipality, working mostly on enforcement of anti-pollution and anti-littering ordinances. After five years, the attorney left the position at the municipality and went to work for the federal Environmental Protection Agency (EPA). In some cases, the EPA intervenes in litigation over pollution in which the same municipality is also a party. In that situation, may the EPA ignore the usual screening requirements that would apply to a lawyer moving to a private firm?

a) Yes, when a lawyer is employed by a city and subsequently is employed by a federal agency, the latter agency does not have to screen the lawyer.

b) Yes, the EPA can always assert federal preemption over a municipality if a conflict arises in litigation.

c) No, because the attorney may know confidential government information that would provide an unfair advantage to the lawyers at the EPA.

d) No, the rules for screening attorneys originally applied only to government lawyers, and the screening requirements are even stricter than they are for lawyers who move to private firms.

Rule 1.11 Cmt. 5

82. The Office of the Attorney General in Texas ordered administrative suspensions of driver's licenses for parents who failed to pay child support, pursuant to state statutes. An attorney worked for the State Office of Administrative Hearings (SOAH), the agency that adjudicated license suspensions like this one. When he decided to leave the SOAH, the attorney surreptitiously copied a database of individuals facing license suspensions and used the names to solicit clients as he started his own firm. The attorney represented clients who wanted to appeal their license suspensions in court, though he did not represent anyone whose case he had personally worked on during his time at the SOAH. Could the attorney be subject to discipline in the cases in which he represents clients appealing their license suspensions?

a) Yes, the attorney had access to confidential government information from his time working for the state.

b) Yes, a former government lawyer cannot represent any clients against the same state entity for whom the lawyer once worked.

c) No, there is no conflict because the lawyer did not participate directly or personally in the client's cases.

d) No, disqualification of former government lawyers does not apply to merely administrative matters such as license suspensions.

Smith v. Abbott, 311 S.W.3d 62
(Tex. App.-Austin 2010);
Model Rule 1.11(c)

RULE 1.12
FORMER JUDGE, ARBITRATOR, MEDIATOR OR OTHER THIRD-PARTY NEUTRAL

83. A certain state has specialized family courts that handle divorces, child custody, child removal cases brought by state social service agencies, and spousal or child support enforcement. An unmarried couple had split up but they had two children, and the family court judge awarded custody of the children to the

single father, and ordered the mother of the children to pay $500 per month in child support to the father. A few months later, the judge left the family court and returned to private practice, specializing in family law, which allowed him to draw on his valuable experience as a former judge in the family court. One day, the father from the case described above came for a consultation, and he explained that the mother of the children had been delinquent for the last two months in paying child support to him. Would it be proper for the judge to represent the father in the action to enforce the child support order?

a) Yes, because Comment to the Model Rules contains a specific exception to the prohibition on contingent fess in divorce and custody cases, allowing contingent fee representation for enforcement of existing child support orders.

b) Yes, because the attorney will not be deciding the enforcement case as a judge, and the merits of the original order are legally irrelevant to the enforcement action.

c) No, because he has a conflicting ethical duty to represent the mother in the case, who lost custody of her own children and must pay child support to the father of the children.

d) No, because the attorney would be representing a party in seeking enforcement of his own order from his time on the bench.

84. A federal judge hired clerk for the first two years after the clerk graduated from law school. During his second year as a clerk, he began applying for associate positions at local law firms, to secure a job that would begin immediately after his clerkship ended. A few of the firms to which he applied had pending matters before the same judge, and these were among the firms that interviewed the clerk for an associate attorney position. During the interviewing process, the clerk refrained from mentioning he knew about their pending matters on his judge's docket, though the interviewers always mentioned the fact that their firms regularly appeared before the judge in whose chambers the applicant was then clerking. Each firm that interviewed the clerk received a letter from the judge recommending the applicant to prospective legal employers. Even though some of these firms had pending matters on the judge's docket, the judge knew from the clerk which firms were interviewing the clerk. Was it

improper for the clerk to apply for positions at firms that have pending matters before the judge for whom she was clerking?

a) Yes, the fact that the judge sent recommendation letters for the clerk to these firms constituted an ex parte contact by the judge and the clerk.

b) Yes, interviewing with firms that have pending matters before the judge, and where this fact was the subject of a comment or discussion in the interview, constituted an ex parte contact by the judicial clerk with a party in a litigation matter.

c) No, a law clerk to a judge may negotiate for employment with a party or lawyer, even if the prospective employer is involved in a matter in which the clerk is participating personally, after the lawyer has notified the judge.

d) No, any lawyers working for the government may always seek private employment with any prospective employer, even if the prospective employer is involved in a matter in which the lawyer is participating personally in a substantial way.

Rule 1.12(b); Rule 1.11(d)(2)(ii)

85. A federal judge hired clerk for the first two years after the clerk graduated from law school. During his second year as a clerk, he began applying for associate positions at local law firms, to secure a job that would begin immediately after his clerkship ended. A few of the firms to which he applied had pending matters before the same judge, and these were among the firms that interviewed the clerk for an associate attorney position. During the interviewing process, the clerk refrained from mentioning he knew about their pending matters on his judge's docket, though the interviewers always mentioned the fact that their firms regularly appeared before the judge in whose chambers the applicant was then clerking. Each firm that interviewed the clerk received a letter from the judge recommending the applicant to prospective legal employers. The judge did not know where the clerk applied, or which firms were interviewing the clerk; the recommendation letter was a general letter that opened with "To Whom It May Concern." Was it improper for the clerk to apply for positions at firms that have pending matters before the judge for whom she was clerking?

a) Yes, interviewing with firms that have pending matters before the judge, and where this fact was the subject of a comment or discussion in the interview, constituted an ex parte contact by the judicial clerk with a party in a litigation matter.

b) Yes, the fact that the judge did not have notice of where the clerk applied, or which firms were interviewing the clerk.

c) No, a law clerk to a judge may negotiate for employment with a party or lawyer, even if the prospective employer is involved in a matter in which the clerk is participating personally.

d) No, any lawyers working for the government may always seek private employment with any prospective employer, even if the prospective employer is involved in a matter in which the lawyer is participating personally in a substantial way.

Rule 1.12(b); Rule 1.11(d)(2)(ii)

86. An attorney served for several years as a professional mediator. She decided to change careers and become a litigator, and one of the parties from her final mediation sought to retain her as their attorney in a matter closely related to the subject of the litigation. The other party, which already had legal representation, provided written, informed consent to this arrangement. Under such circumstances, would it be permissible for the former mediator to represent a party in the same matter in which the attorney served as mediator?

a) Yes, as it appears all parties to the proceeding gave informed consent, confirmed in writing.

b) Yes, a mediator or arbitrator selected as a partisan of a party in a multimember arbitration panel may subsequently represent that party.

c) No, a lawyer who served as a mediator may not represent a client in a matter in which the lawyer personally participated.

d) No, because the other party already had legal representation and therefore did not have the same opportunity to hire the mediator as their lawyer for the trial.

Rule 1.12(a)

87. During a trial recess, the judge asked the lawyers for both parties to meet with him briefly

in chambers. Once there, the judge explained that he planned to retire from the bench soon and was wondering if either of their firms were hiring litigation attorneys, as he might be interested. Could the judge be subject to discipline under the Model Rules of Professional Conduct for making this inquiry?

a) Yes, the judge should not have talked to the two lawyers together, because if one of them immediately offers the judge a job at his firm, the other will also feel compelled to do so, may even feel it necessary to offer a higher salary than the first.

b) Yes, under the Model Rules, a lawyer shall not negotiate for employment with any person who is involved as a party or as lawyer for a party in a matter in which the lawyer is participating as a judge personally and in a substantial way.

c) No, the Model Rules of Professional Responsibility do not apply to judges, because the Code of Judicial Conduct regulates judicial behavior and activities.

d) No, this was merely an initial inquiry, not negotiation for employment at either of the lawyer's firms.

Rule 1.12(b)

88. An attorney served for a while as a municipal court judge, and during that time, she sentenced certain defendants facing criminal charges to terms of probation. Eventually the judge left the court and returned to private practice. Once settled in her new practice, three prospective clients sought to hire her file motions to end their terms of probation early, due to their good behavior and their need to relocate for their jobs. Would it be proper for the attorney to represent them in filing these motions?

a) Yes, sentencing municipal defendants to probation is merely an administrative matter that would not necessitate the disqualification of a former judge who later represents the same individuals in seeking to end their probationary terms.

b) Yes, filing a motion to end probation early due to good behavior is not the same matter as the original crimes for which the received the sentence.

c) No, the attorney may have confidential information from her previous position as the judge in the clients' case that would be prejudicial to the opposing party in the probation-termination hearings.

d) No, a lawyer who served as a judge may not represent a client in a matter in which the lawyer had personal and substantial involvement.

In re Moncus, 733 S.E.2d 330 (Ga. 2012)

89. An attorney served for several years as an appellate court judge. At one point, the judge was on a panel that affirmed two trial orders in an ancillary probate proceeding. Soon thereafter, the attorney left the appellate court and returned to private practice at Boutique Firm. The larger probate matter was still dragging on, and relators brought a mandamus appeal arising out of the same ancillary proceeding and hired Boutique Firm to represent them on the appeal. This necessitated filing a motion to substitute counsel from a previous firm that had provided representation up to that point. Opposing counsel did not oppose the motion, as they did not know Boutique Firm had hired a former appellate judge who had signed earlier orders in the case. Boutique Firm did not screen the former judge from the matter. When opposing counsel eventually realized this fact, the lawyer immediately filed a motion to disqualify Boutique Firm from the appeal. Boutique Firm responded that opposing counsel had already consented to the potential conflict when it did not oppose the motion to substitute counsel; moreover, there was no demonstrated prejudice to the opposing party. How should the court rule on the disqualification motion?

a) The court should deny the motion because the moving party already consented to the conflict by choosing not to oppose the motion to substitute counsel.

b) The court should deny the motion because the former appellate judge had merely affirmed some trial orders in the ancillary probate matter, so there is no actual prejudice to the moving party.

c) The court should grant the motion as the matters related to each other, and the moving party did not have adequate notice about the conflict to give informed consent.

d) The court should grant the motion because relators in a mandamus appeal can easily find substitute counsel.

In re de Brittingham, 319 S.W.3d 95 (Tex. 2010)

THE CLIENT-LAWYER RELATIONSHIP

RULE 1.2
SCOPE OF REPRESENTATION & ALLOCATION OF AUTHORITY BETWEEN CLIENT & LAWYER

90. An attorney grew up in poverty but worked hard to overcome obstacles and achieve success. Now a successful practitioner, the attorney is idealistic and passionate about helping the less fortunate. Every Saturday morning, he uses a small conference room at the local YMCA to assist pro se litigants in divorce and custody matters – the attorney helps them complete their own court forms (court filings) for a nominal fee, gives some advice about their individual situation, and reviews forms they have completed before the individuals themselves file them. The attorney is concerned about these pro se litigants misunderstanding his role and believing he is their lawyer, so the attorney requires each one to sign a printed disclaimer declaring that no attorney-client relationship exists. It reads, in relevant part, "I understand that this attorney has no legal or ethical obligation to provide legal representation to me in this matter." Given that the pro se litigant signed a form acknowledging that no legal representation will follow, is the attorney correct in believing that no lawyer-client relationship exists in these circumstances?

a) Yes, the signed express written disclaimer functions as a contractual agreement that no lawyer-client relationship exists.

b) No, the lawyer is reviewing court documents and providing legal advice about pending legal proceedings, which constitutes the practice of law by the lawyer, even if the representation has a limited scope.

c) No, the pro se litigants described here appear to be unsophisticated users of legal services and potentially do not understand the significance of the written disclaimer.

d) Yes, these pro se litigants will file the documents in court themselves, on their own behalf.

See below[3]

91. A client hired a certain attorney to represent her in a personal injury lawsuit in which the client is the plaintiff. After an initial consultation and two meetings to review the main evidence in case and to discuss the nature of the claims, the attorney drafted the initial pleadings, served the opposing party, and filed the pleadings in the appropriate court. Nevertheless, the attorney did not allow the client to review the pleadings before filing them, and afterward, the client expresses disappointment that she did not have the opportunity to review the pleadings beforehand and make suggested edits, given that it is her case and that the attorney is working for her. Was it proper for the attorney to draft the pleadings based on conversations with the plaintiff and file the documents without first having the plaintiff review them?

a) Yes, because a lawyer may take whatever actions the client has impliedly authorized as part of the representation.

b) Yes, unless the client is an English teacher or a professional editor and might therefore have special expertise in proofreading texts for grammatical errors and stylistic problems.

c) No, because a lawyer shall abide by a client's decisions concerning the objectives of representation and shall consult with the client as to how to pursue these ends.

d) No, because the attorney may have to spend time later revising the pleadings, which could affect the legal fees in the case, and such revisions may have been unnecessary if someone else had proofread the attorney's draft before filing it.

Rule 1.2(a)

---

[3] The facts above are like those described in a 2015 ABA Formal Opinion (state ethics opinions, such as Texas Ethics Opinion 635, reach a similar conclusion). The lawyer is, in practice, providing legal services to the individuals, this constitutes the practice of law, and therefore a client-lawyer relationship exists, even if it is limited in scope. The significance of this conclusion is that the attorney could still be subject to discipline for ethical violations related to the provision of these services, and depending on the situation, sometimes the limited representation still "counts" for purposes of checking for conflicts of interest, unless it is the type of situation described under Model Rule 6.5. Sometimes it is very clear that no attorney-client relationship exists, but there are also confusing situations, as when an attorney gives an oral or written disclaimer stating there is no such relationship, but then provides legal representation anyway.

92. Client is the leader of a radical religious group that protests at the funerals of soldiers who died tragic combat deaths overseas. The protests are not against the war, however, but against society's increasing tolerance of homosexuality and gay marriage. The client and his followers stand outside the funerals as grieving family members arrive, and they hold large picket signs emblazoned with hateful sayings against homosexuals, some of which use shocking language. They also hold signs indicating they are happy that American soldiers die frequently, because they believe these deaths validate their point that the country is on the wrong course morally and has become evil by being more tolerant. The group heckles those attending the funerals, but then disperses once the funeral ceremony starts. The group receives regular national media coverage because of the intentionally sensational and shocking nature of their protests. The client now faces a tort lawsuit by the father of a deceased soldier whose funeral the group picketed; the plaintiff claims intentional and negligent infliction of emotional distress. The client is certain that his First Amendment rights trump such subjective-harm tort claims and has a recent Supreme Court case supporting his position. The client asks an attorney to represent him in the matter. The attorney reluctantly agrees to take the case and the trial court gives an unfavorable verdict against the client. After the case, reporters interview the attorney asking how he could represent such a client and the attorney states during the interviews that he did not necessarily endorse the client's religious, social, moral, or political views, but was merely providing representation. Are the attorney's actions proper in this case?

a) Yes, because the attorney did not win the case on behalf of this client, so justice prevailed in the end, as this client advocates intolerance of others in our society.

b) No, because the attorney has a duty under the Rules of Professional Conduct to refuse representation of a client if he cannot endorse the client's political, social, or moral views, especially those who preach intolerance and hate.

c) No, because the attorney lost the case, and then tried to justify himself in the media by denying any endorsement of the client's political, social, and moral views.

d) Yes, because a lawyer's representation of a client does not constitute an endorsement of the client's political, economic, social, or moral views or activities.

Rule 1.2(b)

93. A certain defendant was indigent and received court-appointed defense counsel in his felony larceny case. The defendant insisted that he was completely innocent and that he would not accept any plea bargains, because he wanted an opportunity to prove his innocence at trial. When the defendant told the attorney his expectations, the attorney explained that there is a special type of plea called an "Alford Plea," in which a defendant may agree to accept a conviction while still contesting his guilt or maintaining his innocence. The defendant refused, and told the attorney, "Do not even contact me with offers from the prosecutor for a guilty plea. I will not plead guilty. I will prove my innocence in a court of law!" The prosecutor indeed made several plea offers, and each time the attorney presented the offer to the defendant, who rejected it and reminded the attorney that he did not want to hear about any offers to "make a deal." The defendant's hard line proved effective as a negotiating strategy, and eventually the prosecutor called the attorney to say they would reduce the charges to a misdemeanor and the sentence to "time served" if the defendant would plead guilty. The attorney thought this was a ridiculously generous offer but simply rejected it without consulting his client. The client proceeded to trial and the jury convicted him, and he received the maximum sentence for the crimes charged. Was it proper for the attorney to reject the final plea bargain offer without informing the client?

a) Yes, because clients have a right to dictate the overall objectives of the representation, but the lawyer has a right to decide the means of achieving that objective.

b) Yes, because the client has previously indicated that the proposal will be unacceptable and has authorized the lawyer to reject the offer.

c) No, because a lawyer who receives from opposing counsel a proffered plea bargain in a criminal case must promptly inform the client of its substance.

d) No, because the ultimate result was a conviction and a severe sentence for the defendant, which he could have avoided by accepting the final plea offer.

Rule 1.2 Cmt 3

40

94. A certain attorney represents a defendant in a murder case. At trial, the jury convicted the client and sentenced him to death, and the appellate courts upheld the conviction as well as the sentence. The attorney has now offered to file a habeas corpus petition in federal court to appeal the case to the United States Supreme Court, if necessary. The defendant, however, has developed terminal cancer, and does not expect to live another six months. The defendant tells the attorney to drop the appeals because even if they won, the defendant would not live long enough to enjoy his freedom. Even so, the defendant does not terminate the representation, because he wants the attorney to handle his estate planning matters while he is on death row, and he has some administrative complaints in progress against the prison where he is living. The attorney strongly opposes the death penalty and believes his client is innocent, so he files the habeas petition anyway. While the habeas petition is making its way through the federal appellate process, the defendant succumbs to his illness and dies in prison. Is the attorney subject to discipline for filing the habeas petition, despite the client's reservations?

a) Yes, because the appeals are clearly a waste of public resources in a case where the defendant will die anyway before the appeals process would be complete.

b) No, because filing appeals is merely a matter of strategy and methods, and lawyers do not have to defer to the client about strategy and methods.

c) No, because the client died before the attorney's actions produced any actual results that could affect the client.

d) Yes, because a lawyer shall abide by a client's decisions concerning the objectives of representation and shall consult with the client as to how to pursue these ends.

95. An attorney represents criminal defendants. One day, a client appeared in the attorney's office and explained that he had been blackmailing his former employer for the last year. The client had hired a prostitute to seduce the former employer in a room with hidden cameras, then showed the embarrassing photographs to his former employer and demanded monthly payments of $500, which the employer paid, not wanting to destroy his marriage. The prostitute subsequently died of a drug overdose. The client's former employer eventually tired of making the monthly

blackmail payments and went to the police about the matter. The client is now worried that he will face charges for blackmail, which would violate his parole and result in a lengthy incarceration. The client retained the only copies of the photographs, as he merely showed them to the former employer a year ago to extort the payments. After the client explained all this to his attorney, he gave the attorney the documents and instructed the attorney to destroy them or hide them so that the police could not find them. Attorney put the photos in a folder marked ATTORNEY WORK PRODUCT - PRIVILEGED AND CONFIDENTIAL, and sent the folder to a secret overseas document storage service in the Caymans. The police obtained an arrest warrant for the client based on the former employer's affidavit, and at trial, the prosecutor obtained a conviction based on the employer's testimony and the bank records showing the monthly transfers. Is the attorney subject to discipline?

a) Yes, because the lawyer was clearly incompetent or negligent if he lost the trial even without the prosecutor having the photographs or the prostitute's testimony to admit as evidence.

b) Yes, because a lawyer shall not assist a client in conduct that the lawyer knows is criminal or fraudulent, such as destroying evidence when there is a pending criminal investigation.

c) No, because the court convicted the client anyway, so the lawyer's feeble attempt to help the client made no difference to the outcome.

d) No, because once the client told the lawyer about the matter privately and gave him the documents, they came under the protections of attorney-client privilege.

Rule 1.2(d)

96. A client hired an attorney to research the legality of a musical "mash-up," a sound recording that includes brief sound clips and samples from many other artists' commercial recordings. The client's unique approach puts it in the gray area around "fair use" and "composite works of art" under prevailing copyright law, and no court has yet ruled on the precise issue, though the question has been the subject of seventeen lengthy law review articles in the last two years, reaching a range of different conclusions. No litigation is pending, and the client has not yet undertaken any activity that could constitute a copyright infringement; he

is seeking reassurance before proceeding that he would not face liability for copyright infringement. Because the client primarily wants a memorandum of law answering his hypothetical legal question, he asks the attorney to limit his research and writing to two hours of billable time. The attorney agrees, spends an hour reading and an hour writing, and gives the client a short memorandum. Given that the client's objective was merely to secure general information about the law the client needs, was it improper for the attorney to agree to this limitation on the scope of representation up front?

a) Yes, because given the complexity of the subject and the uncertainty about this certain point of law, two hours was not a reasonable amount of time to yield advice upon which the client could rely.

b) Yes, because the other artists have a right to receive compensation for their creative work, and the attorney is helping the client potentially infringe on other artists' copyrights.

c) No, because the client had a limited objective of securing general information about the law the client needs, so the lawyer and client may agree that the lawyer's services will be no more than an hour of research and an hour of writing.

d) No, because it would be too costly or burdensome to have the attorney read seventeen tedious law review articles and try to formulate a plausible synthesis of the positions they advocate.

Rule 1.2 Cmt. 7

97. A certain client calls an attorney to ask if it is possible to apply for an extension on filing his annual tax returns, if the deadline for filing returns is still two weeks in the future. This attorney offers to research the matter for a few hours and write a formal legal memorandum for the client about filing extensions. Even so, offhand, the attorney can assure the client over the phone that it is indeed possible to apply for an extension and that the IRS routinely grants them if an application for extension arrives before the regular deadline. The attorney practices tax law and is familiar with the rules. The client thanks the attorney and says that he is satisfied with the "short answer," and that he does not want the attorney to do any more research or writing about it, but to send a bill for the phone call. Then the attorney agrees and bills the client for the telephone conversation and conducts no further research on the matter. Is it proper for the attorney to limit his representation to a single telephone call like this?

a) Yes, because the client's objective is no more than securing general information about the law the client needs to handle a common and typically uncomplicated legal problem, so the lawyer and the client may agree that the lawyer's services will be no more than a brief telephone consultation.

b) Yes, because the lawyer should defer to the client about costs and the objectives of the representation and should not assist a client in committing a crime or fraud, such as tax evasion.

c) No, because such a limitation on the representation does not allot enough time to yield advice upon which the client could rely, and the client could face devastating fines for being late with his tax returns.

d) No, because such an agreement ignores the legal knowledge, skill, thoroughness, and preparation necessary for the representation.

Rule 1.2 Cmt. 7

98. Husband hired a certain attorney to represent him in a divorce; the husband and wife had three adult children. Husband was quite upset when he met with the attorney, because his wife had filed for divorce and he felt deeply betrayed. The couple had a prenuptial agreement that clearly delineated the division of assets in case of divorce, and child custody is not an issue as the children are in their twenties. As part of his routine consultation questions, the attorney asked if there had been any marital infidelity on the part of either the husband or wife. Husband admitted to the attorney that he once had an affair many years ago, that the wife never discovered, and that he wanted to keep secret, if possible. He then speculated that he had no idea if his wife had ever had an affair, then became very emotional as he considered the possibility. Within minutes, he had convinced himself that his wife had been having affairs with other men for years, though he never knew it, and that the three children were unlikely to be his offspring. The attorney had already looked at Husband's photograph of his children, and their resemblance to their father (Husband) was remarkable. the attorney finds repugnant the idea of subjecting the adult children to paternity tests, which would traumatize them unnecessarily, regardless of the result. The attorney also believes that accusing the wife of

42

infidelity would be imprudent, as it will ensure that the family would discover Husband's previous affair, which otherwise might not happen. Without the accusations of infidelity, all the issues of the divorce would come under the prenuptial agreement and not be in dispute. Then the attorney insists on limiting his representation to the divorce and wants to include in the retainer agreement that there will be no accusations of infidelity or paternity testing of the children, unless the other side initiates in this regard. After Husband calms down, he agrees to the attorney's conditions of representation. Is it proper for the attorney to insist on such conditions of representation?

a) Yes, because it would be fraudulent for the husband to accuse the wife of marital infidelity, of which there is no evidence, while hiding the fact that he himself had an affair.

b) No, because there is always a chance that the other party in a divorce was guilty of marital infidelity, and the children should get to know with absolute certainty who is their real father.

c) Yes, the terms of the representation agreement may exclude specific means that might otherwise serve used to accomplish the client's objectives, such as actions that the lawyer regards as repugnant or imprudent.

d) No, because the lawyer should always defer to the client about the objectives of the representation, while the client should defer to the lawyer about the means of achieving the goals of the representation.

Rule 1.2 Cmt. 6

99. A client explains to his attorney that he is operating an illegal website where users can anonymously upload and download pirated music and videos, in violation of copyright laws and other anti-piracy statutes. The website is very lucrative for its operator, and the client has become a multimillionaire by founding and operating the site. The client is concerned about potential criminal charges or civil lawsuits over the website. His attorney explains to the client how he could use a series of dummy limited liability corporations, mail forwarding addresses, and offshore bank accounts to avoid detection. Each of the steps of the process the attorney describes is technically legal – creating the corporate entities, purchasing mail-forwarding

services, and opening bank accounts in Belize. The attorney decides not to charge the client for this advice session but bills the client for other transactional work performed. Is the attorney subject to discipline?

a) Yes, because the attorney did not bill the client for the consultation, in violation of their regular retainer agreement.

b) No, because the individual steps that the attorney proposed would be legal in isolation, and merely gave an honest opinion about the actual consequences that appear likely to result from a client's conduct.

c) Yes, because a lawyer must avoid assisting a client in fraudulent or criminal activity, which includes suggesting how to conceal the wrongdoing.

d) No, because the attorney did not bill the client for the advice, and therefore did not benefit personally from counseling the client.

Rule 1.2 Cmt 9

100. An attorney tells a client that certain features of the client's business proposal would constitute money laundering under current federal statutes. The discussion goes through the statute in detail, and the attorney explains why the course of action would meet the statutory definition of money laundering. In addition, the attorney discusses the various monitoring and reporting mechanisms that federal enforcement agencies have in place to detect money laundering, to convince the client that he would not escape arrest and prosecution if he proceeds. The client absorbs the information and uses it to structure a more elaborate money-laundering scheme. He exploits some ambiguity in the statute and the reporting requirements to make his enterprise much more difficult to detect, and this complicates enforcement and prosecution efforts against him. Overall, the attorney's advice turned out to be incredibly useful to the client in avoiding detection and expanding his criminal enterprise. Is the attorney a party to the client's course of action?

a) No, because the attorney's subjective intentions were not wrong in the situation.

b) No, because the fact that a client uses advice in a course of action that is criminal or fraudulent of itself does not make a lawyer a party to the course of action.

c) Yes, because there is no distinction between presenting an analysis of legal aspects of questionable conduct and recommending how a crime or fraud might be committed with impunity.

d) Yes, because a lawyer may not discuss the legal consequences of any proposed criminal course of conduct with a client and or counsel a client to determine the validity, scope, meaning or application of the law.

Rule 1.2 Cmt. 9

101. Client is an inexperienced drug dealer and consults with his attorney about the legal ramifications of his business. Without explicitly endorsing or encouraging the client in his criminal enterprise, the attorney conducts research at the client's request about various drug laws and sentencing guidelines. The attorney writes a detailed memorandum of law explaining that certain threshold quantities of drugs, according to the relevant statutes, create a presumption of "intent to distribute" or trigger a significant sentencing enhancement. Similarly, the attorney explains that statutes and sentencing guidelines impose higher-grade charges and severe sentencing enhancements if a drug dealer brings a firearm to a transaction. The client mulls over the information and decides to change his business model from bulk sales of narcotics to selling smaller quantities in more individual transactions, such that each sale constitutes only the lowest-level misdemeanor. The client also instructs all his subordinates to avoid carrying firearms and instead to refill pepper spray devices with hydrochloric acid, which they spray in the face of their opponents in any altercation, causing severe disfigurement. Is it proper for the attorney to provide such legal advice to the client?

a) Yes, because a lawyer may discuss the legal consequences of any proposed course of conduct with a client and may counsel or assist a client to make a good faith effort to determine the validity, scope, meaning or application of the law.

b) Yes, because the Rules of Professional Conduct confer upon the client the ultimate authority to determine the purposes or objectives of the legal representation, within the limits imposed by law and the lawyer's professional obligations.

c) No, because off the attorney-client privilege and the duty of confidentiality.

d) No, because a lawyer must to avoid assisting the client in criminal activity by suggesting how to conceal the wrongdoing.

Rule 1.2(d)

102. A certain attorney represents a client in a drug trafficking case. The client asks the attorney to deliver a package to a friend of the client. The client tells the attorney that the package contains illegal drugs, but he assures the attorney that he will not reveal who made the delivery if police discover that the transfer occurred. the attorney advises that he will not participate in the transfer. The attorney does not advise the court of the client's request and remains the client's attorney on the drug trafficking case. Are the attorney's actions improper?

a) No, because an attorney does not have to decline or withdraw from cases unless the client demands that the attorney engage in illegal conduct.

b) No, because the attorney has no obligation to withdraw from a case if he does not engage in illegal activity with or for a client.

c) Yes, because an attorney must decline or withdraw from representing a client if the client asks that the attorney engage in illegal conduct.

d) Yes, because an attorney must notify the court if his client asks or demands that he engage in illegal activity.

RULE 1.4
COMMUNICATIONS WITH THE CLIENT

103. An attorney represented a defendant who was facing criminal charges for violating a newly enacted statute. The statute that made certain activities that had previously been minor misdemeanors into felonies. The district attorney handling the case spoke to the defendant's attorney, explaining that this was an important test case of a new statute, so the D.A.'s office was seeking the maximum penalty. The state did, however, offer a reduced sentence if the defendant would plead guilty, but this would still carry three years of jail time. Outraged, the attorney shouted that this had always been a misdemeanor charge in the past, which carried no jail time at all, and ended the conversation abruptly at that point. Without mentioning the conversation to the defendant, the attorney drafted an impassioned motion to dismiss the charges and filed it with the court. The attorney had a reasonable belief that his motion could be successful, though it was far from certain. The judge agreed with the attorney and granted the motion, dismissing all the charges against the attorney's client. Were the attorney's actions permissible under the Model Rules?

a) Yes, the dismissal of the charges in this case meant that the client was far better off than if he had considered the plea bargain offered by the prosecutor.

b) Yes, the attorney would still have a chance to tell the client about the proffered plea if the judge had not granted the motion to dismiss.

c) No, a defense lawyer who receives a proffered plea bargain in a criminal case must promptly inform the client of its substance, unless the client has previously told the lawyer to accept or to reject the offer.

d) No, the attorney should have given more consideration to the serious public policy reasons for the legislature enacting the new statute.

Rule 1.4

104. A litigation attorney represented a certain defendant in a lawsuit. The client was absent during the final pre-trial hearing about which experts the court would permit to testify at trial for each side. As the hearing was wrapping up,

plaintiff's counsel asked the court to have the record sealed in the upcoming trial, and to have reporters banned from the courtroom. The trial involved sensitive information about the mental health of some of the children involved as parties and witnesses in the case. The court agreed but asked if the defendant had any objections. The defendant's attorney tried to reach his client by phone, but he could not get through. There was no obvious reason to oppose the motion, so the attorney agreed on his client's behalf. The judge ordered the record sealed for the upcoming trial. The client never returned the attorney's phone call, and the attorney forgot to mention what had transpired until they were sitting in court on the first day of trial, two weeks later. The client was upset, having planned to use media publicity about the case to draw attention to the other side's exploitation of children as witnesses in litigation. The attorney told the client that the judge would not reverse the decision now that the trial was underway. Were the attorney's actions permissible, under the Model Rules?

a) Yes, it was proper for the lawyer to defer to the judge on this question, lest he risk angering the judge or unnecessarily inconveniencing the opposing party.

b) Yes, the opposing party's request was reasonable, and even if Attorney had asked Client and Client disapproved, Attorney could not have ethically objected to the request.

c) No, because the importance of the action under consideration and the feasibility of consulting with the client meant the lawyer's duty required consultation prior to acting.

d) No, because even when an immediate decision is necessary during trial, and the exigency of the situation may require the lawyer to act without prior consultation, the lawyer must tell the client about it as soon as possible.

Rule 1.4

105. A certain attorney represents a client in a transactional matter, a complex business merger. The parties have agreed in advance, by contract, to engage in good-faith negotiations, but that if an agreement does not emerge within six months, either party can abandon the deal and cease negotiations. Three months into the negotiations, the parties are close to a final agreement. The attorney has been conducting the negotiations without the client present, checking in with the client from time to time. One day, the other party presents a detailed

proposal that would resolve all remaining issues. This proposal would give each side most of what it wants, but also requires a few concessions from each party. The attorney calls the client immediately and gives a brief overview of the new proposal, hitting most of the highlights and carefully explaining the bottom-line concerning the final buyout price to complete the merger. The client gives the attorney consent to consummate the agreement. Could the attorney be subject to discipline for how he handled the final agreement?

a) Yes, because it is improper for a lawyer to make an agreement in advance to reach a settlement or other final agreement by a certain date, so that parties will abandon negotiations after that point.

b) Yes, when there is time to explain a proposal made in a negotiation, the lawyer should review all important provisions with the client before proceeding to an agreement, and the facts suggest that the attorney did not necessarily explain all the concessions that the client would have to make.

c) No, because the attorney had implied authorization from the client to work out all important provisions of the agreement, and the client does not need to know all the details.

d) No, because the attorney obtained the client's consent about the bottom line before proceeding to a final agreement.

Rule 1.4 Cmt 5

106. A certain attorney represents a client in a litigation matter. The client was not present during the last pre-trial hearing at which the lawyers argued about whether certain experts on each side could testify at trial. The trial was to start the following week. At the end of the hearing, the opposing counsel asked the court to have the record sealed in the upcoming trial, and to have reporters banned from the courtroom. He explained that the testimony at trial would necessarily reveal some of his client's trade secrets, and it was important to the client to keep the trial records sealed. The judge was amenable to this suggestion and asked the attorney if he had any objections. The attorney tried to call the client, but the client did not answer his phone right then. Unfortunately, the attorney could not think of a compelling reason for the client to oppose the motion, so he agreed, and the judge

set the matter for a sealed-record trial. Three hours later, the client returned the attorney's call, and the attorney explained what had transpired. The client felt dismayed because he had planned to use this litigation as a test case for subsequent litigation over the same type of issue, but the attorney explained that it would now be difficult to get the judge to reverse course on this point. Was it proper for the attorney to agree to the request without obtaining the client's prior consent?

a) Yes, because the opposing party's request was reasonable, and even if the attorney had asked the client and the client disapproved, the attorney could not have ethically objected to the request.

b) Yes, because during a trial, when an immediate decision becomes necessary, the exigency of the situation may require the lawyer to act without prior consultation, assuming the lawyer promptly informs the client of actions the lawyer has taken on the client's behalf.

c) No, because the importance of the action under consideration and the feasibility of consulting with the client meant the lawyer's duty required consultation prior to acting.

d) No, because a lawyer must promptly consult with and secure the client's consent prior to taking action unless prior discussions with the client have resolved what action the client wants the lawyer to take.

Rule 1.4 Cmt 3

107. An attorney represented a client in a criminal matter. The client had a history of mental illness, and the court ordered a psychological examination to determine if the client would be competent to stand trial. The case did not involve an insanity defense or a defense of diminished capacity. The psychologist who evaluated the client spoke privately to the attorney and explained that the client was indeed competent to stand trial, but that in his opinion, the client also suffered from delusional narcissism, paranoia, and oppositional-defiant syndrome. The psychologist pleaded with the attorney not to tell the client about this diagnosis, because the disclosure could harm the client, triggering an episode of paranoia in which the client would suspect that everyone around him was conspiring to institutionalize him, and he would become uncooperative at trial and mistrustful of his own

lawyer. Then the attorney told the client that the psychologist had deemed him competent to stand trial and did not disclose the rest of the psychologist's assessment. Was it proper for the attorney to conceal the psychologist's diagnosis from the client?

a) Yes, a lawyer may delay transmission of information when the client would be likely to react imprudently to an immediate communication, including a psychiatric diagnosis of a client when the examining psychiatrist indicates that disclosure would harm the client.

b) Yes, because the psychologist's duty was only to evaluate for competence to stand trial, so his additional diagnosis was outside the scope of his assignment.

c) No, because the information must be appropriate for a client who is a comprehending and responsible adult, and if the client is competent to stand trial, he is competent to receive the rest of the psychologist's diagnosis.

d) No, because full communication between the lawyer and the client is necessary for the client effectively to participate in the representation.

Rule 1.4 Cmt 7

108. An attorney prepared a contract for a client in 2016. The matter is nearing competition, so the representation regarding that matter has not ended. In 2018, while using that agreement as a template to prepare an agreement for a different client, the attorney discovers a material error in the agreement. The error does not, however, furnish a colorable claim for malpractice, because the client did not suffer any injury, and the client in the meantime canceled the agreement with the other party due to other factors. Even so, any reasonable client who learned of this mistake would lose confidence in their lawyer's competence or diligence. On those facts, do the Model Rules require the lawyer to inform the client of the error?

a) Yes, because Rule 1.4 requires that lawyers disclose material errors made during the representation to current clients, whenever the error would predictably cause a client to consider terminating the representation even in the absence of harm or prejudice.

b) Yes, because Model Rule 1.16(d) requires that a lawyer, upon termination of a

representation, must "take steps to the extent reasonably practicable to protect a client's interests, such as giving reasonable notice to the client."

c) No, because the Model Rules do not require disclosure of material errors to clients after the representation in that matter has ended.

d) No, because it is not clear on these facts that the former client has suffered any actual injury or prejudice, even if the error was material.

ABA Formal Op. 481

109. An attorney was a partner at Big Firm, which represented Conglomerate Corporation and Giant Company in corporate merger negotiations. Big Firm had state-of-the-art network firewalls, virus protection, password protection, and other data security features in place. Nevertheless, one Friday evening some hackers managed to breach Big Firm's networks and access client information and partner emails, for purposes of engaging in insider trading. The firm detected the breach within a few hours and notified state and federal law enforcement. The stock exchange had closed for the weekend, and law enforcement managed to apprehend the hackers over the weekend, before they had a chance to review the stolen information and share useful data or engage in illegal stock trades. The clients suffered no losses or adverse effects, but they could have. Big Firm is worried about how news of the breach would affect their reputation, and that it might invite other hackers to target their firm, so they would prefer to keep the incident a secret. The partners at Big Firm claim they have no duty to disclose to its clients that the breach occurred, given that no harm resulted. Are they correct?

a) Yes, the firm's need to keep the incident secret outweighs any reasons to disclose the breach to the clients.

b) Yes, the firm fulfilled its duties to the clients by having reasonable measures in place to safeguard confidential client information, so no further disclosures to the clients are necessary.

c) No, a firm's competence in preserving a client's confidentiality is a strict liability standard that requires the lawyer to be invulnerable or impenetrable.

d) No, when a data breach occurs involving, or having a substantial likelihood of involving, material client confidential information a lawyer has a duty to notify the client of the breach.

Rule 1.4; ABA Formal Op. 18-483

110. An attorney prepared a contract for a client in 2015. The matter has concluded, the representation has ended, and the person for whom the contract was prepared is not a client of the attorney or law firm in any other matter. In 2018, while using that agreement as a template to prepare an agreement for a different client, the attorney discovers a material error in the agreement. On those facts, do the Model Rules require the lawyer to inform the former client of the error?

a) Yes, because Rule 1.4 requires that lawyers disclose material errors made during the representation to the clients.

b) Yes, because Model Rule 1.16(d) requires that a lawyer, upon termination of a representation, must "take steps to the extent reasonably practicable to protect a client's interests, such as giving reasonable notice to the client."

c) No, because the Model Rules do not require disclosure of material errors to former clients after the representation has ended.

d) No, because it is not clear on these facts that the former client has suffered any actual injury or prejudice, even if the error was material.

ABA Formal Op. 18-481

111. An attorney prepared a contract for a client in 2013. The matter concluded, and the representation regarding that matter has ended, though the attorney continues to represent the same client on some unrelated matters. In 2017, while using that agreement as a template to prepare an agreement for a different client, the attorney discovers a material error in the agreement. On those facts, do the Model Rules require the lawyer to inform the client of the error?

a) Yes, because Rule 1.4 requires that lawyers disclose material errors made during the representation to current clients, and the attorney's ongoing representation on other matters means a client-lawyer relationship still exists.

b) Yes, because Model Rule 1.16(d) requires that a lawyer, upon termination of a representation, must "take steps to the extent reasonably practicable to protect a client's interests, such as giving reasonable notice to the client."

c) No, because the Model Rules do not require disclosure of material errors to clients after the representation in that matter has ended.

d) No, because it is not clear on these facts that the former client has suffered any actual injury or prejudice, even if the error was material.

ABA Formal Op. 18-481

112. An attorney prepared a contract for a client in 2016. The matter is nearing conclusion, so the representation regarding that matter has not ended. In 2018, while using that agreement as a template to prepare an agreement for a different client, the attorney discovers a material error in the agreement. The error does not, however, furnish a colorable claim for malpractice, because the client has not yet suffered any injury, and it is not clear that the attorney's error falls far enough below the industry standards to meet the legal standards for negligence. On those facts, do the Model Rules require the lawyer to inform the client of the error?

a) Yes, because Model Rule 1.16(d) requires that a lawyer, upon termination of a representation, must "take steps to the extent reasonably practicable to protect a client's interests, such as giving reasonable notice to the client."

b) Yes, because Rule 1.4 requires that lawyers disclose material errors made during the representation to current clients, even though the error does not furnish the basis for a valid malpractice claim.

c) No, because the Model Rules do not require disclosure of material errors to clients after the representation in that matter has ended.

d) No, because it is not clear on these facts that the former client has suffered any actual injury or prejudice, even if the error was material.

ABA Formal Op. 18-481

RULE 1.5   FEES

113. An attorney agreed to represent a plaintiff in a personal injury lawsuit, and the client agreed to pay the attorney a contingent fee based on a percentage of the award in the case. The attorney put all the terms of the fee agreement in written form in a letter to the client. The letter explained the percentage that should accrue to the attorney the event of settlement, trial, or appeal; litigation and other expenses that the attorney would deduct from the recovery; and that such deductions would come out of the total before the calculation of the contingent fee. The letter also explained all potential expenses for which the client could be liable, if the client prevailed in the case or not. The client received the letter, read it carefully, and called the attorney to give verbal assent and confirmation to all the terms. The client's spouse later discarded the letter, and the attorney proceeded with the representation. Could the attorney be subject to discipline, based on these facts?
a)   Yes, because the client did not sign the fee agreement.
b)   Yes, because the attorney arranged to deduct expenses from the total award before the calculation of the contingent fee, rather than after the determination of the fee.
c)   No, because the letter constituted a written fee agreement stipulating all the terms of the contingent fee arrangement, and the client gave full consent and authorization over the phone.
d)   No, under the Model Rules, a written fee agreement signed by the client is preferable but not a requirement.

Rule 1.5(c)

114. Boutique Firm charges its clients fifteen cents per page for photocopies done in-house on the firm's copiers. All new clients receive a schedule of fees before the representation begins that clearly specifies such charges, and client bills clearly itemize photocopying charges. The charge applies even if the client never sees the photocopies, as when associates conducting research must copy sections of cases, statutes, and regulations, or circulate draft memoranda to other lawyers working on the case. The charge also applies when the firm must produce documents for the other party in response to a discovery request. Boutique Firm set the amount at fifteen cents per page because that approximates the firm's own costs in leasing the high-tech photocopiers, purchasing paper and toner cartridges, and paying for frequent maintenance and repairs of the machines by technicians. Could Boutique Firm be subject to discipline for charging clients per page for photocopies done in-house?
a)   Yes, because lawyers may charge clients only for the lawyer's time (legal fees), expert fees, and court costs.
b)   Yes, because a lawyer may not charge a client for overhead expenses normally associated with properly maintaining, staffing, and equipping an office.
c)   No, a lawyer may seek reimbursement for the cost of services performed in-house, such as copying, or for other expenses incurred in-house, such as telephone charges, either by charging a reasonable amount to which the client has agreed in advance or by charging an amount that reasonably reflects the cost incurred by the lawyer.
d)   No, it is permissible to pass charges through to the client if the lawyer is charging the client on an hourly (itemized) basis, but not if the lawyer is charging a contingent fee or a fixed fee for the representation.

Rule 1.5 Cmt. 1; ABA Formal Op. 93-379

115. An attorney represented a client in a divorce case and charged the client an hourly fee for the representation. The client won primary custody of the child from the marriage, and the ex-spouse (the child's other parent) would take the child during school vacations. A year after the case ended, the client wanted to reopen the case to seek additional child support, because in the intervening months, the child had developed a disability that imposed high medical care costs on the client, and at the same time, the ex-spouse had won the Mega-Millions lottery, and was living a luxurious, profligate lifestyle. Would it be permissible for the attorney to represent the client in this matter on a contingent fee basis, given that the divorce was already final?
a)   Yes, the Model Rules do not preclude a contract for a contingent fee for legal representation in connection with the recovery of post-judgment balances due under support, alimony, or other financial orders.
b)   Yes, because the circumstances have changed, given that the client now must pay

unexpected medical bills for the child, and the ex-spouse has won the lottery.

c) No, the Model Rules preclude a contract for a contingent fee for legal representation in connection with the recovery of post-judgment balances due under support, alimony, or other financial orders.

d) No, the attorney may not enter into an arrangement for, charge, or collect any fee in a domestic relations matter, the payment or amount of which is contingent upon the securing of a divorce or upon the amount of alimony or support, or property settlement in lieu thereof

Rule 1.5(d)

116. A certain defendant was facing charges for assault with a deadly weapon. A local criminal defense attorney offered to represent this defendant on a contingent fee basis. In other words, the attorney would charge no fee (the client would pay nothing) if the case resulted in a conviction, but he would pay only if the lawyer won an acquittal. Having no funds on hand to hire a lawyer by any other means, the client was eager to do this and consented to the arrangement, in writing. Which of the following best describes the lawyer's situation?

a) The attorney is subject to discipline for charging a contingent fee in a criminal matter.

b) The attorney is not subject to discipline because the client consented and confirmed it in writing.

c) The attorney is subject to discipline for failing to include a third option, a partial fee if the case ends with a plea bargain to a lesser charge that requires no jail time.

d) The attorney's arrangement would constitute ineffective assistance of counsel in a criminal case.

Rule 1.5(d)(2)

117. Big Firm raises its hourly billing rate for all clients annually, on the first day of the year, by two percent. The initial engagement documents at the outset of representation explain this practice clearly, but Big Firm does not inform clients in writing each time the annual rate increase occurs. Is it proper for Big Firm to handle its billing and rate increases in this manner?

a) Yes, unless the clients object, their acquiescence to the rate increases constitutes acceptance of the new contractual term.

b) Yes, periodic, incremental increases in a lawyer's regular hourly billing rates are permissible if understands and accepts such practice at the commencement of the client-lawyer relationship, and the periodic increases are reasonable under the circumstances.

c) No, Big Firm had an ethical duty to remind the clients of the rate increase whenever it occurred.

d) No, it is unethical to change fees after the representation has begun, unless the attorney complies with the disclosure and documentation requirements for business transactions with clients.

Rule 1.5(b); ABA Formal Op. 11-458

118. A new federal Treasury Regulation provides that attorneys who prevail in tax cases on behalf of their clients against the Revenue Service may receive attorneys' fees at the fixed rate of $100 per hour, not to exceed $100,000. A certain attorney lives in a state that allows "reasonable" fees, and he makes a written fee agreement with the client for an additional $100 fee per hour, on top of whatever fees the Treasury Regulations allow in their case. If the client provides written informed consent, could the attorney be subject to discipline for this fee agreement?

a) Yes, because state rules about legal fees are subject to limitations by applicable law, such as government regulations regarding fees in certain tax matters.

b) Yes, because tax matters require a contingent fee agreement, not an hourly rate, lest attorneys have a temptation to drag out the case to drive up their collectable fees.

c) No, so long as the fee agreement incorporates the federal regulation by reference, it is permissible for clients and lawyers to make a private agreement for additional compensation to the lawyer.

d) No, so long as the total fees paid do not exceed $100,000.

Rule 1.5 Cmt 3

119. An attorney worked as a purchaser for Conglomerate Corporation for many years before law school. After graduating and becoming a licensed practitioner, the attorney opened his own firm and represented many of Conglomerate Corporation's outside vendors in their

contractual disputes with Conglomerate. In fact, the attorney advertised every month in local trade journals that he was a former purchaser for Conglomerate Corporation and could provide "affordable and experienced legal representation" to vendors who had legal disputes with corporations like Conglomerate. Regarding fees, the attorney would tell prospective clients that he sometimes billed hourly and sometimes charged a flat fee, depending on the complexity and time demands of each matter, and that this was difficult to predict beforehand. If this uncertainty was acceptable to the client, the attorney would agree to represent the individual. After the representation was complete, the attorney would decide how to bill the client. Is it proper for the attorney to handle fees in this manner?

a) Yes, so long as the fees and expenses are consistently reasonable, and each client consents.

b) Yes, so long as the attorney does not base the decision on whether to charge an hourly rate or a flat fee on which will be higher.

c) No, the attorney must inform the client of the basis or rate of the fee and expenses before or within a reasonable time after commencing the representation.

d) No, hourly fee agreements must be in writing, signed by the client at the outset of the representation.

Rule 1.5(b)

120. An attorney had her own firm, and she employed a paralegal who had previously worked for another firm. The attorney agreed to represent two new clients: a plaintiff in a personal injury lawsuit, and a seller in commercial real estate transaction. The personal injury plaintiff had a case that was unlikely to succeed due to evidentiary problems, though it was legally valid and factually plausible. The attorney wanted to charge a fixed, non-contingent fee up front for this case, and the client reluctantly agreed. The seller of the commercial real estate, on the other hand, was in a hurry to complete the deal and wanted to liquidate the asset for more than its fair market value, which was possible but also unlikely to succeed. The attorney offered to handle the transaction on a contingency fee basis. If she

could negotiate with prospective buyers and convince one to buy the property immediately for a price above the appraised value, she would receive thirty percent of the sale price as a fee, but if it sold at or below the market value, or took more than two months to sell, the attorney would receive only reimbursement for the transaction's costs and expenses. The paralegal told the attorney that these fee agreements were impermissible, because personal injury plaintiff's normally paid contingent fees, and real estate transactions had to be on a fixed or hourly fee basis. The attorney disagreed, but she did not check the ethical rules herself to confirm this. Which of the following is correct?

a) The attorney may charge a contingent fee in the personal injury case but not in the real estate transaction.

b) It is improper to charge a plaintiff in a personal injury case a flat fee regardless of the case outcome, but it is permissible to charge the seller a contingent fee in a real estate transaction.

c) It is improper to charge a plaintiff in a personal injury case a flat fee regardless of the case outcome, and it is impermissible to charge the seller a contingent fee in a real estate transaction.

d) It is proper to charge a plaintiff in a personal injury case a flat fee regardless of the case outcome, and it is permissible to charge the seller a contingent fee in a real estate transaction.

Rule 1.5(c)

121. An attorney worked as an associate for several years at Big Firm, and while she worked there, she started a sexual relationship with one of the clients of the firm, whom the firm had already been representing before she began working there. Nevertheless, the attorney did not make partner at the firm due to this incident, even though it had not resulted in a disciplinary action, so she eventually left and started her own practice. She then made radio commercials to attract new clients to her firm, in which she boasted that she had been an associate at Big Firm, but that she did not make partner there merely because she had sex with a client a few times. This advertisement brought many new male clients to her firm. One day, the attorney was flying cross-country to attend a deposition

on behalf of one client. This counted as travel time she would ordinarily bill to that client, as permitted by the ethical rules. During the flight, she decided not to watch the movie or read a book, but to work instead on drafting a motion for another client. Would it be permissible for her to charge both clients, each of whom agreed to hourly billing, for the time during which she was traveling on behalf of one and drafting a document on behalf of the other?

a) Yes, each client is receiving the legal services they paid for during that time.

b) Yes, the Model Rules encourage this type of efficiency, because it allows lawyers to provide legal representation to more people who need it.

c) No, if the attorney flies for six hours for one client, while working for five hours on behalf of another, she has not earned eleven billable hours.

d) No, because the work for which she is charging each client does not relate to the type of legal services she advertised.

Rule 1.5; ABA Formal Op. 93-379

122. Big Firm hired associates from the top of their class at the most prestigious law schools. Big Firm's partners often boasted to their clients, truthfully, that all their associates did federal judicial clerkships before joining Big Firm as lawyers. Conglomerate Corporation retained Big Firm regularly as outside legal counsel, partly in reliance on these representations from Big Firm's partners about the credentials and experience of their associates. On one occasion, an associate at Big Firm did several hours of legal research on a certain topic for one client, Conglomerate Corporation. The research later turned out to be relevant to another client's legal matter. Would it be permissible for Big Firm to bill the second client, who agreed to pay fees based on the time spent on the case, the same amount for the recycled work product that it charged Conglomerate, the first client, if Conglomerate consented?

a) Yes, each client is receiving the legal services they paid for during that time.

b) Yes, the Model Rules encourage this type of efficiency, because it allows lawyers to provide legal representation to more people who need it.

c) No, attorneys who reuse old work product have not re-earned the hours previously billed and compensated when they first

generated that work product.

d) No, it is a conflict of interest for a lawyer to use information gleaned from the representation of one client to benefit another client.

Rule 1.5; ABA Formal Op. 93-379

123. A certain employee at Big Bank faced criminal charges for alleged embezzlement of bank funds, so she retained an attorney to defend her against the charges for a flat fee of twenty thousand dollars, which the client could pay in monthly installments. The next day, a different Big Bank employee confessed to having taken the money, so the prosecutor dropped the charges against the first suspect, that is, the employee who had hired the attorney. The attorney had done nothing on the case except the original consultation with the bank employee as a prospective client, checking for conflicts of interest, and drafting an appearance for the court. The prosecutor was not aware that the original defendant had retained counsel; the withdrawal of the charges was due solely to another individual confessing to the crime. The attorney did not have to decline any other potential clients when he agreed to undertake the representation. After confirming with the client that the matter was over and further representation was unnecessary, the attorney sent the client a bill for the $15,000 flat fee. Was it proper for the attorney to do this?

a) Yes, the fee was reasonable given how quickly the attorney was able to obtain the full amount the client was hoping to recover.

b) Yes, but the attorney must share the fee with whatever lawyer is representing the bank employee now facing charges for the same crime, because it was a flat fee for solving a specific legal problem.

c) No, the Model Rules prohibit flat fees in criminal cases, as well as monthly repayment plans from criminal defendants.

d) No, it would be unreasonable for the attorney to charge twenty thousand dollars for doing so little.

RESTATEMENT §34 - Reasonable and Lawful Fees

124. An attorney filed a lawsuit on behalf of a client against Conglomerate Corporation as the

defendant. The attorney's contingent fee contract stipulated that the attorney would receive thirty percent of recovery, if the case settled before trial, and a higher percentage if a trial was necessary. The client and the attorney signed an engagement contract for the provision of legal representation, which stipulated these terms. The document that the client signed clearly explained the percentage that should accrue to the attorney the event of settlement, trial, or appeal; litigation and other expenses that the attorney would deduct from the recovery; and that such deductions would come out of the total before the calculation of the contingent fee. The letter also discussed all potential expenses for which the client could be liable, if the client prevailed in the case or not. While the case was still in the discovery phase, Conglomerate Corporation offered the client a structured settlement. Under the settlement terms, Conglomerate would pay the client one million dollars up front, which would cover the plaintiff's medical costs, and the defendant would also purchase an annuity for the client. The annuity would cost Conglomerate $153,000, and it would guarantee the client monthly disbursements of $1000 until the client's death. The client is thirty years old. In terms of fees, how much should the attorney receive?

a) The attorney should receive $300,000 when Conglomerate's million-dollar lump sum payment arrives, but none of the subsequent disbursements from the annuity.

b) The attorney must choose between thirty percent of the initial million-dollar payment and thirty percent of the monthly annuity payments.

c) The attorney should receive $333,300 from combined value of the initial lump sum payment and the expected annuity payments.

d) The attorney should receive $300,000 when Conglomerate's million-dollar lump sum payment arrives, and $300 of each subsequent disbursement from the annuity, when the disbursements occur, until the client's death.

RESTATEMENT §35 Contingent-Fee Arrangements

125. A client hired an attorney to represent him in suing his employer for wrongful termination. The attorney proposed a fee arrangement that made the fees contingent on the outcome, and he included in the fee agreement that the attorney would advance the costs of litigation. The attorney lost the case at trial, and the client then refused to pay back the costs that the attorney had advanced beforehand. Can the attorney force the client to repay the litigation costs that the attorney advanced to him?

a) Yes, because even where the fee agreement stipulates that it is a contingent fee, this does not apply to litigation costs that a lawyer advances to a client.

b) Yes, because losing the case nullified the contingent fee agreement and created a quantum meruit situation.

c) No, because under the fee agreement, the client had to repay the attorney only if they won the case.

d) No, because the parties never made a legally binding fee agreement.

126. An attorney provides itemized billing to her clients: hours worked by partners and associates, expert fees, international phone call charges, court costs, stenographers used in depositions, and so forth. She also includes some itemized prorated charges for overhead costs. Her mobile phone, which she uses exclusively for work, has a plan with a fixed monthly charge and unlimited minutes and data, so she divides her monthly phone bill into hourly increments for each day of the month, and for each hour of time she works on a client's matter, she bills the client for an hourly increment of her phone bill, even if she did not use the phone during that hour. She reasons that she was paying to have a phone available during that time in case clients needed to reach her, so the clients can share the costs. She takes a similar approach with other fixed overhead costs, like the salaries of her support staff – each client bill has a ten-dollar charge for "general staffing costs." A nominal charge on each bill is for the administrative costs of billing clients. Could the attorney be subject to discipline for charging clients a share of her overhead costs and operating expenses?

a) Yes, because lawyers may charge clients only for the lawyer's time (legal fees), expert fees, and court costs.

b) Yes, because a lawyer may not charge a client for overhead expenses normally associated with properly maintaining, staffing, and equipping an office.

c) No, a lawyer may seek reimbursement for the cost of services performed in-house, such as copying, or for other expenses incurred in-house, such as telephone charges, either by charging a reasonable amount to which the client has agreed in advance or by charging an amount that reasonably reflects the cost incurred by the lawyer.

d) No, it is permissible to pass charges through to the client if the client receives a written, itemized bill that specifies the nature of each charge.

Rule 1.5; ABA Formal Op. 93-379

127. Boutique Firm charges its clients five dollars per page for photocopies done in-house on the firm's copiers. All new clients receive a schedule of fees before the representation begins that clearly specifies such charges, and client bills clearly itemize photocopying charges. The charge applies even if the client never sees the photocopies, as when associates conducting research must copy sections of cases, statutes, and regulations, or circulate draft memoranda to other lawyers working on the case. The charge also applies when the firm must produce documents for the other party in response to a discovery request. Boutique Firm set the amount at five-dollar per page, even though photocopies cost the firm only fifteen cents or so per page, because the surcharge generates a side revenue stream for the firm that enables it to charge lower legal fees, and to discourage clients from wasting paper. Boutique Firm is environmentally conscious. Is it permissible for Boutique Firm to assess clients a surcharge per page for photocopies done in-house?

a) Yes, a lawyer may seek reimbursement for the cost of services performed in-house, such as copying, or for other expenses incurred in-house, such as telephone charges, either by charging a reasonable amount to which the client has agreed in advance or by charging an amount that reasonably reflects the cost incurred by the lawyer.

b) Yes, it is permissible to pass charges through to the client if the lawyer is charging the client on an hourly or itemized basis, but not if the lawyer is charging a contingent fee or a fixed fee for the representation.

c) No, because lawyers may charge clients only for the lawyer's time (legal fees),

expert fees, and court costs

d) No, a lawyer may charge the client no more than the actual cost of making a copy on the photocopy machine plus a reasonable allocation of overhead expenses directly associated with the provision of the service, such as the salary of a full-time photocopy machine operator.

Rule 1.5 Cmt. 1; ABA Formal Op. 93-379

128. An attorney consulted with a potential client, a plaintiff in a personal injury lawsuit, and the client agreed to pay the attorney a contingent fee based on a percentage of the award in the case, which appeared to be a complicated matter that would necessitate the testimony of experts at trial, and depositions of the experts and other witnesses beforehand. As the consultation concluded, the client and the attorney signed an engagement contract for the provision of legal representation, which stipulated that the attorney would a contingent fee based on a percentage (one-third) of the award in the case. The document that the client signed clearly explained the percentage that should accrue to the attorney the event of settlement, trial, or appeal; litigation and other expenses that the attorney would deduct from the recovery; and that such deductions would come out of the total before the calculation of the contingent fee. The letter also discussed all potential expenses for which the client could be liable, if the client prevailed in the case or not. To impress the client, the attorney called the defendant's counsel in the matter, at the end of the consultation, while the client was still sitting in his office. Over the phone, the attorney explained the plaintiff's injuries, the medical expenses the plaintiff had incurred, and the one-million-dollar recovery they would seek in the lawsuit they planned to file. The defendant's lawyer checked with the defendant, who was standing next to him at the time, and then immediately agreed to pay the full amount that the client was seeking to recover – a million dollars – without litigation. Would it be permissible for the attorney to charge the client one-third of the million dollars as a fee, given these facts?

a) Yes, a fee may be contingent on the outcome of the matter, and the attorney complied with all the requirements in the Model Rules for written disclosures about the terms of the fee.

b) Yes, the fee was reasonable given how quickly the attorney was able to obtain the full amount the client was hoping to recover, and the attorney complied with all the requirements in the Model Rules for written disclosures about the terms of the fee.

c) No, it is not reasonable for the attorney to charge over three hundred thousand dollars in fees for making one phone call at the end of the first consultation with the client.

d) No, an attorney cannot charge a contingent fee without first initiating litigation by filing pleadings in court.

Rule 1.5(a); ABA Formal Op. 94-389

129. An attorney had her own firm, and she employed a paralegal who had previously worked for another firm. The attorney agreed to represent two new clients: a plaintiff in a personal injury lawsuit, and a seller in commercial real estate transaction. The personal injury plaintiff had a case that was unlikely to succeed due to evidentiary problems, though it was legally valid and factually plausible. The attorney wanted to charge a fixed, non-contingent fee up front for this case, and the client reluctantly agreed over the phone, though the fee agreement was not in writing. The seller of the commercial real estate, on the other hand, was in a hurry to complete the deal and wanted to liquidate the asset for more than its fair market value, which was possible but not likely to happen. The attorney offered to handle the transaction on a contingency fee basis - if she could negotiate with prospective buyers and convince one to buy the property immediately for a price above the appraised value, she would receive thirty percent of the sale price as a fee, but if it sold at or below the market value, or took more than two months to sell, the attorney would receive only reimbursement for the transaction's costs and expenses. The client agreed to this arrangement over the phone, after the attorney had carefully explained it, though the fee agreement was not in writing. The attorney was successful in both matters, and both clients were satisfied with the results of the attorney's representation. The paralegal told the attorney that these fee agreements were impermissible, because personal injury plaintiff's normally paid contingent fees, and real estate transactions had to be on a fixed or hourly fee basis. The attorney disagreed, but she did not check the ethical rules herself to confirm this.

Which of the following is correct?

a) It was impermissible for the attorney to represent the plaintiff in a personal injury case without a written fee agreement, signed by the client, stating shall state the method of determining the fee.

b) It was permissible, though not preferable, for the attorney to represent the seller in a commercial real estate transaction on a contingent fee basis without a written fee agreement, signed by the client, stating the method of determining the fee.

c) In any representation related to civil litigation, the fee agreement must be in writing, signed by the client, and must state the method of determining the fee, but in representation for a transaction, without litigation, written fee agreements are preferable but not obligatory.

d) It was impermissible for the attorney to represent the seller in a commercial real estate transaction on a contingent fee basis without a written fee agreement, signed by the client, stating the method of determining the fee.

Rule 1.5(c)

130. Big Firm bills most of its clients on an hourly-billing basis, measured in fifteen-minute increments. Most of the firm's clients are large corporations. Big Firm's associates have burdensome billable hour requirements, so they spend as many hours as possible on every case, working every angle possible, taking an exhaustive approach to research memoranda, depositions of potential witnesses, and daily written updates to the corporate clients about their matters. The managing partners at Big Firm assign a dozen or more associates to every matter, no matter how small, even if that means some associates are merely double-checking or proofreading the work of other associates. The corporate clients and their insurers pay for these services, and whenever the clients prevail in litigation, they seek attorney's fees from the losing party. Could Big Firm (or its managing partners) be subject to discipline for charging unreasonable fees?

a) Yes, lawyers should not exploit fee arrangements based primarily on hourly charges by using wasteful procedures.

b) Yes, even though the corporate clients are willing purchasers of expensive legal services, when opposing parties lose and must pay attorney's fees to Big Firm's clients, they may end up paying law fees they would never have agreed to pay themselves.

c) No, corporate clients and liability insurers place a premium on excellent, comprehensive legal work and would prefer their lawyers give too much attention to their matters, rather than not enough.

d) No, the alternative is that inexperienced associates would make mistakes and might commit malpractice.

Rule 1.5 Cmt. 5.

131. An elderly retiree was reading the newspaper one morning, and he noticed an advertisement by a local attorney offering to write simple wills for $500. The attorney's name was unfamiliar, but the retiree called the phone number in the ad and asked the attorney to write a simple will for him, and the attorney agreed. Neither party, however, mentioned the advertisement or discussed the attorney's fees. The lawyer drafted the will, met with the client for signing, and then sent a bill for $1500. Under these circumstances, is the client entitled to pay only $500?

a) Yes, given that the attorney advertised for that amount and the client had seen the ad, the parties have an implicit contract under which the attorney must write the will in exchange for $500.

b) Yes, because the client is elderly, and charging $1500 would be unconscionable.

c) No, because the client never mentioned the advertisement, and the attorney's $1500 fee is reasonable.

d) No, because fee agreements must be in writing, signed by the client.

Restatement § 18 - Client–Lawyer Contracts

132. A client hired an attorney to represent her in business litigation, as the plaintiff, for a set hourly rate for the fees. By agreement, the fees were not due until the conclusion of the matter and the end of the representation. During the pleading phase of the lawsuit, however, the other party unexpectedly impleaded a third party, which made the case far more complicated and time-consuming for the attorney. The attorney

explained the problem to the client, and the two agreed to shift to a contingent-fee arrangement. The attorney carefully explained the tradeoffs involved in the different fee arrangements, and offered to continue, on an hourly basis, but both the client and attorney thought that contingent fees were now more appropriate. The attorney fully complied with the written notice requirements of Rule 1.8(a) for changing fees mid-representation. The following day, in another unexpected development, the opposing party offered to settle for a generous sum, more than the parties thought the case was worth, and the client immediately accepted. Must the client now pay the contingent fee to the attorney, even though the client would have paid significantly less under the original hourly fee agreement?

a) Yes, because the parties made a valid modification to a contract, which is legally enforceable.

b) Yes, the fee change was reasonable under these circumstances, and the attorney followed the notice requirements of the Model Rules.

c) No, lawyers may not change fee structures mid-representation if the original fee was reasonable at the time the representation began.

d) No, the client has a right to pay either the original fee or the modified fee, whichever is lower.

Restatement § 18 - Client–Lawyer Contracts

133. A certain attorney was a solo practitioner with many years of experience. For the last few years, the attorney represented a local cupcake shop, jointly owned by Susan and Diane. Susan was in a traffic accident while doing a personal errand, but she was driving the delivery van of the cupcake shop. Susan was co-owner of the shop and was therefore free to use the shop's vehicle for occasional person errands. The police who arrived on the scene determined that Susan was not at fault in the accident. The attorney did not do personal injury litigation, so Susan asked him to refer her to a personal injury lawyer who could represent her at trial. At the same time, Susan insisted that the attorney who handled the business transactional work for the cupcake shop should receive a referral fee, and the attorney is willing to accept joint responsibility for the matter but will not assist in the litigation. The attorney has a reasonable belief that the cupcake shop will not become a

party to the matter. Could the attorney be subject to discipline for making the referral and accept a referral fee without first obtaining written, informed consent of the cupcake shop, Diane, and Susan for a potential conflict of interest?

a) Yes, because the cupcake shop owns the vehicle that was in the accident, and Diane is co-owner of the shop and its assets, including the vehicle.

b) Yes, because the attorney has done other legal work for the cupcake shop and has confidential information that could be prejudicial to the new client.

c) No, representation of one client is not directly adverse to another client, and there is not a significant risk that the referral of Susan will be materially limited by attorney's responsibility to the cupcake shop.

d) No, because the attorney is merely referring the case to another lawyer and not handling the representation, even though he assumes joint responsibility for his passive involvement.

ABA Formal Op. 16-474

134. A certain attorney was a solo practitioner with many years of experience. For the last few years, the attorney represented a local cupcake shop, jointly owned by Susan and Diane. Susan was in a traffic accident while doing a personal errand, but she was driving the delivery van of the cupcake shop. Susan was co-owner of the shop and was therefore free to use the shop's vehicle for occasional person errands. There is a dispute among the parties involved in the accident about who was at fault. The attorney did not do personal injury litigation, so Susan asked him to refer her to a personal injury lawyer who could represent her at trial. At the same time, Susan insisted that the attorney who handled the business transactional work for the cupcake shop should receive a referral fee, and the attorney is willing to accept joint responsibility for the matter but will not assist in the litigation. The attorney expects the other driver in the accident to file a claim against Susan, and eventually against the cupcake shop as well, as the owner of the vehicle. In that case, the attorney's duty of loyalty to Susan and the cupcake shop could be in tension, and the attorney could have a material limitation in the representation. Can the attorney make the

referral and accept a referral fee, under these circumstances?

a) Yes, if the attorney obtains the informed consent, confirmed in writing, of both the cupcake shop and Susan as potential co-defendants, and otherwise meets the requirements of Model Rule 1.7(b).

b) Yes, if Diane gives her personal consent, confirmed in writing, and the other driver also consents.

c) No, the clients are likely to become adverse parties in the same litigation.

d) No, because there is no way for a solo practitioner to screen himself from the matter and avoid receiving a share of the fees earned for the referral.

ABA Formal Op. 16-474

135. A certain attorney was a solo practitioner with many years of experience. For the last few years, the attorney represented a local cupcake shop, jointly owned by Susan and Diane. Susan was in a traffic accident while doing a personal errand, but she was driving the delivery van of the cupcake shop. Susan was co-owner of the shop and was therefore free to use the shop's vehicle for occasional person errands. There is a dispute among the parties involved in the accident about who was at fault. The attorney did not do personal injury litigation, so Susan asked him to refer her to a personal injury lawyer who could represent her at trial. At the same time, Susan insisted that the attorney who handled the business transactional work for the cupcake shop should receive a referral fee, and the attorney is willing to accept joint responsibility for the matter but will not assist in the litigation. The other driver has already filed a claim against Susan and the cupcake shop, and the attorney can see that Susan's interests in the suit are adverse to the cupcake shop's interests. Even though the attorney does not plan to represent the cupcake shop in the lawsuit, the cupcake shop will continue to be the attorney's client for business and transactional matters. Can the attorney make the referral and accept a referral fee, under these circumstances?

a) Yes, if Diane gives her personal consent, confirmed in writing, and the other driver also consents.

b) Yes, if the attorney obtains the informed consent, confirmed in writing, of both the cupcake shop and Susan as potential co-

57

defendants, and otherwise meets the requirements of Model Rule 1.7(b).

c) No, the clients are likely to become adverse parties in the same litigation.

d) No, because there is no way for a solo practitioner to screen himself from the matter and avoid receiving a share of the fees earned for the referral.

ABA Formal Op. 16-474

RULE 1.16
DECLINING OR TERMINATING REPRESENTATION

136. An attorney injured his back and leg badly in a car accident. In the aftermath, the attorney became chemically dependent on prescription pain medications. This addiction progressed until it began to affect the attorney's relationships and work habits. The partners in his firm eventually insisted that the attorney seek professional help, so he enrolled in an outpatient rehab program and a twelve-step support group for painkiller addicts. The supervising psychiatrist in the outpatient program expressed concern about the attorney's complete dependence on the painkillers and his diminished ability to function physically or mentally. He advised the attorney to take a leave of absence from work, because he did not believe the attorney could competently fulfill his obligations to his clients. This same concern had prompted the attorney's partners to insist that he seek professional help. Just before enrolling in the outpatient program, a new client had approached the attorney about representing her in a tax dispute with the Internal Revenue Service. The attorney had handled such cases before, but it was not his specialty. The client is so desperate that he tells the attorney privately that he is considering shredding documents to hide some of his tax fraud from the IRS, which the attorney says he should not do, but worries that the client might do it anyway. May the attorney undertake the representation?

a) Yes, assuming the attorney can acquire the necessary knowledge or expertise through additional research to handle the complexity of the matter on the client's behalf.

b) Yes, because the attorney is getting help for his addiction problem and should recover soon.

c) No, because the client has proposed engaging in fraud or criminal activity.

d) No, because a physical or mental condition currently materially impairs the lawyer's ability to represent the client.

Rule 1.16(a)(2)

137. An attorney represented a municipality for several years, in accordance with a contract for legal services. The contract term ended, and the municipality published a new request for proposals, and in the end chose a different lawyer to provide legal services for the next several years. The municipality requested that the attorney (the one whose contract expired) provide the municipality's new counsel with all files - open and closed. The municipality has already paid the attorney in full for all his legal work. Which of the following would the attorney NOT have to provide to the municipality?

a) The materials provided to the lawyer by the municipality

b) Third party assessments, evaluations, or records paid for by the municipality.

c) A general assessment of the municipality or the municipality's matter

d) Legal documents filed with a tribunal, or documents completed and ready for submission to the tribunal.

ABA Formal Op. 15-471

138. An attorney represents a client in a family law matter. A hearing is set for Monday. On the Wednesday prior to the scheduled hearing, the client calls the attorney and advises that the client no longer wants the attorney to represent her; the attorney's representation is over as of the date and time of the call. The client advises that she intends to retain another attorney prior to the hearing. After receiving the call from the client, the attorney schedules another matter for Monday, does not appear at the hearing, and does nothing further on the case. Is the attorney subject to discipline?

a) Yes, if representation has begun, the attorney must to withdraw from the case and take reasonable steps to mitigate consequences to client if discharged by client.

b) Yes, the attorney must continue representation of client until attorney receives notice of discharge in writing and signed by client.

c) No, if the attorney receives notice of discharge directly from client, whether oral or in writing, attorney can cease work entirely on the case if client is aware of all hearings or other important dates scheduled as of the date of the discharge.

d) No, if the attorney has a reasonable belief that the client will have representation by other counsel soon, and that client will not have any consequences as a result of the immediate discharge, then the attorney may discontinue all work on case.

139. An attorney has already represented a certain client on several matters. Most recently, the attorney has represented the client in a litigation matter against the city's largest manufacturer. The manufacturer, whom the attorney is suing on behalf of the client, is both the city's largest employer and the largest purchaser of goods and services from small businesses in the area. As the discovery phase winds to a close and the court sets a trial date, the attorney learns that the client misused the attorney's services in the past to perpetrate fraud by having the attorney submit falsified documents to government entities and to insurance companies. The attorney is furious and yells at the client, using profanity. the attorney then petitions the court to let him withdraw from the representation, stating the reasons in general terms that do not betray specific client confidences. The client strongly objects to the attorney withdrawing from the representation, because the trial is only two months away, and all the other litigation firms in the city have conflicts of interest that prevent them from taking a case against the large manufacturer. It is indisputable that the withdrawal is materially prejudicial to the client, who may have to proceed into the trial pro se or must find a new lawyer from out of town. The court is willing to postpone the trial by three weeks to give the client time to find a new lawyer or prepare to represent himself. Is it proper for the attorney to withdraw from representation in this case, if the court has no objection?

a) Yes, because if a court or tribunal has no objection to an attorney withdrawing from a case, then the attorney has no ethical duty to continue the representation.

b) Yes, because withdrawal is permissible if the client misused the attorney's services in the past, even if the withdrawal would materially prejudice the client.

c) No, because a lawyer cannot withdraw from representation, if doing so would have a materially adverse impact on the client.

d) No, because the attorney yelled at the client and used profanity, which is completely unprofessional.

Rule 1.16 Cmt. 7

140. A trial judge is going through a divorce, and he hired an attorney to represent him. The attorney's law firm partner is representing another client who is appearing before the same judge in his personal injury lawsuit. The judge and the litigation client both give written informed consent to the representation despite the potential conflicts of interest. Even so, the judge is trying to keep the divorce quiet until after the upcoming elections, because this occurs in a state with elected judges. The judge therefore refuses to disclose to the parties in the personal injury case that counsel for one side is from the same firm as the lawyer representing the judge in his pending divorce. Neither the attorney nor his partner can reveal to opposing counsel in the personal injury case that their firm represents the judge, due to their duty of confidentiality. The judge believes he will be unbiased in the personal injury case, even though he is the client of a partner of one of the lawyers in the case, so the judge does not need to disqualify himself from the case. The Code of Judicial Ethics does require, however, that the judge disclose the representation to the litigants appearing before him, which the judge has refused to do at this time. Can the attorney continue representing the judge in his divorce?

a) Yes, if the judge and the litigation client both provided written, informed consent, then the attorney can continue with the representation.

b) Yes, because in a case where the judge does not need to disqualify himself, the attorneys would not need to withdraw merely because the judge refuses to disclose the representation to the other litigants appearing before the judge in the tort case.

c) No, because the attorney would need the judge's permission to withdraw from representing him in the divorce case, and the judge is unlikely to agree to that.

d) No, because the attorney must withdraw from the representation of the judge under these circumstances.

ABA Formal Ethics Op. 07-449

141. An attorney had to abandon his home and his vehicle to take refuge in a FEMA rescue shelter following a natural disaster in his area. Some of the attorney's clients required immediate legal services that the attorney was unable to provide. What would be the attorney's ethical duty in this situation?

a) The attorney must temporarily withdraw from the practice of law, and the attorney may seek reinstatement with the bar after the situation returns to normal.

b) The attorney must withdraw from representing the clients mentioned.

c) The attorney must find a way to contact the clients and request their patience.

d) The attorney must notify the bar immediately of his situation and request that the bar intervene on behalf of his clients.

Rule 1.16(b)(7); ABA Formal Op. 18-482

RULE 6.2
ACCEPTING/DECLINING
COURT APPOINTMENTS

142. An attorney had a firm that specialized in criminal defense work. He managed a team of young lawyers that worked on DUI cases and other noncomplex cases; while he would handle the more complicated or high-profile cases himself. The attorney received a court appointment to represent a defendant charged in a series of automobile thefts, and quickly reached an impasse with the defendant about whether he should maintain his innocence in the face of overwhelming evidence of his guilt. The appointee-client declared that he would gladly represent himself and maintain his own innocence rather than accept the attorney's

advice of agreeing to a guilty plea in exchange for leniency. The attorney knew that the county did not pay well for taking court appointments, and the defendant did not accept his advice, so he petitioned the court for permission to withdraw from the representation, and the court reluctantly agreed, but ordered the attorney to stay on the case as standby counsel. The defendant proceeded pro se, the jury convicted him, and the judge applied the maximum sentence. Could the attorney be subject to discipline for withdrawing from the representation?

a) Yes, assuming the client can prove that he would have been likely to prevail in the case if the attorney had not withdrawn

b) Yes, because he took advantage of the client's willingness to go pro se and left the client with ineffective representation

c) No, because the court attempted to force the attorney to work for much less than he can earn working for a non-appointed client

d) No, the attorney may ask for permission to withdraw as counsel, or to serve merely as standby counsel in this scenario.

143. A defendant faced criminal charges for running a Ponzi scheme and an elaborate conspiracy to help others commit tax fraud. The government seized all his accounts and assets, so he had no funds to hire defense counsel. The court, therefore, appointed a local attorney to represent the defendant in the case. The attorney had spent his entire career up to that point exclusively handling traffic-court charges and driving-while-intoxicated cases. Realizing that the complex case was far outside his range of experience or ability, the attorney tried to decline the appointment, but the court required a "showing of incompetence." The attorney followed through with the showing and the court granted the request to withdraw. Were the attorney's actions proper?

a) Yes, an attorney can seek withdrawal for good cause, such as lack of competence to handle certain specialized legal matters.

b) Yes, because an appointed attorney may withdraw at any time for any reason

c) No, because an attorney does not have to be an expert in a specific field of law to provide competent representation

d) No, the attorney has not sufficiently proven good cause for withdrawal

144. A court appointed a local solo practitioner to represent and indigent criminal defendant. The attorney sought to decline the appointment on the basis that he did not have legal malpractice insurance; normally, he explained, he could manage his risk of liability by carefully selecting clients whose legal needs were safely within his area of expertise, but the new court appointment involved some unfamiliar legal issues. Moreover, clients who select their attorney themselves are far less likely to blame or sue the attorney than clients who have no choice about the representation. Is the attorney's motion to decline the court appointment likely to succeed?

a) Yes, because lack of malpractice insurance is always good cause for withdrawal

b) Yes, because a court may not force an attorney to provide representation in a case over the attorney's objection, as the attorney's diligence and attention will inevitably suffer as a result.

c) No, attorneys may not seek to withdraw or decline from representation of indigent defendants, because this would leave too many indigent defendants without representation.

d) No, because lack of malpractice insurance is not good cause for withdrawal.

RULE 1.18
DUTIES TO PROSPECTIVE CLIENTS

145. An attorney was representing a criminal defendant, and he agreed to meet with one of the defendant's co-conspirators to learn more about what happened and to discuss what to expect as the case proceeded. At the beginning of the meeting, the co-conspirator gave the attorney a dollar bill, saying, "This is to establish attorney-client privilege." The discussions then proceeded as planned. Later, the co-conspirator turned state's witness against the attorney's client, and near the end of the proceedings, the prosecution moved to disqualify the attorney due to his conflict of interest. Did it establish attorney-client privilege and a conflict of interest problem when the co-conspirator gave the attorney a dollar?

a) Yes, giving the lawyer any amount of money before a conversation constitutes a token retainer and creates an attorney-client relationship.

b) Yes, giving the lawyer any amount of money before a conversation constitutes a token retainer and creates attorney-client privilege for the conversation, even if the attorney never provides legal representation afterwards.

c) No, giving money to the attorney did not create any attorney-client relationship.

d) No, the dollar was an insufficient amount to create attorney-client privilege.

Rule 1.18 Cmt. 2; United States v. Carlisle, No. 3:13-CR-012 JD, 2014 WL 958027, 2014 BL 67492 (N.D. Ind. Mar. 12, 2014)

146. In response to an attorney's advertising, which describes the attorney's education, experience, areas of practice, and contact information, and individual sent an email to the attorney describing their legal problem at length, including many personal details. Some of the information was unfavorable to the individual's legal interests. The attorney, who had never met or had any contact with the individual, read the long email in its entirety, and immediately sent a terse reply declining the representation. There was no consultation with the individual, and the attorney did not promise to provide representation. A few days later, the attorney received an inquiry from the opposing party in the case, and he agreed to represent the opposing party, and used information gleaned from the other individual's email to prevail in the matter. Was the attorney's conduct proper?

a) Yes, because the attorney declined to provide representation.

b) Yes, because the individual who sent the original email was not a prospective client for purposes of the Model Rules, and the attorney had no duty to keep the information confidential.

c) No, because written, oral, or electronic communications, constitute a consultation and meant the first individual was a prospective client.

d) No, because advertisements have the effect of soliciting such contacts from prospective clients, which normally include disclosures of confidential information the attorney should protect.

Rule 1.18 Cmt. 2

61

147. A family law attorney represented a client in a divorce proceeding. Early in the representation, before the client's spouse had retained counsel, the attorney advised her client to meet with other lawyers in the area for the sole purpose of creating a conflict of interest, that is, so that the client's spouse would be unable to retain the other lawyers for representation in the divorce. The client did so, and scheduled consultations with several other divorce attorneys in a "taint shopping" campaign, but he never intended to retain any of their services. Could the attorney be subject to discipline for instructing the client to do this?

a) Yes, because lawyers are normally vicariously liable for their client's actions.

b) Yes, because this is dishonest, interferes with the administration of justice, and has no purpose other than to interfere with the opposing party's ability to form a client-lawyer relationship.

c) No, because the other lawyers will still be able to represent the spouse if the spouse can simply show that the client engaged in taint-shopping.

d) No, because the lawyer merely counseled the client, and is not liable for the decisions and actions of the client after that.

Rule 1.18 Cmt. 2; Ill. Ethics Op. 12-18 (2012)

148. A family law attorney represented a client in a divorce proceeding. Early in the representation, before the client's spouse had retained counsel, the attorney advised her client to meet with other lawyers in the area for the sole purpose of creating a conflict of interest, that is, so that the client's spouse would be unable to retain the other lawyers for representation in the divorce. The client did so; the client scheduled consultations with several other divorce attorneys in a "taint shopping" campaign, but he never intended to retain any of their services. Could one of the other lawyers be subject to discipline for representing the spouse anyway, if they were lucky enough to have evidence to show that the original consultation was merely taint-shopping?

a) Yes, the person was not genuinely seeking legal representation, so the lawyer would have no duty to protect the confidentiality of the information disclosed and no conflict of interest.

b) Yes, because the other lawyers all declined the representation immediately.

c) No, because a lawyer shall not represent a client with interests materially adverse to those of a prospective client in the same or an overlapping matter if the lawyer received information from the prospective client that could be significantly harmful to that person in the matter.

d) No, because the client can easily find other representation, and therefore has suffered no injury.

Rule 1.18 Cmt. 2; Ill. Ethics Op. 12-18 (2012)

149. A prospective client consulted with an attorney about the possibility of securing legal representation in a matter. During the conversation, the client shared openly with the attorney about the strengths and weaknesses of her legal claims, including some personal information that would be embarrassing if it became public. Some of the information indicated the prospective client may have already waived some of her legal claims, and she may have been partly at fault on other points. The attorney considered it for a few minutes and then declined the representation, because he felt he could not devote adequate time to the case, and he thought the case was too problematic. In addition, he was skeptical that the prospective client would be able to pay his fees. A few weeks later, some of the attorney's other matters settled sooner than expected, freeing up his schedule, and another prospective client came for a consultation, who turned out to be the opposing party in the legal matter that the attorney had recently declined. This new prospective client had already gathered some convincing evidence supporting his side, and was wealthy, so paying the attorney's fees was not an issue. Would it be proper for the attorney to proceed with representing this new prospective client?

a) Yes, because no attorney-client relationship formed with the previous consultation, and the reasons for declining that case do not seem to apply now to the new prospective client.

b) Yes, because the information learned from the first consultation with the other party will be quite helpful to the new client.

c) No, because the information learned from the first consultation with the other party would be so helpful to the new client, and so harmful to the individual the attorney declined to represent.

d) No, because when the attorney's schedule freed up, he had a duty to contact the client he turned away and offer to represent her first.

150. An attorney undertook the representation of a client in a breach of contract claim and began working on the matter. A few weeks later, the opposing party in the litigation consulted with another lawyer in the attorney's firm about the same matter, but during the consultation, disclosed no confidential information except the identity of the other party and the nature of the claim. The other lawyer did a routine conflict check, quickly discovered the conflict with this new potential client, and immediately declined to represent the party. The lawyer and the attorney already representing the first client discussed the situation. Would it be proper for the attorney to disclose to his client that the opposing party had come in for a consultation with another lawyer in his firm?

a) The attorney has an ethical duty to inform his client that his firm conducted an uninformative initial consultation with the opposing party and declined the representation immediately.

b) The attorney has an ethical duty to withdraw from the representation because another lawyer at his firm consulted with the opposing party after the representation began.

c) The attorney may disclose to his client that the opposing party had an initial consultation with another lawyer in his firm, and that the other lawyer immediately declined the representation.

d) The attorney may not disclose to the client that the opposing party consulted with another lawyer in the firm but may continue to represent the client if the attorney does not use any information gleaned from the other party's consultation against the other party.

ABA Formal Op. 90-358, Rule 1.18

63

LITIGATION & OTHER FORMS OF ADVOCACY

RULE 3.1
MERITORIOUS CLAIMS & CONTENTIONS

151. An attorney agreed to represent a plaintiff in a claim against the client's employer for intentional infliction of emotional distress, because of insulting remarks the supervisor makes about his subordinates' intelligence and maturity. The attorney researched past court decisions and concluded that intentional infliction of emotional distress claims usually lose in employment settings like this. Moreover, in his various discussions with the client, the story has changed a little each time. The attorney now suspects that the client either is lying or is so confused that he will not be a credible witness at trial. The attorney would like to withdraw before filing an answer to the lawsuit asserting a defense of mistake of fact, because he knows they are unlikely to win, and he is not even sure if his client is telling the truth. Nevertheless, the client insists that the attorney should file the complaint before withdrawing from the case, so that the client does not miss the statute of limitations and forfeit the potential claim, but the client does not mind if he must find another lawyer to handle the discovery and trial phase. Would it be permissible, under the Model Rules, for the attorney to file the complaint, alleging intentional infliction of emotional distress?

a) Yes, because the client's defense has some basis in fact and law, even if it seems improbable in both regards.
b) Yes, because filing the answer contradicts the lawyer's duty of candor to the court.
c) No, because the attorney's research has led him to the conclusion that courts usually disfavor such defenses as a rule.
d) No, because the attorney suspects his client is either lying or is confused about the facts.

Model Rule 3.1

152. An attorney licensed in Texas represented a group of plaintiffs in a foreign court – a third-world dictatorship with no enforcement of lawyer licensing requirements. The lawsuit claimed that a former United States President was personally responsible for international terrorism, colonial imperialism, climate change, the worldwide malaria epidemic, human trafficking, and narcoterrorism. The local court in the third-world dictatorship found the former President liable on all charges, even though he was not present or aware of the proceedings and awarded damages of ten billion dollars to the local plaintiffs. The attorney then filed an action in the United States jurisdiction where the former U.S. President had a ranch and a personal bank account, seeking to execute on the foreign judgment. The state court immediately dismissed the action with prejudice, and the attorney appealed this decision, still hoping to execute the billion-dollar judgment against the former President. Is the attorney subject to discipline for bringing a frivolous action and appeal?

a) Yes, even though it was permissible to seek execution of the judgment, it was frivolous for the attorney to appeal a dismissal with prejudice in this situation.
b) Yes, it was impermissible for the attorney to bring the action for executing the judgment, and to appeal the dismissal, as there was basis in law or fact for doing so.
c) No, he made a good faith effort to appeal a summary dismissal of his claim in the lower court.
d) No, because they are seeking enforcement of a foreign judgment based on the facial reading of the foreign court's entered judgment.

In re Girardi, 611 F.3d 1027 (9th Cir. 2010).
Model Rule 3.1

153. A certain client was an indigent defendant and received court-appointed counsel for his trial. The trial ended in a conviction. A certain attorney served as his appointed counsel in the case. The client wanted to appeal his conviction, but the attorney believes, for several reasons, that there is no merit to an appeal. The client insisted that the attorney file an appeal before he missed the deadline and agreed that the attorney could withdraw from the case without the client's objection if he would simply file the appeal and provide the client with the opportunity to pursue the appeal pro se or with another lawyer. The

attorney presented a "no-merit" letter to the appellate court explaining that his client was appealing his conviction but that the attorney could see no merit in the appeal. Was the attorney's conduct proper, according to the United States Supreme Court?

a) Yes, because a lawyer shall not bring or defend a proceeding, or assert or controvert an issue therein, unless there is a basis in law and fact for doing so that is not frivolous.

b) Yes, assuming the letter preserves the client's right to proceed with the appeal on his own, and the client has agreed to terminate the representation after that.

c) No, because if the lawyer believed, with good reason, there was no merit to the appeal, he had an ethical duty to refuse to file the appeal or do anything to facilitate the defendant's abuse of the court system.

d) No, because a lawyer must prepare a brief referring to anything in the record that might potentially support the appeal and leave it to the appellate court to decide whether the appeal is truly frivolous.

> Anders v. California, 386 U.S. 738 (1967)

154. Client hired an attorney to represent her federal court litigation, defending against antitrust enforcement actions by the Federal Trade Commission and the Department of Justice. The attorney adopts a "quagmire" strategy, burying the government lawyers in several dozen motions to limit or compel discovery, to compel admissions or stipulations, to limit the admissibility of certain evidence or witness testimony. The strategy also includes maximizing the number of depositions and repeated requests for extensions of time and postponements of proceedings. On a few occasions, the attorney even re-filed a motion after the court ruled on the motion in the government's favor, merely to make the government lawyer spend the time filing objections or replies based on the court's previous ruling on the same issue. The government lawyers filed a complaint against the attorney with the state bar authorities, but the state disciplinary authority decided not to pursue the matter, in part because it was in federal court and involved exclusively federal issues. Could the attorney also face sanctions or penalties

under federal law, if the state bar rejected the complaint?

a) Yes, but only because some of the motions were redundant, and may have come after the state disciplinary authority rendered its no-action decision.

b) Yes, a federal statute authorizes federal courts to require a lawyer to pay all the excess costs, expenses, and legal fees incurred because of the lawyer "unreasonably and vexatiously" multiplying the proceedings.

c) No, because discipline of lawyers over frivolous or vexations litigation is exclusively a matter of state law, so the judge should simply refer the matter again to the state disciplinary authorities, who are more likely to take it seriously if it comes from a federal judge.

d) No, because the Free Speech Clause of the constitution gives lawyers an absolute right to file motions on their clients' behalf in federal court.

> 28 U.S.C.A. § 1927

RULE 3.2
EXPEDITING LITIGATION

155. A certain client hired an attorney to represent a client in a litigation matter, but after he filed the notice of representation and the initial pleadings in the case, the opposing party hired Big Firm to represent it. The attorney has already completed three rounds of job interviews with Big Firm and is now simply waiting for their answer, which he hopes will be an offer of employment. Rather than notify the client that an unforeseen conflict of interest has possibly emerged, the attorney simply slows down his work on the case, because if the job offer comes through, he will have to transfer the client's case to another lawyer anyway, and if he does not receive an offer, the potential conflict disappears and he can proceed with the litigation. The attorney thus waits until the last day to respond to any filings or discovery requests, and frequently calls the opposing party asking for more time, which they always grant. Is it proper for the attorney to stall the progress of the case for a while, to allow time for the conflict either to disappear or for him to need to transfer the case to some other lawyer?

a) Yes, because the conflict of interest will disappear if Big Firm rejects the attorney's application for employment before the case proceeds any further.
b) Yes, because the attorney may need to transfer the case to another lawyer anyway, and addressing the potential conflicting of interest directly, instead of simply stalling, could create unnecessary expenses for the client.
c) No, because a lawyer has a duty to make reasonable efforts to expedite litigation consistent with the interests of the client.
d) No, because a lawyer has a duty to withdraw from the representation immediately if a potential conflict of interest emerges.

ABA Formal Op. 96-400

156. A certain client hired an attorney to represent him in litigation because of the attorney's reputation for being the meanest, most aggressive litigator in town. The client is the defendant and the attorney bills by the hour. The judge in the case orders the parties to participate in a "caucused mediation" to encourage a settlement before trial. Then the attorney begins the mediation by declaring that his client is unwilling to compromise at all, even though the client had told him that they might settle the case for a reasonable amount. The attorney overstates the strength of the client's case and grossly understates the strength of the opposing party's position in what everyone knows is a close case. The attorney is merely posturing or bluffing in hopes of obtaining a more favorable settlement for his client. Due to the attorney's hardline approach, the mediation drags on for several sessions spanning several days, and proves to be futile, so the parties schedule a trial. Is the attorney potentially subject to discipline for this approach in court-ordered mediation?
a) Yes, because overstating the strength of his case or downplaying his client's willingness to compromise are misstatements of material fact.
b) Yes, because even if the statements were not material facts, lawyers must make reasonable efforts to expedite litigation consistent with the interests of the client.
c) No, because a lawyer can advocate zealously to obtain the most favorable outcome possible for his client.

d) No, because this is court-ordered mediation, meaning the parties did not willingly agree to it and therefore have no duty to negotiate in good faith.

ABA Formal Op. 06-439 fn. 18

157. An attorney works for a firm that handles mortgage lenders in foreclosure actions; she handles foreclosure matters in mediation and at trial. Some close friends of the attorney form a real estate investment company, which buys properties in foreclosure, and sells the properties later at a profit. The friends include the attorney as a passive partner, so she receives a small share of the company's net revenues. The attorney's role in mediation conferences puts her in a position to speed up or slow down foreclosure proceedings, because she negotiates with the defaulting mortgagee for a loan modification. Delayed or failed modifications provide an opportunity for other interested investors, such as her friends' company, to purchase the property at a short sale. The lenders, who are the attorney's clients, often agree to these delays because a short sale may yield a better payoff for the lender than a loan modification. Would it be impermissible for the attorney to drag out the loan modification negotiations with the owner-in-default so that prospective buyers may have the chance to purchase the properties at a short sale?
a) Yes, the attorney is a passive owner of the real estate company and therefore has a nonconsentable conflict of interest.
b) Yes, even with the consent of the attorney's clients, this is an impermissible dilatory litigation tactic with no substantial purpose other than to delay or prolong the proceeding.
c) No, if the attorney's clients (the lenders) give written, informed consent to the proposed delays, the attorney may proceed accordingly.
d) No, delay may, in fact, benefit the lender-clients, when the short sale yields a higher or more certain payoff than a loan modification for the original owner.

NY Ethics Opinion 991 (2013)

158. An attorney represented a client in a case for violation of federal employment laws by the client's former employer. The employer filed a motion for summary judgment because the attorney's client had left the company prior to the effective date of the relevant statute. The attorney requested repeated extension for more time to respond to the summary judgment motion, which the court at first granted, but eventually denied. It turned out that the attorney knew the statute as enacted was not retroactive, but he was hoping some case law might develop during the delay that would help his case. There were no pending appellate cases considering the issue of retroactivity for this statute. Was it permissible for the attorney to request more time to file a response when the sole reason for doing so was the remote chance that some courts would modify the law that governed the case?

a) Yes, a lawyer may request reasonable delays in the proceedings consistent with the interest of the client.

b) Yes, postponing a decision until other courts had an opportunity to consider the issue is a reasonable basis for delaying the proceedings.

c) No, given that the issue was not pending before any appellate courts at the time, it was improper for the attorney to request these extensions.

d) No, the extensions could only benefit the client, and would disadvantage the other party.

In re Boone, 7 P.3d 270 (Kan. 2000)

159. An attorney represented an immigrant who was facing deportation. At one point in the proceedings, the immigration judge ordered the attorney to file various documents and forms necessary to the case. The attorney simply ignored the judge's order, knowing that the judge would not close the case and issue a deportation order without these important documents in the record. The client's deportation was inevitable, given the facts of the case and the relevant law, so the only thing the attorney could do to help the client was delay the deportation for as long as possible. Months passed, and the immigration judge repeatedly re-issued the orders for production of the documents, and the attorney continued to ignore them. Was it permissible for the attorney to hold off on filing the documents that would have hastened the deportation of his client?

a) Yes, an attorney may seek reasonable continuance of a proceeding in the client's best interest.

b) Yes, the prohibitions on lawyers using dilatory tactics do not apply in administrative proceedings like deportation hearings.

c) No, the lawyer has no right to try to prolong the stay of a client whom the law deems deportable.

d) No, the attorney's failure to file the papers was not a legitimate litigation strategy to prevent or delay the deportation.

In re Howe, 843 N.W.2d 325 (N.D. 2014)

160. An attorney had a dispute with her nonlawyer siblings about the guardianship of their elderly mother. One of the siblings filed a petition for the appointment as the mother's legal guardian, which the court granted. The attorney then filed an appearance on behalf of her mother in the matter to contest the guardianship. Bitter fighting between the siblings continued, and at one point the attorney filed a motion to withdraw, which the court granted, even though it was not clear that the attorney had ever had a client-lawyer relationship with her mother. As the moths went by, the attorney grew increasingly concerned about how her sibling was treating their elderly mother, and began filing various motions, petitions, and appeals on the mother's behalf seeking judicial relief and the appointment of a different legal guardian. Could the attorney be subject to discipline, given these facts?

a) Yes, filing petitions and appeals on behalf of someone no longer legally one's client imposes unnecessary delays in court proceedings.

b) Yes, given the mother's age and limitations, the litigiousness was pointless.

c) No, the attorney was not delaying the proceedings on behalf of an actual client, but merely her own mother.

d) No, the attorney had a good faith belief that her actions were necessary to prevent substantial bodily harm to her mother.

State ex rel. Counsel for Discipline v. Herzog, 762 N.W.2d 608 (Neb. 2009)

161. An attorney agreed to represent a client who wanted to contest the will of her recently deceased aunt. The matter turned out to be much more complicated than the attorney imagined, however, and he already had an overwhelming number of cases for other clients. The attorney received interrogatories from the opposing parties in the matter regarding the will, and he put them off, and then put them off again, as he was busy with other cases. After several months without a response to the interrogatories, the court dismissed the client's case. The client planned to file a malpractice action against the attorney, but the evidence in her case and the relevant law meant she had been unlikely to succeed on her original claim. Could the attorney be subject to discipline for failing to expedite the proceedings, if the court already punished the attorney by dismissing the client's case?

a) Yes, the fact that the court dismissed the client's case means the attorney is automatically subject to discipline.

b) Yes, the attorney did not make reasonable efforts to expedite the litigation consistent with the interests of the client.

c) No, an attorney cannot be subject to discipline for a mere omission, if there was no overt act that violated a rule.

d) No, imposing disciplinary sanctions on the attorney would be unnecessarily duplicative after the adverse action already taken by the court against the client based on the attorney's neglect of the matter.

In re Roggeman, 779 N.W.2d 520 (Minn. 2010)

RULE 3.3
CANDOR TOWARD THE TRIBUNAL

162. A client hired an attorney to represent him in litigation, and he explained to the attorney his version of the incident that gave rise to the dispute with the other party. In response, the attorney took notes on the account that the client provided, and drafted pleadings that alleged the facts as alleged by the client. The attorney did no investigation before filing the pleadings to provide independent verification of the client's version of the story, because he thought that discovery would bring to light the necessary facts to reveal the truth of the matter. Similarly, the attorney submitted as evidence the various documents the client provided to him, without doing his own assessment of the authenticity of the evidence so that he could vouch for the evidence himself. It turned out, as the other side submitted its evidence, that the client's account of what happened was full of fabrications, and some of the evidence was invalid. The attorney did not know the client was being untruthful, but he neglected to make any efforts to verify the client's story before presenting it in court. Could the attorney be subject to discipline for undermining the integrity of the adjudicative process?

a) Yes, because the lawyer as an advocate is responsible for pleadings and other documents prepared for litigation, and therefore must have personal knowledge of matters asserted therein.

b) Yes, because a lawyer in an adversary proceeding has an ethical duty to vouch for the evidence submitted in a cause of action.

c) No, because the discovery phase and the trial will bring to light which side is telling the truth.

d) No, because a lawyer need not have personal knowledge of matters asserted in pleadings, for litigation documents ordinarily present assertions by the client, and not assertions by the lawyer.

Rule 3.3. Cmt. 3

163. An attorney represents a client in a civil litigation matter. As they prepare for trial, at which the client will testify as a witness on his own behalf, the attorney realizes that the client is unlikely to tell the truth, even though the client insists he will be completely truthful. Even so, the attorney believes there is some chance that the client is indeed telling the truth, but he is about 70% certain that the client is being untruthful, despite the client's protestations. Does the attorney have an ethical duty to try to prevent the client from presenting testimony that the attorney believes is unlikely to be true?

a) Yes, a lawyer cannot suborn perjury, or even risk that the testimony he is eliciting via direct examination is perjury.

b) Yes, a lawyer must disclose to the court that he does not believe the client's testimony and have the court give the client an opportunity to testify in a narrative mode.

c) No, because the prohibition against offering false evidence only applies if the lawyer knows that the evidence is false, and a lawyer's belief that evidence is false does not preclude its presentation to the trier of fact.

d) No, because the opposing party will have an opportunity to impeach the witness and the testimony during cross-examination.

Rule 3.3 Cmt. 8

164. A client is a defendant in a criminal prosecution, and a certain attorney is his court-appointed defense lawyer. The client wants to testify at his own trial, despite the attorney's recommendations that he not do so. As they are preparing for trial, the attorney asks the client what he plans to say on the stand. The client's story seems suspicious to the attorney – he has serious doubts about its veracity – but the client insists that he is telling the truth, and the attorney is not sure. Does the attorney have an ethical duty to allow the client to give this improbable testimony at trial?

a) Yes, because in a criminal case, a lawyer cannot refuse to offer the testimony of a client where the lawyer believes, but does not know, that the testimony will be false; unless the lawyer knows that the testimony will be false, the lawyer must honor the client's decision to testify.

b) Yes, because a lawyer cannot control what a client will say once the client is on the stand under oath.

c) No, because a lawyer should refuse to offer testimony or other proof that the lawyer believes is false; offering such proof may reflect adversely on the lawyer's ability to discriminate in the quality of evidence and thus impair the lawyer's effectiveness as an advocate.

d) No, because the lawyer has a duty of candor to the court and cannot allow a criminal defendant to abuse the legal process by testifying falsely to obtain a wrongful acquittal.

Rule 3.3. Cmt. 9

165. A certain attorney is a criminal defense lawyer, and he represents a client, who is facing charges for burglary of a private residence. The client has asserted an alibi – he claims that on the evening of the burglary, he was 100 miles away on a romantic getaway with his girlfriend. Naturally, the attorney interviews the client's girlfriend, who recounts a similar story about being on a romantic getaway, but a few details do not match the client's account, such as what they ordered for dinner when they stopped at a restaurant, and whether they had to stop for gas along the way. The attorney suspects the girlfriend is lying to protect the client, and that they rehearsed an alibi story without working through the fine details together. The attorney lectures both the client and his girlfriend about the wrongfulness of perjury and the fact that they do not have to testify at all, as well as the hazard of having their stories crumble under rigorous cross-examination. Is it permissible, under the Rules of Professional Conduct, for the attorney to call the client and his girlfriend as witnesses during trial?

a) Yes, because the attorney does not know with certainty that they are lying, he must allow the client to testify, and it is permissible to call the girlfriend as a witness as well.

b) Yes, because a lawyer in a criminal case has no duty to screen witnesses based on whether they plan to tell the truth.

c) No, because the attorney may not call the girlfriend as a witness, but he has no choice about allowing the client to testify.

d) No, because it would be improper for the attorney to call either the client or the girlfriend to testify if he is not mostly certain that each one will tell the truth.

Rule 3.3 Cmt. 9

166. An attorney represented a defendant in a criminal proceeding. While preparing for trial, the defendant told the attorney that the main witness for their side, the defendant's friend who planned to corroborate his alibi, intended to lie on the witness stand. The attorney tried to dissuade the client and the witness from this course of action. He explained that committing perjury could subject the client to additional criminal changes, and that a rigorous cross-examination from the prosecutor would certainly expose the lies. Even so, the witness insisted on testifying at trial and stated his intention to present a fabricated version of the alibi. Should the attorney allow the witness to testify, and examine the friend as a witness, under these circumstances?

a) Yes, because the attorney fulfilled his ethical duty by trying to dissuade his client and the friend from perjury, and the prosecutor has an opportunity to cross-examine the witness.

b) Yes, if the untruthful testimony is not

69

material to the case and is unlikely to affect the outcome of the litigation.

c) No, the attorney must withdraw from representation before the testimony occurs.

d) No, the attorney must either disclose the contemplated perjury to the tribunal, or refuse to call the witness, or withdraw from the representation.

Model Rule 3.3(b)

167. An experienced attorney represented a new client in civil litigation. The client lied extensively on the witness stand during the trial, but the attorney was not aware of the untruthfulness of the statements at the time. The verdict was favorable to the client and there was no appeal. A year later, the client boasted to the attorney about lying convincingly to the court and winning the lawsuit as a result. Is it permissible for the attorney to keep this information confidential, and not disclose to the tribunal that the perjury occurred?

a) Yes, unless the judge specifically asks the attorney if his client committed perjury after the attorney learns about it.

b) No, because when a lawyer represents a client in an adjudicative proceeding and knows that a person has engaged in fraudulent conduct related to the proceeding shall take reasonable remedial measures.

c) Yes, because a lawyer's duty to take remedial measures after perjury occurs continue only to the conclusion of the proceeding.

d) No, because if a witness called by the lawyer has offered material evidence and the lawyer comes to know of its falsity, the lawyer shall take reasonable remedial measures, including, if necessary, disclosure to the tribunal.

Model Rule 3.3(c) Cmt.13

168. A litigation attorney represented a client in a lawsuit. The case was still at the pre-trial phase, and the parties had filed cross-motions for summary judgement. While researching the case law to write a responsive brief, the attorney discovered, to her dismay, a new decision from highest court in a sister jurisdiction that is directly adverse to her position in the case. In the attorney's own jurisdiction, the issue presents a case of first impression. The briefs from opposing counsel never mentioned this new decision, presumably because the other lawyer

had not yet seen it. Is it improper for the attorney to keep this information confidential, and not disclose the unfavorable authority to the court?

a) Yes, a lawyer must disclose to the tribunal legal authority in the controlling jurisdiction known to the lawyer to be directly adverse to the position of the client and not disclosed by opposing counsel.

b) Yes, because it is very common for litigators to recycle their briefs for years at a time, and everyone should help each other out with updating their legal research on issues that arise frequently in that area of litigation.

c) No, because it would be a breach of the attorney's duty of loyalty to his own client to disclose a case unnecessary that undermines their position.

d) No, the case is not controlling authority in that jurisdiction.

Model Rule 3.3(a)(2)

169. An experienced attorney represented a client in commercial litigation. During a deposition, the client gave answers that the attorney knew to be false, regarding a matter of great relevance to the case. The attorney sat silently and permitted the client to give these answers in the deposition. At the subsequent trial, opposing counsel submitted convincing evidence showing that the client had lied during the deposition. It was evident from the circumstances that the attorney must have known that the client's statements were untruthful at the time. Opposing counsel then filed a grievance against the attorney for allowing the client to give false testimony and failing to rectify it. When the attorney filed a response to the grievance, he explained that alleged ethical violation took place during a deposition, long before the trial, so the duty of candor to the tribunal was inapplicable at that point. Is the attorney correct in this argument?

a) Yes, the Model Rules require a lawyer to take remedial measures when a client offers false statements even during a deposition.

b) Yes, unless it appears that opposing counsel already knows that the statements are false and is planning to impeach the witness.

c) No, if the client was testifying in a deposition, it is not testimony before a tribunal for purposes of the ethical rules requiring candor.

d) No, the duty to protect client confidentiality

and a duty of loyalty to the client would prohibit such a disclosure.

Rule 3.3 Cmt. 1

170. An attorney represented a client in civil litigation. Early in the trial, the attorney had to testify briefly about an uncontested point. The testimony was necessary to establish a minor antecedent point for more critical issues in the case. The attorney made statements that she believed to be true at the time. The next day, while the trial was still underway, the client fired the attorney. When the attorney tried unsuccessfully to dissuade the client from doing so, the client told the attorney that the attorney's testimony was incorrect, and the client also explained some previously unknown information. Under these circumstances, could the attorney keep this information confidential, instead of taking remedial measures to rectify the false statements?

a) Yes, because the attorney was not aware at the time that the statements were false, and therefore did not knowingly mislead the tribunal.

b) Yes, because the lawyer has a duty of confidentiality that continues even after a client discharges the lawyer.

c) No, because a lawyer must correct a false statement of material fact or law previously made to the tribunal by the lawyer

d) No, because the client discharged the attorney, and no duty of confidentiality remains after the termination of representation.

Model Rule 3.3(a)(3)

171. Early in the pre-trial phase of a civil lawsuit involving multiple crossclaims, the court enjoined the parties from transferring any assets out of the jurisdiction. The next day, an attorney heard that his client had transferred millions of dollars to a confidential Swiss bank account. The attorney did not make any affirmative representations to the court about following the court's order. It was clear to the attorney, however, that the court and the opposing party were under the impression that the client was complying with the court's order, and they were relying upon that fact in the ongoing proceedings. The client did not use the attorney's services in any way to make the transfers, and the attorney did not recommend it

or know about it until after it occurred. Would it be improper for the attorney to do nothing and say nothing about the matter at this time, to protect the client's confidential information?

a) Yes, because this is a circumstance where failure to make a disclosure is the equivalent of an affirmative misrepresentation.

b) Yes, because a lawyer always has a duty to inform the court if a client is engaged in illegal or fraudulent conduct, even if it is unrelated to the attorney's representation.

c) No, because the client has not made any false statements to the court.

d) No, because the attorney has not made any material misrepresentations to the court.

ABA Formal Op. 98-412, Rule 3.3.

172. A litigation attorney normally represented clients at trial or in binding arbitration, but in some instances, she will represent a client in a mediation. In one mediation, the attorney knowingly made untrue statements of fact to the other party and opposing counsel. Has the attorney violated her ethical duty of candor to the tribunal, as delineated in Model Rule 3.3?

a) Yes, a lawyer shall not knowingly make a false statement of fact to a tribunal or fail to correct a false statement of material fact.

b) Yes, in mediation, a lawyer shall not knowingly offer evidence that the lawyer knows to be false.

c) No, the duty of candor in Model Rule 3.3 is inapplicable to mediation; nevertheless, other rules such as Rule 4.1 may apply to the lawyer's untruthfulness here.

d) No, the lawyer does not have a duty to avoid making false statements to other parties, only to a judge.

Rule 3.3; ABA Formal Op. 06-439 Fn. 2; Rule 2.4 Cmt. 5

RULE 3.4

FAIRNESS TO OPPOSING PARTY AND COUNSEL

173. A client is on trial for a theft case. A certain witness was with the client at the time police state that the client committed the crime at a location far from the crime scene. The client chooses to take the case to trial. For the witness's attendance at trial, the attorney pays the witness a lump sum amount. Are the attorney's actions proper?

a) Yes, because lawyers may pay witnesses for their attendance and expenses incurred for attending and testifying at a hearing or trial.
b) Yes, because contingency fees are the only kinds of fees not permissible for lawyers to pay witnesses for their attendance and testimony at a hearing or trial; lump sum payments are permissible.
c) No, because lawyers may not pay a witness to attend and testify at a hearing or trial.
d) No, because an attorney cannot pay for witnesses' attendance at a trial or hearing; rather, the client must pay the fees to the witness directly.

Rule 3.4

174. An attorney responded to a distressed call from a client asking that he meet him immediately on the street behind the attorney's office. Immediately, the attorney rushes downstairs to meet the client outside his building. The client is very distraught and has blood splattered on his clothes, hands, and face, and is holding a pistol. The client stammers, "You will not believe what just happened." Quietly, the attorney takes the pistol and throws it down the closest storm gutter on the street, and they can hear the gun clanging against concrete as it tumbles deep down into the storm sewer. Then the attorney says, "It is late, and you are too upset to talk. Go home and clean yourself up and do your laundry – you are a mess. We can discuss this tomorrow morning when you are in a better frame of mind." The client goes home to shower and launder his clothes, and the attorney returns to his office and resumes his work on the brief he was writing. Did the attorney's conduct constitute a violation of his ethical duties?

a) Yes, because he had a duty to inquire about what had happened and to call the police or emergency services if someone had been hurt.

b) Yes, because the attorney concealed or obstructed the police's access to potential evidence by discarding the gun, and he counseled the client to destroy the evidence on his clothes.
c) No, because the attorney does not know if the client has perpetrated a crime or if he was the victim of a crime, so he has not destroyed evidence knowingly; perhaps the client just saved someone else from a violent attacker.
d) No, because the gun is still retrievable from the storm sewer, and the attorney could still testify about his observations of the client's appearance when they met.

Rule 3.4(a)&(b)

175. During trial, the plaintiffs complained that the attorney's client had not fully complied with certain production requests during discovery. The judge ordered the attorney to produce the specific records. Yet the attorney believed that his client had no legal obligation to produce the records in question, because they included important trade secrets and were not relevant or material to the current litigation in any way. The attorney openly refused to produce the records and explained his position to the judge. The judge disagreed and ordered the attorney to bring the records to the courtroom the next day. Of course, the attorney did not obey the judge's order. Apart from any potential contempt-of-court sanctions, could the attorney be subject to discipline for violating the Rules of Professional Conduct?

a) Yes, because a lawyer must not knowingly disobey an obligation under the rules of a tribunal.
b) Yes, because the proper response would be to produce the records and then object to their admissibility at trial.
c) No, because a lawyer may disobey an order from a tribunal when the lawyer has made an open refusal based on an assertion that no valid obligation exists.
d) No, because in an adversarial proceeding, the judge should rely on the evidence that the parties present, rather than meddling with discovery and production of evidence.

Rule 3.4(c)

72

176. An attorney represented a client in a lawsuit over a traffic accident. The client told the attorney about a certain eyewitness who had been present at the scene and who had said at the time that the client was not at fault. The attorney tracked down this witness, but soon discovered that the eyewitness did not want any involvement in the litigation or trial. The witness was necessary to corroborate the client's version of what happened in the accident, so the attorney offered to pay $500 honorarium in cash if the witness would testify at trial. The eyewitness was out of work needed the cash, so he begrudgingly agreed. Would the Model Rules prohibit the attorney from paying the eyewitness an honorarium to testify at trial?

a) Yes, because an attorney cannot pay for witnesses' attendance at a trial or hearing; rather, the client must pay the witness directly.

b) Yes, it is impermissible for a lawyer to pay an eyewitness to attend and testify at a hearing or trial.

c) No, so long as the sum offered is a percentage share of the expected verdict in the case.

d) No, a lawyer may pay an occurrence witness for attending and testifying at a hearing or trial.

Model Rule 3.4(b)

177. An attorney represented a client in commercial litigation. One component of the case necessitated expert testimony about the economic losses suffered, interest calculations, and potential mitigation costs. The attorney hired the most famous expert witness that he could find on such matters, one who would easily be able to counter the opposing party's expert at trial. With the client's consent, the attorney agreed to pay the expert a six-figure retainer fee to review the case documents plus $2000 per hour for any courtroom time. Would the attorney be subject to discipline for paying the expert witness a huge sum to help with the case?

a) Yes, a lawyer may not offer an inducement to a witness, especially an expert witness, who is supposed to provide a purely objective assessment.

b) Yes, a lawyer may not hire an expert witness unless he pays the witness a contingent fee that depends on the outcome of the case.

c) No, it is proper to compensate an expert witness on terms permitted by law, so long as it is not a contingent fee.

d) No, the Model Rules put no restrictions on what kind of compensation a lawyer may pay an expert witness.

Rule 3.4 Cmt. 3

178. An attorney represented a defendant facing criminal charges. The client was concerned that his estranged brother would testify against him at trial to impeach the defendant's own credibility if the defendant chose to testify. The rift between them had begun in high school, with a fight over a girlfriend, and had escalated over the years, so that the estranged brother was always ready to list several of the defendant's greatest failures or lapses in character whenever the two interacted. The attorney approached the brother privately and explained that his client was facing serious jail time that would have long-term consequences for the entire family. He then pleaded with the brother not to testify against the client or even talk to the prosecutors about it. The brother found this entreaty moving and agreed to keep quiet. Could the attorney be subject to discipline for this conversation with the brother?

a) Yes, because a lawyer may not request a person other than a client to refrain from voluntarily giving relevant information to another party.

b) Yes, if the brother already has an adverse attitude or position toward the client, the attorney may not approach him and request that he not testify.

c) No, because a lawyer may ask anyone to refrain from voluntarily giving relevant information to another party.

d) No, the Model Rules do not forbid a lawyer from asking a family member to refrain from giving information to the other party.

Rule 3.4(f)

179. A certain client hired an attorney to represent him in civil litigation. The client's own testimony at trial would be crucial to the case, and the client was concerned that his embittered former business partner would testify against him as a negative character witness to impeach his credibility. The two had been quite close early in their partnership, but then had a falling out and were no longer on speaking

terms. The attorney approached the former partner privately, explained the client's situation, and offered the client's former partner several thousand dollars not to testify or even talk to the opposing counsel in the case. The former partner jumped at the chance to make some easy money by doing nothing, and he accepted the attorney's offer. Could the attorney be subject to discipline for his actions, as described here?

a) Yes, the Model Rules do not permit lawyers to offer witnesses money to refrain from testifying or providing information about the matter, with exceptions that do not apply here.

b) Yes, the lawyer should not have approached the former partner privately without opposing counsel present.

c) No, a lawyer may ask various potential witnesses to refrain from disclosing information to keep the proceedings from becoming unnecessarily acrimonious or protracted.

d) No, if the client consents the lawyer can ask former business associates, employees, or employers to refrain from offering unfavorable testimony.

Rule 3.4(f)(1)

180. Conglomerate Corporation became the subject of an enforcement action by the Department of Labor for violating certain wage-and-hour laws protecting workers' rights. Conglomerate's general counsel interviewed many of the company's employees, in groups of eight or ten at a time, and explained that there was litigation pending with the Department of Labor that could hurt their employer in the long run. General counsel then asked each groups of workers that they decline to discuss the case with anyone, especially lawyers from the government. Did general counsel violate the Model Rules by asking the employees not to talk to the other party?

a) Yes, as party of the duty of zealous advocacy for the client, an attorney should to encourage every potential witness to talk openly and honestly with the lawyers on both sides of the case.

b) Yes, it was not reasonable for the general counsel to believe that refraining from giving such information would not impinge on the employees' interests.

c) No, the employees are free to ignore the request and talk to whomever they want about the case or about the company.

d) No, there is an exception in the Model Rules permitting in-house to advise company employees against giving information to an opposing party in litigation.

Rule 3.4(f)(2)

181. During the discovery phase of business litigation, Conglomerate Corporation receives a discovery request asking for "all documents, memoranda, emails, or other internal correspondence related to the transaction that is the subject of this dispute." A certain attorney represents Conglomerate Corporation. Thousands of documents stored in electronic format on Conglomerate's computers and servers would potentially fall under this request for production. Then the attorney proposes to opposing counsel that they produce the requested documents in electronic form on a set of compact discs, and the opposing counsel readily agrees. Long before the litigation began, the attorney began using software to scrub the metadata from documents – electronically embedded information about the name of the user whose computer created the document, the date and time of creation, redlined changes from each stage of editing, and comments that other readers added to the document before it took its final form. Proposed contracts, letters to business partners, and correspondence with opposing counsel are all free from embedded metadata. Was it proper for the attorney to scrub the metadata from electronic documents that could potentially be subject to a discovery or production request in future litigation?

a) Yes, because the printed copies of the documents would not have had such information.

b) Yes, because a lawyer may take measures to eliminate metadata from documents that could later fall into the hands of an opposing party.

c) No, because the main reason for scrubbing metadata is to conceal information that might be useful to an opposing party or tribunal in the future.

d) No, because the metadata is often necessary for determining who created a document, when they created it, or how the document changed from its original draft to its final form.

ABA Formal Op. 06-442

182. During the discovery phase of business litigation, Conglomerate Corporation receives a discovery request asking for "all documents, memoranda, emails, or other internal correspondence related to the transaction that is the subject of this dispute." An attorney represents Conglomerate Corporation. Thousands of documents stored in electronic format on Conglomerate's computers and servers would potentially fall under this request for production. The attorney proposes to opposing counsel that they produce the requested documents in electronic form on a set of compact discs, and the opposing counsel readily agrees. After receiving the production request, the attorney began using software to scrub the metadata from documents – electronically embedded information about the name of the user whose computer created the document, the date and time of creation, redlined changes from each stage of editing, and comments that other readers added to the document before it took its final form. Proposed contracts, letters to business partners, and memoranda between managers all have their embedded metadata erased. Was it proper for the attorney to scrub the metadata from electronic documents before delivering them to the other party in response to a discovery request?

a) Yes, because the printed copies of the documents would not have had such information.
b) Yes, because a lawyer may take measures to eliminate metadata from documents that could later fall into the hands of an opposing party.
c) No, because the main reason for scrubbing metadata is to conceal information that might be useful to an opposing party or tribunal in the present litigation.
d) No, because the metadata is often necessary for determining who created a document, when they created it, or how the document changed from its original draft to its final form.

ABA Formal Op. 06-442

RULE 3.5
IMPARTIALITY AND DECORUM OF THE TRIBUNAL

183. A family law attorney represented a client in a child custody dispute. The divorced parents lived in neighboring states, and the dispute involved allegations of child abuse by the client's ex-husband, the opposing party in the case. The case was complex and involved related petitions in two separate courts. The client received an unfavorable preliminary ruling regarding custody in the initial stages of the proceedings. With her client's consent, the attorney then took her zealous advocacy online, using Twitter and other social media platforms to denounce the injustice of the unfavorable preliminary custody ruling, to urge the judges to uphold the law, and to urge readers to write to the judges in the case or advocate for the children's safety themselves through Twitter. The attorney also created online petitions on websites like Change.org, with names like "Demand Justice for These Children!" The judges presiding over the various petitions in the case received hundreds of letters, emails, and phone calls in response to the attorney's efforts. Many of these communications by concerned citizens to the judges were hostile and vulgar. Could the attorney be subject to disbarment for such zealous advocacy online?

a) Yes, the lawyer was attempting to communicate with the judges and potential jurors through public commentary.
b) Yes, if the lawyer's client received an unfavorable preliminary ruling, the lawyer should have known she was advocating for the wrong side in this case.
c) No, the attorney was conducting zealous advocacy and exercising her First Amendment rights.
d) No, the attorney had her client's consent, so using public commentary was appropriate, especially given the seriousness of the allegations.

In re Joyce Nanine McCool, 2015-B-0284 (Sup. Ct. La. 2015); ABA Formal Op. 18-480 (2018)

184. During a lunchtime recess of a case, the attorney representing the plaintiffs walked with his expert witness to a nearby delicatessen, which full. By coincidence, the server seated the

attorney and his expert at the adjoining table to two of the jurors in the case. The attorney recognized the two women from the jury and greeted them, and they chatted for a few minutes about the weather, their favorite sandwiches, and how long the case was taking. They did not discuss the merits of the case itself. Two secretaries from opposing counsel's firm were also eating at the delicatessen and observed this conversation, which they promptly reported to their supervising attorney, who reported it to the judge. The judge ordered a mistrial, dismissed the jurors, and ordered the attorney to reimburse the county for the jurors' fees. Could the attorney also be subject to disciplinary sanctions for running into the two jurors at lunch and making friendly conversation?

a) Yes, but only if the attorney intended to influence their decisions in the case.
b) Yes, regardless of the attorney's intentions, the conversation violated the prohibition on ex parte communication with jurors.
c) No, the attorney did not plan the incident, it was just a coincidental meeting, and they did not discuss the merits of the case.
d) No, punishment already occurred in the form of the mistrial and the attorney paying the fees for the dismissed jurors, so additional sanctions for the same incident would constitute double jeopardy for the attorney.

Fla. Bar v. Peterson, 418 So. 2d 246 (Fla. 1982)

185. Police arrested several protestors who were advocating a cause that an attorney strongly supported. One of the protestors had a violent altercation with police, and she was facing criminal charges. This attorney practices corporate transactional law and not litigation. The news media reported that jury selection would begin the following Monday in the protestor's prosecution. The attorney waited outside the courthouse where prospective jurors were reporting for jury service, and a long line formed at the metal detectors for entering the courthouse. For a long time, the attorney waited in line and started conversations with the prospective jurors in front of him and behind him in the line, during which he explained that he was a lawyer and that the case against the protestor was ridiculous from a legal standpoint. He told them that he hoped the jury would follow the laws of the state and acquit the protestor. Once the attorney made it through the

security line, he walked out of the courthouse and got back in the security line again and had similar conversations with more prospective jurors. During voir dire, the prosecutor asked the prospective jurors if anyone had spoken to them directly about the case, and three people mentioned their conversations with a lawyer in the security line waiting to get into the building. None of the individuals with whom the attorney spoke ended up on the jury in the case. The prosecutor eventually determined the attorney's identity and filed a grievance with the state disciplinary authority. Could the attorney be subject to discipline?

a) Yes, because the attorney should have explained both sides of the case as evenhandedly as possible to the prospective jurors.
b) Yes, because a lawyer shall not seek to influence a judge, juror, or even a prospective juror.
c) No, because he spoke to prospective jurors, and they did not end up serving on the case.
d) No, because he was not representing a party in the case, and he was not even a litigator.

Rule 3.5(a)

186. A judge lost his temper with an attorney and spoke very abusively to him in open court, in front of a jury, using profanity and calling the attorney "an embarrassment to the profession and a menace to his own clients." Defensively, the attorney shot back that the judge was completely out of line, that the judge should have retired years ago; the attorney also made a mildly obscene gesture at the judge. Eventually, both calmed down and apologized to each other profusely. Opposing counsel reported the attorney to the state bar disciplinary authority, but did not report the judge, before whom opposing counsel appears regularly. Could the attorney be subject to discipline?

a) Yes, because he escalated the fiery exchange by making an obscene gesture.
b) Yes, because a lawyer may stand firm against abuse by a judge but should avoid reciprocation; the judge's default is no justification for similar dereliction by an advocate.
c) No, because the opposing counsel who reported the matter did not report the judge, who instigated the exchange, and

presumably reported the attorney merely to make trouble for his opponent in litigation.

d) No, because the attorney apologized to the judge immediately, and a lawyer does not have to passively accept abuse or inappropriate attacks from a judge or other lawyer.

Rule 3.5 Cmt. 4

187. An attorney received a call from his cousin, who lives in another city, one evening after work. The cousin was serving on a jury in a misdemeanor criminal case, and deliberations were set to begin the following morning. The cousin explained that part of the jury instructions focused on whether the defendant committed the act "knowingly." She is confused about whether that means that the defendant knew that he was committing the act, or that the defendant knew he was doing something illegal at the time. She called the attorney hoping for some clarification. The attorney practiced real estate law and had never handled a criminal case, but he vaguely remembered something about this from his first-year law school course in criminal law. Given that there was no time for him to research the subject, or to create an agreement for representation, and the fact that he had very limited information, the attorney offered the best explanation he could. Was it proper for the attorney to answer her question under these circumstances?

a) Yes, because he has no involvement with the case, and the juror is his relative.

b) Yes, because the Supreme Court has held that any restrictions in this area violate the First Amendment.

c) No, because he communicated with a juror about a pending case.

d) No, because there is a chance his cousin could repeat a garbled version of his informed opinion to the other jurors during deliberations.

Rule 3.5(b)

188. A certain client hired an attorney to represent her at trial. After voir dire, the attorney wanted to learn as much as possible about each of the jurors, such as their views on political and social issues that might be relevant to issues in the case, so the attorney found each juror's social media accounts and reviewed their postings and comments. One juror, the foreperson of the jury, had limited the access of some of her social media accounts so that only her friends or connections on that platform could view what

she shared. The attorney sent a connection request to the juror in hopes of gaining access to the juror's shared photos, commentary, and so on. The attorney did not otherwise engage in conversations online with the juror, did not discuss the case with the juror, and did not respond to or "like" anything the juror shared or posted through social media. Was it permissible for the attorney to request access to the juror's social media posts, if the attorney has no other communication with the juror?

a) Yes, a lawyer may review a juror's Internet presence, which may include postings by the juror or potential juror in advance of and during a trial.

b) Yes, if the lawyer believes reviewing the juror's social media activity is necessary to reveal juror bias or prejudice.

c) No, a lawyer may not send an access request to a juror to review of the juror's electronic social media.

d) No, a lawyer may not invade the juror's privacy by reviewing a juror's Internet presence, which may include postings by the juror or potential juror in advance of and during a trial.

Rule 3.5(b). ABA Formal Op. 14-466

189. A certain client hired an attorney to represent her at trial. After voir dire, the attorney wanted to learn as much as possible about each of the jurors, such as their views on political and social issues that might be relevant to issues in the case, so the attorney found each juror's social media accounts and reviewed their postings and comments. One juror, the foreperson of the jury, had limited the access of some of her social media accounts so that only her friends or connections on that platform could view what she shared. The attorney asked his law student intern to send a connection request to the juror in hopes of gaining access to the juror's shared photos, commentary, and so on. There would be no reason for the juror to know the intern worked for the attorney in the case, as the intern was never present in the courtroom, and her own social media accounts did not mention her internship. The intern did not otherwise engage in conversations online with the juror, did not discuss the case with the juror, and did not respond to or "like" anything the juror shared or posted through social media. Was it permissible for the attorney to have his intern request access to the juror's social media posts, if the attorney has no other communication with the juror?

a) Yes, if the lawyer believes reviewing the juror's social media activity is necessary to reveal juror bias or prejudice.

b) Yes, a lawyer may review a juror's Internet presence, which may include postings by the juror or potential juror in advance of and during a trial.

c) No, a lawyer may not invade the juror's privacy by reviewing a juror's Internet presence, which may include postings by the juror or potential juror in advance of and during a trial.

d) No, a lawyer may not send an access request to a juror to review of the juror's electronic social media, even vicariously through an intern.

Rule 3.5(b). ABA Formal Op. 14-466

190. A certain client hired an attorney to represent her at trial. After voir dire, the attorney wanted to learn as much as possible about each of the jurors, such as their views on political and social issues that might be relevant to issues in the case, so the attorney found each juror's social media accounts and reviewed their postings and comments. Was it permissible for the attorney to review all the social media posts and comments by the jurors, even back to their high school days, if the attorney has no other communication with the juror?

a) It is permissible for a lawyer to review a juror's Internet presence, which may include postings by the juror or potential juror in advance of and during a trial.

b) It is permissible for the lawyer to review a juror's social media activity only if the lawyer shares the information with opposing counsel.

c) It is impermissible for a lawyer to review a juror's Internet presence, unless the juror has sent the lawyer a request to connect as friends or contacts on that social media platform.

d) It is impermissible for a lawyer to invade the juror's privacy by reviewing a juror's Internet presence, which may include postings by the juror or potential juror in advance of and during a trial.

Rule 3.5(b). ABA Formal Op. 14-466

191. A litigation attorney represented Conglomerate Corporation as the defendant in a personal injury lawsuit. Proceedings were underway, and the discovery phase was nearing conclusion. Cross motions for summary judgment were pending. One day, the attorney received a phone call from the judge presiding over the matter, asking to meet the attorney for coffee. When the attorney met with the judge, the judge asked the attorney how much harm it would cause if Conglomerate if the company had to go to trial instead of winning at summary judgment. The attorney explained that the trial would cost his client millions of dollars in expert witness fees, and that settlement seemed impossible at this point, so summary judgment was the only way for his client to avoid a major financial setback that could affect their share price and solvency. Opposing counsel was not present and the two agreed not to mention their meeting to her. The next day, the judge granted summary judgment in favor of Conglomerate Corporation, the attorney's client. Could the attorney be subject to discipline for his conduct in this situation?

a) Yes, the attorney had an impermissible ex parte communication with the judge presiding over the attorney's case.

b) Yes, the attorney and the judge kept a secret from the opposing counsel.

c) No, the judge initiated the contact and asked the question, so the attorney did not violate the Model Rules, though the judge could be subject to discipline.

d) No, if the information the attorney told the judge was already available or obvious to the other party, which seems to be the case in this scenario, then the other party suffered no prejudice or injury from the ex parte conversation.

Rule 3.5(b)

192. A certain client hired an attorney to represent her at trial. After voir dire, the attorney wanted to learn as much as possible about each of the jurors, such as their views on political and social issues that might be relevant to issues in the case, so the attorney found each juror's social media accounts and reviewed their postings and comments. Some of the social media platforms notify the account holder whenever someone views their profile, so jurors with these social media accounts received notifications that the attorney had visited their profile page and reviewed items there. Which of the following is true, given this scenario?

a) A lawyer may review a juror's social media profile only if the social media network setting notifies the juror of such review, but otherwise the review is a violation of Rule 3.5(b).

b) The fact that a juror or a potential juror may become aware that the lawyer is reviewing his Internet presence when a social media network setting notifies the juror of such review does not constitute a communication from the lawyer in violation of Rule 3.5(b).

c) The fact that a juror or a potential juror may become aware that the lawyer is reviewing his Internet presence when a social media network setting notifies the juror of such review constitutes a communication from the lawyer in violation of Rule 3.5(b).

d) It is impermissible for a lawyer to review a juror's Internet presence, unless the juror has sent the lawyer a request to connect as friends or contacts on that social media platform.

Rule 3.5(b). ABA Formal Op. 14-466

193. A prosecutor learned that his cousin was serving jury duty in a criminal trial in the prosecutor's own district, although another lawyer from the prosecutor's office was handling that trial. Nevertheless, before and during the trial, the prosecutor repeatedly communicated with his cousin about the trial, even though the prosecutor himself was not involved in the matter. Was it permissible for the prosecutor to have this contact with the juror?

a) Yes, the prosecutor and the juror are relatives, so naturally it is permissible for them to have conversations.

b) Yes, the prosecutor is not the advocate in the proceeding in which the cousin is a juror, so the conversations would not constitute ex parte communication.

c) No, prosecutors are subject to stricter rules than other lawyers about contact with jurors, so the usual exceptions for family members and relatives would not apply.

d) No, even though a colleague of the prosecutor was handling the trial in which the cousin was a juror, the prosecutor's conversation violated the ethical prohibitions on ex parte communication with jurors.

In re Nelson, 750 S.E.2d 85 (S.C. 2013)

RULE 3.6   TRIAL PUBLICITY

194. An attorney is representing the defendant in a highly publicized civil trial between two celebrities. On his way into the courthouse on the day of jury selection, reporters gather around the attorney hoping for comments. The attorney explains that his client has agreed to take a polygraph test proving that he is telling the truth about the disputed matter, but that the opposing party has refused to take a polygraph test, which suggests that the other person is hiding something. The attorney has his client's permission to talk to the media. Opposing counsel is standing nearby waiting for his turn to talk, and he expresses no objection to the first attorney giving interviews like this, or to the attorney's comments. Were the attorney's statements proper?

a) No, because there is a presumption of prejudicial effect on the proceedings when a lawyer comments publicly about the performance or results of any examination or test or the refusal or failure of a person to submit to an examination or test.

b) Yes, because the other lawyer is present and did not object to the comments at the time.

c) No, because it violates the rules to talk to crowds of reporters near a courthouse entrance on the day when potential jurors are entering the building for voir dire.

d) Yes, because polygraph tests are inadmissible, so commenting on these tests is irrelevant to the trial itself.

Rule 3.6 Cmt. 5(3)

195. A certain attorney is representing the defendant in a highly publicized criminal trial. On his way into the courthouse on the day of jury selection, reporters gather around the attorney hoping for comments. The attorney explains that his client is still considering whether to enter a guilty plea to lesser charges, as the prosecutor's offer is still open, and that they are waiting to see how jury selection goes before deciding whether to plead guilty or proceed to trial. The attorney also explains that his client has never actually confessed to the crime charged, despite several lengthy interviews with the police and the client's admitting that he was near the scene of the crime when it occurred. The attorney has his client's permission to talk to the media, and the prosecution has expressed no objection to him giving interviews like this on

the courthouse steps in previous cases. Were the attorney's statements proper?

a) Yes, because the rules about trial publicity explicitly allow the attorney to explain the offense or defense involved, and the prosecutor has not objected.

b) Yes, because the attorney's statements clearly fall under the protection of his First Amendment rights, and he has his client's consent.

c) No, because it violates the rules to talk to crowds of reporters near a courthouse entrance on the day when potential jurors are entering the building for voir dire.

d) No, because there is a presumption of prejudicial effect on the proceedings when a lawyer comments publicly about the possibility of a guilty plea, or a party's refusal to confess to a crime

Rule 3.6 Cmt. 5(2)

196. A certain attorney is representing the defendant in a highly publicized trial. On his way into the courthouse on the day of jury selection, reporters gather around the attorney hoping for comments. The attorney explains that his client has a perfectly clean criminal record, while the state's star witness is already serving time on a felony drug conviction. In his opinion, he says, the client is innocent and should receive an acquittal, but he does not explain the defense theory of the case. The attorney declares that he has his client's permission to talk to the media, which is true, and that the prosecution expressed no objection to him giving interviews like this on the courthouse steps in previous cases. Were the attorney's statements proper?

a) Yes, because the rules about trial publicity explicitly allow the attorney to explain the offense or defense involved, and the prosecutor has not objected.

b) Yes, because the attorney's statements clearly fall under the protection of his First Amendment rights, and he has his client's consent.

c) No, because it violates the rules to talk to crowds of reporters near a courthouse entrance on the day when potential jurors are entering the building for voir dire.

d) No, because the official Comment to the Model Rules says that expressing an opinion about a party's guilt or innocence, or about the criminal record of a party or witness, is

more likely than not to have a material prejudicial effect on a proceeding.

Rule 3.6 Cmt. 5(4)

197. An attorney defended a client in a criminal proceeding that attracted low-level media attention on the local evening news and a few local-interest blogs. A semi-retired reporter for the local evening news called the attorney at his office and asked for a quote about the client's case. Then the attorney stated that the client had no prior criminal record and that they planned to put on a rigorous defense, and he hoped the prosecutor would drop all the charges before trial. Was it improper for the attorney to make these statements?

a) Yes, because lawyers involved in a criminal proceeding may not make any statements to the media about the case or the parties involved.

b) Yes, because a lawyer should not make extrajudicial comments about the criminal record of a party during a criminal matter.

c) No, because a lawyer may state the claim, offense or defense involved and, except when prohibited by law, the identity of the persons involved.

d) No, because the matter received only low-level media attention and the reporter was semi-retired.

Rule 3.6 Cmt. 5(1)

198. An attorney defended a client in a criminal proceeding that attracted low-level media attention on the local evening news and a few local-interest blogs. One of these bloggers called the attorney at his office and asked for a quote about the client's case. The attorney stated that a member of the local clergy, as well as the Principal of the local high school, would testify as to the client's good character and volunteer activities. Was it proper for the attorney to discuss such things with a blogger?

a) Yes, because a local-interest blogger is not an official public communication and does not constitute dissemination by means of public communication.

b) Yes, because a lawyer may state the expected testimony of a party or witness in a criminal matter.

c) No, because in a criminal matter, there is a presumption of prejudice when a lawyer makes extrajudicial statements about the expected testimony of a party or witness.

d) No, because a criminal defense lawyer may not make any extrajudicial statements except to state the claim, offense or defense involved and, except when prohibited by law, the identity of the persons involved.

Rule 3.6 Cmt. 5(1)

199. At a press conference about the prosecution of an accused serial killer, the prosecutor stated that the police arrested the defendant at the scene of one of the crimes soon after the crime occurred, at 11 pm on Saturday. Was it proper for the prosecutor to disclose such information about the case to reporters?
a) Yes, because a lawyer in a criminal case may state the fact, time, and place of arrest.
b) Yes, because a prosecutor represents the people, and the public disclosures are necessary communications between a lawyer and his clients, the taxpayers.
c) No, because the defendant is on trial for murder, so special ethical duties automatically apply to the prosecutor's public statements.
d) No, because a lawyer in a criminal case may not disclose the time and place of arrest

Rule 3.6(b)(7)(i)

200. At a press conference about the prosecution of a notoriously vice-prone celebrity, the prosecutor stated that the District Attorney's office had filed charges against the celebrity for shoplifting and drug possession. The prosecutor then said he had no further comments and took no further questions. Was it proper for the prosecutor to disclose such information about the case to reporters?
a) Yes, because the prosecutor took no further questions and merely stated the nature of the case.
b) Yes, because in a criminal case, a prosecutor may state publicly that the government has charged a certain defendant with a crime if the statement includes a reminder that the charge is merely an accusation and that the defendant has a presumption of innocence.
c) No, because a prosecutor should not make any public statement about a criminal case, unless the prosecutor has express authorization from a tribunal.

d) No, because in a criminal case, there is a presumption of prejudice when a prosecutor states publicly that a defendant is the subject of criminal charges, unless he includes a statement explaining that the charge is merely an accusation and that the defendant still has a presumption of innocence.

Rule 3.6 Cmt. 5(6)

201. After a terrorist attack that claimed many lives, authorities identified and arrested someone they believed to be the perpetrator of the attack. After the arrest, the prosecutor held a press conference, stating that the suspect was single and lived with his mother in a specific apartment complex in the city, and that the suspect would face charges related to the attacks. Could the prosecutor be subject to disciplinary action by the state bar for disclosing such information about the case to reporters?

a) Yes, because the defendant is on trial for murder, so special ethical duties automatically apply to the prosecutor's public statements.
b) Yes, because a lawyer in a criminal case may not disclose the residence, occupation, or family status of the accused.
c) No, because a lawyer in a criminal case may state the identity, residence, occupation, and family status of the accused.
d) No, because a prosecutor represents the people, and the public disclosures are necessary communications between a lawyer and his clients, the taxpayers.

Rule 3.6(b)(7)(i)

202. A flamboyant billionaire who founded a tech company faced charges of violating securities laws and regulations, and he became the target of an enforcement action by the Securities and Exchange Commission. Reports of the alleged crime generated significant media coverage and commentary, and the arrest and prosecution led to even more media attention. His attorney spoke to the press that assembled on the court house steps, and he gave the following statement: "I'm sure the only one guilty of anything here is the media – everyone knows my client is innocent, that the police framed him." Would it be permissible for the attorney to make such statements to the media, under the Model Rules?

a) Yes, because a lawyer may make a statement that a reasonable lawyer would believe is necessary to protect a client from the substantial undue prejudicial effect of recent publicity not initiated by the lawyer or the lawyer's client.

b) Yes, because it was unlikely to have a materially prejudicial effect on an adjudicative matter.

c) No, because a lawyer participating in a criminal proceeding shall not make any extrajudicial statement that the lawyer knows or should know that the media will disseminate

d) No, because a lawyer should not publicly express any opinion as to the guilt or innocence of a defendant or suspect in a criminal case or proceeding that could result in incarceration.

Rule 3.6 Cmt. 5 & 7

RULE 3.7
LAWYER AS WITNESS

203. An attorney represented the seller in a commercial real estate transaction. During the negotiations over the sale, the only parties present were the attorney, the client (seller), the buyer, and the buyer's lawyer. After the consummation of the purchase, the buyer sought to rescind the sale, alleging that the seller and the attorney had made fraudulent misrepresentations before and at the closing. Each side had completely different versions of what each party said during the negotiations and at the closing. Could the attorney represent the seller in the litigation over rescinding the sale for fraud?

a) Yes, if the attorney is not a co-defendant and has no conflict of interest, he may represent his transactional client at the trial.

b) Yes, the attorney's interests and the seller's interests align sufficiently in the matter to provide representation at trial.

c) No, the attorney is a material witness for the seller in the upcoming trial.

d) No, the attorney is a transactional lawyer and must refer the case to another lawyer for the trial.

RESTATEMENT § 108; Rule 3.7

204. An attorney represented a client in transactional matters, and another lawyer in the same firm represented the client in pending litigation. The attorney did not appear on a list of counsel for the litigation matter and was not planning to sit at counsel table or otherwise physically appear in support of advocacy. On the other hand, the litigation involves a transaction that the attorney handled previously for the client. Would it be impermissible for the attorney serve as a witness in support of the client's position in the trial?

a) Yes, a lawyer shall not act as advocate at a trial in which the lawyer is likely to be a necessary witness.

b) Yes, the testimony relates to a contested issue

c) No, if all the parties provide informed consent, confirmed in writing.

d) No, a lawyer serving in a capacity other than that of a courtroom advocate may serve as a witness for the lawyer's client.

Restatement of the Law Governing Lawyers § 108; Rule 3.7

205. An attorney represented a client in pending litigation that had just begun. A magistrate judge held a preliminary hearing in the matter to settle whether the matter should remain under seal for the time being; a regular trial judge would later conduct the jury trial on the merits. The attorney's testimony was necessary to establish a matter at the preliminary hearing, so another lawyer from his firm represented the client at the hearing and conducted the direct examination of the attorney as a witness. After the attorney has served as a witness at a preliminary matter, could he then represent the client at the trial, the following year?

a) Yes, a lawyer who testifies before a judicial officer concerning only a preliminary motion may still serve serving as advocate at a subsequent trial before a jury.

b) Yes, the advocate-witness rule does not apply to proceedings in which a magistrate presides.

c) No, a lawyer shall not act as advocate at a trial in which the lawyer is likely to be a necessary witness.

d) No, the attorney would have a conflict of interest because another lawyer from his firm already conducted the preliminary hearing.

RESTATEMENT § 108; Rule 3.7

206. An attorney represented a criminal defendant facing extortion charges. The state's star witness against the defendant was a former co-conspirator who had agreed to testify in exchange for a plea deal. To establish the witness' reliability and knowledge of the conspiracy, the prosecution planned to introduce a recorded conversation of an intercepted conference call, from a wiretap, in which the defendant, the witness, and other co-conspirators discussed and planned the conspiracy. The attorney was also part of the recorded conversation, at least at the beginning, though left the call before the later part when the participants agreed to commit their crimes. Even though the attorney was not facing charges as a co-conspirator, his voice would be among others in the recorded conversation when it played at the trial. Given this situation, does the attorney have an ethical duty to have another lawyer represent the defendant at the trial?

a) Yes, unless the client gives informed consent, confirmed in writing to the potential conflict of interest.

b) Yes, the attorney is in the uncomfortable position of being a potential witness and an advocate in the same trial.

c) No, the attorney's voice on the recording does not make the attorney a witness in the proceedings.

d) No, a lawyer serving as the advocate for a party at trial can also be a witness for purposes of impeaching a witness for the opposing party.

U.S. v. Lucio, 996 F.Supp.2d 514 (S.D Tex. 2013)

207. An attorney normally represents a client in commercial litigation matters, but in one specific case, the attorney had to testify as a witness during the trial, so he arranged for another firm to represent the client during the trial at which the attorney testified. The client prevailed at trial, and the opposing party filed an appeal. In this instance, the attorney's testimony from the trial is not an issue in the appeal; instead, the appeal focuses on the apportionment of fault and certain guarantees in a commercial contract. The firm that handled the trial did not do appellate work and ended their termination of the client after the trial ended in a favorable verdict. May the attorney represent the client in the appeal, even though the attorney testified at the trial?

a) Yes, because the advocate-as-witness rule applies only to representation during the

trial, unless the lawyer's testimony is an issue on appeal.

b) Yes, because the opposing party brought the appeal after the attorney's client obtained a favorable verdict at trial using other trial counsel.

c) No, because a lawyer shall not act as advocate at a trial in which the lawyer is likely to be a necessary witness.

d) No, because combining the roles of advocate and witness can prejudice the tribunal and the opposing party and can also involve a conflict of interest between the lawyer and the client.

Rule 3.7

208. An attorney was a criminal defense lawyer and she represented a client, who was a defendant in a criminal prosecution. The prosecution called the attorney to the witness stand to authenticate a piece of evidence, which the attorney was willing to do because the authenticity of the evidence was not really in dispute; the attorney planned to use alibi evidence to defeat the charges against the client, which would make this piece of evidence relatively unimportant to the case. May the attorney testify in this manner in a case in which she represents the defendant?

a) Yes, because the testimony relates to an uncontested issue.

b) Yes, because testifying as a witness will give the lawyer a good opportunity to advocate on behalf of his client.

c) No, because a lawyer shall not act as advocate at a trial in which the lawyer is likely to be a necessary witness.

d) No, because this is a criminal prosecution.

Rule 3.7(a)(1)

209. A certain client is an indigent criminal defendant and a certain attorney is his court-appointed counsel. The trial is taking place in a rural county where only a handful of lawyers practice law. Before appointing the attorney to represent the client, the court had tried to appoint five other local criminal defense lawyers, one after the other, but each was unable to provide representation due either to a conflict of interest or because their current caseload would have precluded them from providing competent representation. In fact, the attorney was the last lawyer on the court appointments list.

Unfortunately, the attorney also needed to serve as a witness during part of the trial, to authenticate a piece of evidence, and the authenticity of the evidence was a matter of dispute in the case. In addition, the attorney realized that his testimony would radically contradict the testimony of his own client, though the attorney still believed he could obtain an acquittal by impeaching the prosecution's star witness. May the attorney continue to represent the client and testify as a witness in this matter?

a) Yes, because the testimony relates to a contested issue, so the ambiguities in the dual role are purely theoretical.

b) Yes, because disqualification of the lawyer would work substantial hardship on the client.

c) No, because there is likely to be substantial conflict between the testimony of the client and that of the lawyer, so the representation involves a conflict of interest that requires compliance with the rules about conflicts.

d) No, because a lawyer shall not act as advocate at a trial in which the lawyer is likely to be a necessary witness, and it may not be clear whether a statement by an advocate-witness should serve as proof or as an analysis of the proof.

Rule 3.7 Cmt. 6

210. An attorney is representing himself in his divorce proceeding. Would it be proper, under the advocate-witness rule, for the attorney to testify as a witness on his own behalf in the proceeding in which he represents himself?

a) Yes, because disqualification of the lawyer either from representing himself or from testifying would work substantial hardship on the client.

b) Yes, because the advocate-witness prohibition does not apply to pro se litigants who are attorneys.

c) No, because a lawyer shall not act as advocate at a trial in which the lawyer is likely to be a necessary witness.

d) No, because he will be unable to make objections to improper questions by opposing counsel during cross-examination.

See Ayres v. Canales, 790 S.W.2d 554 (Tex. 1990); Horen v. Bd. Of Educ., 882 N.E.2d 14 (Ohio Ct. Appl. 2007); Conn. Informal Ethics Op. 05-03 (2005)

211. A famous professional athlete faced charges for murdering his wife and her male companion one evening outside their Beverly Hills home. The defendant assembled a legal "dream team" of the five most famous criminal defense lawyers from around the country. One of the lawyers was in possession of a handwritten letter from one of the murder victims saying that a drug cartel had been making death threats against the victim for a few weeks. The evidence might have been exculpatory for the defendant, but the lawyer would have to take the witness stand briefly during the trial to authenticate the document or explain how he received it. The document was a hotly contested piece of evidence in the case, but it was not the only evidence pointing toward the defendant's innocence or guilt. The prosecutor wanted the court to disqualify the lawyer from representing the defendant if he testified about the letter. The defendant insisted that this would work a substantial hardship on him, because this lawyer was the only criminal defense lawyer in the county with an undefeated record – he had obtained acquittals in hundreds of criminal trials and had never lost a case. Should the court side with the defendant in this case and allow the lawyer to continue as part of his defense team?

a) Yes, because disqualification of the lawyer would work substantial hardship on the client.

b) Yes, because this is a criminal prosecution and the client has a Sixth Amendment right to counsel.

c) No, because disqualification of the lawyer would not work substantial hardship on the client.

d) No, because a lawyer may act as advocate in a trial in which another lawyer in the lawyer's firm is likely to testify as a witness.

Rule 3.7(a)(3)

RULE 3.8

SPECIAL RESPONSIBILITIES OF A PROSECUTOR

[NOTE: The bar examiners include this as a subtopic under "Lawyers' Duties to the Public and the Legal System," the least-tested category of subjects. I include them here because in a law school course, the subject fits with the others immediately preceding it]

212. A certain attorney works as a prosecutor and brings charges against a defendant. In this instance, the attorney clearly has probable cause for alleging that the defendant committed the crime, but he also doubts that a judge or jury will find that the evidence satisfies the standard of "beyond a reasonable doubt." Yet the attorney brings the case anyway, and the defendant wins an acquittal. Has the attorney acted improperly, under the Rules of Professional Conduct?

a) Yes, because a prosecutor in a criminal case shall not seek a conviction unless the prosecutor believes in good faith that the defendant is guilty beyond a reasonable doubt.

b) Yes, because the prosecutor should have conducted more investigation before commencing the proceedings so that he could ensure a conviction, if he already has probable cause to believe the defendant is guilty.

c) No, because when a prosecutor knows of clear and convincing evidence establishing a wrongful conviction of an innocent defendant in the prosecutor's state, the prosecutor shall seek to remedy the conviction.

d) No, because a prosecutor may bring charges if the prosecutor knows the charges have probable cause.

Rule 3.8(a)

213. An Assistant U.S. Attorney (federal prosecutor) is working for the Department of Justice, and he must prosecute the defendants arrested in a high-profile sting operation against a terrorist cell. This attorney faces tremendous political and media pressure to win convictions at any cost. As a result, the attorney argues with his supervisor that he is not subject to local ethics rules, as he is litigating exclusively in federal court in cases involving federal law, and that he should therefore be immune from state

bar disciplinary proceedings. Is the attorney correct?

a) Yes, because of federal preemption of state law, a federal prosecutor who litigates exclusively in federal court, under federal law, does not come under the jurisdiction of the local bar disciplinary authorities.

b) Yes, because under the USA Patriot Act, federal prosecutors are immune from disciplinary actions for their decisions in antiterrorism prosecutions.

c) No, because the attorney will inevitably have cases that involve questions of state law or will have cases transferred to state court.

d) No, because federal statute, as well as Department of Justice regulations, subject federal prosecutors to the ethics rules of the state where such the attorney engages in that the attorney's duties.

28 U.S.C. § 530B; 28 C.F.R. §77.3

214. A prosecutor sees the backlog of prosecutions coming from his office and feels concern about whether all the cases will come to trial in time to comply with the Speedy Trial Act. To expedite some of the simpler cases, the prosecutor asks arrestees to waive their right to a pre-trial hearing, which saves up to a week due to scheduling complications and allows the defendants' cases to come to trial sooner. Because most of the defendants in these cases are unrepresented by counsel, the prosecutor explains that they have a right to a preliminary hearing, but that defendants without a lawyer usually accomplish little or nothing at such hearings, and that the defendant will have a full trial at which to argue his innocence. He also explains that if the defendant believes he can win an acquittal, waiving a preliminary hearing might bring about the defendant's moment of freedom a bit sooner. Most defendants without representation agree to waive their preliminary hearings, which relieves some of the pressure on the local criminal docket and makes this more manageable for everyone. Is the prosecutor behaving properly in this regard?

a) Yes, because he is making a good-faith effort to expedite the proceedings, which is good for the defendants who are innocent and want to get their trials done sooner rather than later.

b) Yes, because he is apprising them of their

rights before asking them to waive the right to a preliminary hearing.

c) No, because it is improper for a prosecutor to have any direct contact with an unrepresented defendant before trial.

d) No, because a prosecutor must not seek to obtain from an unrepresented accused a waiver of important pretrial rights, such as the right to a preliminary hearing.

Rule 3.8(c)

215. A prosecutor in New York is engaged in plea bargain negotiations with a defendant and defense counsel. The defendant offers to confess to a much more serious crime, committed several years ago in California, if the prosecutor will drop the current charges, which will put the defendant in danger of retaliation from his gang once he is in prison. The prosecutor agrees, and the defendant confesses to a notorious armored car robbery in California ten years earlier that made national news, and for which another wrongfully convicted man was serving his sentence. The defendant describes the crime with enough detail that the prosecutor doubts that he could be fabricating the story. Does the prosecutor have any ethical duties about what to do with this information?

a) Yes, the prosecutor must notify the defense counsel of the wrongfully convicted man and must investigate to see if there is corroboration for the new confession to the crime by the New York defendant.

b) Yes, the prosecutor must promptly disclose that evidence to an appropriate court or authority.

c) No, the prosecutor does not have to take any action unless there is clear and convincing evidence that a wrongfully convicted person is in prison.

d) No, because the prosecutor cannot breach his duty of confidentiality, but he should urge the defendant to contact the authorities in California directly so that the wrongfully convicted man can get out of prison.

Rule 3.8(g)

216. Three years after prosecuting a defendant and obtaining a conviction for murder, another individual comes to the police station and confesses to committing the very murder for which the defendant is already serving time. The defendant always maintained his innocence and the basis of his conviction was an identification (in a lineup) by a single eyewitness. The person now confessing to the crime also fits the description given by the eyewitness and had a plausible motive for committing the murder. Does the prosecutor have a duty report this to the convicted defendant's lawyer?

a) Yes, when a prosecutor knows of new, credible and material evidence creating a reasonable likelihood that a convicted defendant in his jurisdiction did not commit an offense of which the defendant was convicted, the prosecutor shall promptly disclose that evidence to the defendant unless a court authorizes delay, and undertake further investigation, or make reasonable efforts to cause an investigation, to determine whether the defendant was convicted of an offense that the defendant did not commit.

b) Yes, the prosecutor shall seek to remedy the conviction.

c) No, assuming the defendant received a fair trial and had presentation by counsel, a judgment of the court is final, and the new evidence is irrelevant.

d) No, the prosecutor should report it to the defendant himself and urge him to file a habeas corpus petition in federal court.

Rule 3.8(g)

217. A prosecutor obtained an indictment from a grand jury against a defendant on a multiple-count assault and robbery of a woman, that is, a violent mugging in which the perpetrator stole the woman's purse. The victim did not know her assailant, but afterward she identified the defendant in a photo array and then picked him out of a line-up. A bystander made the same identification from a photo array and a subsequent lineup. At the same time, the police informed the prosecutor that two other eyewitnesses viewed the same line-up, but those witnesses stated that they did not see the perpetrator. Moreover, a confidential informant attributed the assault to someone else. Concerned, the prosecutor interviewed the other two eyewitnesses, but he decided that they did not get a good enough look at the perpetrator to testify reliably. The prosecutor also interviewed the confidential informant, but he learned that the informant had previous convictions for fraud, and therefore was not credible. Does Rule 3.8(d) require the prosecutor to disclose to defense counsel that two bystanders failed to identify the

defendant and that an informant implicated someone other than the defendant?

a) If the information is not "material" for purposes of constitutional case law under the Brady doctrine, the prosecutor does not have to inform defense counsel about the other unreliable witnesses.

b) The prosecutor would have to disclose that two eyewitnesses failed to identify the defendant as the assailant and that an informant attributed the assault to someone else, because the prosecutor knew that information from communications with the police.

c) If the prosecutor has a reasonable belief that defense counsel will find these witnesses on his own, he has no independent duty to inform the other lawyer.

d) Under these circumstances, the Model Rules require the prosecutor to conduct further inquiry or investigation to discover other evidence or information favorable to the defense.

ABA Formal Op. 09-454, Rule 3.8(d)

218. A defendant faced charges in a white-collar crime case – corporate espionage, securities fraud, and so forth. The police brought the prosecutor voluminous files, with the file boxes filling an entire storage room at the district attorney's office. These dozens of file boxes were only part of the evidence the police had amassed before making the arrest, so they inform the prosecutor that they have another room full of corporate records documenting the crimes in the basement of their precinct. Unbeknownst the to the prosecutor, some of the files in both locations have a few documents that case doubt on the defendant's role in some of the crimes, and others that might tend to mitigate the some of the other charges. If the prosecutor has not yet reviewed voluminous files or obtained all police files, however, does Rule 3.8 require the prosecutor to review or request such files before the plea bargaining, so that the defense can make better-informed decisions during the plea negotiations?

a) Yes, the rule requires prosecutors to find and disclose favorable evidence immediately so that the defense can decide on its utility.

b) Yes, the prosecutor at least has a duty at the outset of the plea negotiations to inform

defense counsel that he has not yet reviewed the voluminous files of corporate records, so he does not know whether there will be exculpatory evidence in the files.

c) No, Rule 3.8 does not require the prosecutor to review or request such files unless the prosecutor knows or infers from the circumstances, or it is obvious, that the files contain favorable evidence or information.

d) No, there is no constitutional right to plea bargain, so the Brady rule does not apply until the trial begins.

ABA Formal Op. 09-454, Rule 3.8(d)

219. A grand jury indicted a defendant on a multiple-count assault and robbery of a woman, a violent mugging in which the perpetrator stole the woman's purse. The victim did not know her assailant, but afterward she identified the defendant in a photo array and then picked him out of a line-up. A bystander made the same identification from a photo array and a subsequent lineup. At the same time, the police informed the prosecutor that two other eyewitnesses viewed the same line-up, but those witnesses stated that they did not see the perpetrator. Moreover, a confidential informant attributed the assault to someone else. Concerned, the prosecutor interviewed the other two eyewitnesses, but he decided that they did not get a good enough look at the perpetrator to testify reliably. The prosecutor also interviewed the confidential informant, but he learned that the informant had previous convictions for fraud, and therefore was not credible. Given the early state of the proceedings, the prosecutor decides that if the case goes to trial, he will inform defense counsel about the other witnesses, because defense counsel may want to call them to testify. On the other hand, it seems unnecessary to mention the other witnesses during the plea-bargaining negotiations, because they are not part of the evidence the prosecutor would use in the case. Has the prosecutor acted within the parameters of the Model Rules?

a) Yes, there is no constitutional right to plea bargain, so the Brady disclosure rule does not apply until the trial begins.

b) Yes, the existence of the other witnesses does not matter at the plea-bargaining stage, but only if they are necessary at trial to contradict the testimony from the victim and the other eyewitness.

c) No, the Model Rules require the prosecutor to conduct further inquiry or investigation to discover other evidence or information favorable to the defense before proceeding with the plea negotiations.

d) No, to allow the defendant to make a well-advised plea at the time of arraignment, prior to a guilty plea, the prosecutor must disclose known evidence and information that would be relevant or useful to establishing a defense or negating the prosecution's proof.

ABA Formal Op. 09-454, Rule 3.8(d)

220. A major city has large district attorney's office with many prosecutors. In most cases, several prosecutors share responsibility for parts of a single criminal case, so different prosecutors have responsibility for investigating the matter, presenting the indictment, and trying the case. Inevitably, some less important or immaterial information learned by the prosecutor conducting the investigation, or the grand jury presentation, does not pass along to the other prosecutor in the subsequent proceedings. As a result, the prosecutor handling the trial does not know certain minor details that might be helpful to the defendant's case, and therefore cannot disclose the information to defense counsel. Does it constitute a violation of the Model Rules for cases to pass from prosecutor to prosecutor, with the defendant and the prosecutor being unaware of some minor details (whether inculpatory, exculpatory, or mitigating) lost in the process?

a) Yes, within the district attorney's office, supervisory lawyers must establish procedures to ensure that each prosecutor involved has the exculpatory evidence to disclose.

b) Yes, the Model Rules require that the same prosecutor handle a criminal matter from the indictment through its conclusion, to avoid this very problem.

c) No, the information is unknown to both the prosecutor and the defense counsel at trial, so it does not help or hurt either side.

d) No, the prosecutors are responsible only for disclosing information they know about.

ABA Formal Op. 09-454, Rule 3.8(d)

RULE 3.9
ADVOCATE IN NONADJUDICATIVE PROCEEDINGS

221. An attorney testified before a state legislative committee about the need for the state to privatize its dysfunctional prison system. The attorney said he was there to testify as a concerned citizen of the state and a taxpayer, and the attorney did in fact believe that prison privatization was smart public policy. Yet the attorney did not disclose that he was representing Alcatraz Incorporated, the largest private prison company in the country, which hoped to secure the lucrative contracts to operate the state's prisons after the legislature votes to privatize them. Was it improper for the attorney to neglect to disclose his representation of the private prison company?

a) Yes, because a lawyer representing a client before a legislative body or administrative agency in a nonadjudicative proceeding shall disclose that the appearance is in a representative capacity.

b) Yes, because the lawyer pretended that he was hoping to save on his taxes, but the privatization of prisons often turns out to be more expensive than having state-run prisons.

c) No, because what the lawyer told the committee was factually accurate – he is a concerned citizen, a taxpayer, and he believes strongly in privatizing prisons.

d) No, because a lawyer's duty of candor pertains to tribunals, not to legislative subcommittees.

Rule 3.9

222. An attorney represented Conglomerate Corporation in the company's regulatory compliance work. The Environmental Protection Agency (EPA) proposed new pollution emission regulations through notice-and-comment rulemaking procedures as proscribed under the Administrative Procedure Act. The proposed new regulations would impose burdensome financial costs on Conglomerate Corporation. During the public comment period, the attorney submitted comments arguing that the proposed rules made only marginal improvements to public health but imposed devastating costs on the regulated industry, which would violate the "feasibility" requirement in the relevant

governing statute. The attorney relied entirely on published scientific studies to argue that the health benefits were minimal, but knowingly exaggerated how much it would cost his client to comply with the proposed standards. Any member of the public could submit comments during the comment period; there were no public hearings and none of the submissions to the agency were under oath. Could the attorney be subject to discipline for his conduct regarding the submission of comments to the agency?

a) Yes, lawyers have a duty to argue in the interest of the public when making submissions to a regulatory agency, rather than advocate for a special interest group, such as a client.

b) Yes, a lawyer cannot submit false statements or comments to a regulatory agency functioning in its rulemaking capacity.

c) No, this was not an adjudicative or adversarial proceeding, so there was no duty of candor or fairness to other parties.

d) No, any member of the public could submit unsworn statements and comments, so the agency could not have a reasonable expectation in the reliability or truthfulness in all the contents.

Rule 3.9 Cmt. 1

223. An attorney worked as in-house general counsel for Big Bank. The Federal Trade Commission was holding a series of hearings about the consolidation of the industry and anticompetitive activities, and certain consumer protection groups were advocating in the hearings for regulatory reforms. In one instance, the consumer protection groups persuaded the Commission to subpoena certain corporate from the largest banks to show that they had engaged in undetected predatory pricing and price gouging following natural disasters. After hearing about the request for this subpoena, but before receiving service of it from the Commission, the attorney deleted several computer archives about the company's pricing patterns, and shredded printed records pertaining to the same subject. Big Bank was not currently the target of an enforcement action, and no litigation was pending or immediately contemplated regarding this information. Was it permissible for the attorney to clean up the company archives before receiving a subpoena from the Commission for its public hearings?

a) Yes, a lawyer should act with commitment and dedication to the interests of the client

and with zeal in advocacy upon the client's behalf.

b) Yes, this was not an adjudicative proceeding or appearance before a tribunal, so the attorney's duty to protect client confidentiality was paramount.

c) No, lawyers have a duty when representing a client before an agency in a nonadjudicative proceeding to collaborate with other interested parties and cooperate fully with their requests for information.

d) No, the attorney obstructed another party's access to evidence and destroyed documents or other material having potential evidentiary value.

Rule 3.9 Cmt. 1

224. An attorney represented a large pharmaceutical company that was part of an industry consortium. The industry consortium was pressuring the Food and Drug Administration (FDA) to relax its requirements for approval of new drugs. Regulators within the FDA had divergent views on this from a policy standpoint. The issue did not pertain to any individual drug or company; it concerned procedures for new drug approval as a general matter. Representatives from different companies within the industry would meet as a group with a team of regulators tasked with reviewing the FDA's policies in this regard, and during these meetings the regulators would ask the industry representatives probing questions about their research and development costs, market share, and retail pricing of drugs after approval. When executives from the attorney's company were preparing to attend one of these "negotiated rulemaking" meetings, the attorney coached him to say, "I do not recall" whenever the regulators asked questions that would reveal information unfavorable to the company's position. Was it permissible for the attorney to counsel the corporate executives to give evasive or vaguely untruthful answers at an industry meeting like this?

a) Yes, the Model Rules governing advocacy in nonadjudicative proceedings do not apply to representation of a client in a negotiation or other bilateral transaction with a governmental agency or in connection with an application for a license or other privilege.

b) Yes, the executives were not testifying under oath before a tribunal in this situation,

or committing fraud, so the answers were
lawful.

c) No, a lawyer may not submit false
statements or false evidence through another
to a rulemaking agency, which should be
able to rely on the integrity of the
submissions made to it.

d) No, the coached answers could give the
company an unfair advantage over its
competitors in the negotiations.

Rule 3.9 Cmt. 1

DILIGENCE, COMPETENCE, LEGAL MALPRACTICE, & OTHER CIVIL LIABILITY

RULE 1.1 COMPETENCE

225. An attorney had graduated from law school near the bottom of his class, but he told himself that every year someone at graduation had to be at the bottom of their class. Besides, his mentor always told him that law school classes have nothing to do with the actual practice of law. The attorney was unaware that his 1L Civil Procedure Professor had miscalculated his grade two full letter grades higher than he deserved, and otherwise he would have failed out before his second year. The attorney invested a reasonable amount of time preparing for his clients' cases, and put in normal effort for an attorney, but still was far behind his fellow lawyers in his ability. He lacked knowledge of settled principles of Law and was not aware of recent developments in case law and legislation in his area of practice, even though he tried and made an earnest effort, often trying even harder than the lawyers around him, who seemed to coast along effortlessly by comparison. His intentions were always good, and he genuinely cared about his clients. Could the attorney be subject to discipline, including disbarment, for incompetent representation?

a) Yes, if he was never supposed to graduate from law school in the first place, but for that professor's mistake that inured to his benefit.

b) Yes, he lacks basic knowledge and skills necessary, despite his efforts and good intentions.

c) No, the evaluation of competence takes into consideration how hard the lawyer tries and whether he has the right intentions.

d) No, because for many clients, he certainly knows enough to get by, given that most cases settle quickly.

Rule 1.1

226. An attorney has spent his entire career practicing family law, and he has never done a criminal trial before. When asked to take a pro bono criminal case, he whimsically agreed, because the attorney was going through a midlife crisis and wants to try

something new. The attorney invested time studying and researching the relevant law and court procedures so that he knows how to proceed and how to advise the client, but still feels nervous doing this for the first time, and certainly does not have the same expertise as the most experienced lawyers in the area. Could the attorney be subject to discipline for his lack of competence?

a) Yes, he has never done a criminal trial before and a defendant is completely depending on him.

b) Yes, he did not spend time carefully considering the decision before agreeing to take the case, and took the case because of a midlife crisis, which is improper.

c) No, an attorney can provide competent representation in an entirely new area with adequate study and preparation.

d) No, the client is pro bono, so the attorney does not have to meet usual standards of competency.

Rule 1.1 Cmts. 2, 4

227. An attorney was highly knowledgeable and skillful, but he lost every case that he undertook, either because the law was unfavorable to his clients, or the other side could afford an entire army of elite lawyers, or because he was an unattractive person. He also regularly took on clients that no other lawyer wanted to represent because they seemed likely to lose. Over time, the attorney's clients lost their homes, lost custody of their children, lost their inheritances, and sometimes even went to jail. Despite his vast knowledge, skills, and thorough preparation, could the attorney nevertheless be subject to discipline for lack of competence, because he is consistently losing every time?

a) Yes, clients have a contractual expectation of effective representation, which means some of the outcomes should be favorable.

b) Yes, it is incompetent to take on clients whose cases seem likely to lose, or where the opposing party has far greater resources to hire the most elite law firms.

c) No, even though the clients received an unfavorable outcome, their results might have been even worse without the attorney's help.

d) No, the attorney seems competent, based on the facts given, regardless of the pattern of unfavorable outcome in his cases, which could be due to other factors.

Rule 1.1 Cmt. 2

228. A very winsome, likable attorney was objectively incompetent in providing representation to his client, but he was lucky - the other side had a terrible case on the merits, and opposing counsel was unlikable and abrasive, so the attorney prevailed in his client's case. Could the attorney nevertheless be subject to discipline for lack of competence?

a) Yes, a lawyer shall provide competent representation to a client, regardless of the outcome.

b) Yes, because it is not fair to other lawyers who are competent if an incompetent lawyer can win.

c) No, the attorney's ability to prevail in the matter on behalf of his client, notwithstanding the efforts of opposing counsel, is per se evidence of his competence.

d) No, the client received effective representation and a favorable outcome, which is what the client bargained for when he retained counsel.

Rule 1.1

229. An attorney has spent his entire career practicing family law, and he has never done a criminal trial before. When asked to take a criminal case, he agreed to do only the preliminary pre-trial work, such as the arraignment or bond hearing, initial rounds of plea negotiations, and some basic factual investigation. The client was facing charges for various white-collar crimes, brought under federal statutes, and would involve complex jurisdictional and procedural issues at trial. The attorney knew that he would not be competent to represent the client at such a trial, so he contractually agreed to limit his representation to the few preliminary tasks described above, to allow the client time to find another lawyer with more experience and expertise in this area. Once the representation began, the attorney confined himself to the parts of the matter that he had agreed to handle. Is it permissible for the attorney to be incompetent in certain matters but still provide representation to a client in a more limited capacity?

a) Yes, clients and lawyers have wide latitude in their contractual agreements, and a lawyer can contract with a client to provide representation that would seem objectively incompetent to most other lawyers.

b) Yes, agreements between the lawyer and the client regarding the scope of the representation may limit the matters for which the lawyer is responsible.

c) No, a lawyer may not avoid the duty of competence by limiting the scope of the representation through an agreement with the client.

d) No, the attorney could have achieved the requisite level of competence to handle the entire matter by reasonable preparation.

Rule 1.1 Cmt. 5

230. A brilliant attorney graduated at the top of his class from Harvard Law School. He was supremely intelligent and well-studied in the law, remarkably handsome, witty, and well-spoken. As he progressed through his career, he was in such high demand that he could afford to take only the cases he knew were mostly likely to win. Regardless of the complexity of the matter, he always won based on his wit, looks, and eloquence. He has been so successful that he has not needed to read a new case in fifteen years, nor has he needed to keep abreast of changes in law. He has never faced disciplinary action or a malpractice lawsuit. Assuming his winning streak continues indefinitely, is he providing competent representation, according to the Model Rules?

a) Yes, the Model Rules use an objective, outcomes-based standard for evaluating competence.

b) Yes, the Model Rules measure competence based on the education, experience, and reputation of the lawyer.

c) No, the Model Rules measure the required attention and preparation primarily by what is at stake.

d) No, a lawyer should keep abreast of changes in the law and its practice and engage in continuing study and education.

Rule 1.1 Cmt 8

231. An attorney had just graduated and passed the bar when he agreed to represent a certain client. Even though he was new to the practice of law, he devoted plenty of time to study and preparation to understand the relevant statutes and case law, correctly identified all the issues in the case, and conducted a thorough investigation of the facts. His knowledge and skills were normal for newer lawyers in his area. Unfortunately, he was simply no match for the counsel, one of the most famous lawyers in the state, and reputed to be the best in his field. The case went overwhelmingly in favor of the opposing party, so the client ended up worse off than before the matter began. Opposing counsel would have had an advantage over any other lawyer in the area, though an experienced lawyer might have obtained a less adverse result for the new attorney's client. Could the new attorney be subject to discipline for his lack of competence?

a) Yes, expertise in a specific field of law is a requirement in some circumstances, as when opposing counsel is a renowned expert.
b) Yes, the most fundamental legal skill consists of determining what kind of legal problems a situation may involve, a skill that necessarily transcends any specific specialized knowledge.
c) No, a newly admitted lawyer can be as competent as an experienced practitioner, even if the outcome in this case was unfavorable.
d) No, because now that he has learned a hard lesson, in the future he can provide competent representation through the association of a lawyer of established competence in the field in question.

Rule 1.1 Cmt 2

232. An attorney graduated from law school in the early 1970's, and he spent his career in solo practice in a small rural town, mostly drafting wills and simple contracts for sale for farm machinery. He has a landline phone in his office and home, but has never had or needed a cell phone, does not use a computer, and has never used email or the Internet. The attorney has an extensive library of law books and treatises. Could the attorney be subject to discipline for not keeping abreast of changes in technology that are relevant to the practice of law?
a) Yes, to maintain the requisite knowledge and skill, a lawyer should keep abreast of changes in the law and its practice, including the benefits and risks associated with relevant technology.
b) Yes, unless the client gives informed consent, confirmed in writing, to the fact that the attorney does not know how to use a cell phone or the Internet.
c) No, a practitioner with long experience can be just as competent as a newly admitted lawyer.
d) No, the most fundamental legal skill consists of determining what kind of legal problems a situation may involve, a skill that necessarily transcends any specific technology.

Rule 1.1 Cmt. 8; ABA Formal Op. 18-483

233. An attorney specialized in transactional work for corporate clients, and he focused his practice on this area for many years. An emergency arose in which an attorney needed to give immediately telephone advice to an individual client who had to make an urgent decision. Referring the case to another firm, or even consulting with another lawyer, was not practical in the moment. The attorney did not have

the requisite skill or knowledge for the matter, because it was far outside the attorney's regular area of practice, and he explained this to the client before offering any advice. He then gave his best educated guess about what the client should do, based on analogous situations in areas of law more familiar to him. The attorney took the opportunity to give the client extensive advice about the net several steps the client should take, and advice about the subsequent appeal of the matter, all of which was completely outside the attorney's range of knowledge or experience. The client relied on the attorney's uninformed advice, all of which turned out to be wrong, and resulting in several lawyers of harm to the client's legal interests. If the attorney had limited his emergency advice to the minimum necessary in the moment, the client would have suffered less harm. Could the attorney be subject to discipline for lack of competence?
a) Yes, even in emergencies, a lawyer should limit assistance to what is necessary in the circumstances, for ill-considered action under emergency conditions can jeopardize the client's interest.
b) Yes, competent handling of a specific matter includes inquiry into and analysis of the factual and legal elements of the problem, and the use of methods and procedures meeting the standards of competent practitioners.
c) No, an agreement between the lawyer and the client regarding the scope of the representation may limit the matters for which the lawyer is responsible.
d) No, in emergencies a lawyer may give advice or assistance in a matter in which the lawyer does not have the skill ordinarily required where referral to or consultation or association with another lawyer would be impractical.

Rule 1.1 Cmt.3

234. An attorney specialized in transactional work for corporate clients, and he focused his practice on this area for many years. An emergency arose in which an attorney needed to give immediately telephone advice to an individual client who had to make an urgent decision. Referring the case to another firm, or even consulting with another lawyer, was not practical in the moment. The attorney did not have the requisite skill or knowledge for the matter, because it was far outside the attorney's regular area of practice, and he explained this to the client before offering any advice. He then gave his best educated guess about what the client should do, based on analogous situations in areas of law more familiar to him, and confined his comments to the minimum

necessary in the circumstances. The client relied on the attorney's (mostly uninformed) advice, which turned out to be wrong, and the outcome was harmful to the client's legal interests. Could the attorney be subject to discipline for lack of competence?

a) Yes, according to the Model Rules, a lawyer must not give advice or assistance in a matter in which the lawyer does not have the skill ordinarily required.

b) Yes, competent handling of a specific matter includes inquiry into and analysis of the factual and legal elements of the problem, and the use of methods and procedures meeting the standards of competent practitioners.

c) No, in emergencies a lawyer may give advice or assistance in a matter in which the lawyer does not have the skill ordinarily required where referral to or consultation or association with another lawyer would be impractical.

d) No, an agreement between the lawyer and the client regarding the scope of the representation may limit the matters for which the lawyer is responsible.

Rule 1.1 Cmt.3

235. Conglomerate Corporation decided to hire Big Firm to represent it in litigation for an important but complex matter. First, however, Conglomerate offered a proposed a budget for the entire litigation. A partner at Big Firm explained to Conglomerate's in-house counsel that such a limited budget would be feasible only if the firm restricted how much discovery it conducted before trial. The partner also warned that restricting their time and money expenditures during discover could negatively impact their chances of prevailing at trial. Nevertheless, Conglomerate's directors decide that the corporation would be better off having the talents and reputation of Big Firm's attorneys at a limited expense, even though they knew they could have spent more for more thorough and expensive representation. According to the Restatement, may Conglomerate waive its right to more thorough representation?

a) Yes, if a corporate client has in-house counsel, there are no restrictions on what types of agreements the corporation can make with outside counsel.

b) Yes, a client and lawyer may agree to limit a duty that a lawyer would otherwise owe to the client if the client has enough information and consents, and the terms of the limitation are reasonable in the circumstances.

c) No, because eventually, such restrictions could become a standard practice that constricts the rights of clients without compensating benefits.

d) No, the administration of justice may suffer from distrust of the legal system that may result from such a practice.

RESTATEMENT § 19 - Agreements Limiting Client or Lawyer Duties

RULE 1.3 DILIGENCE

236. An attorney represented a client as the plaintiff in a legal malpractice action against another lawyer for simple negligence. The plaintiff's attorney sent a demand letter to the other lawyer, who immediately notified his malpractice insurer. The insurer offered to settle immediately, for the full amount that the client was demanding, mostly to avoid the publicity and attention that would result if litigation ensued, including the risk that the claim would inspire others to file lawsuits against the same firm. The attorney had received prior authorization from the client, during the initial consultation, to accept a settlement offer for that amount whenever it might come as the matter progressed. The attorney did not file pleadings in court and did not file a grievance with the state bar against the other lawyer. Did the attorney violate his ethical duty of zealous advocacy by not filing pleadings or a grievance?

a) Yes, a lawyer should pursue a matter on behalf of a client despite opposition or personal inconvenience, taking whatever lawful and ethical measures might be necessary to vindicate a client's cause or endeavor.

b) Yes, a lawyer must also act with commitment and dedication to the interests of the client and with zeal in advocacy upon the client's behalf.

c) No, if a client has clearly expressed a preferred settlement amount, the lawyer has no obligation except to obtain than amount.

d) No, a lawyer does not have to press for every advantage that might be realized for a client, having professional discretion to determine how a matter should be pursued.

Rule 1.3 Cmt. 1

237. The Office of the Public Defender in a large urban center lacked the budget to hire the number of lawyers they needed. The number of indigent

defendants who requiring representation always exceeded the capacity of the lawyers there. An attorney worked as a prosecutor for a few years to get experience, then became a public defender at this office. He soon found himself with an overload of cases, so it was impossible to provide full representation to each client. The attorney, like the other public defenders there, encouraged all his clients to accept a plea bargain, with rare exceptions. Going to trial on any one case meant turning away about two dozen indigent clients, most of whom could reach a plea agreement within an hour or two. The attorney reasoned that it was better for indigent criminal defendants to have a little representation rather than none. Besides, he knew that many of the defendants would lose if they went to trial. Given these facts, is the attorney violating his ethical duty of diligent representation to the clients?

a) Yes, every criminal defendant has a constitutional right to a jury trial, and lawyers should not advise them to waive this important right and accept a plea bargain instead.

b) Yes, lawyers must control their workload so that each matter receives competent, diligent representation.

c) No, there is a special exception to the workload-limit rules for public defenders, in light of the pressing need for representation of indigent defendants.

d) No, if most of the clients would indeed be worse off if they went to trial, then the attorney's minimal representation is better for them.

Ruel 1.3, Cmt. 2

238. A litigation attorney represented Big Bank in a lawsuit involving many complex issues and numerous expert witnesses. At a preliminary hearing, opposing counsel requested a three-month postponement of the previously scheduled trial date, to allow more time for deposing expert witnesses and the top managers from Big Bank. The attorney for Big Bank acquiesced, relieved that the extension of time would allow him to focus on other urgent client matters. The next day, the attorney notified Big Bank that the judge had postponed the trial. Big Bank's directors were frustrated, as they had hoped to resolve the case sooner, and would have objected to the postponement if the attorney had checked in before agreeing to it. On the other hand, Big Bank suffered no financial or reputational harm from the postponement, and the directors had not instructed the attorney to refuse requests for more time. Was it proper for the attorney to agree to the postponement of the trial?

a) Yes, a lawyer's duty to act with reasonable promptness does not preclude the lawyer from agreeing to a reasonable request for a postponement that will not prejudice the lawyer's client.

b) Yes, the attorney had a duty to accommodate the request for a more time, assuming the delay will not prejudice the client in the eventual outcome.

c) No, the Model Rules require lawyers to act with reasonable diligence and promptness in representing a client.

d) No, because a client's interests suffer by the passage of time or the change of conditions, and unreasonable delay can cause a client needless anxiety and undermine confidence in the lawyer's trustworthiness.

Rule 1.3, Cmt. 3

239. An experienced litigation attorney represented Small Business as a client in a civil lawsuit. The trial resulted in an unfavorable verdict for the client, who then hoped to reverse the decision on appeal. Nevertheless, the attorney and the client had never agreed that the attorney would handle the appeal, so the attorney simply closed out his file for that client. The deadline for the client to appeal the verdict passed, and only afterward did the client discover that the attorney had not filed a timely appeal. Did the attorney fulfill his ethical duty of diligence to the client in this instance?

a) Yes, the same lawyer cannot represent a client at trial and on appeal, and the client should have been aware of this rule.

b) Yes, a lawyer does not have to continue working on a case for a client after trial unless the attorney and the client specifically agreed that the attorney would continue to be employed as the attorney for the appeal process.

c) No, an attorney must discuss the possibility of an appeal prior to relinquishing responsibility for a client's case, unless there was a prior agreement about whether the lawyer would handle the appeal process.

d) No, a lawyer should complete an entire case for a client, including the appeal process, unless the parties have agreed in writing that the attorney's employment terminates after trial.

Rule 1.3 Cmt. 4

240. An attorney worked for Big Firm for several years, but he failed to make partner there because he was unable to recruit any new clients to the firm. He also observed numerous minor ethical violations occurring regularly at Big Firm, but none seemed

serious enough to warrant a report to the state bar disciplinary authority. He left Big Firm and started his own solo practice, but struggled to attract clients, despite heavy investments in advertising. As a last resort, he tried using an online coupon app, called PleaseTryThis, to market his law practice. The attorney would offer the same "Deal of the Day" every weekday, stating that he would do the first ten hours of legal work at half his usual hourly rate. The ad also noted that many routine legal matters take ten hours or less. The response to his PleaseTryThis ad far exceeded the attorney's expectations. His waiting room was full every day, throughout the morning and afternoon, with new clients, eagerly awaiting their initial consultation for half-price legal representation. The attorney was agreeing to represent ten or more new clients every day, week after week. Are the attorney's actions here proper, according to the ABA Model Rules?

a) Yes, if the lawyer indeed gives the discount to each client bearing the PleaseTryThis coupon, because the Model Rules allow lawyers to advertise their services, assuming the communications are truthful.

b) Yes, but only if the lawyer gives the same deal to every new client who comes in during the PleaseTryThis advertising campaign, so that no clients pay a higher rate merely because they did not see the PleaseTryThis ad.

c) No, the attorney has an ethical duty to limit the number of deals offered, to devote adequate time and attention to each matter.

d) No, the advertising rules do not allow lawyers to advertise lower fees than usual as a special promotion.

> Rule 1.3; ABA Formal Ethics Op. 465 (2013)

241. An attorney agreed to represent a client before the Tax Court, to challenge the amount the Internal Revenue Service said he owed in unpaid taxes. The attorney filed an appearance in the matter and the initial pleadings and forms. Nevertheless, when the client did not pay even the first installment of fees, and did not return the attorney's phone call, the attorney assumed the client did not want his representation. The attorney moved on to other cases and forgot about it. He "failed to appear for a discovery conference, failed to give opposing counsel key documents, failed to show up for trial, and went missing again when the hearing was rescheduled." When the Tax Court asked the attorney to show cause why he should not face discipline, he explained that

he no longer represented the client, and had never received any legal fees from the individual. Is it proper for the Tax Court to reprimand him?

a) Yes, because he has violated the requirement of diligent representation under Rule 1.3, and courts have inherent authority to discipline attorneys who appear before the court in a matter.

b) Yes, because his reason for abandoning the cases was purely profit-motivated, rather than out of a genuine concern for the integrity of the legal process.

c) No, because the Tax Court is not an Article III court, and therefore lacks the inherent authority to discipline attorneys.

d) No, because if the client has never even paid a first installment of fees, and did not return the lawyer's phone call, the client-lawyer relationship has not been fully consummated.

> Aka v. United States Tax Court, 854 F.3d 30, 33 (2017)

LEGAL MALPRACTICE

242. An attorney undertook the representation of represent a new client, but the attorney's firm forgot to screen for conflicts of interest. The attorney normally relied on her firm to screen for conflicts with clients of the other attorneys, and assumed this had occurred, so she drafted and filed a complaint at the client's behest, and then began planning to file a motion for a preliminary injunction. Before filing for the preliminary injunction, however, the attorney discovered that one of her partners at the firm previously represented the opposing party in a closely related matter, which would have been obvious beforehand if the firm had conducted a routine conflict check. The respective clients would not consent to the conflict, so the attorney had to withdraw from representing the new client. Her withdrawal forced the client to search for another lawyer and start over, which delayed the issuance of a preliminary injunction by several weeks, and the client suffered financial losses as a result. Would the attorney be liable to the new client for a breach of fiduciary duty?
a)   Yes, law firms have strict liability for their fiduciary duties, so the reasonableness of the attorney is irrelevant.
b)   Yes, the attorney is subject to liability to the client for negligent breach of fiduciary duty.
c)   No, she is not liable for a breach of fiduciary duty, but the firm could be subject to disqualification from the other client's matter.
d)   No, a lawyer has no fiduciary duty if she withdraws from the representation.

Restatement § 49

243. An attorney undertook the representation of represent a new client, and the attorney's firm searched for potential conflicts of interest. Unfortunately, despite conducting an otherwise adequate conflict search, the opposing party in the new matter had changed its name in the two years since the prior representation (by the same firm), and the attorney's firm was unaware of the name change. The attorney normally relied on her firm to screen for conflicts with clients of the other attorneys, but in this instance a competent search had not revealed the conflict. The attorney then drafted and filed a complaint at the client's behest, and then began planning to file a motion for a preliminary injunction. Before filing for the preliminary injunction, however, the attorney discovered that one of her partners at the firm previously represented the opposing party, under another name, in a closely related matter. The

respective clients would not consent to the conflict, so the attorney had to withdraw from representing the new client. Her withdrawal forced the client to search for another lawyer and start over, which delayed the issuance of a preliminary injunction by several weeks, and the client suffered financial losses as a result. Would the attorney be liable to the new client for a breach of fiduciary duty?
a)   Yes, law firms have strict liability for their fiduciary duties, so the reasonableness of the attorney is irrelevant.
b)   Yes, the attorney is subject to liability to the client for negligent breach of fiduciary duty.
c)   No, she is not liable for a breach of fiduciary duty, but the firm could be subject to disqualification from the other client's matter.
d)   No, a lawyer has no fiduciary duty if she withdraws from the representation.

Restatement § 49

244. An attorney undertook the representation of a client, but the representation was in the client's capacity as trustee of an express trust for the benefit of a beneficiary. The client informed the attorney that he wanted to transfer funds into the client's own account, which would legally constitute embezzlement. The attorney explained to the client that the transfer would be illegal and subject to criminal charges. Disregarding the attorney's counsel, the client made the transfer, and informed the attorney what he had done. The attorney took no measures to mitigate or prevent the financial losses sustained by the beneficiary, for example, he did not inform the beneficiary or the supervising court, which would have been permissible under the exceptions to the confidentiality rules. The attorney believes he should not be subject to liability to the beneficiary, whom he does not represent. Is the attorney correct?
a)   Yes, the attorney had no attorney-client relationship with the beneficiary, and therefore owes no legal duties to that party that could be the basis of liability.
b)   Yes, the attorney told the client not to make the transfer, and the client disregarded the attorney's instructions.
c)   No, the attorney could have prevented the breach of fiduciary duty without violating the ethical duty to protect client confidentiality.
d)   No, attorneys have strict liability when a client uses the lawyer's services in furtherance of crime or fraud.

RESTATEMENT § 51

245. An attorney undertook the representation of a client, but the representation was in the client's capacity as trustee of an express trust for the benefit of a beneficiary. The client informed the attorney that he wanted to transfer funds into a certain account, which the client says is the trust account, even though it is the client's personal account. The client's intended action would constitute embezzlement. Due diligence by the attorney would have revealed that the client was lying about the accounts, but the attorney forgot to check, gave the client no guidance, and the client proceeded with the illegal transfer. The beneficiary sustained financial losses because of the illegal transfer, and eventually sued the attorney for a breach of fiduciary duty. The attorney believes he should not be subject to liability to the beneficiary, whom he does not represent. Is the attorney correct?

a) Yes, for the attorney did not owe the beneficiary a duty to use care because attorney was unaware that appropriate action was necessary to prevent a breach of fiduciary duty by the client, even though further investigation would have revealed this.

b) Yes, the attorney cannot be liable to third party beneficiaries unless the attorney directed the client to take the actions that injured the beneficiary.

c) No, the attorney could have prevented the breach of fiduciary duty by conducting a diligent check to ensure that the accounts were proper for the receipt of the transferred funds.

d) No, attorneys have strict liability when a client uses the lawyer's services in furtherance of crime or fraud.

RESTATEMENT § 51

246. An attorney undertook the representation of a client, but the representation was in the client's capacity as trustee of an express trust for the benefit of a beneficiary. The client informed the attorney that he wanted to invest trust funds in a way that would be unlawful, but it would not constitute a crime or fraud under applicable law. The client did not use the attorney's services in finalizing the investment. At the same time, the attorney said nothing to discourage the client from making the unlawful (though not criminal) investment. The beneficiary sustained financial losses due to the bad investment by the client, and eventually sued the attorney for a breach of fiduciary duty. The attorney believes he should not be subject to liability to the beneficiary, whom he does not represent. Is the attorney correct?

a) Yes, a lawyer never owes a duty of care to a nonclient such as the beneficiary.

b) Yes, a lawyer owes a duty to the nonclient beneficiary to intervene only where the breach is a crime or fraud or the lawyer has assisted or is assisting the breach.

c) No, the attorney had a fiduciary duty to protect the fiscal interests of the third-party beneficiary.

d) No, a lawyer owes a duty to use care to a nonclient when and to the extent that the lawyer's client is a trustee, guardian, executor, or fiduciary acting primarily to perform similar functions for the nonclient

RESTATEMENT § 51

247. At a real estate closing, the seller's attorney offered to record the deed for the buyer. Could the lawyer be subject to liability to the buyer for negligence in doing so, even if the buyer did not thereby become a client of the lawyer?

a) No, lawyers cannot be subject to liability for negligence to nonclients.

b) No, lawyers cannot be subject to liability for negligence to nonclients in transactional scenarios, even if they could be liable to nonclients in litigation matters.

c) Yes, but only if the seller had independent representation by counsel at the hearing.

d) Yes, lawyers who invite reasonable reliance from another party in a transactional setting can be subject to liability to nonclients who rely on the lawyer's promises.

RESTATEMENT § 51

248. An attorney provided representation to a plaintiff in a personal injury lawsuit against Conglomerate Corporation. During the discovery phase of the litigation, the attorney felt overwhelmed with other client cases and distracted by family issues at home, and she did not conduct a thorough factual investigation. Her misunderstanding of the facts led the attorney to include a groundless claim in the complaint, which was otherwise valid and had appropriate factual support. The defendant successfully persuaded the court to dismiss that specific claim, but the defendant incurred costly legal expenses in doing so. Assume there is no "loser pays" rule for this type of litigation in this state. Could the plaintiff's attorney be liable in a subsequent negligence action to the defendant for the groundless claim?

a) Yes, lawyers whose negligence in their legal work imposes unnecessary costs on the opposing party are liable for legal malpractice to the party that suffered the injury.

b) Yes, lawyers who undertake the representation of a litigant have strict liability for failures to conduct an exhaustive factual investigation during litigation.

c) No, lawyers must balance their duties to the current client with their duties to other clients and their own personal needs.

d) No, as a rule, lawyers have no duty of care to the opposing party in litigation that could furnish the basis for liability to that party.

RESTATEMENT § 51

249. A certain client retained an experienced attorney for the drafting and execution of a will. The client wanted the will to leave the client's entire estate to her favorite professor from her law school, the one who had taught her Professional Responsibility course in her 3L year. The attorney prepared the will naming the professor as the sole beneficiary, but negligently arranged for the client to sign it without the correct number of witnesses present at the signing. After the client died, a probate court held the will to be ineffective due to the lack of witnesses, and the nonclient beneficiary thereby suffered monetary loss. The client's intent to benefit her favorite law professor appeared on the face of the will executed by the client. Assuming the majority rule, is the attorney subject to liability to the nonclient beneficiary for negligence in drafting and supervising the execution of the will?

a) Yes, the attorney knew that the client intended, as one of the primary objectives of the representation, that the attorney's services benefit the nonclient beneficiary.

b) Yes, the attorney invited the nonclient to rely on the attorney's opinion or provision of other legal services, and the nonclient so relied.

c) No, because there was no breach of fiduciary duty involving a crime or fraud.

d) No, because there was no privity between the attorney and the intended beneficiary of the will.

RESTATEMENT § 51

250. A certain client retained an experienced attorney for the drafting and execution of a will. The client wanted the will to leave the client's entire estate to her favorite professor from her law school, the one who had taught her Professional Responsibility course in her 3L year. The attorney prepared the will by copying from previous will she had prepared for

other clients, and then she arranged for the client to sign the will before the proper number of witnesses. The client's intent to benefit the law professor thus did not appear on the face of the will, which instead listed the sole beneficiary merely as "the legal heir." The professor inherited nothing when the will went through probate, and then he accused the attorney of negligently writing the will to name someone other than professor as the legatee. Can the professor, as the intended beneficiary, recover from the attorney in a negligence-malpractice lawsuit?

a) Yes, the attorney had an automatic fiduciary duty to the beneficiary when the client expressed the desire to benefit the nonclient beneficiary.

b) Yes, but only by producing clear and convincing evidence that the client communicated her intent to the attorney that the professor should be the legatee.

c) No, because there was no breach of fiduciary duty involving a crime or fraud.

d) No, because there was no privity between the attorney and the intended beneficiary of the will.

RESTATEMENT § 51

251. A certain client retained an experienced attorney for the drafting and execution of a will. The client wanted the will to leave the client's entire estate to her favorite professor from her law school, the one who had taught her Professional Responsibility course in her 3L year. The attorney drafted the will accordingly, and she arranged for the client to sign the will before the proper number of witnesses. Nevertheless, after the client's death, a disinherited relative sued and had the will set aside, claiming client was incompetent at the time of the signing. The relative, who had then become the heir of the estate, sued the attorney for her legal expenses in challenging the will successfully. The heir argued that the attorney was negligent in assisting the client in the execution of the will, despite the client's mental incompetence. Is the attorney liable to the heir for negligence, if the heir has already obtained a court verdict that the testator-client was incompetent?

a) Yes, a lawyer drafting a will has an implied fiduciary duty to whomever the legitimate heirs may be.

b) Yes, if a court has already determined that the client was mentally incompetent, this establishes the attorney's negligence as a matter of law.

c) No, the attorney is not subject to liability for negligence to the heir who set aside the will.

d) No, lawyers cannot be liable to nonclient heirs.

RESTATEMENT § 51

252. A client asked her attorney to draft a will leaving a bequest in trust to a specific beneficiary, and to do so within one day, as the client was on her deathbed. The attorney wrote the will accordingly. After the client's death, however, the bequest was set aside. The invalidity of the will was due to a defect that most competent lawyers would not have been able to discover within one day. Later, the beneficiary sued the attorney for professional negligence. Can the beneficiary recover damages from the attorney for the invalidity of the will?

a) Yes, a lawyer owes a duty of care to beneficiaries of testamentary instruments that the lawyer drafts.

b) Yes, a lawyer owes a fiduciary duty to beneficiaries of testamentary instruments that the lawyer drafts.

c) No, the beneficiary was not a client of the attorney, and without privity, the attorney owed no duty of care to the beneficiary.

d) No, even though the attorney owed some duty of care to the beneficiary, the original client's time constraints are relevant to what constitutes ordinary competence, and the beneficiary cannot exact from the attorney greater care than the attorney owed the client.

RESTATEMENT § 52 Standard of Care

253. A client was selling some property to a buyer, and they reached an agreement that, as a condition for the sale, the client would supply an opinion letter by her attorney regarding liens on the property. The attorney knows about the agreement. Nevertheless, the client privately instructs the attorney to rely on the client's own information or assertions in preparing the opinion letter, and not to spend time searching the public lien records, as customary practice would require. The attorney relied on the client's information, so the opinion letter did not mention a recorded lien that the buyer would later discover, after the purchase was complete. Could the attorney be liable to the buyer for lack of diligence in a subsequent malpractice action?

a) Yes, it was reasonable for the buyer to rely upon the opinion letter, as the client invited this reliance, so the attorney had a duty to follow customary practice in rendering the opinion.

b) Yes, a lawyer preparing opinion letters has fiduciary duties to anyone who reads and relies upon the lawyer's written declarations.

c) No, there was no attorney-client relationship between the buyer and the attorney, and the attorney owed a duty of diligence to follow the seller's (the client's) instructions.

d) No, the buyer should have asked whether the attorney had followed customary practice and searched for liens on the property.

RESTATEMENT § 52 Standard of Care

254. A client hired an attorney to represent her as the plaintiff in a contract action. The client sought to recover $100,000 under the contract. The attorney agreed to provide representation on an hourly basis, at a rate of two hundred dollars per hour. The attorney spent ten hours working on the matter, and then withdrew from the representation to go on vacation, on the eve of trial. The client did not have time to find another lawyer, and tried to proceed pro se, resulting in a dismissal of her case with prejudice. The plaintiff then sued the attorney for malpractice and showed that she would have prevailed in her contract claim, but for the attorney's withdrawal. The court in her malpractice action awarded her the full $100,000 in damages that she would have won in the contract case. The attorney then argues that if the client is receiving the full amount she sought to recover originally, then the attorney should receive the two thousand dollars in attorney's fees for the hours she worked, if not the full amount the client anticipated paying the attorney from the beginning. How much should the attorney deduct from the damages owed to the client, toward the attorney's fees for the representation?

a) The attorney should keep two thousand, for the hours she in fact worked on the matter and should pay the client $98,000 in damages.

b) The attorney should keep however much the client originally anticipated paying in attorney's fees, when the representation began, and should pay the remainder to the client in damages.

c) The attorney should have forfeited her right to fees by committing malpractice and must pay the full award amount to the client.

d) The attorney does not have to pay the client anything in the malpractice action if the client has not yet paid the attorney any legal fees.

RESTATEMENT § 52 Standard of Care

255. The state bar association operated peer-support program. As a participant in the program, Attorney Stevenson consulted with another lawyer in confidence about a thorny issue that Attorney Stevenson was having with his representation of a client. The other lawyer gave Attorney Stevenson some bad advice, which Attorney Stevenson followed. The result was that the client fired Attorney Stevenson, which was a major setback for

his law firm. Attorney Stevenson wants to sue the other lawyer for giving him bad advice, and he can make a plausible claim that it was reasonable for him to follow the advice, given the other lawyer's expertise and Attorney Stevenson's inexperience. Does Attorney Stevenson have a potentially valid claim against the other lawyer for malpractice?

a) Yes, the other lawyer gave harmful advice, and it was reasonable for Attorney Stevenson to follow the advice.

b) Yes, consultations between attorneys create strict liability for malpractice claims, because a higher standard of care applies in such situations.

c) No, Attorney Stevenson is a lawyer and can think for himself and take responsibility for his own decisions.

d) No, there was no client-lawyer relationship between Attorney Stevenson and the other lawyer, at least under the facts delineated here.

256. A potential client called an attorney's office and told the receptionist that he wanted to hire the attorney to represent him at his drivers-license revocation hearing, which was set for two weeks from that date. The attorney regularly represented clients at license revocation hearings and appeals. The receptionist instructed the potential client to send or drop off all the papers concerning the proceeding but did not tell the caller whether the attorney would take the case. The individual dropped off the papers the next day. The attorney did not communicate with potential client until the day before the hearing, at which point the attorney declined to take the case. When the individual subsequently sues the attorney for malpractice, could a court find that a client-lawyer relationship existed in this situation?

a) Yes, if someone at the firm has a live telephone conversation with a potential client, a client-lawyer relationship has commenced until the lawyer expressly declines the representation or withdraws.

b) Yes, the individual relied on the attorney by not seeking other counsel when that was still practicable, and this reliance was reasonable because the attorney practiced in this area, the receptionists solicited the individual's papers needed for the proceeding, and the hearing was imminent.

c) No, if the attorney had never talked to the individual before the conversation in which he declined the case, then it was not reasonable for the individual to think that a client-lawyer relationship existed.

d) No, because malpractice actions must have a basis in a more substantial harm to the injured party than merely having to go to a license revocation hearing without a lawyer.

257. A potential plaintiff sent an email to an attorney that described a medical-malpractice suit that sender wanted to bring. The email asked the attorney to represent the victim in the matter. The attorney read but never responded to the email. Fourteen months later, the applicable statute of limitations on the claim expired. The plaintiff then sued the attorney for legal malpractice for not having filed the suit on time. Is the attorney liable for malpractice for missing the statute of limitations?

a) The attorney could not be liable under these facts because no client-lawyer relationship existed.

b) The attorney could not be liable under these facts because malpractice actions are due to conflicts of interest, not missing the statute of limitations.

c) The attorney could be liable because it was reasonable for the potential client to assume that the attorney would protect her interests, unless the attorney stated otherwise.

d) The attorney could be liable because he read the email and should have known the statute of limitations might expire in the next year or so, but the attorney failed to respond.

258. A state disciplinary authority issued a public reprimand of an attorney for a clear violation of the state's rules about solicitation of clients, and the tribunal ordered the attorney to pay a modest sum for costs and penalties. One of the attorney's improperly solicited clients, whose matter the attorney had handled competently, resulted in an unfavorable outcome for the client. The client brought a malpractice action against the attorney, based on the state bar's finding of an improper solicitation in her case, and she sought to recover damages. Is the client likely to prevail in this malpractice claim?

a) Yes, the state disciplinary authority has already determined that the attorney violated the ethical rules, so the attorney's representation was malpractice per se.

b) Yes, the client received an unfavorable outcome after hiring the attorney in response to an improper solicitation.

c) No, it would constitute double jeopardy to punish the attorney a second time in the malpractice action for the same conduct that the state bar already sanctioned.

d) No, the attorney's violation of the solicitation rule does not prove that the attorney negligently mishandled the representation of the client.

Allen v. Allison, 155 S.W.3d 682 (Ark. 2004)

259. A client called the same attorney that had previously represented her, asking the attorney to handle a pending antitrust investigation. She requested that the attorney come to the client's corporate headquarters to explore litigation strategies. The attorney visited the headquarters and spent four hours meeting with the client and her management team to discuss strategy, but never gave a definitive answer about whether he would represent the client in the matter. Is it reasonable for the client to assume that an attorney-client relationship exists?

a) If the attorney never explicitly agreed to represent the client in the matter, no attorney-client relationship exists.

b) The potential client merely asked the attorney to discuss strategy, so no attorney-client relationship exists.

c) The attorney communicated a willingness to represent the client by her actions.

d) If the attorney has represented the client on more than one matter in the past and had a discussion with the client about a new matter, then an attorney-client relationship already exists.

RESTATEMENT § 14

260. An attorney agreed to represent a client, but the attorney's firm did not search for potential conflicts of interest. The attorney filed the lawsuit in court. During the pleading and motion stage, the attorney discovered that one of her law firm partners formerly represented the opposing party in a closely related matter. As a result of this conflict of interest, the attorney had to withdraw from representing the client. A competent conflicts search would have revealed the conflict. Due to the attorney's withdrawal, the client had a significant delay in obtaining a preliminary injunction against the other party, resulting in financial losses for the client. Which of the following is true, given these facts?

a) The attorney could not face malpractice liability because the client cannot show damages over a delayed preliminary injunction, as opposed to the eventual outcome on the merits.

b) The attorney properly withdrew when the conflict of interest arose, so there should be no malpractice liability to the client.

c) The attorney is liable to the client for a negligent breach of fiduciary duty.

d) Second-hand conflicts of interest, such as one described here with the attorney's partner, are too attenuated to furnish the basis for a liability claim.

Restatement § 49 Breach of Fiduciary Duty

PART
II

[**NOTE:** In the author's law school courses on Professional Responsibility, PART II is material covered in the second half of the semester. If the class has a midterm exam, the material after this point is <u>not</u> on the midterm.]

CLIENT CONFIDENTIALITY & PRIVILEGE

RULE 1.6 - CONFIDENTIALITY

261. An attorney represents a client who went through a divorce several years ago in another state, and the divorce resulted in a court order for child support and spousal maintenance. The client then moved to the attorney's state, started a new career in politics, and formed new relationships. She has kept her previous marriage a divorce a secret, except from her closest friend and her attorney, because she is afraid it will affect her new career and public image. Recently, she hired her attorney to handle various legal matters for her, which included issuing a press release about her withdrawal from a political campaign. When news media outlets posted online about the client's withdrawal from the race, the attorney responded to some of the comments that readers posted, to clear up some misunderstandings. In one of the attorney's responses, he mentioned the client's previous marriage and divorce. Did the attorney violate the duty of confidentiality?

a) It depends on whether there was a sealed record in the client's divorce case.

b) No, because the divorce and court order regarding child support are a matter of public record.

c) No, because the client authorized the attorney to issue the press release, which impliedly authorized the disclosure of other helpful information.

d) Yes, because even disclosures of information contained in the public record must have client authorization.

ABA Formal Op. 18-480

262. An attorney is representing a corporate client on a variety of litigation matters. The attorney receives a subpoena (compulsory process) for information and a document relating to one of her corporate clients. The attorney promptly produces the information and document required by the subpoena, and then informs the client. Could the attorney be subject to discipline for this action?

a) Yes, because she did not consult first with the client before making the disclosure.

b) Yes, because it was incompetent for her to believe that a subpoena could have legal force binding a corporate entity, as opposed to individuals.

c) No, because the client is a corporation, not an individual.

d) No, because she was acting under a subpoena.

ABA Formal Op. 16-473

263. An attorney is a partner in a seven-lawyer firm. The client retained the attorney to handle his workers' compensation matter. Yet the attorney did not discuss with the client that he would normally disclose to the other partners in the firm some of the details about his cases and clients. At the weekly meeting of the partners, as everyone discussed their pending cases, the attorney explained the client's case and solicited input from the partners. One partner had an ingenious suggestion that would have been quite helpful to the client's case. The attorney mentioned to the client in their next phone call that one of his partners had made a brilliant suggestion that could turn the case in the client's favor. The client was upset that the attorney had discussed the case with anyone else. Is the client correct that the attorney should not have discussed the case with the others at the firm?

a) Yes, because a lawyer has a duty to preserve the confidentiality of client information, even from other lawyers in his law firm, unless the client expressly authorizes disclosure.

b) Yes, because the disclosure automatically created potential conflicts of interest for the other lawyers in the firm who might represent clients with adverse interests to this client.

c) No, because lawyers in a firm may disclose to each other information relating to a client of the firm, unless the client has instructed that certain information be available only to specified lawyers.

d) No, because in this case the disclosure yielded a brilliant suggestion from another lawyer that was immensely helpful to the case, which offsets any potential injury to the client from the disclosure.

Rule 1.6 Cmt. 5

264. Client, a large auto dealer, retains an attorney to represent him in a bankruptcy case. This attorney's firm represents a bank, through which the client has several large loans that covered loans for the dealership. The loans are all contained in the bankruptcy. The attorney is concerned about whether there is a conflict, so he contacts a lawyer friend of his. While explaining his dilemma, the attorney tells Friend the name of the dealer. Is the attorney subject to discipline?

a) Yes, because the attorney disclosed more than what details were necessary to accomplish his purpose.
b) Yes, because attorneys shall not discuss client matters with other lawyers not also serving as counsel for their client.
c) No, because attorneys may discuss their cases with other lawyers to ensure they are following the rules of professional conduct.
d) No, because the restrictions regarding confidentiality only apply in criminal cases.

265. A client hired an attorney to represent her in a burglary charge. During a meeting with the attorney and with the understanding that any information would be confidential, the client advised the attorney about a murder she committed. A wrongfully accused man was presently on trial for that same murder. Eventually, the attorney was able to negotiate a plea deal for the client on her burglary charge. They finalized the plea deal and the attorney's representation ended. Soon thereafter, the attorney discovered that a jury had convicted an innocent man for the murder the client had committed and confessed to the attorney. The wrongfully convicted men received a life sentence, without the possibility of parole. The attorney contacted the District Attorney's office that handled the murder trial and left an anonymous tip stating that the client confessed to committing the murder. Was the attorney's conduct proper?

a) Yes, because attorneys have a duty to reveal information, even if confidential, that relates to a crime or fraud committed by his client.
b) Yes, because attorneys no longer have a duty not to disclose information relating to the representation of a client once the attorney's representation of that client terminates.
c) No, because an attorney must not leave such tips anonymously, but must make themselves available for questioning and for testifying if making any tip regarding a crime or fraud committed by one of his clients.
d) No, because attorneys cannot disclose client representation information and the death had

already occurred, therefore, the disclosure would not prevent certain death or substantial bodily injury.

266. An attorney has been practicing for many years, and he is now representing a client who is a notorious celebrity-turned-criminal in a criminal case involving drug charges. The attorney is confused about whether he may publicly disclose information that he learned in confidence from his client if the information is already a matter of public record, and his research indicates there is a split of authority on this question. Seeking clarification, the attorney calls another lawyer who specializes in lawyer malpractice and lawyer disciplinary matters to seek advice about what course of action would comply with the Rules of Professional Conduct. The other lawyer, an expert in legal ethics, agrees to provide an opinion and to keep the conversation a secret. The attorney tries to use a hypothetical to explain the problem, but given the client's national reputation and celebrity status, the other lawyer knows immediately who the client is, and can easily surmise the nature of the confidential information. In addition, the attorney mentions that his client is secretly a bisexual and has been having an affair with both the male and female hosts of a nationally televised morning talk show, though neither of them is aware that the other is having an affair with the same person. Is the attorney subject to discipline for disclosing confidential information about his client?

a) Yes, because the attorney used a hypothetical that was obvious enough that the other lawyer immediately knew the identity of the client and the client's information that the attorney was supposed to protect.
b) Yes, because the lawyer revealed more client information than was necessary to secure legal advice about the lawyer's compliance with the Rules
c) No, because a lawyer may reveal information relating to the representation of a client to secure legal advice about the lawyer's compliance with the Rules, even when the lawyer lacks implied authorization to make the disclosure.
d) No, because a lawyer may disclose confidential information to another lawyer, assuming the other lawyer promises to keep the conversation secret, and the other lawyer has a reputation for complying with the ethical rules.

Rule 1.6(b)(4) & Cmt 9

267. While representing a client, an attorney learned confidential information about the client's previous marriage and divorce, which occurred many years before in another country. Before the attorney could conclude the matter, the client terminated the representation. Over the next three years, the now-former client became a well-known celebrity, and her prior marriage and divorce received widespread public attention in that region. Very recently, the state bar journal interviewed the attorney about his career and his greatest achievements. One question pertained to the representation of the client who became a celebrity. The attorney mentioned that at the time, the client was an unknown figure and her previous marriage were family secrets. The interviewer was not well-informed about this celebrity and was surprised to hear that the individual had been married and divorced in another country. The former client had never authorized the attorney to discuss her legal matters, but the Model Rules provide a "generally known" exception to the duty of confidentiality to former clients. Would that exception apply to the attorney's disclosure of the marriage and divorce during the interview?

a) Yes, because the information received widespread public attention in that area.

b) Yes, because the representation ended when the client fired the attorney, and the duty of confidentiality no longer applied.

c) No, because the "generally known" exception applies only after the client's death.

d) No, because the "generally known" exception does not apply to disclosures by the attorney about former clients.

ABA Formal Op. 479

268. Small Firm is considering hiring an attorney, who currently works for Big Firm, in a lateral move. The attorney is a transactional lawyer, so none of the information he possesses is "privileged" in that it was not in anticipation of litigation. To facilitate the checks for conflicts of interest, the attorney discloses to Small Firm the clients he has represented while at Big Firm. This includes the names of persons and issues involved in the matters, as well as names and issues for matters handled by other lawyers in the firm about which the attorney had overheard or otherwise acquired some confidential information. Small Firm uses the information solely for checking about potential conflicts of interest before making an offer of employment to the attorney. The attorney did not ask any of the clients for authorization to

disclose the representation or the nature of the issues involved in their matters. Was it proper for the attorney to disclose this confidential information without the consent of the clients?

a) Yes, so long as the attorney informs the clients subsequently that such disclosures have occurred.

b) Yes, because the attorney disclosed the information solely to detect and resolve conflicts of interest arising from the lawyer's change of employment.

c) No, because the attorney did not obtain consent or authorization from the clients before disclosing this information.

d) No, because the attorney disclosed not only the clients that he himself represented, but also clients of other lawyers in his firm.

Rule 1.6(b)(7); ABA Formal Op. 09-455

269. An attorney works for a state-operated legal aid clinic, which under a state statute counts as a social service agency. The state has a mandatory reporting law for child abuse, which statutorily requires employees of social service agencies to report any instances of child abuse they discover among their clients or constituents. The attorney met with a prospective client and her child to discuss potential representation at a welfare termination hearing. The prospective client did not meet the agency's guidelines to be eligible for free legal representation, however, so the attorney had to decline the case. Nevertheless, it was evident during the interview that the prospective client's child was the subject of serious physical abuse – a black eye, cigarette burns on her arms and neck, bruises on the backs of her legs, and a demeanor of cowering in fear around adults. The attorney wanted to talk to the mother about it, but the attorney has been unable to reach her since declining to represent her. Must the attorney report the prospective client for child abuse?

a) Yes, because state law requires the disclosure, and a lawyer may reveal information relating to the representation of a client to the extent the lawyer has a reasonable belief that it is necessary to comply with other law.

b) Yes, because the mother was only a prospective client who was ineligible for representation by the attorney, so the attorney owed her no duty of confidentiality.

c) No, because the exceptions to the duty of confidentiality merely permit disclosure, so the attorney "may" report the incident, but there is no duty to do so.

d) No, because the attorney met the prospective client only once, and does not know if the abuse occurred at the hands of her mother, or if the child was the victim of a crime at the hands of someone else, and it is not the mother's fault.

Rule 1.6(b)(6)

270. An employee of Conglomerate Corporation retained an attorney to advise her about a potential claim against her employer. Like most corporate employees, this client has a cubicle workstation with a computer assigned for her exclusive use at work. Conglomerate Corporation's written internal policy states that the company has a right of access to all employees' computers and e-mail files, including those relating to employees' personal matters. Nevertheless, all the employees sometimes use of their computers for personal matters, and most send some personal e-mail messages, whether from their personal or office e-mail accounts. The attorney expects that the employee will sometimes use her computer at work to communicate with the lawyer. Does the attorney have an affirmative ethical duty to warn the employee about the risks this practice entails?

a) The attorney does not need to warn the client because any correspondence between the client and the attorney would have already the protection of attorney-client privilege, even if the employer reads the emails.

b) The attorney does not need to warn the client because the pre-existence of the written, internal policy means there is no reasonable expectation of privacy in the emails, and therefore the information would not be confidential.

c) The attorney has an ethical duty to warn the client, and a duty to warn the employer that the client's communications with her attorney are privileged and exempt from the company's internal policy.

d) The attorney has an ethical obligation to warn the client not to communicate about the matter via her work computer through any email account, and a duty to refrain from emailing the client's workplace email account or responding to emails from the client's workplace email account.

ABA Formal Op. 11-459

271. An insurance company retained an attorney to defend both the insured employer and one of its employees, whose conduct is at issue and for which the employer might be vicariously liable. During a private consultation with the attorney, the employee recounts some facts about the incident that are self-incriminating. In fact, the confidential information that the employee shared with the attorney suggests that the employee was acting outside the scope of his employment at the time, and his actions were also outside the scope of the employer's insurance coverage. The employee had a reasonable belief that he had client-lawyer relationship with the attorney, and the employee did not understand the legal implications of his admissions. In subsequent interviews with other witnesses, the attorney corroborated this information. It appeared to the attorney that the insurance company could have a contractual right to deny coverage for the employee's conduct, and the employer could invoke scope-of-employment principles to defend against its own liability to the plaintiff. What would the ethical rules require the attorney to do under these circumstances?

a) The attorney must disclose the information to the other clients in the representation, that is, the insurer and the employer, because the facts directly impact their legal rights and liabilities.

b) The attorney cannot disclose the information to anyone, and must withdraw from representing the employer, the employee, and the insurer.

c) The attorney must make a "noisy withdrawal" from representing the employee and the employer, disaffirming any previous statements, information, or opinions rendered in the matter.

d) The attorney should reveal only enough information to obtain informed, written consent from the insurer and the employer to continue representing all three in the matter.

ABA Formal Op. 08-450

272. A wealthy client invited his attorney to visit the client's lavish home, so that they could update the client's will and other estate planning instruments. They updated these documents every year. On this occasion, a few others were present during their conversation about the client's estate planning issues: the client's longtime business partner, the client's new girlfriend, a housekeeper, one of the client's grown children, and the client's personal physician, who had stopped by for a social visit. Two individuals would be necessary to witness the execution of an updated will, so the attorney was glad to have others present. During the conversation, as an aside, the business partner mentioned some upcoming litigation that was in the news, a lawsuit

between a major insurance carrier and a pharmaceutical company related to the current epidemic in opioid abuse. No one present was a party to the anticipated litigation, but many investors were following it with great interest. Afterward, the attorney wrote personal notes about the meeting, including who was present and what each person had said. A year later, the client died, and litigation ensued over the client's estate. Which of the following would apply to the attorney's notes and mental recollections about the conversation with the client and others that were present?

a) The attorney's ethical duty of confidentiality to the client.
b) The attorney work product doctrine.
c) Attorney-client privilege.
d) A duty of loyalty to the others present.

273. An attorney was the managing partner at a firm. The firm had current, up-to-date network security, firewalls, password protection, anti-virus software, and email encryption. As managing partner, the attorney would revisit this issue every year in January, checking with the relevant vendors to see if there were important software updates or new products that the firm needed. One January, a vendor was installing new software and discovered that the firm had suffered a significant data breach the previous summer that went unnoticed. Hackers had used sophisticated methods to bypass conventional firewalls and other mainstream security features, and they had accessed confidential client information. The vendor explained to the managing partner that there was no reason for such events to go unnoticed, because low-cost products and services were available to monitor for data breaches. Could the firm, or at least the managing partner, be subject to discipline for failing to monitor for any breaches in data security?

a) The firm is not subject to discipline, but the clients may demand contractually that the firm constantly monitor for a data breach, and the firm could be liable for malpractice.
b) No, the Model Rules require lawyers to have adequate protections against a data security breach, not necessarily to monitor constantly for attacks and breaches.
c) Yes, lawyers must employ reasonable efforts to monitor the technology and office resources connected to the internet, external data sources,

and external vendors providing services relating to data and the use of data.
d) Yes, competence in preserving a client's confidentiality is a strict liability standard and requires the lawyer to be invulnerable or impenetrable

Rule 1.6; ABA Formal Op. 18-483

274. An attorney was a partner at Big Firm, which represented Conglomerate Corporation in their corporate merger negotiations with Giant Company. Big Firm had state-of-the-art network firewalls, virus protection, password protection, and other data security features in place. Nevertheless, one Friday evening some hackers managed to breach Big Firm's networks and access client information and partner emails, for purposes of engaging in insider trading. The firm detected the breach within a few hours and notified state and federal law enforcement. The stock exchange had closed for the weekend, and law enforcement managed to apprehend the hackers over the weekend, before they had a chance to review the stolen information and share useful data or engage in illegal stock trades. The clients suffered no losses or adverse effects, but they could have. The partners at Big Firm maintain that they should not be subject to discipline for failure to protect their clients' confidential information, because they had all the latest data security measures in place, though technology is constantly changing. Are they correct?

a) Yes, unauthorized access to, or disclosure of, client information does not constitute a violation of the Model Rules if the lawyer has made reasonable efforts to prevent the access or disclosure.
b) Yes, even if their network security was inadequate, the clients did not in fact suffer any harm to their legal or commercial interests, and the firm responded to the incident promptly enough.
c) No, a firm's competence in preserving a client's confidentiality is a strict liability standard that requires the lawyer to be invulnerable or impenetrable.
d) No, it depends on whether the customers had the level of protection they expected when they hired the firm to represent them.

Rule 1.6(c) Cmt. 18; ABA Formal Op. 18-483

ATTORNEY-CLIENT PRIVILEGE

[NOTE: the best resource for students on attorney-client privilege is §§ 68-86 of the RESTATEMENT (THIRD) OF THE LAW GOVERNING LAWYERS, and many of the following questions reflect the RESTATEMENT'S examples and illustrations. In practice, states vary in how they apply privilege and its exceptions. The RESTATEMENT normally reflects the majority rule and is the safest point of reference for answering privilege questions that appear on the MPRE.]

275. Two clients, an entrepreneur and a venture capitalist, jointly consulted an attorney about establishing a business. The two clients had not yet agreed on the confidentiality of their separate communications with the attorney. The entrepreneur later sent the attorney a confidential memorandum outlining his own proposed business arrangement. The venture capitalist knew that the entrepreneur had sent the memorandum but did not know its contents. Eventually, the joint representation ended. Two years later, the venture capitalist filed suit against the entrepreneur to recover damages arising out of the failed business venture. Each hired a new lawyer for the litigation. The venture capitalist then requested a copy of the memorandum during discovery, and the entrepreneur responded that this was a privileged communication. The entrepreneur asserted that the venture capitalist never knew the contents of the letter during the joint representation, so he had waived his right to this item. How should the court rule on this discovery issue?
a) In this litigation, the memorandum from the entrepreneur to his previous attorney is not privileged and is therefore discoverable.
b) In this litigation, the memorandum from the entrepreneur to his previous attorney is privileged and is therefore not discoverable.
c) The venture capitalist would need to show hardship and that the document is necessary to obtain it in discovery.
d) The memorandum is discoverable but not admissible at trial.

276. An attorney drafted a confidential email to a client offering legal advice on a tax matter. The client had sought the attorney's legal opinion on the question. The attorney's answer relied partly on information that the client had provided, partly on information the attorney himself obtained from third parties, and partly on the attorney's own legal research on Westlaw. When the IRS later brought an enforcement action against the client, the government lawyers sought discover of this email, hoping to find useful evidence about the defendant's financial activities and whether the defendant had knowingly violated the tax code. Can the government lawyers obtain the email through discovery?
a) The portions of the email relying on information from third parties is discoverable, but the parts relying on the client's information or the attorney's own research are privileged.
b) Both the attorney and the client would have to disclose the email or testify its contents.
c) Neither the attorney nor the client would have to disclose or testify about any of its contents.
d) The client does not have to disclose the email, but the attorney would have to produce it if he still has it.

277. A client kept in his files an old memorandum that the client had prepared for his attorney during an earlier representation by the attorney. After some time, the client takes the memorandum to another lawyer, in confidence, to obtain legal services on a different matter. The memorandum qualified as a privileged communication in the earlier matter. While in the hands of the new lawyer, does the memorandum remain under the protection of privilege?
a) Yes, privilege still applies to the document due to its originally privileged nature.
b) Yes, because once privilege attaches to a document, it remains privileged permanently.
c) No, the client waived privilege by showing it to another lawyer.
d) No, the privilege for the communication with the first attorney ended when the client switched to another lawyer.

278. A client confidentially delivered his own business records to his attorney, who specializes in tax matters, to obtain the attorney's legal advice about taxes. The business records were routine bookkeeping files, not prepared for obtaining legal advice. When the IRS eventually brought an enforcement action against the client and sought production of the business records that the client had provided to the attorney, the attorney asserted that attorney-client privileged protected them from

disclosure. Is the attorney correct?

a) Yes, the records gain privileged status by the fact that the client delivered them privately to the attorney to obtain legal advice.

b) No, the records gain no privileged status by the fact that the client delivered them to the attorney to obtain legal advice.

c) Privilege applies to the records only if the client was anticipating litigation at the time he gave them to the attorney, as opposed to seeking advice about claiming deductions and exemptions.

d) Privilege does not apply if the client committed a crime or tax fraud.

279. The police arrested Professor Stevenson and would not permit him to communicate directly with his attorney. Professor Stevenson asked his longtime friend and confidant, Sisyphus, to convey to his attorney that the attorney should not permit the police to search Professor Stevenson's home. Later, the prosecution calls the friend to testify about the contents of the message he related from Stevenson to his attorney. The attorney claims this information is privileged. How should the court rule?

a) The contents of the message transmitted through the friend are privileged and therefore both undiscoverable and inadmissible at trial, because the friend was acting as an agent of the client.

b) The contents of the message are not privileged because the client disclosed them to a third party to transmit the information to the attorney.

c) The attorney waived privilege for the information by receiving it from a third party without the client present.

d) The friend has a right to testify and disclose the information if he chooses, but neither the client nor the attorney should have to disclose it themselves.

280. A client who spoke only Spanish hired a local attorney who spoke English and no other languages. The client used an interpreter to communicate an otherwise privileged message to the attorney. The interpreter was an acquaintance of the client. The opposing party later tried to have the interpreter testify at trial about the contents of the conversation he interpreted. The attorney objected that the information falls under the protection of attorney-client privilege. Is the attorney correct?

a) Yes, but only if the interpreter signed a nondisclosure agreement and understood that the conversation was privileged.

b) Yes, because the interpreter acted as an agent of the client in facilitating the provision of legal services.

c) No, the interpreter was unnecessary, because a client could easily find another lawyer who speaks Spanish.

d) No, because the client and attorney had the conversation in the presence of a third party, thereby waiving privilege.

281. An attorney agreed to represent an underage client in a legal matter. The client was fifteen years old, and the youth's parents were present at the consultations and other meetings with the attorney. Would the presence of the parents during confidential communications between the attorney and the underage client waive the protection of attorney-client privilege for the conversation?

a) Yes, because the attorney is discussing confidential matters with a client in the presence of nonclients.

b) Yes, unless the parents have previously signed a nondisclosure agreement and understand that they must preserve the privilege on behalf of the client.

c) No, because the parents are there to facilitate the representation on behalf of their minor child.

d) No, if the parents are paying the attorney's legal fees, then they are co-clients with the minor child.

282. An accountant advised Professor Stevenson to consult a lawyer about a legal problem involving complex questions of tax accounting. Professor Stevenson is easily distractible, and he and does not fully understand the nature of the accounting questions, and he asks his accountant to accompany him to a consultation with his attorney so that the accountant can explain the nature of Professor Stevenson's legal matter to the attorney. The accountant helps to explain the attorney's legal advice in business or accounting terms more understandable to Professor Stevenson. Would attorney-client privilege still protect these consultations against subsequent discovery by government lawyers in a tax enforcement action against Professor Stevenson?

a) Yes, because the client and the attorney consented to having the accountant present.

b) Yes, because the accountant is acting as the client's agent in this scenario, just as if her were a foreign language interpreter.

c) No, the presence of the accountant means the conversation was not confidential and privilege did not attach to the conversation.

d) No, because the accountant suggested that the client consult the attorney in the first place, so the client was not the true initiator of the conversation.

283. An attorney agreed to represent a client who suffered from severe mental illness that had resulted in his institutionalization. The client complained that the staff mistreated her and wanted the attorney to litigate. At the end of this litigation, the court appointed a family member as the legal guardian for the client and her assets. Subsequently, a question arose concerning the client's ownership rights in certain intellectual property, and the attorney agreed to represent the interests of the client in the property. The client's legal guardian participates in the conversations between the attorney and the client, and he serves as an intermediary for confidential correspondence or messages between the client and the attorney. Would attorney-client privilege still apply to these communications, if the guardian is present or serves as an intermediary?
a) Yes, the legal guardian is necessary for rendering legal services to the client, and functions as the client's agent in this scenario.
b) Yes, privilege applies to the oral communications, but not to messages relayed by the guardian between the client and the attorney.
c) No, privilege does not apply to legal incompetent clients.
d) No, the presence of the third-party guardian waives privilege for these communications.

284. An attorney represented a defendant in a personal-injury action. The client made a confidential communication to the attorney concerning the circumstances of the accident. Later, in the judicial proceedings, the attorney was conducting direct examination of the client, and the client testified about the occurrence. She did not, however, make any reference in her testimony to what she told the attorney previously about the same matter. When the plaintiff's lawyer began his cross-examination of the client, he asked whether the defendant's testimony was consistent with the account she previously gave to her attorney in confidence. The defendant's attorney objects that privilege applies to this conversation, but the plaintiff's lawyer asserts that the defendant waived privilege by discussing the same things in her court testimony. Which one is correct?
a) It depends on whether the facts in question would constitute material questions of fact in the case.

b) It depends on whether the client claimed attorney-client privilege for all prior conversations with her attorney before she began testifying about the same events.
c) The defendant's attorney is correct that his client did not waive attorney-client privilege by testifying regarding the same facts at trial.
d) The plaintiff's lawyer is correct that the defendant opened the door by discussing the same events that she previously discussed with her attorney, thereby waiving privilege for the prior conversations.

285. An attorney represented a defendant in a personal-injury action. The client made a confidential communication to the attorney concerning the circumstances of the accident. Later, in the judicial proceedings, the attorney was conducting direct examination of the client, and the client testified about the occurrence. When the plaintiff's lawyer began his cross-examination of the client, he asked whether the defendant's testimony was consistent with the account she previously gave to her attorney in confidence. The defendant declared, "I have testified exactly as I told attorney two days after this awful accident occurred. I explained to my attorney then that the skid marks made by the plaintiff's car were 200 feet long, and I have said the same things here." The plaintiff's attorney then proceeds to ask questions about the discussions with her attorney, and the defendant's attorney objected that privilege applies to this conversation. The plaintiff's lawyer insisted that the defendant waived privilege by discussing the same things in her court testimony. Which one is correct?
a) It depends on whether the facts in question would constitute material questions of fact in the case.
b) It depends on whether the client claimed attorney-client privilege for all prior conversations with her attorney before she began testifying about the same events.
c) The defendant's attorney is correct that his client did not waive attorney-client privilege by referencing the previous privileged conversations at trial.
d) The plaintiff's lawyer is correct that the defendant opened the door referencing the previous privileged conversations at trial, thereby waiving privilege for the prior conversations.

286. Professor Stevenson was walking alone through a high-crime neighborhood late at night, carrying his briefcase, which contained copies of confidential and

111

privileged correspondence between the Professor Stevenson and his attorney. Robbers mugged Professor Stevenson and ran off with his briefcase, which they soon discarded when they discovered that it contained no cash or valuables. The police recovered the briefcase, but to identify its owner, they opened it and read the documents. Some of the documents were very incriminating, so the police turned them over to the district attorney. Professor Stevenson and his attorney claim attorney-client privilege protects the documents from admission as evidence in any criminal proceedings, but the prosecution claims privilege disappeared when the police had a good reason to inspect the contents of a lost briefcase. Which side is correct?

a) The prosecutor is correct that attorney-client privilege no longer protects the documents, now that they easily available exposed to the public.

b) The attorney is correct that privilege would still apply, and the documents are inadmissible.

c) It depends on whether the brief case remained locked when the police recovered it.

d) It depends on whether Professor Stevenson told the robbers that the documents in his brief case came under attorney-client privilege.

287. An attorney represented a client in a license-revocation hearing before an administrative law judge. At one point, the government lawyer asked the client a question about a confidential communication with the client's attorney, and the attorney objected that the conversation clearly came under attorney-client privilege. The administrative law judge overruled the attorney and ordered the client to answer the question, and the client testified about the prior communications with his attorney. On appeal, the attorney claims that the ALJ wrongly overruled his objection and that privilege should in fact apply. The tribunal questioned whether privileged could reattach to a communication after its disclosure, even if the disclosure was the result of an incorrect ruling by a lower tribunal. In subsequent unrelated litigation with another party, opposing counsel seeks to introduce the client's testimony at the administrative hearing that disclosed the information, and the attorney against objects that the original communications were privileged, that he objected to the disclosure at the time, and that the administrative law judge and wrongly overruled his objection. What is the result?

a) The appellate tribunal is correct that privilege cannot reattach even if the disclosure was in response to an incorrect ruling by another tribunal, and the disclosure-under-protest also waived privilege for subsequent litigation.

b) The appellate tribunal is correct that privilege cannot reattach even if the disclosure was in response to an incorrect ruling by another tribunal, but the wrongfully ordered disclosure did not waive privilege for subsequent litigation.

c) The appellate tribunal is incorrect that privilege cannot reattach if the disclosure was in response to an incorrect ruling by another tribunal, but the wrongfully compelled disclosure did indeed waive privilege for subsequent litigation.

d) The appellate tribunal is incorrect that privilege cannot reattach even if the disclosure was in response to an incorrect ruling by another tribunal, and the disclosure did not waive privilege for subsequent litigation.

288. An attorney represented a client who was a potential defendant in a personal injury lawsuit. The victim of the accident has threatened the client with litigation unless the client can convince the victim's lawyers that the client is not at fault. The victim also gives a deadline for producing such evidence, after which litigation will proceed. The client authorized the attorney produce a large batch of documents. The attorney reviewed the files before sending, but she overlooked one confidential memorandum by the client to the attorney that was in the batch of documents produced. This oversight occurred even though the attorney conducted a more thorough pre-production review than most lawyers would do – the attorney was not negligent, but the mistake still happened. As soon as the attorney discovered her mistake, she reasserted privilege on behalf of the client for that document. The victim's lawyer claims that the attorney waived privilege by disclosing it, even inadvertently. Which side is correct?

a) Opposing counsel is correct that the attorney waived privilege by disclosing the confidential document during discovery.

b) Privilege does not apply because the plaintiff has not yet filed a claim in court.

c) The attorney who made the inadvertent disclosure, without negligence, can properly reassert privilege.

d) Waiver cannot occur because the plaintiff has not yet filed a claim in court.

289. A soda company had a delivery truck that collided with a school bus full of children on a field trip. The soda company's distribution manager wrote a report of the accident and provided it to the company's litigation counsel. The manager did not share the report with anyone except the attorney.

When lawsuits from the injured children begin against the company, one of the plaintiffs requests the distribution manager's report. Will a court order the attorney or the company to produce the report during discovery?

a) Yes, due to the business records exception to attorney-client privilege.
b) Yes, the report constitutes an admission of a party opponent.
c) No, because the distribution manager is not one of the corporate directors.
d) No, it is privileged communication from a client to a lawyer.

290. A small independent soda company had a delivery truck that collided with a school bus full of children on a field trip. The company's owner and the driver, who were co-defendants in the first lawsuit over the incident, met with their litigation attorney – the owner agreed to pay the fees for representing them both. As they were discussing the accident, the attorney called in his own accident scene investigator to join the discussion, and the investigator took notes. As the litigation progressed, the driver eventually filed a cross-claim against the owner for indemnification if the driver has to pay damages to the plaintiff. At that point, the plaintiff sought to depose the attorney's accident investigator to discover what admissions the co-defendants made in the previous conversation. The owner objected. How is the court likely to rule?

a) The deposition can go forward, and the investigator's disclosures will be admissible, because his presence in the conversation as a non-client waived attorney-client privilege for the others.
b) The deposition can go forward, and the investigator's disclosures will be admissible, because the driver and the owner are now adverse parties in the litigation.
c) The conversation comes under the protection of attorney client privilege because at the time it occurred, the driver and owner were both clients and the investigator was there to assist the attorney.
d) The investigator's notes will be admissible, even if the participants in the conversation do not have to disclose what they said.

291. A small independent soda company had a delivery truck that collided with a school bus full of children on a field trip. The company's owner and the driver, who were co-defendants in the first lawsuit over the incident, met with their litigation attorney – the owner agreed to pay the fees for

representing both. As they were discussing the accident, the attorney called in his own accident scene investigator to join the discussion, and the investigator took notes. As the litigation progressed, the driver eventually filed a crossclaim against the owner for indemnification if the driver has to pay damages to the plaintiff. At that point, the driver sought to depose the attorney's accident investigator to have him testify about the admissions the owner made in the previous conversation. The owner objected. How is the court likely to rule?

a) The deposition can go forward, and the investigator's disclosures will be admissible, because his presence in the conversation as a non-client waived attorney-client privilege for the others.
b) The deposition can go forward, and the investigator's disclosures will be admissible, because the driver and the owner are now adverse parties in the litigation.
c) The conversation comes under the protection of attorney client privilege because at the time it occurred, the driver and owner were both clients and the investigator was there to assist the attorney.
d) The investigator's notes will be admissible, even if the participants in the conversation do not have to disclose what they said.

292. Conglomerate Corporation hired outside counsel to represent the organization in a lawsuit, but part way through the representation, Conglomerate's managers decided to fire the attorney and hire someone else with more experience. Conglomerate's former attorney then sued the organization for her unpaid legal fees for the representation up to that point. Conglomerate's new lawyer subpoenaed the attorney's time sheets for the billable hours he claimed to have worked for Conglomerate, because the organization believed the attorney was overbilling. The attorney claimed that the time sheets came under attorney-client privilege and refused to disclose them. Is the attorney correct?

a) Yes, the attorney's hourly records are her own work product.
b) Yes, because the client and the attorney have become adverse parties in litigation.
c) No, because a lawyer cannot invoke privilege without the relevant client's consent.
d) No, documents and information about billable hours, scheduling, and so forth are not privileged.

293. A client consulted with his attorney privately about how to wire funds to an offshore bank account legally, in a manner that would not violate tax laws or draw the attention of federal regulators. The attorney was not aware at the time that his client was engaged in illegal activity, and thought he merely wanted a secure investment. Later, however, the client became the target of a federal prosecution on corruption charges. The prosecution subpoenaed the attorney to answer questions about the conversation with the client regarding wire transfers to offshore accounts. The attorney objected that this was a privileged communication between the client and the attorney. How is the court likely to rule?

a) The conversation is privileged, because it was a private conversation between a client and lawyer to obtain legal advice.

b) The conversation is privileged, because the attorney was unaware that the client was engaged in illegal conduct.

c) The conversation is not privileged because of the client's illegal purpose in seeking the information.

d) The conversation is not privileged because it pertained to a business transaction rather than a legal matter.

294. An attorney heard from one of his clients in county jail that the client's cellmate did not have a lawyer, so the attorney sent a message offering to represent him, and the cellmate agreed and hired the attorney. The new client was under investigation for a variety of financial crimes, so the attorney hired a private financial forensics investigator to assess the client's potential criminal liability. This investigation, conducted at the behest of the attorney, involved the investigator interviewing the client alone for over an hour about certain bank transfers and backdated checks. Later, the prosecutor subpoenaed the private financial forensics investigator to testify at the criminal proceedings against the client, and the investigator refused to answer any questions about the conversation with the defendant. Would attorney-client privilege apply to the investigator's private conversation with the attorney's client?

a) Yes, because the investigator was acting as an agent of the attorney, and the conversation was a confidential communication with a client for the purpose of obtaining legal services.

b) Yes, but only if the attorney in fact reviewed a recording or transcript of the conversation afterward, which would make the investigator his proxy-after-the-fact.

c) No, because the attorney solicited the client, offering to represent him in a manner that

violated the solicitation rules, which voided the subsequent claim of attorney-client privilege.

d) No, because the attorney was not present during the non-lawyer investigator's conversation with the client.

295. The parents of an autistic child submitted a complaint to a vaccine manufacturer, claiming that its early childhood inoculation for Mumps-Measles-Rubella had caused the child's autism. The vaccine producer referred the complaint to its legal department. Its in-house counsel investigated the complaint, and eventually concluded that the matter posed no legal issues for the company, because of a federal statute that shields vaccine manufacturers from tort liability, which in turn would preempt any lawsuits in state courts. The attorney wrote a legal memorandum to the company's management describing his research and conclusions. He included in the memorandum a section about the alleged facts, and another section presenting the legal analysis. If the parents of the child later file a lawsuit anyway, would the facts that the attorney's memorandum included be discoverable, and admissible at a subsequent trial?

a) Yes, because the lawyer who wrote the memorandum was in-house counsel at the manufacturer, so the company never communicated with an outside law firm seeking legal advice.

b) Yes, because attorney-client privilege does not apply to underlying facts, even if those facts were under discussion in an otherwise privileged communication.

c) No, because a state statute shielded the manufacturer from liability for injuries from this type of product.

d) No, because the communication was part of a private communication between a lawyer and a client who was seeking legal advice.

Bruesewitz v. Wyeth LLC, 562 U.S. 223 (2011)

296. Conglomerate Corporation has several overseas facilities, and a mid-level manager at one of these locations bribed local government officials to obtain lucrative government contracts. The matter came to the attention of Conglomerate's top management and Board, who recognized that the incident was an egregious violation of the Foreign Corrupt Practices Act. An internal corporate investigation of the matter

ensued, and the corporation's directors asked their in-house General Counsel to send written inquiries to the wrongdoer's counterparts in each of its overseas branches, asking whether similar payments or bribes were occurring elsewhere. After reviewing the responses to these inquiries and following up with phone calls and meetings, the corporate directors self-reported any questionable transactions to the relevant federal agencies. When one of those agencies brought an enforcement action against Conglomerate Corporation, the Department of Justice lawyers sought discovery of all the original written responses to these internal inquiries. The corporate directors and General Counsel refused, claiming that the information was privileged. Should Conglomerate Corporation be able to resist production of these documents as privileged?

a) Yes, because the corporate directors requested the information from the in-house attorney, and the information was work-related, and was necessary for obtaining legal advice

b) Yes, because providing the information to an attorney made privilege attach.

c) No, because the inquiries and written responses are underlying facts in the case, and therefore not covered by attorney-client privilege.

d) No, because lower level employees at a corporation, who play no part in controlling the corporate decision making, do not count as part of the "client" for purposes of attorney-client privilege.

Upjohn Co. v. United States, 449 U.S. 383 (1981)

297. An attorney prepared the policy manuals for a corporate client, an insurance company. The manuals guide the client's claims adjusters about claims reporting procedures, such as assigning counsel, closing files, reporting bad-faith claims, maintaining records, settlement authority, and so forth. These attorney-drafted policies served the purpose of facilitating the rendition of competent claims handling by the insurer's employees. When a litigation opponent requests production of these manuals during pre-trial discovery, would they come under attorney-client privilege?

a) Yes, because the attorney prepared them on behalf of the client, at the client's request.

b) Yes, because the attorney prepared them as part of rendering legal services to the client, and the manuals were for internal, nonpublic use by the insurance adjusters.

c) No, because attorney-client privilege applies only to conversations, not to written documents.

d) No, because the documents were not part of rendering legal advice, but rather for the employees to use in processing claims, and they were not confidential enough to create privilege.

Medallion Transport & Logistics, LLC v. AIG Claims, Inc., 2018 WL 3608568 (E.D. Tex. June 23, 2018)

298. An attorney met a small business proprietor at a social event, and the proprietor mentioned that he routinely hires lawyers for lease and contract issues. The attorney offered to provide representation for such matters in the future, and gave him his business card, and the proprietor called the next day to engage the attorney to provide these types of legal services. The new client later dropped of boxes of files with documents relating to the matters that the attorney was handling. A few weeks into the representation, the attorney noticed some serious discrepancies and legal issues while reviewing the documents in one of the boxes, and he sent the client an email explaining that he might face regulatory fines and even criminal sanctions if the client did not resolve the matter immediately. The client sent a reply email directing the attorney to shred the entire contents of that box of files, and he did so. A year later, law enforcement officials investigated the client and sought to compel disclosure of the emails between the client and the attorney regarding the boxes of files, including the now-missing files. The attorney claimed attorney-client privilege for the private email communications he had with his client. Should a court compel the production of the emails?

a) Yes, because the privilege belongs to the client, so only the client could assert it, not the attorney.

b) Yes, because the communications, though confidential, were in furtherance of committing a crime or fraud.

c) No, the communication comes squarely under the protection of attorney-client privilege.

d) No, the producing the emails would violate the client's right against self-incrimination and the attorney's duty of confidentiality.

299. Howard Hamlin is a partner at the law firm Hamlin, Hamlin, & McGill (HHM). HHM's computer network automatically inserts the firm's "Hamlindigo Blue" logo and letterhead into every email sent from the firm's email accounts, as well as a legal disclaimer at the end of every email that reads, "NOTICE: This email may contain PRIVILEGED

and CONFIDENTIAL information and is only for the use of the specific individual(s) to which it is addressed. If you are not an intended recipient, you must not review, copy, or show the message and any attachments to anyone. Please reply to this e-mail and highlight the mistaken transmission to the sender, and then immediately delete the message." Attorney Hamlin believes that every email sent by anyone at the firm to anyone outside the firm should be undiscoverable, under the doctrine of attorney-client privilege, because each email automatically includes this disclaimer under the sender's signature line. Is Hamlin correct?

a) Yes, because the disclaimer informs anyone who reads the email that it is a private communication between the lawyers at the firm and individuals seeking legal assistance.
b) Yes, the disclaimer asserts the privilege explicitly, but any emails from a law firm would automatically trigger the attorney-client privilege, even without such a disclaimer.
c) No, because the disclaimer appears automatically in every email, so the sender might not have had a subjective intent for the communication to be confidential.
d) No, blanket privilege inscriptions on law firm correspondence do not guarantee that privilege will apply to the contents of the email, because emails sent to non-clients (or copying non-clients as additional recipients) would not be privileged.

300. Conglomerate Corporation has several offices around the state. After receiving a few employee complaints about workplace discrimination from one office, Conglomerate's corporate officers asked the company's attorney to advise them about potential liability in the matter. The attorney conducted a careful investigation and wrote a thorough memorandum summarizing her findings and legal conclusions. Because the matter involved a commonplace scenario, the attorney thought it would be helpful to give all the company's human resources managers, in each of its offices statewide, guidance about the issue, so she sent the memorandum to all sixty-two HR managers in Conglomerate's offices nationwide. When litigation eventually ensued over the alleged discrimination, the plaintiffs sought discovery of the attorney's memorandum, but Conglomerate attorney asserted attorney-client privilege. Is Conglomerate's position correct?

a) Yes, because the communication was part of a private communication between a lawyer and a client who was seeking legal advice.
b) Yes, because the memorandum was prepared in anticipated of upcoming litigation, and therefore qualifies as attorney work product.
c) No, the attorney was investigating a few separate complaints, so the memorandum did not pertain to any specific lawsuit; rather, it was a general inquiry.
d) No, because sending the memorandum to so many employees who had no connection to the matter waived the privilege.

301. An attorney specialized in criminal defense work, and at one point she agreed to represent a client who was multiple charges for gang-related criminal activities. While the client was in county lockup, inmates there from a rival gang assaulted him, necessitating his hospitalization. The attorney visited her client in the hospital to discuss a pending plea offer from the prosecutor. Both the client and the attorney believed, with good reason, that they were having a confidential conversation. Unbeknownst to them, however, a doctor was eavesdropping on their conversation, and the doctor subsequently contacted the prosecutor and repeated the entire conversation. Armed with this new evidence, the prosecutor revoked the pending plea offer, proceeded with the prosecution, and called the doctor to testify at trial about the conversation. The attorney argued that her conversation with her client came under attorney-client privilege and was therefore inadmissible at trial. Is the attorney correct in this assertion?

a) Yes, the attorney and the defendant were reasonable in believing that the conversation was confidential.
b) Yes, the information relates to the attorney's representation of the defendant.
c) No, the fact that a third party heard the conversation waived attorney-client privilege.
d) No, in overhearing the conversation, the doctor did not engage in illegal conduct.

302. A former employee is suing Conglomerate Corporation. The employee claims that Conglomerate fired him as retaliation for uncovering internal corruption at the company. While he still worked for Conglomerate, the employee had several

email exchanges with Conglomerate's in-house counsel about the problems he had uncovered and the consequences for reporting them. Now that litigation has ensued after his termination, he requests production of all his email exchanges with in-house counsel (he no longer has access to the company's email server). Conglomerate's lawyers assert that these conversations are privileged, because the emails were between a Conglomerate employee and its corporate counsel. Would the emails come under the protection of attorney-client privilege, given these facts?

a) Yes, if they were confidential exchanges between a corporate employee and corporate counsel seeking legal advice.

b) Yes, if the employee had received instructions from his superiors at Conglomerate to email corporate counsel about his concerns.

c) No, because the privilege belongs to the client, and the plaintiff here owns the privilege.

d) No, one may presume that other individuals have seen the emails, besides the plaintiff and the lawyer by this point.

303. Two codefendants stood trial on an arson charge, each represented by separate counsel. The first defendant, through his attorney, offered to tell the prosecutor about some valuable eyewitnesses that would help the prosecution's case against the other defendant, in exchange for a plea agreement that included no jail time for the first defendant. The prosecutor declined the offer and continued with the prosecution of both defendants. The first defendant, who had offered to make the disclosures, died unexpectedly in a violent prison fight. The prosecutor then called the deceased defendant's attorney and asked him to disclose whatever information he had about these additional witnesses that would strengthen the case against the remaining defendant. The attorney was unsure about whether attorney-client privilege applied, but the prosecutor insisted it did not apply after the defendant's death. Is the prosecutor correct?[4]

---

[4] *See, e..g., Swidler & Berlin v. United States*, 524 U.S. 399, 118 S.Ct. 2081, 141 L.Ed.2d 379 (1998) (under federal evidence rules, privilege survives death of client); *State v. Macumber*, 544 P.2d 1084 (Ariz.1976) (on prosecutor's objection, lawyer for deceased client could not testify to confession for crime for which another person now on trial); *In re John Doe Grand Jury Investigation*, 562 N.E.2d 69 (Mass.1990) (lawyer had privilege for pre-death conversations with suicide victim suspected of killing wife); *People v. Modzelewski*, 611 N.Y.S.2d 22 (N.Y.App.Div.1994) (privilege precluded testimony of lawyer of deceased co-perpetrator); RESTATEMENT OF THE LAW: THE LAW

a) Yes, the privilege belongs to the client and only a living client can assert privilege.

b) Yes, because the client had offered to make the disclosure before his death, and the client's death makes that offer the final word on the client's intention about the disclosure.

c) No, because the prosecutor declined the offer of disclosure at the time, and the privilege survives the client's death.

d) No, because attorney-client privilege does not apply as to co-defendants in the same proceeding.

304. The corporate officers of a large hospital were trying to decide whether to provide free HBO and Showtime (and other subscription cable channels) to all the televisions in the patient rooms. Corporate counsel participated in these meetings due to his familiarity with the pricing of these channels and what other hospitals in the area were doing in this regard. Later, the hospital finds itself in contract litigation with its cable provider, and the opposing party requests disclosure of the comments and discussion in this meeting. The hospital's corporate counsel objects that this meeting was privileged communication because of the participation of the attorney in the meeting. Is he correct?

a) Yes, if the meeting was confidential and the hospital has not waived privilege in the meantime.

b) Yes, because the participation of corporate counsel in a management meeting ensures that the discussions are privileged.

c) No, because the cable company owns the privilege in this case.

d) No, because the attorney was participating as a business advisor in this meeting, not providing legal services.

305. An attorney represented a personal injury plaintiff in a lawsuit. While trying to find potential witnesses to support the client's litigation claims and personal credibility, the attorney met with several people neighbors and friends of the client, asking about the incident that injured the client, as well as the client's character and past behavior. One of the client's neighbors told the attorney several disturbing stories about wild parties at the client's house, and disreputable character who frequently visited the home. Later, at trial, the defendant sought to compel

---

GOVERNING LAWYERS § 77 - Duration of the Privilege.

the attorney to disclose the information conveyed by the client's neighbors. The attorney objected that this information falls under the attorney-client privilege and is therefore inadmissible. Is the attorney correct in this assertion?

a) Yes, because the stories are confidential information related to the representation.
b) Yes, assuming the client wants the attorney to keep the information confidential, because the client is the holder of the privilege.
c) No, because the information did not come from the client, and therefore attorney client privilege does not apply.
d) No, because the attorney-client privilege does not apply during trials, but only to communication outside the courtroom.

306. A client had a confidential conversation with his attorney seeking legal advice. The client died a few weeks later. The client had pending litigation at the time of his conversation with the attorney, and the opposing party seeks disclosure of the conversation, because opposing counsel believes the client had instructed the attorney to accept the opposing party's settlement offer, up to a certain amount. The attorney is continuing the claim on behalf of the client's estate, and he refuses to settle or to disclose the contents of the conversation. Should the court compel the attorney to reveal whether the client wanted to settle the case before he died?

a) Yes, because the client has absolute control over whether to settle a case or proceed to trial.
b) Yes, if the opposing party has some evidence that the deceased client intended to accept the settlement offer that the attorney is now rejecting.
c) No, because the decision whether to settle is now up to the decedent's estate.
d) No, because privilege normally survives the death of the client.

307. An attorney sometimes recorded his interviews with clients, after obtaining permission from the client, especially when the client was recounting a long narrative about events that transpired, which had given rise to litigation. The opposing party in one lawsuit sought discovery of the recording of the client's narrative of the events to the attorney. Which

of the following is most likely to result in the recording being discoverable?

a) The client played the recording at home for his friend to get his advice and input.
b) There was good reason to believe that the client had told contradictory versions of the story on different occasions.
c) The client has died and is unavailable to testify at trial.
d) The lawsuit involved some criminal behavior by the client at some point.

308. Attorney Stevenson works in-house as General Counsel for Conglomerate Corporation. Conglomerate's Chief Financial Officer (CFO) resigned suddenly. Due to his background in corporate finance and economics, Conglomerate's Board of Directors asked Attorney Stevenson to serve temporarily as the acting Chief Financial Officer, until they could find a permanent replacement to fill the position. Attorney Stevenson divided his time evenly between corporate financial operations and legal tasks for the company, such as contract review, regulatory compliance, and supervising the outside firms that handle the company's litigation. His financial responsibilities at Conglomerate included reviewing financial reports and forecasts, investment strategy proposals, and various emails or memoranda relating to the firm's financial affairs. An opposing party in antitrust litigation against the corporation seeks to compel production of some of Attorney Stevenson's financial reports and strategy proposals, but he claims these come under attorney-client privilege, as he simultaneously serves as the in-house lawyer for Conglomerate Corporation. Are the documents discoverable at trial?

a) Yes, because there is no indication that the attorney marked these documents as "privileged and confidential" at the time of drafting.
b) Yes, because these are business communications, not legal advice from the lawyer to the client.
c) No, because these are internal communications are between corporate managers and their in-house counsel.
d) No, because assuming the documents were not available to all the lower-level employees at the company.

309. An attorney handled the estate planning for an elderly client, which included the creation of a

spendthrift trust, with the client's grandchildren as the beneficiaries. The trust document stipulated that disbursements to the beneficiaries were discretionary until they reach the age of 25. The client has now died, and the attorney who drafted the trust document for the client serves as the trustee. The beneficiaries, ages 21-23, have sued, seeking larger and more frequent disbursements from the trust. During discover, the plaintiffs request production of all documents relating to the creation of the trust and the testator's intentions about disbursements – emails and memoranda between the deceased client and the attorney. The attorney, now the trustee, claims that these communications come under the protection of attorney-client privilege. How should the court rule?

a) The court should compel disclosure because it was improper for the same attorney to draft the trust document giving the trustee discretion about disbursements, and then serve as the trustee himself.

b) The court should compel disclosure because attorney-client privilege normally does not apply in disputes between trustees and beneficiaries.

c) The court should apply the privilege to these documents, because they were confidential communications between a client and his lawyer, seeking legal advice and representation.

d) The court should apply the privilege because the trust document itself is controlling, and the requested documents are immaterial to the litigation.

310. Walter White conferred confidentially with his attorney, Saul Goodman, about how to resolve a specific legal problem. Attorney Goodman suggested shredding documents and hiring some thugs to beat up the other party in the matter, leaving them with a warning to stay away from Walter White. White, the client, proceeds with this plan. Later, when White faces criminal prosecution for the assault-for-hire, the prosecutor seeks disclosure of any conversations he had with his attorney about hiring thugs to carry out the assault. Predictably, Attorney Goodman argues that the conversation comes under the protection of attorney-client privilege. Is the prosecutor correct to demand disclosure?

a) Yes, given these facts, the crime-fraud exception to attorney-client privilege would potentially apply.

b) Yes, because attorney-client privilege normally does not apply in criminal prosecutions.

c) No, the crime-fraud exception to attorney-client privilege in this case would mean that the conversation was not discoverable.

d) The privilege belongs to Attorney Goodman in this case, so he can decide whether to make the disclosure without conferring with his client.

311. Conglomerate Corporation's recent litigation has received unfavorable media attention, so the corporate directors have hired a public relations firm (Afflatus, Inc.) to handle media relations and help boost the company's image. The directors have also asked their attorney, who is handling their litigation, to meet with the Afflatus staff, explaining the company's litigation position and how to answer media inquiries without giving statements that might bind the corporation to a disadvantageous legal position. The attorney opened his presentation with a declaration that the meeting was confidential, and that some of the information shared would be privileged. A few months later, the opposing party learns that this meeting occurred and seeks discovery of the PowerPoint slides the attorney used in the presentation to the public relations firm. Given these facts, would these the slides be discoverable at trial?

a) Yes, because the public relations firm is not the client.

b) Yes, because attorney-client privilege would apply only to discussions at the meeting, not to the PowerPoint slides, which anyone could forward to individuals who were not at the private meeting

c) No, because the communication was private, between a lawyer and an agent of the client at the client's direction, and it related to litigation.

d) No, because the lawyers explained at the beginning of the private meeting that the contents of their presentation would be privileged and confidential.

312. Conglomerate Corporation had an accident occur at one of its chemical manufacturing facilities – a large explosion killed several workers and injured many others. Soon after the incident, at the behest of Conglomerate's corporate managers, the general counsel obtained statements from employees and other witnesses about what happened, memorializing the statements in written form. Later, the family of an employee killed in the accident sued Conglomerate, and the plaintiffs' interrogatories

included a demand for the contents of the written statements taken by the corporate general counsel. Must Conglomerate Corporation disclose the statements taken by its attorney after the accident? [pick the best answer]

a) Yes, because Conglomerate Corporation is a party to the case.
b) Yes, because the statements are relevant to material issues in the litigation.
c) No, because the statements are communications protected by the attorney-client privilege.
d) No, because the statements are protected work product, and no exceptions could ever apply.

313. An attorney represented Conglomerate Corporation, and she made a confidential report to Conglomerate's CEO, describing Conglomerate's contractual relationship with Supplier Systems, a large vendor. The attorney advised the CEO that Conglomerate could terminate its contract with Supplier without facing any liability. The CEO then sent a confidential memorandum to Conglomerate's purchasing manager, explaining the parts of the attorney's advice necessary for understanding the issue at hand, and asking whether termination of the contract would nonetheless be inappropriate for business reasons. Months later, Conglomerate finds itself in litigation over a related matter, and the opposing party seeks discovery of what the attorney reported to the Conglomerate CEO regarding Supplier's contract. Conglomerate asserts attorney-client privilege for the report and its contents, but opposing counsel responds that Conglomerate waived privilege by sharing crucial aspects of the report with the purchasing manager, while asking for a business judgment. How is the court likely to rule?

a) The purchasing manager can decide whether to keep or waive privilege at this point.
b) The attorney's report remains privileged if Conglomerate was already anticipating litigation over the contract with Supplier, but not if litigation was not a concern at the time.
c) The CEO indeed waived privilege for the attorney's report by sharing it with a manager in the context of a business judgment inquiry, rather than a legal position.
d) The attorney's report to the CEO would remain privileged notwithstanding that CEO shared it with the purchasing manager.

314. An attorney represented Conglomerate Corporation. An officer of Conglomerate Corporation communicated in confidence with the attorney about deals between Conglomerate and one of its creditors, Big Bank. Conglomerate later declared bankruptcy, and the court appointed a in bankruptcy for Conglomerate. Then the attorney became a necessary witness in the litigation between Big Bank and Conglomerate's bankruptcy trustee. Conglomerate's trustee in bankruptcy waived privilege on behalf of Conglomerate with respect to testimony by the attorney regarding statements by the officer to the attorney. The officer, knowing that the statements would embarrass or even incriminate him, tried to prevent the attorney from testifying, claiming the conversation was a privileged communication to the corporation's attorney. Big Bank's lawyer responded that former officers and directors of a corporation cannot claim privilege after control of the corporation has passed to a bankruptcy trustee. Should the court side with the officer in this situation?

a) Yes, because the officer spoke as the legal agent of Conglomerate in a confidential conversation with Conglomerate's attorney about legal matters of the corporation.
b) Yes, because trustees in bankruptcy cannot waive privilege retroactively on behalf of the Corporation and its directors for conversations that occurred before the bankruptcy.
c) No, if there is a chance that the communication could incriminate the officer, he can assert privilege under the crime-fraud exception.
d) No, the officer cannot assert privilege because he was not a client of the attorney in the representation.

315. An attorney's client was a member of a drug cartel that imported and distributed illegal narcotics. The client promised the other cartel members that the client would provide anyone in the cartel with legal representation whenever the need arose. The client then offered the attorney a generous monthly retainer if the attorney would stand ready to provide legal services whenever the client or the cartel associates encountered legal difficulties during the operation of the cartel. In a confidential communication that would normally otherwise qualify as privileged, the client told the attorney the identities of the other cartel members. The client continued the cartel operations for some time after this communication.

Would government lawyers, in a subsequent law enforcement action, be able to compel the attorney to disclose the identities of the other cartel members?

a) Yes, the crime-fraud exception renders nonprivileged the communications between the client and the attorney, including identification of the client's confederates.

b) Yes, because the other members of the cartel are not clients of the attorney.

c) No, the conversation was a confidential communication between a client and a lawyer to obtain legal services.

d) No, the privilege belongs to the client, so the government lawyers should instead subpoena the client to reveal the contents of the communication.

316. A client consults an attorney about the client's indictment for the crimes of theft and unlawful possession of stolen goods. Applicable law treats possession of stolen goods as a continuing offense. The client is still hiding the stolen items in a secret place. The prosecutor then tries to subpoena the attorney to testify about the conversations with the client regarding the charges and the legal proceedings. Would attorney-client privilege apply to the conversation, if the client's crime is still ongoing?

a) Yes, privilege covers all communications between an attorney and a client.

b) Yes, privilege covers the confidential communications between the attorney and the client regarding the indictment for theft and possession.

c) No, the crime-fraud exception defeats attorney-client privilege if the crime is still ongoing.

d) No, attorney-client privilege does not apply until the representation has ended.

317. A client consults an attorney about the client's indictment for the crimes of theft and unlawful possession of stolen goods. Applicable law treats possession of stolen goods as a continuing offense. The client is still hiding the stolen items in a secret place, and the client asks the attorney about in which client can continue to hold onto the stolen goods. During the conversation, the client describes the present location of the stolen items. The prosecutor then tries to subpoena the attorney to testify about the location of the stolen goods. Would attorney-client

privilege apply to the conversation, if the client's crime is still ongoing?

a) Yes, privilege covers all communications between an attorney and a client.

b) Yes, privilege covers the confidential communications between the attorney and the client.

c) No, the crime-fraud exception defeats attorney-client privilege for this conversation, as the crime is still ongoing.

d) No, attorney-client privilege does not apply until the representation has ended.

318. A client consults an attorney about the client's indictment for the crimes of theft and unlawful possession of stolen goods. Applicable law treats possession of stolen goods as a continuing offense. The client is still hiding the stolen items in a secret place, and the client asks the attorney about how the client might lawfully return the stolen items. The prosecutor then tries to subpoena the attorney to testify about conversation. Would attorney-client privilege apply to the conversation, if the client's crime is still ongoing?

a) Yes, privilege covers all communications between an attorney and a client.

b) Yes, confidential communications about ways in which Client might lawfully return the stolen goods to their owner are privileged.

c) No, the crime-fraud exception defeats attorney-client privilege for this conversation, as the crime is still ongoing.

d) No, attorney-client privilege does not apply until the representation has ended.

319. A federally recognized tribe of Native Americans, the Jicarilla Apache Nation, brought an action against the Department of the Interior for mismanagement of tribal trust funds, in violation of federal statutes. During discovery, the plaintiffs requested production of certain government documents, but the government had a plausible claim that the documents in question came under the protection of attorney-client privilege. The plaintiffs countered that the fiduciary exception to privilege applied in this case because of the trust relationship between the United States government and the Native American tribes. How should the court rule?

a) The fiduciary exception to privilege does not

apply to trusts, so compelled production is appropriate.
b) The court should give more weight to the position of a governmental entity as a party when resolving disputes over privilege.
c) The fiduciary exception applies to situations in which the federal government acts as a trustee of tribal resources.
d) The fiduciary exception to the attorney-client privilege does not apply to the general trust relationship between the United States and the Indian tribes.

U.S. v. Jicarilla Apache Nation, 564 U.S. 162 (2011)

WORK PRODUCT DOCTRINE

[NOTE: the best resource for students on the attorney work product doctrine is §§ 87-93 of the RESTATEMENT (THIRD) OF THE LAW GOVERNING LAWYERS, and many of the following questions reflect the RESTATEMENT'S examples and illustrations. In practice, states vary in how they apply privilege and its exceptions. The RESTATEMENT typically reflects the majority rule for each point, and it is the safest point of reference for answering privilege questions that appear on the MPRE.]

320. Which of the following is NOT one of the elements of the work product doctrine?
a) anticipation of litigation applies to almost any legal work performed for a client, because litigation could eventually arise over any contract, will, or property disposition
b) the materials normally must be documents or tangible things
c) the materials must be prepared in anticipation of litigation or for trial – that is, the party had reason to anticipate litigation and the primary motivating purpose behind the creation of the document was to aid in potential future litigation.
d) the materials must be prepared by or for a party's representative

321. Prosecutors from the Department of Justice (DOJ) began an antitrust investigation into Conglomerate Corporation, and the DOJ began questioning some of Conglomerate's business customers. Conglomerate's attorney prepared a memorandum analyzing the antitrust implications of Conglomerate's standard contract form with commercial purchasers. Soon thereafter, some Conglomerate employees received subpoenas to testify before a grand jury that was investigating the same antitrust issues in their industry. The attorney worried that the grand jury would indict Conglomerate, so she interviewed the employees herself and prepared a debriefing memorandum. Would the attorney's two memoranda described above come under the protection of the work product doctrine?
a) The memorandum analyzing the contract is work product, but not the memorandum summarizing the employee statements.
b) The memorandum summarizing the employee statements is work product, but not the memorandum analyzing the contract.
c) Both the lawyer's memorandum analyzing the contract form and the lawyer's debriefing

memorandum were prepared in anticipation of litigation, because a grand jury proceeding is itself litigation.

d) Neither the lawyer's memorandum analyzing the contract form and the lawyer's debriefing memorandum were prepared in anticipation of litigation.

322. The law school casebook industry was heavily consolidated. Several witnesses testified before a grand jury investigating this specialized publishing industry. Shortly afterward, an attorney for East Publishing Company debriefed the witnesses and wrote memoranda of those interviews in anticipation of the potential indictment of East Publishing, and the anticipated civil suits that could follow. Five years later, some plaintiffs representing a class of law school casebook consumers filed an antitrust class action against East Publishing and sought discovery of the non-opinion work-product portions of the attorney's debriefing memoranda. The plaintiffs were careful in preparing their case and gathering evidence through other means, and they can show that the witnesses in question were no longer able to remember some of the events to which they testified at the previous grand jury proceeding. Should a court order the attorney to produce the memorandum?

a) Yes, this situation falls under the need-and-hardship exception to the work product doctrine.

b) Yes, because the witness statements are only facts, not the attorney's own thoughts.

c) No, because the memorandum is attorney work product.

d) No, because the witnesses are still available to testify, even if their memories are fading as time passes, as is true with all witnesses in litigation.

.

323. A defendant accused of bank robbery hired an attorney. The attorney interviewed a bank teller, who witnessed the robbery. The attorney memorialized the conversation in a written memorandum that qualified as work product. Later, during the trial, the same teller testified for the prosecution, and the attorney cross-examined the bank teller by quoting from the teller's prior statement, as memorialized in the memorandum. The bank teller then denied making the statements. In turn, the prosecutor demanded a copy of the document from which the attorney had read statements during the cross-examination, and the attorney objected that the document was attorney work product and therefore not subject to discovery. Is the attorney correct?

a) Yes, if the attorney prepared the document in anticipation of litigation, the memorandum is

work product and is not subject to discovery or compelled disclosure.

b) Yes, disclosure would violate the criminal defendant's right to confront witnesses, guaranteed in the Confrontation Clause of the Sixth Amendment, and the right against self-incrimination, guaranteed in the Fifth Amendment.

c) No, when the attorney chose to ask the teller questions with direct reference to the memorandum, it waived work-product immunity for the portion of the memorandum discussing the teller's story, and any other parts of the document that are necessary to place all the testimony fairly into context.

d) No, the entire document merely summarizes the factual statements of an eyewitness, and it contains no attorney work product.

324. The DOJ brought an antitrust suit against Conglomerate Corporation. Giant Company separately sued Conglomerate, mostly alleging the same facts that the DOJ had alleged in its case, and Giant sought parallel relief. An attorney for Giant Company showed the DOJ lawyers some documents that constituted part of the attorney's work product in Gian Company's parallel lawsuit against Conglomerate. Giant Company and the DOJ formally agreed that the DOJ would use documents only in litigation against Conglomerate Corporation. Later, however, in the government's case, Conglomerate Corporation sought discovery of Giant Company's work product, that is, the documents that Giant's attorney had shared with the DOJ. How should the court rule on this discovery request?

a) Only Giant Company but not the DOJ (government) may properly assert Giant's work-product protection for the documents.

b) Only the DOJ but not Giant Company may properly assert Giant's work-product protection for the documents.

c) Neither Both Giant Company and the DOJ (government) may properly assert Giant's work-product protection for the documents.

d) Both Giant Company and the DOJ (government) may properly assert Giant's work-product protection for the documents, under the common-interest doctrine.

325. An attorney had many years of experience in handling personal injury litigation, and in a certain case, the attorney represented a plaintiff in litigation

over injuries sustained in a car accident. In preparation for trial, the attorney interviewed each of the eyewitnesses of the accident, and afterward wrote a memorandum summarizing what each witness said. The witnesses themselves agreed to swear and sign the statements, as if they were affidavits. The statements contained no mental impressions of the attorney, only facts communicated by the witnesses. Opposing counsel eventually learned of these interviews and sought discovery of the witness statements that the plaintiff's attorney had drafted. Unsurprisingly, the attorney objected that these documents were attorney work-product doctrine. Should the court compel the production of the witness statements?

a) Yes, the witnesses themselves have a right to assert protection from disclosure of their statements, but not the attorney.

b) Yes, witness statements contain only factual information, and underlying facts do not come under the protection of the work-product doctrine.

c) No, lawyers may not discover any materials prepared by the other lawyer in anticipation of litigation.

d) No, because the attorney prepared the witness statements on behalf of the plaintiff in anticipation of the litigation.

326. An attorney agreed to represent a plaintiff who sustained serious injuries three months earlier when she fell through a defective staircase on the defendant's premises. Her hospitalization after the incident prevented the plaintiff from securing legal representation for twelve weeks. The attorney filed a personal injury lawsuit immediately, and the defendant retained counsel for the litigation in response. The defendant's lawyer visited the accident scene immediately and took photographs. By that time, the defendant had completely rebuilt the staircase, adding additional handrails, bannisters, and other safeguards. Later, as the litigation proceeded through the discovery phase, the plaintiff's attorney sought production of defense counsel's photographs of the scene, and defense counsel objected that the photographs were non-discoverable attorney work product. The attorney for the plaintiff explained in a motion to the court that the lapse of time since the accident prevented the attorney from viewing the accident scene as it was at the time, invoking the need-and-hardship doctrine. Moreover, the plaintiff's

delay in securing counsel was due to her injuries and hospitalization, which were not her fault. How should the court rule?

a) The court should deny the motion because the photos depict a completely different staircase than the one that caused the accident, so they are no more helpful than photos the plaintiff could take now.

b) The court should compel production of the photographs because there is no other way for the plaintiff to establish the condition of the staircase at the time of the accident.

c) The court should compel production of the photographs because the images themselves do not constitute attorney work product, as they contain no opinions, ideas, or impressions of the lawyer.

d) The court should deny the motion because discovery would discourage lawyers from taking their own photographs of accident scenes.

Fint v. Brayman Construction Corp., Case No. 5:17-cv-04043, 2018 U.S. Dist. LEXIS 103772 (S.D.W. Va. June 21, 2018)

327. An attorney represented a client in litigation. During the discovery phase of the matter, the opposing party sought to discover communications from a meeting that the attorney had previously organized to prepare for the case. The attorney, an accountant, certain interested creditors, and the bankruptcy liquidation committee members had all attended the meeting, as well as a few others. The attorney resisted discovery based on the work product doctrine. The opposing party countered that the presence of other parties besides the attorney, the client, and their necessary agents waived the privilege. How should the court rule?

a) The court should compel discovery because the presence of third parties negated to confidentiality requirement for privilege.

b) The court should deny the request and not force the attorney to violate the ethical duty of confidentiality.

c) The court should first determine whether the discussions pertained primarily to the legal interests of the party seeking discovery.

d) The court should deny discovery because the work product doctrine protects the information from disclosure.

Firefighters' Retirement System v. Citco Group

Limited, Civ. A. No. 13-373-SDD-EWD, 2018 U.S. Dist. LEXIS 79034 (M.D. La. May 10, 2018)

328. An attorney agreed to represent a plaintiff who sustained serious injuries three months earlier when she fell through a defective staircase on the defendant's premises. Her hospitalization after the incident prevented the plaintiff from securing legal representation for twelve weeks. The attorney filed a personal injury lawsuit immediately, and the defendant retained counsel for the litigation in response. The defendant's lawyer, however, had visited the accident scene immediately after the accident and took photographs. Two weeks later, the defendant completely rebuilt the staircase, adding additional handrails, bannisters, and other safeguards. Later, as the litigation proceeded through the discovery phase, the plaintiff's attorney sought production of defense counsel's photographs of the scene, and defense counsel objected that the photographs were non-discoverable attorney work product. The attorney for the plaintiff explained in a motion to the court that the lapse of time since the accident prevented the attorney from viewing the accident scene as it was at the time, invoking the need-and-hardship doctrine. Moreover, the plaintiff's delay in securing counsel was due to her injuries and hospitalization, which were not her fault. How should the court rule?

a) The court should compel production of the photographs because there is no other way for the plaintiff to establish the condition of the staircase at the time of the accident.

b) The court should compel production of the photographs because the images themselves do not constitute attorney work product, as they contain no opinions, ideas, or impressions of the lawyer.

c) The court should deny the motion because the photos depict a completely different staircase than the one that caused the accident, so they are no more helpful than photos the plaintiff could take now.

d) The court should deny the motion because discovery would discourage lawyers from taking their own photographs of accident scenes.

329. An attorney had a series of private meetings with a client about incorporating the client's new business venture as an LLC. The attorney kept careful notes of these discussions. Which of the following is true regarding these notes about the conversations between the attorney and the client?

a) The attorney's notes would come under the protection of the attorney's duty of confidentiality but not the work product doctrine.

b) The attorney's notes would come under the protection of attorney-client privilege and the work product doctrine.

c) The attorney's notes would come under the protection of the attorney's duty of confidentiality but not attorney-client privilege.

d) The attorney's notes would not come under the protection of the work product doctrine, nor attorney-client privilege.

330. An attorney had a series of private meetings with a client about the subject matter of the representation. The attorney kept careful notes of these discussions, along with the attorney's reflections and concerns. Sometime later, an opposing party in litigation moved to compel production of these notes. Which of the following is most likely to be a reason that the attorney would assert attorney-client privilege for these notes, rather than claim they are attorney work product?

a) The client's friend had been present during the conversations.

b) The representation pertained to anticipated litigation that seemed immediate at the time.

c) The client had recounted the conversations to a friend immediately afterward.

d) The need and hardship exception.

331. An attorney had a series of private meetings with a client about the subject matter of the representation. The attorney kept careful notes of these discussions. Sometime later, an opposing party in litigation moved to compel production of these notes. Which of the following is most likely to be a reason that the attorney would try claiming that they are attorney work product, rather than asserting attorney-client privilege for these notes?

a) The representation pertained to anticipated litigation that seemed immediate at the time.

b) The notes are written documents rather than the attorney's mental recollections of the meetings.

c) The need and hardship exception.

d) The client's friend had been present during the conversations.

332. An attorney had a series of private meetings with a client about the subject matter of the

representation. The attorney kept careful notes of these discussions, along with some of the attorney's reflections and ideas. Sometime later, an opposing party in litigation moved to compel production of these notes. Which of the following is most likely to be a reason that the attorney would assert attorney-client privilege for these notes, rather than claim they are attorney work product?

a) The client's friend had been present during the conversations.
b) The client had recounted the conversations to a group of friends immediately afterward.
c) The attorney's firm had an unexpected data breach, despite the firm's updated firewalls and password protection, and the breach allowed an unknown hacker to access the notes before the litigation began.
d) The representation pertained to an employee manual that the attorney was drafting for the client's business.

333. For purposes of attorney work product protection, which of the following is NOT likely to create an objectively and subjectively reasonable "anticipation" of litigation:

a) An outside event certain to generate litigation
b) An adversarial party's explicit threat
c) In some circumstances, a corporate client's own internal actions gearing up to sue an industry rival
d) A client who has a history of being extraordinarily litigious

REGULATION OF THE LEGAL PROFESSION

RULE 5.1
RESPONSIBILITIES OF A PARTNER OR SUPERVISORY LAWYER

334. An attorney served as the director of the Environmental Enforcement Division of the state Attorney General's office, which brought legal actions against polluters in the state. The Attorney General's Office hired only lawyers with three years' experience or more – they never hired new law school graduates. In the Environmental Enforcement Division, all the lawyers had many years of experience as litigators in that field. The attorney who served as director oversaw the prioritization of cases and implementation of the Attorney General's policy objectives, and assigned cases to the lawyers in her Division, but did not need to monitor their work, train them in legal ethics, or watch for ethical violations, because all the lawyers were competent and experienced. It turned out, however, that one of the lawyers committed some ethical violations, such as testifying as the key witness in a trial in which he was the attorney of record for the state, which was the plaintiff or prosecuting party in the cases. In another instance, the lawyer brought an enforcement action that had no factual basis in retaliation against an entity that had defrauded the lawyer of a substantial amount of money. When these violations received attention in a local new station expose, the lawyer resigned in disgrace, and the Attorney General took the position that the director of the Environmental Enforcement Division is not responsible for the actions of this individual lawyer, whom he described as a "bad apple" in the Division. Is he correct?

a) Yes, even though the Model Rules state that lawyers in supervisory positions can be subject to discipline for the ethical violations of their subordinates, these rules contain an explicit exemption for government agencies.

b) Yes, because all the lawyers in the Division were competent and experienced, and it was reasonable for the Division director not to monitor their activities or provide ethical training like she would for newly licensed lawyers.

c) No, lawyers having comparable managerial authority in a government agency must make reasonable efforts to ensure that the firm has in effect measures giving reasonable assurance that all lawyers in the agency or department conform to the Rules of Professional Conduct.

d) No, even though the Model Rules merely require that lawyers in regular supervisory positions take reasonable steps to ensure that their subordinates follow the rules, there is a higher standard for supervisory lawyers in government agencies, who have strict liability for abuses of government power by their subordinates.

Rule 5.1(a) Cmt. 1

335. A certain attorney worked at Big Firm, and she was supervising a new associate lawyer there. During a negotiation for the sale of a company, in which Big Firm represented the seller, the associate informed the buyer's lawyers that certain assets of the company had no liens or other encumbrances on them, and that she had verified this herself. This was a misrepresentation – the properties had significant encumbrances, which the purchase price should have reflected, but it did not. The supervising attorney, who was part of the conversation when the associate made the misrepresentation, did not correct her, because she did not want to humiliate her in front of the opposing party, or reveal an internal discord among Big Firm's lawyers. Instead, the supervising attorney lectured the associate about the misrepresentation privately the next day, and he told her not to let it happen again. Then they agreed to drop the matter, and the supervising attorney instructed the associate to watch for a good opportunity to bring up the mistake and clarify the matter for the buyer. The associate never did so. Could the supervising attorney be subject to discipline for failing to correct the resulting misapprehension by the buyer?

a) Yes, the supervising attorney had a duty during the conversation in which the misrepresentation occurred to correct the associate in front of the opposing party.

b) Yes, the supervising attorney had a duty to take affirmative steps to correct the misapprehension of the other party, sometime before the consummation of the purchase.

c) No, it was the associate's duty to correct her own

misrepresentation, and the supervising attorney instructed her to do so.

d) No, it was not an ethical violation for the associate to misstate that she had checked for liens and encumbrances herself, as opposing counsel would normally do their own check for this.

Rule 5.1(c) Cmt. 5

336. An associate worked at Big Firm. Even though she had only recently graduated from law school, the associate had earned the respect of the partners at the firm, and she was involved in several projects for multiple lawyers and clients. Overwhelmed with looming deadlines on multiple matters, she realized that she could not devote enough attention to each client's issues - she could not provide competent, diligent representation to so many clients at once. She approached the partner who was her mentor at the firm and explained her concerns, and he responded that she was just experiencing a learning curve, and that her workload was in fact normal, and that she should stop complaining. A few weeks later, the associate was conducting research on a client matter, and she overlooked an important case related to her issue, despite her conscientious work ethic. At the time, she was racing against deadlines on two other projects, was working long hours, and was sleeping only five hours a night on average. Big Firm has a managing partner and a committee of senior partners. Could the partner who was her mentor be subject to disciplinary action for the associate's mistake?

a) Yes, the partners at a firm have strict liability for ethical violations of their associates or subordinates.

b) Yes, partners and others in a supervisory role at a firm are responsible to monitor the workload of their subordinate attorneys.

c) No, overlooking a case while conducting research does not constitute an ethical violation.

d) No, only the managing partner at the firm has responsibility for monitoring the workload of the associates.

Rule 5.1; *see* example in Arthur J. Lachman, *What You Should Know Can Hurt You: Management and Supervisory Responsibility for the Misconduct of Others Under Model Rules 5.1 and 5.3*, 18 PROF. LAW. 1 (2007)

337. An attorney had supervisory responsibilities for a new lawyer at her firm, but she had her own cases and clients to handle. It was a busy season for the firm, so the attorney did not check on the associate herself, but she would take time to answer questions if the associate approached her. The associate needed more oversight and direction that she received, and she committed several serious ethical violations. The supervising attorney had no way of knowing about these because the associate was always careful to cover up her mistakes or blame others when something went wrong. Could the supervising attorney avoid responsibility for the associate's ethical violations even if she did not direct, ratify, or have knowledge of the associate's misdeeds?

a) Yes, because the Model Rules require actual knowledge of a subordinate's ethical violations to trigger disciplinary liability for the supervising attorneys.

b) Yes, the Model Rules require actual knowledge of the violations to trigger a duty to report the violations of another lawyer in one's firm.

c) No, an attorney having direct supervisory authority over another lawyer must make reasonable efforts to ensure that the other lawyer conforms to the ethical rules, even apart from the supervising attorney directing, ratifying, or even knowing about a specific violation.

d) No, supervisory attorneys are automatically responsible for ethical violations by their subordinates if the subordinate engages in a repeated pattern of hiding, covering up, or blaming others for her actions.

Model Rule 5.1 Cmt. 6

338. An attorney was the District Attorney for a local prosecutor's office, and she had several subordinate lawyers working under her authority and oversight. This office had a series of appeals from defendants they prosecuted, and in several cases, the appellate courts reversed the convictions over <u>Brady</u> violations, that is, withholding exculpatory material evidence from defense counsel. Is the District Attorney immune to discipline for these violations?

a) Yes, the Model Rules impose an ethical duty of disclosure on prosecutors only for exculpatory evidence that is "clear and convincing," so a <u>Brady</u> reversal does not necessarily indicate an ethical violation by the prosecutor in the case.

b) Yes, the remedy for <u>Brady</u> violations is for the court to impose direct sanctions on the government lawyers in the case, and this judicial remedy preempts disciplinary action by the state bar in an administrative proceeding.

c) No, because a series of reversed convictions over Brady violations from the same office indicates a lack of training or supervision regarding the ethical duties of prosecutors.

d) No, if there were more than three clear instances of prosecutors withholding exculpatory evidence within her office during a five-year period.

ABA Formal Op. 14-467; Rule 5.1

339. An attorney worked as an entry-level prosecutor. She did not have a supervisory position or title in her office hierarchy, but merely worked on her assigned cases under the direction and oversight of the higher-ranked lawyers in the office. On one occasion, however, a case arose involving an issue that was important to her, so she asked to be the lead prosecutor on this one case. The District Attorney agreed, and assigned one other lawyer in the office, who was also an entry-level prosecutor, to assist her on the matter. The case had two defendants, and at one point, the attorney leading the prosecution was in one room negotiating a plea arrangement with the first defendant, and the lawyer assisting her was negotiating with the other defendant at the same time in the next room. The state's main witness against the two defendants was a third co-conspirator who had become an informant in exchange for a favorable plea that involved no jail time. The lawyer assisting in the case lied to the second defendant and denied that the state's witness had agreed to a deal. The lawyer had told the lead attorney on the case that he planned to do this beforehand, and she informed him that this would be unethical, but she did not try to stop him from doing so, because she was not his boss. After the negotiations, they met to debrief, and he informed her that he had indeed lied to the defendant and defense counsel about the state's arrangement with their main witness in the case. She reminded him that this violated the ethical rules, but she took no further action, because she was only an entry-level prosecutor, at the same rank as the lawyer assisting on the case. Could the attorney, as lead prosecutor on the case, be subject for the ethical violations in this case?

a) Yes, all the lawyers working together on a case are responsible for the actions of the others regarding their conduct related to that matter.

b) Yes, even if a lawyer is not a partner or other general manager, she directly supervises the work of the other lawyer as lead prosecutor in this proceeding.

c) No, ordinarily a lawyer will not be subject to discipline for the actions of other lawyers who are at the same level in the office.

d) No, because she did not have a supervisory position or title in her office hierarchy.

Rule 5.1(b); ABA Formal Op. 14-467

RULE 5.2
RESPONSIBILITIES OF A SUBORDINATE LAWYER

340. An insurance company routinely hired outside counsel to represent its policyholders in litigation under liability policy. An inexperienced attorney worked for the firm. The firm's partners charged the policyholders fees for the representation even though the insurer was already paying their legal fees; this and other aspects of their fee arrangements violated state insurance laws, as well as the ethical rules about reasonable fees. The inexperienced acted as the partners directed him to do and charged clients these fees that were illegal and unreasonable, but at one point he raised concerns about the practice with one of the partners. The partner said he would check into it. Would the safe harbor provision of Model Rule 5.2(b) absolve the attorney of a duty to research the fee issue?

a) Yes, a subordinate lawyer does not violate the ethical rules when acting upon a partner's reasonable resolution of an arguable question of professional duty.

b) Yes, because the attorney raised his concerns with the partner, who agreed to investigate the issue, so the attorney should wait until the partner has time to research it.

c) No, the attorney had a duty to research the issue himself and would have discovered that the fees were clearly illegal and unreasonable.

d) No, the safe harbor provision does not apply when a firm is serving as outside counsel for an insurance company or a bank.

Disciplinary Counsel v. Smith, 918 N.E.2d 992 (Ohio 2009)

341. An attorney had recently graduated from law school and entered the practice of law. After a federal clerkship, he went to work for Big Firm, which paid the highest associates' salaries in the state. A partner at Big Firm gave the attorney an assignment to represent the teenage daughter of one Big Firm's most important clients, a billionaire social media entrepreneur. The daughter had been part of a group of student protesters that the police had arrested the previous week for trespassing. When arrested, the daughter had given the police a friend's driver's license and identified herself as the friend, who had a similar appearance. The police mistakenly charged the daughter under the friend's name, and the district attorney proceeded to prosecute her under the mistaken identity. The friend, whose name and driver's license the daughter had used, was unaware that she was the named defendant in a misdemeanor criminal case, and the billionaire's daughter, who was now the attorney's client, continued with the ruse even as she remained in custody along with the other protestors. During a private consultation with her, the attorney asked about the name discrepancy, as he was expecting to represent the daughter of Big Firm's client, and the girl explained the false identification, and insisted that the attorney not disclose her real identity to the police or the court. Back at the firm's office, the attorney approached the partner who had assigned the case, but before the attorney could finish explaining the name problem, the partner said, "Do not mess this up, her father is an important client of the firm. Convince the court to drop the charges as quickly as possible. Close this matter quickly." The attorney spoke to the prosecutor and convinced her to dismiss the case, but the attorney never told her about the misidentification of his client. After the dismissal of the case, the attorney met with the billionaire's daughter and her mother, together with the friend whose name she had used and the friend's parents, who were upset that their daughter had been a named defendant in the matter in the first place. Despite the attorney's efforts to reassure the friend's parents that the state dropped the charges, the friend's parents contacted the prosecutor's office in hopes of removing the arrest from their daughter's record. When the prosecutor realized what had transpired, he reported the attorney to the state bar disciplinary authorities. Could the attorney, as an inexperienced new associate at Big Firm, be subject to discipline for this matter?

a) Yes, because the attorney had a duty to consult with the friend who was the named defendant in

the case before negotiating the terms of the dismissal with the prosecutor.

b) Yes, regardless of the directions the attorney received from the partner at Big Firm or from the client, he is subject to discipline for failing to disclose a material fact to a tribunal when disclosure was necessary to avoid assisting a criminal or fraudulent act by a client.

c) No, because the attorney acted in accordance with a supervisory lawyer's reasonable resolution of an arguable question of professional duty.

d) No, the attorney tried to bring his claimed ethical dilemma to the partner for his advice, and the partner failed to provide adequate guidance to the respondent.

People v. Casey, 948 P.2d 1014 (Colo. 1997)

342. An attorney works exclusively as a contract lawyer for other firms that need extra help for big cases, whether in pre-trial document review or in background research and writing of briefs. She has no direct contact with the clients of these firms, and she does not participate in important decisions about any of the matters for which she performs legal tasks. Can the attorney avoid being be subject to discipline if a firm uses her contract work in a way that constitutes misconduct, either regarding clients or before a tribunal, assuming she either knows or could have known about the misconduct?

a) Yes, because she is not an employee of the firm and therefore cannot control how the firm uses her legal work product.

b) Yes, if her contract with the firm includes a provision in which the firm takes full responsibility for misconduct, malpractice, or ethical violations.

c) No, a contract lawyer has a duty to comply with the requirements of the Rules of Professional Conduct, notwithstanding that the lawyer acted at the direction of another person.

d) No, if the clients in the matters agree that they will not hold her responsible for the work product she contributes to their representation.

Rule 5.2; Phila. Ethics Op. 2010-4 (2010);
S.C. Ethics Op. 10-08 (2010)

343. An attorney who had only recently graduated from law school, and she received a job offer from a newly elected County Attorney, after volunteering for his campaign. The new attorney did not directly

handle cases but assisted trial lawyers with clerical work and non-legal tasks, such as creating public service announcements for websites, social media, and press interviews. The County Attorney soon began a series of highly publicized attacks, including lawsuits and investigations, against political rivals on the County Board and County Courts. At one point, the County Attorney decided to file a federal civil racketeering lawsuit against several of the County Board members. There was no factual support for the allegations. When all the other lawyers in the office refused to be involved in the matter, the County Attorney assigned the case to the new attorney, who had no trial experience, and who was completely unfamiliar with the racketeering statute or case law. She took the case enthusiastically because she was eager to prove herself to the County Attorney; she even tried to amend the complaint to add additional racketeering charges, which were merely duplicative of the existing frivolous charges. She also filed several preemptive pre-trial motions seeking to qualify her expert witnesses and suppress evidence the defendants might try to submit. The court denied the motion to amend the complaint and dismissed the original complaint for having no basis in fact or law. The judge took the additional step of filing a grievance with the state bar against the attorney. In her hearing before the disciplinary committee, the attorney claimed that she was too inexperienced to know that the racketeering charges in her case had no basis in fact or law, and that she merely deferred to the guidance and instructions of the County Attorney. Could she be subject to discipline despite these mitigating factors?

a) Yes, because she had no trial experience and knew she could not have handled a complex racketeering case competently.

b) Yes, regardless of the directions of her superiors or her inexperience, she had a duty not to bring a frivolous proceeding or assert a frivolous issue in litigation.

c) No, because a lawyer need not necessarily have special training or prior experience to handle legal problems of a type with which the lawyer is unfamiliar; even a newly admitted lawyer can be as competent as a practitioner with extensive experience.

d) No, a subordinate lawyer does not violate the ethical rules she acts in accordance with a supervisory lawyer's reasonable resolution of an arguable question of professional duty.

In re Alexander, 300 P.3d 536 (Ariz. 2013); Rule 5.2

RULE 5.3
RESPONSIBILITIES REGARDING NONLAWYER ASSISTANCE

344. An attorney works for a mid-size law firm that employs two or three law students every year as summer associates. The manager of the student associates assigns one of them to work on the attorney's pending antitrust case, in addition to assignments for other lawyers at the firm. While researching a central issue in the case, the summer associate discovered an older Supreme Court decision that was unfavorable to their client. The summer associate decided not to tell anyone about the case, as the opposing party seemed to have overlooked it in their briefs. The attorney was not aware of any of this until they were on a break during their hearing. The hearing was going well for their side, and the associate boasted to the attorney about "burying" that Supreme Court case he had found. The attorney said, "Well, you should have told me about it at the time, but there is no point in bringing it up now, as it appears opposing counsel overlooked it and the hearing is going our way." The judge's clerks, however, found the case, and the judge queried the lawyers about how they could have missed it. Opposing counsel admitted he had been negligent in doing legal research on the matter, and the attorney recounted the story about the summer associate hiding the case from him. Is the attorney now subject to discipline for what the summer associate did?

a) Yes, because lawyers are automatically liable for the misconduct of nonlawyer employees at their firm; the lawyer had an affirmative duty to find the case himself and disclose it.

b) Yes, even though he was unaware of the violation at the time, the attorney ratified the summer associate's conduct after he learned about it.

c) No, because the attorney did not know about the associate's conduct at the time it occurred, or while submitting briefs, or even when the hearing began.

d) No, because opposing counsel was negligent in failing to research the issue, and if he had, he would have been likely to discover the case on his own.

Rule 5.3

345. An attorney hired Receptionist because of her good looks and because her brother was in the attorney's college fraternity, but he did not check into her background at all or ask for references. Receptionist had access to all files, records, and accounts in the firm, and three months later, there arose a problem with funds missing from client trust accounts. Circumstantial evidence pointed to Receptionist as the culprit, and at this point the attorney learns that Receptionist has an arrest record for theft and embezzlement on several occasions in the past. The attorney lectures Receptionist about it but allows her to keep her job because nobody can prove her guilty - the firm does not keep the type of records that would enable anyone to prove where the missing funds went. When additional complaints arise over misappropriated client trust funds, would the attorney be subject to discipline?

a)   Yes, because he was negligent in the hiring and supervision of nonlawyer employees.

b)   Yes, because lawyers face strict liability (automatic responsibility) for misappropriations of client trust funds.

c)   No, because it is implausible that the attorney could have known about the arrest record of someone merely interviewing for a receptionist position, and there is still no way to prove that Receptionist actually stole the money.

d)   No, because Receptionist is not a lawyer and therefore not subject to the Rules of Professional Conduct.

Rule 5.3

346. A certain attorney is a fifth-year associate at a large national law firm. As a senior associate, the attorney can attend business meetings of the firm, but cannot vote on any decisions. The attorney is aware that the firm has no measures in effect that would give reasonable assurance that the paralegals are observing the confidentiality and conflict of interest rules that are part of the professional obligations of lawyers. The attorney mistakenly believes, however, that the rules apply only to the lawyers in the firm, not to the clerical staff of paralegals. When a paralegal in a separate practice group from the attorney violates the rules and the state disciplinary authority investigates the firm's ethical compliance measures, will the attorney be subject to discipline?

a)   Yes, because any attorney with enough seniority to attend firm business meetings with the partners has shared responsibility to ensure that measures are in effect to keep the paralegals in compliance with the rules.

b)   No, because the attorney is not a partner nor in a comparable managerial position to implement

such measures, nor does it appear that the paralegal was under the attorney's direct supervision

c)   Yes, because the attorney is aware that the firm has no measures in effect that would give reasonable assurance that the paralegals are observing the confidentiality and conflict of interest rules

d)   No, because the attorney honestly believed that the Rules of Professional Conduct do not apply to the paralegals, and therefore falls under the good-faith exception to the rule.

Rule 5.3

347. An attorney employs an experienced legal assistant to manage administrative matters in the firm, including the client trust accounts. The attorney provided the legal assistant with detailed instructions about client trust accounts, including the specific kinds of records to keep, what funds to deposit there, and under what circumstances to withdraw funds. The attorney also sent the legal assistant to attend CLE courses and workshops on IOLTA accounts and managing firm records. Due to the legal assistant's thorough training, competence, and experience, the attorney reviewed the client account books cursorily once a year during the annual review of the employee. Eventually, an audit by the state disciplinary authority revealed numerous discrepancies in the bookkeeping regarding the IOLTA accounts and some prohibited commingling of client funds with the firm's funds. The attorney had no actual knowledge of the discrepancies or problems regarding the client trust accounts. Is the attorney subject to discipline?

a)   Yes, because the attorney must manage all client trust accounts personally and cannot delegate such matters to support staff at the firm.

b)   Yes, because the attorney did not make reasonable efforts to ensure that the legal assistant's conduct was compatible with the professional obligations of a lawyer.

c)   No, because the attorney made reasonable efforts to ensure that the legal assistant's conduct was compatible with the professional obligations of a lawyer by providing extensive training and periodic reviews.

d)   No, because the attorney lacked actual knowledge of the discrepancies, and the legal assistant is not subject to the Rules of Professional Conduct.

Rule 5.3

RULE 5.4
PROFESSIONAL INDEPENDENCE OF A LAWYER

348. An attorney was part of a partnership before he died. He left his nephew as his sole heir. The partnership agreement, as written, provides that the firm should pay the certain amounts to the nephew. Those amounts are $210,000, for the attorney's share of the firm's assets; a $500,000 death benefit, provided for all shareholders in the partnership; and $17,500 for fees that the attorney earned on recent cases, but had not yet received. Under the Model Rules, which of the following represents the most that the firm may properly pay to the decedent's nephew?
a) Only the $210,000 for the attorney's share of the firm's assets.
b) $727,500, for the attorney's share of the firm's assets, his of uncollected fees, and the death benefit
c) Only $17,500 for the attorney's uncollected fees.
d) Only $500,000 for the death benefit, as death benefits come under a special exception under the Rules of Professional Conduct.

349. Attorney Barrett was the managing partner at a small law firm. Barrett hired Cooper, an ordained minister who had been unemployed, as a legal assistant at the firm. Cooper's main job at the firm, however, was to bring in new clients. Cooper received a minimum-wage base salary, but also received large bonuses for bringing in clients who generated fees for the firm, and the combined bonuses each year exceeded $100,000. The firm paid for Cooper to complete a certification course to become a hospital chaplain, which gave Cooper chaplain's access to emergency areas of hospitals to visit accident victims and their families. He would offer to pray with them, but he would also give them a business card from Barrett's firm. In this way, Cooper brought several high-payoff personal injury clients to the firm. Cooper also recruited clients from the local church where he served as a "biblical counselor." Is it proper for the firm to pay Cooper bonuses for bringing fee-generating clients to the firm?
a) Yes, because Cooper is merely recommending the firm to individuals he meets while conducting his ministry activities.
b) Yes, because Cooper is doing recruiting clients as an employee of the firm, under the direct supervision of Attorney Barrett.
c) No, the arrangement constitutes an improper sharing of fees with a nonlawyer.
d) No, because it is unethical to use Cooper's chaplain status to gain access to hospital patients and their families.

Based on Florida Bar v. Barrett, 897 So.2d 1269 (2005)

350. An attorney could not find a full-time job after law school, so instead he works on a contract basis for other firms. The attorney also signs up with a legal temp-work agency, a company owned by nonlawyers that places lawyers in temporary assignments at law firms that need an extra associate on a short-term basis. Law firms contact the legal temp-work agency when they need lawyers for a special project or assignment, and the agency sends them several resumes from which to choose the temporary associates they want. Through this temp-work agency, the attorney receives a three-month assignment at Big Firm conducting document review as part of litigation discovery. The firm pays the attorney $75 per hour, and it pays the temp-work agency a placement fee of 7% on whatever the attorney earns. Big Firm, in turn, passes the attorney's $100/hour fees and the 7% placement fee through to its clients as an item on the client's bill. Is this arrangement proper?
a) It is proper for Big Firm to pay the placement fee to the agency, to pass the fees through to the clients, and to pay the attorney's hourly rate out of the fees it receives from clients.
b) It is proper for Big Firm to hire the attorney on an hourly, short-term contract basis and to pass his fees through to the client, but it is improper for Big Firm to pay the temp-work agency a percentage, as this constitutes sharing legal fees with the nonlawyers who own the temp-work agency.
c) It is proper for Big Firm to pay the attorney and the temp-work agency, but it is improper for Big Firm to pass the costs through to their clients.
d) It is proper for Big Firm to pay a temp-work agency and to pass these costs through to the clients, but it is improper for the attorney to work on a case on an hourly-fee basis without becoming an associate at Big Firm.

ABA Formal Opinion 88-356

351. After a long, distinguished career as a solo practitioner in a major city, an elderly attorney agrees to join a newer law firm on the condition that the firm would pay $1000 per month after the attorney's death to his sister, who is 74 years old, until her death. The attorney's sister is not a lawyer. The firm agrees to this arrangement, in addition to making the attorney a partner with a 15% share in the firm. Is this arrangement proper?

a) Yes, because it is the payment of money over a reasonable period after the lawyer's death to a specified person.

b) Yes, because the Contracts Clause of the Constitution guarantees the freedom of contract, so lawyers and firms can make whatever compensation arrangements they want.

c) No, because the sister is not a lawyer and therefore cannot share in the legal fees received by the firm.

d) No, because payments that continue until the sister's death could go on indefinitely, and this goes beyond the Model Rules' stipulation of "a reasonable period of time."

352. An attorney agrees to buy the successful law firm of a fellow lawyer who recently succumbed to terminal cancer. The sale includes the office building, the library and furnishings, and the good will of the firm, and conforms to the provisions of Rule 1.7. The purchasing attorney pays $100,000, the agreed-upon purchase price, to the executor of the deceased lawyer's estate, but the executor is not a lawyer. The funds for the purchase came from the contingent fees in a recent personal injury case won by the purchasing attorney. Was this transaction improper?

a) Yes, because the attorney is sharing legal fees with a nonlawyer, the executor.

b) Yes, because the funds for the purchase came from a contingent-fee case.

c) No, because an attorney purchasing the firm of a deceased lawyer may pay the executor the agreed-upon purchase price.

d) No, because even a nonlawyer executor of a firm functions temporarily in the role of a lawyer for purposes of the Model Rules.

353. Three law partners have decided to incorporate their firm instead of continuing as a partnership, as their malpractice insurer has offered them a lower rate on their premiums if they incorporate and thereby reduce some of their joint liability. They also want to make a clearer track for associates to become shareholders after reaching certain performance benchmarks. The articles of incorporation provide that when a shareholder dies, a fiduciary representative of the estate may hold stock in the corporation for a reasonable time during administration of the estate before transferring it to the heirs. Which of the following may the partners properly do as they incorporate?

a) They may incorporate their law practice and convey an interest in the corporation to their heirs, such as spouses or children.

b) They may stipulate that the corporation will hold all funds in a single operating account, and thereby avoid holding client funds in separate IOLTA accounts.

c) They may provide, as stated, that when a shareholder dies, a fiduciary representative of the estate may hold stock in the corporation for a reasonable time during administration of the estate before cashing out the shares and transferring the funds to the heirs.

d) They may not have a plan whereby associates acquire shares merely by working at the firm for a certain number of years and bringing in a certain number of clients.

Rule 5.4(d)(1)

354. A church retains an attorney to challenge a new zoning regulation that would prohibit the church from constructing a new, expanded sanctuary on its property, attached to the existing church. The church cannot afford to pay the attorney, and it is seeking only a declaratory judgment (that the regulation is invalid) rather than money damages. The attorney agrees to take the case and then split any court-awarded legal fees with the church if they prevail. They win a favorable judgment; the court declares the regulation unconstitutional and awards legal fees, which the attorney shares with the church. Is the fee sharing proper?

a) No, because a lawyer or law firm shall not share legal fees with a nonlawyer.

b) No, because the award of legal fees to a church violates the separation of church and state, and a lawyer is under oath to uphold the Constitution.

c) Yes, because a lawyer may share court-awarded legal fees with a nonprofit organization that retains the lawyer in a matter.

d) Yes, assuming the attorney takes only 30% of the legal fees and does not claim a tax deduction for the 70% shared with the church.

RULE 5.5
UNAUTHORIZED PRACTICE OF LAW; MULTIJURISDICTIONAL PRACTICE OF LAW

355. An attorney is a licensed lawyer in a New England state, but has an office and represents clients exclusively in a southern state. The attorney confines her practice to immigration law, representing foreign-born clients in immigration hearings. A relevant federal statute permits nonlawyers to appear as representatives for immigrants when they appear before the immigration agency. Many of the attorney's clients have applied for a spousal visa after marrying an American citizen, and some clients had a Notary Public from their home country or an un-ordained lay minister from their home church conduct their wedding ceremony. In addition, some were previously married and divorced in their home country, where such transactions are informal and have no official documentation. There is often some question about whether the marriage is valid under local state law, which is a prerequisite for obtaining certain types of visas. Which of the following is correct?

a) The attorney's conduct is proper, because she is merely providing services authorized by federal law, which preempts state licensing requirements.

b) The attorney's conduct is proper because she has specialized in immigration law, which is entirely federal and involves no questions of state law.

c) The attorney could be subject to discipline for the unauthorized practice of law in this southern state.

d) The attorney's conduct is improper if she does not file a pro hac vice appearance in each case.

356. A husband and wife are both attorneys in Puerto Rico, though they attended law school in Florida. They have practiced in Puerto Rico for ten years and have a license to practice there. Last year, they moved to Florida, where the wife took the state bar exam and gained admission to the Florida bar. They have now opened a law office in Florida with both of their names listed on the firm letterhead, followed by the phrase "Attorneys at Law." The husband confines his practice exclusively to Puerto Rican clients who are living in Florida or are visiting there; the wife handles all other legal matters. It is proper for them to use such letterhead?

a) Yes, because Puerto Ricans are U.S. Citizens, and they both attended an American law school.

b) Yes, because the husband confines his practice to Puerto Rican immigrants and visitors, whom he would be able to represent if they were back in Puerto Rico.

c) No, because the letterhead reveals that the wife is aiding her husband in the unauthorized practice of law.

d) No, because identifying themselves as law firm partners is misleading, and does not apprise readers to the fact that they are indeed married.

357. An attorney obtained a license to practice law in the state where she attended law school. After a few years, the attorney took a job in a neighboring state, moved there, and obtained a license to practice law in her new state. She kept her original license, in her former state, but went on inactive status there to avoid the burdensome annual bar membership fees in a state where she no longer practiced. Eventually, her new firm loses its anchor clients and recommends that the attorney drum up some new business among her former clients. Then the attorney sends letters to all her former clients in her former state, offering to represent them in any new legal matters they have, or in updating wills or contracts that she previously did for them. She travels about once per week to her home state and meets with clients in a library study room at the law school she attended. A few of her former clients refer her to friends or relatives who become new clients, and the attorney's new employer is thrilled. Which of the following is true?

a) The attorney is subject to discipline for practicing law in her home state while on inactive status, but her supervising lawyer is not subject to discipline because she had a license in that state when he hired her.

b) Neither the attorney nor her supervising lawyer would be subject to discipline, because she merely went on inactive status in the other state, but she still holds her license there.

c) Only the supervising lawyer is subject to discipline, because he encouraged his subordinate to solicit out-of-state clients in a state where he is unlicensed, but the attorney can still practice law there.

d) Both the attorney and her supervising lawyer are subject to discipline because she is on inactive status in her home state but is soliciting clients and handling their matters there regularly.

358. A client retains his attorney, who has represented the client in the past, to represent him in litigation in another state, where the attorney is unlicensed. The matter requires some knowledge of the law of the state where the trial will occur. His attorney files a pro hac vice appearance in the matter, which the local court accepts, and begins preparing for trial there. The attorney and the client never discuss the particulars of filing a pro hac vice appearance; nor did they discuss why it would be necessary. The client never asked if the attorney could practice law in the other jurisdiction, and the attorney never explained the licensing requirement and that he would need permission from the court there to handle the case. Then the attorney prevailed in the matter on behalf of the client, kept his agreed-upon contingent fee, and gave the client the remaining proceeds and unused retainer funds. Which of the following is true?

a) The attorney is subject to discipline for accepting a contingent fee in a proceeding in another state where the attorney does not have a license to practice law.

b) The attorney's conduct was proper, as the court accepted the pro hac vice appearance, and it made no difference to the client whether the attorney had a license to practice there on an ongoing basis or appeared only on a pro hac vice basis.

c) The attorney's conduct was proper, assuming the attorney can acquire the necessary knowledge of local laws with a reasonable amount of study.

d) It was improper for the attorney to fail to disclose to the client that he was unlicensed in the other state and would need to file a pro hac vice appearance, especially given that the matter required some knowledge of local laws.

359. An attorney is a joint owner of a collection agency. Whenever the agency's initial efforts to collect prove unsuccessful, the staff at the agency sends the delinquent debtor a demand letter on the attorney's law firm letterhead, threatening to commence litigation if the matter does not reach a resolution within 30 days. The attorney authorized the staff at the agency to send these demand letters, but the attorney is too busy to review all the letters himself. The collection agency staff signs the letters on behalf of the attorney's firm. Will the attorney be subject to discipline for authorizing these letters?

a) Yes, because the letter contains a specific threat of litigation and the facts do not specify whether the attorney will indeed follow through and file any claims in court.

b) No, because the collection agency has other owners besides the attorney, so it is not necessarily his responsibility to supervise the employees there.

c) No, because the staff at the collection agency are acting on the attorney's behalf with his explicit authorization

d) Yes, because the attorney is merely facilitating the collection agency in the unauthorized practice of law.

360. An attorney hired a second-year law student as a clerk. The law student is unlicensed. The attorney has the law student perform a variety of tasks. Which of the following tasks, if performed by the law student, would mean that the attorney is subject to discipline?

a) Conducting online legal research and writing research memoranda.

b) Drafting a customized retainer agreement for the attorney to use with clients pursuing claims against a government agency

c) Interviewing accident witnesses and potential character witnesses; and asking them to certify the accuracy of the student's written notes.

d) Reaching settlement agreements with insurance companies before the attorney indeed files any lawsuit in the matter.

Rule 5.5(b) & Cmt 2

361. An experienced attorney has an office in State X, and she is duly licensed to practice law in that state. The attorney's office is in a city on the border of State Y, and the attorney does not have a license to practice there. Over the years, some of the attorney's clients have in fact been residents of State Y, and their legal issues sometimes involve research into the laws or judicial precedents of State Y. For the convenience of these clients, and to attract business of other clients there, the attorney rents a small office space, hires nonlawyer clerical staff, and otherwise prepares premises for the general practice of law at a branch-office location in State Y. Apart from the issues raised by opening the new branch office, was it improper for the attorney to represent residents of State Y in her office in State X?

a) Yes, the clients are coming to the attorney in her office in the state where she has a license to practice law.

b) Yes, the Supreme Court has held that the privileges and immunities clause should permit lawyers to practice across state lines.

c) No, the attorney is unlicensed in State Y, so she

should not advise clients on matters that come under the laws of State Y.

d) No, because as a policy matter she is taking clients away from licensed lawyers in State Y.

Restatement § 3 Jurisdictional Scope of the Practice of Law by a Lawyer

362. An experienced attorney has an office in State X, and she is duly licensed to practice law in that state. The attorney's office is in a city on the border of State Y, and the attorney does not have a license to practice there. Over the years, some of the attorney's clients have in fact been residents of State Y, and their legal issues sometimes involve research into the laws or judicial precedents of State Y. For the convenience of these clients, and to attract business of other clients there, the attorney rents a small office space, hires nonlawyer clerical staff, and otherwise prepares premises for the general practice of law at a branch-office location in State Y. Is it permissible for the attorney to open the branch office in State Y?

a) It is permissible because she is doing so primarily for the convenience of clients whom she is already representing in the state where she has a law license.

b) It is impermissible because she does not have a license to practice in State Y and she has established an office or other systematic and continuous presence in this jurisdiction for the practice of law.

c) It is permissible because the Supreme Court has held that the privileges and immunities clause should permit lawyers to practice across state lines.

d) It is impermissible because the new office does not have any lawyers on staff there, and she will not be able to provide competent, diligent representation in two places at the same time.

Restatement § 3

363. An experienced attorney has an office in State X, and she is duly licensed to practice law in that state. The attorney's office is in a city on the border of State Y, and the attorney does not have a license to practice there. The attorney represents a regulated utility, which operates a power plant in State X near the border with State Y. The attorney's representation of the utility mostly pertains to environmental issues, obtaining necessary permits, and complying with federal and state regulations of utilities. Occasionally, the utility also has issues relating to compliance with the environmental and permitting laws of State Y because of those same activities. Is it

permissible for the attorney to travel to State Y to deal with governmental officials regarding regulatory issues arising out of the utility's activities?

a) It is impermissible because the attorney is practicing law without a license in State Y.

b) It is impermissible because if the attorney represents one client in some matters in State Y, she must be available to represent any other within State Y who have the same legal issues there.

c) It is permissible because the legal issues arise out of or relate closely to the attorney's practice in a jurisdiction in which the lawyer is admitted to practice.

d) It is permissible because the Supreme Court has held that the privileges and immunities clause should permit lawyers to practice across state lines.

Restatement § 3

364. An experienced attorney has an office in State X, and she is duly licensed to practice law in that state. The attorney's office is in a city on the border of State Y, and the attorney does not have a license to practice there. The attorney represents a regulated utility, which operates a power plant in State X near the border with State Y. The attorney's original work for the utility in State X related to rate-setting proceedings before a utility commission in that state, and before the Federal Energy Regulatory Commission (FERC). New legislative changes now permit the utility to make retail sales of electricity to consumers in multiple states. Given the attorney's extensive knowledge of the utility's rate-related financial information, the utility asks the attorney to handle its new rate applications in several other states, but in none of these states does the attorney have a license to practice law. The attorney's work in those matters would frequently require her presence for legal activities in each of the other states until the new rate work is complete. Is it permissible for the attorney to conduct those activities in the other states on behalf of the utility?

a) It is impermissible because if the attorney represents one client in some matters in State Y, she must be available to represent any other within State Y who have the same legal issues there.

b) It is impermissible because the attorney is practicing law without a license in State Y.

c) It is permissible because the Supreme Court has held that the privileges and immunities clause should permit lawyers to practice across state lines.

d) It is permissible because the legal issues arise out of or relate to the attorney's practice in a jurisdiction in which the lawyer has a license to practice.

Restatement § 3

RULE 5.6
RESTRICTIONS ON RIGHTS TO PRACTICE

365. An attorney wants to retire from practice due to a chronic illness, and he decides to sell his practice to another lawyer. The sale agreement complies with the Model Rules regarding the sale of a law practice. As part of the sale agreement, however, the attorney stipulates that he will not resume the practice of law in that jurisdiction, even if medical breakthroughs cure his chronic illness and restore him to perfect health. The purchaser of the firm is aware that research for a cure of the attorney's illness is well underway, and he is concerned because it is foreseeable that the attorney would recover and want to return to the practice of law in a few years. Is it proper for the attorney and his buyer to include this provision of the sales agreement for the law firm?
a) Yes, because the rule against restrictions on the right to practice does not apply to the sale of a law practice.
b) No, because a lawyer shall not participate in offering or making an agreement that restricts the right of a lawyer to practice.
c) No, because a lawyer shall not participate in offering or making an agreement in which a restriction on the lawyer's right to practice is part of the settlement.
d) Yes, because the Contracts Clause of the U.S. Constitution would prohibit a state from restricting the right for a lawyer to include certain contract provisions in a sale agreement.

Rule 5.6 Cmt. 3

366. An attorney agrees to join a new firm as one of its shareholders, and to merge his practice with that of the new firm. The shareholder agreement includes a provision that if the attorney retires from the firm and begins collecting the firm's retirement benefits, he cannot practice law with another firm, government entity, or as a solo practitioner. Otherwise, the agreement stipulates, the attorney will forfeit the retirement benefits. The firm is concerned that the attorney will want to represent clients occasionally in

his retirement, and that he may steal some clients from the firm. Is this agreement proper?
a) No, because prohibiting a lawyer from practicing after retiring from the firm is a restriction on the right of the lawyer to practice, in violation of the Model Rules.
b) No, because the intent is to keep the attorney from "poaching" clients, and thus limits the freedom of clients to choose a lawyer.
c) Yes, because the Contracts Clause of the U.S. Constitution would prohibit a state from restricting the right for a lawyer to include certain contract provisions in a sale agreement.
d) Yes, because the rule against restrictions on the right to practice have an exception for agreements concerning benefits upon retirement.

367. Big Bank hires outside counsel to handle its mortgage foreclosure cases against borrowers who are in default. An attorney agrees to handle a matter for Big Bank, but the engagement contract between the attorney and Big Bank specifies that the attorney may not represent clients in the future who have adversarial claims against Big Bank, and that the attorney agrees to disqualification in any case in which Big Bank would be the opposing party in litigation. The attorney recognized that this term would be unenforceable in court, and he accepted the appointment as outside counsel. Were the attorney's actions improper, under the Model Rules of Professional Conduct?
a) Yes, because the attorney has entered into an agreement in which a restriction on the lawyer's right to practice is part of the settlement of a client controversy.
b) Yes, because the attorney has entered into an employment agreement that restricts his right to represent future clients who sue Big Bank or whom Big Bank sues.
c) No, because courts consistently hold such clauses to be unenforceable, so the attorney has not agreed to an actual restriction on his right to practice.
d) No, because this is not an employment agreement with a law firm or partnership, nor is the attorney agreeing to the term to help settle another client's case.

Model Rule 5.6(a); ABA Formal Op. 94-381 (1994)

368. An attorney specializes in helping his business clients obtain business loans from commercial lenders. While assisting one client in obtaining an unusually large commercial loan from Big Bank, the attorney noticed a clause in the loan contract by

which the borrower promised that its attorney would not seek to obtain similar loans for other parties from Big Bank's primary market competitor in that state. The clause required evidence of a contractual agreement by the attorney – whether with Big Bank or with the client – to this effect. The client desperately needed the loan to survive a temporary downturn in its own industry, and the attorney could easily direct future clients to this same lender, Big Bank, to obtain loans on comparable terms to what the competitor bank offered. In fact, most of the attorney's clients ended up getting their financing through Big Bank, and only rarely had the attorney succeeded in securing loans for clients through the competitor. The contract provision seemed harmless to the attorney, though it would be enforceable. Is it proper for the attorney to sign off on these loan documents for this client, including this clause in the contract?

a) Yes, because the attorney has a fiduciary duty to consider the client's best interests before the personal interests of the attorney or the attorney's potential future clients.

b) Yes, because the bank is the party to the contract that includes the provision in question, not the attorney.

c) No, because an attorney must not make an agreement restricting the attorney's right to practice.

d) No, because the provision is clearly an illegal action against the competitor bank.

369. Big Bank routinely hired lawyers as outside counsel on various matters, and it required each one to sign an Outside Counsel Agreement (OCG) as part of its contract of engagement for legal representation. Big Bank's OCG included the following provision:

> Notwithstanding the rules and opinions set forth in ABA or state ethical opinions, regulations, or cases applicable to outside counsel, outside counsel agrees to treat Big Bank and all its subsidiaries as one entity for analyzing conflicts of interest. Big Bank will ordinarily give informed consent, confirmed in writing, to waive conflicts in transactional matters, whenever the bank's interests will not be impaired. For conflicts of interest, Big Bank shall include all organizations and entities delineated in the attached APPENDIX, which Big Bank may amend at any time.

An attorney has an opportunity to work as outside counsel for Big Bank on a specific matter, but she is concerned about this provision. Would it be proper for the attorney to accept this OCG by contractual agreement?

a) Yes, even though the OCG provision goes beyond the requirements of the Model Rules for conflicts screening, lawyers may contractually agree to such limitations on their practice.

b) Yes, because the OCG provision merely reflects the duties already imposed on lawyers by the Model Rules of Professional Conduct and similar state codes.

c) No, because this agreement impermissibly restrains the attorney's right to practice.

d) No, because the entities relevant for conflicts of interest screening must not be subject to change after the representation begins.

https://www.americanbar.org/publications/professional
_lawyer/2016/volume-24-number-
2/the_new_battle_over_conflicts_interest_should.html

370. Conglomerate Corporation routinely hires outside counsel for representation on legal matters, and it requires the lawyers to sign an Outside Counsel Agreement (OCG) that contains the following provision:

> ATTORNEY agrees not to represent any party adverse to CONGLOMERATE CORP., or any entity in the APPENDIX, without prior written consent. In no event may ATTORNEY represent an adverse party against CONGLOMERATE in litigation. The APPENDIX contains a confidential list of entities ATTORNEY must use in screening for conflicts. The APPENDIX includes some entities that may be affiliated with CONGLOMERATE's parent companies, as well as entities that may not be controlled by CNOGLOMERATE or its parent companies, but in which they may have an ownership interest.

Would it be improper for an attorney to enter into this agreement, if it includes this OCG provision?

a) Yes, because the OCG provision creates an impermissible restraint on the attorney's right to practice law.

b) Yes, because attorneys may not enter into any OCG agreements when serving as outside counsel.

c) No, because lawyers are free to include contractual obligations to their clients that go beyond the normal duties found in the Model Rules.

d) No, because the provision merely reflects the duties already set forth in the Model Rules for conflicts of interest.

https://www.americanbar.org/publications/professional_lawyer/2016/volume-24-number-2/the_new_battle_over_conflicts_interest_should.html

371. Conglomerate Corporation offered to hire an attorney as outside counsel for a specific legal matter. Conglomerate's OCG (outside counsel agreement) with all outside lawyers it hires includes the following provision:

> ATTORNEY agrees that it would constitute an impermissible conflict of interest to represent a significant competitor of CONGLOMERATE CORP. or its subsidiaries or affiliates. The APPENDIX attached to this document includes a list of CONGLOMERATE CORP. subsidiaries. Before ATTORNEY'S representation begins, ATTORNEY must disclose in writing the names of any national or regional retailers or any significant competitors of CONGLOMERATE CORP. or its subsidiaries or affiliates that ATTORNEY represents, as well as a general description of the type of representation that ATTORNEY'S firm provides to such client(s).

Is it proper for Conglomerate's in-house counsel to require outside counsel to agree to this provision in the OCG?

a) Yes, even though the OCG provision goes beyond the requirements of the Model Rules for conflicts screening, lawyers may contractually agree to such limitations on their practice.
b) Yes, because the OCG provision merely reflects the duties already imposed on lawyers by the Model Rules of Professional Conduct and similar state codes.
c) No, because only the Board of Directors can request that outside counsel sign an OCG, not in-house counsel.
d) No, because this agreement impermissibly restrains the attorney's right to practice.

https://www.americanbar.org/publications/professional_lawyer/2016/volume-24-number-2/the_new_battle_over_conflicts_interest_should.html

372. An attorney worked as in-house counsel at Conglomerate Corporation. Her employment agreement with Conglomerate Corporation that she would not, following her employment there, represent any client in litigation against Conglomerate. General Counsel for Conglomerate maintained that this was necessary to prevent lawyers who left there from using confidential information they learned during their time at Conglomerate against the company in litigation thereafter. In other words, the contractual provision merely mirrored the duties a lawyer in that situation would have under the conflicts of interest rules. Would this agreement be enforceable, if the attorney left Conglomerate Corporation and then represented a client who had a contract claim against the company?

a) Yes, because the agreement could be binding as a matter of contract law, even if it somehow violated the Model Rules of Professional Conduct.
b) Yes, because the agreement does not restrict the attorney's ability to practice law or represent clients, it merely reflects the conflict of interest rules that prohibit a lawyer from switching sides in litigation.
c) No, the agreement places an impermissible restriction on the attorney's ability to practice law, and it goes beyond the constraints of the conflict of interest rules.
d) No, because the agreement was between two lawyers, and the future client was not a party to the contract.

ABA Formal Op. 94-381 (1994)

373. An attorney worked as in-house counsel at Conglomerate Corporation. Conglomerate had a problem with lawyers who left its legal department to work for its suppliers – the lawyers would contact their friends who still worked for Conglomerate to solicit additional supply contracts, or to negotiate more favorable terms on existing contracts. Worse, the lawyers could also make strategic use of their knowledge of Conglomerate's internal procurement practices (such as the time of year when certain major supplier contracts were up for renewal). General Counsel for Conglomerate started including in its contracts with all new in-house counsel a prohibition on departing lawyers who work for Conglomerate's corporate vendors, either as in-house counsel or with a law firm representing the vendor, from contacting any of Conglomerate's employees. Is this agreement proper, under the Model Rules?

a) Yes, because it does not restrict the departing lawyers' ability to practice law, but merely protects against vendors using unfair competition methods to obtain or manipulate their contracts with Conglomerate.

b) Yes, because it does not restrict the departing lawyers' ability to represent clients who want to sue Conglomerate, or even from working for Conglomerate's major corporate customers.

c) No, because it is overbroad, and interferes with the departing employees' ability to continue their friendships or personal relationships with other employees at Conglomerate, even for non-legal contact.

d) No, the agreement imposes an impermissible restriction on lawyers' ability to practice law.

Pa. Ethics Op. 2012-006 (2012) (corporation requires departing lawyer who becomes affiliated with its vendors to obtain general counsel's consent before communicating with any of corporation's employees).

374. An attorney represented a plaintiff in a claim against Conglomerate Corporation and was remarkably effective in her efforts, mostly because she hired Professor Stevenson as an expert witness. After the deposition of Stevenson, Conglomerate realized they needed to settle the case before trial. Conglomerate offered a very generous settlement to the plaintiff, including the full amount the plaintiff sought as recovery in its pleadings, plus reasonable attorney's fees, and even some additional stock options in Conglomerate Corporation. Conditions of the settlement included a waiver and release of all the plaintiff's claims, including potential claims not part of this lawsuit, and an agreement by the attorney never to use Professor Stevenson again as an expert witness in a case against Conglomerate. The settlement imposed no other restraints on the attorney, and it did not restrain Professor Stevenson from serving as a fact witness (as opposed to expert) in the future. Assume for this question that Professor Stevenson is not a licensed attorney in this jurisdiction. Is this agreement proper, under the Model Rules?

a) Yes, because it did not impose any restraint on the attorney's ability or right to practice law, but merely restricted a non-lawyer expert witness from testifying again against a specific defendant.

b) Yes, because if the client exercised her stock options, the attorney would not be able to represent her in an action against Conglomerate again anyway, due to the conflict of interest rules, rendering moot any other restraints on the attorney's practice of law.

c) No, because even limiting the attorney's ability to use a specific expert witness against this defendant would be an impermissible restriction on the attorney's ability to practice law.

d) No, because the agreement includes a waiver and release of potential claims by the plaintiff that the lawyer has not yet brought, which would be an impermissible restraint on the attorney's freedom to practice law.

Colo. Ethics Op. 92 (1993)

375. An attorney made a lateral move to Small Firm. The managing partner had the attorney sign an employment contract on his first day, which included a provision under which the attorney agreed that upon leaving employment, he would pay his former employer ninety-five percent of any attorney fees earned in a contingent-fee settlement from any Small Firm clients who might follow the attorney when he left. The attorney worked for Small Firm for seven years, then left to start his own practice. Before the attorney left Small Firm, however, he had begun representation of a client who was an accident victim, and the client choose to follow the attorney to his new firm, to continue the representation. The attorney eventually obtained a generous settlement for the client; the attorney's contingent fee was one-third of the award, after deducting fees and expenses. The managing partner immediately notified the attorney that he had a contractual obligation to pay Small Firm ninety-five percent of the fee from the settlement, and notified the defendant's insurer, that it should send its check to Small Firm as the loss payee rather than the attorney's new firm. What is the proper result in this case?

a) The insurer should send the check to the attorney at his new firm as the loss payee, and the attorney should then send his former employer, Small Firm, ninety-five percent of his one-third, after fees and expenses.

b) The insurer should send the check to Small Firm as the loss payee, as Small Firm initiated the claim, and Small Firm should then send disburse two-thirds to the original client, after deducting costs and expenses, and five percent of the remaining one-third to the attorney.

c) The insurer should send the check to the attorney's new firm as loss payee, and the attorney should send no money at all to Small Firm.

d) The insurer should send the check to the client as loss payee, and the client cover outstanding bills for costs and expenses, and then should give ninety-five percent of one third to Small Firm, and the remainder to the attorney.

Hackett v. Moore, 939 N.E.2d 1321 (Ohio 2010) (Employment contracts that require attorneys to give contingent fees to their previous firm when clients follow the attorney to a new firm violate Model Rule 5.6)

376. An attorney brought a class action lawsuit against Conglomerate Corporation and was remarkably effective in her efforts, mostly because she was brilliant about forum shopping. After discovery, Conglomerate realized they needed to settle the case before trial. Conglomerate offered a very generous settlement to the plaintiff class, including the full amount sought as recovery in the pleadings, plus reasonable attorney's fees. Conditions of the settlement included a nondisclosure agreement about the terms of the settlement, and an agreement with this attorney limiting venue and forum options in future cases against Conglomerate brought by non-settling plaintiffs. The settlement imposed no other restraints on the attorney. Assume that the attorney did not care anymore about forum and venue, because she had learned enough about Conglomerate Corporation's activities that she thought she could easily win future cases in any court. Is this agreement proper, under the Model Rules?

a) Yes, because it did not impose any restraint on the attorney's ability or right to practice law, but merely functioned as a forum selection clause in a contract.
b) Yes, because the attorney knew that she could win future cases regardless of the forum or venue.
c) No, because even limiting the attorney's ability to shop for forum or venue in future cases for other plaintiffs would be an impermissible restriction on the attorney's ability to practice law.
d) No, because the plaintiff cannot agree to settlement conditions that might affect other plaintiffs who have not yet settled their claims.

Colo. Ethics Op. 92 (1993)

377. Conglomerate Corporation was a defendant in multidistrict litigation, and a plaintiff's attorney represented many different plaintiffs in these related cases against Conglomerate. The attorney and Conglomerate reached a settlement agreement for one group of claimants. The settlement was generous toward those plaintiffs, but it included an agreement by the attorney to withdraw as counsel from representing the other plaintiffs in related cases who had not yet settled their claims. Is the attorney correct in believing it would be improper to sign this agreement with this group of plaintiffs?

a) Yes, because it creates a nonconsentable conflict of interest between the different plaintiffs the attorney represents.
b) Yes, because the agreement would be an impermissible restriction on the right to practice law.
c) No, but only if the attorney returns any unused portion of the fees those clients have already paid.
d) No, because withdrawing from representing clients whose claims have already gone forward does not constitute a future restriction on the right to practice law.

Ala. Ethics Op. 92-01 (1992)

378. An attorney represented a plaintiff in a wrongful death case arising out of a prison riot, which included many claims and crossclaims. The case ended in settlement. The defendant's settlement offer included two conditions: first, the commonplace requirement that the attorney and client not disclose the amount of the settlement; and second, that the attorney give defendant counsel her entire file to keep under seal, meaning the attorney could not keep copies of her own work product in the case. She would have to turn over her own personal notes and internal memoranda in the file from her interns and associates. Would it be proper for the attorney to agree to this as a condition of a large monetary settlement for her client?

a) Yes, because turning over the file from one completed case places no restrictions on a lawyer's future practice of law.
b) Yes, because it is in the best interest of the client to accept the settlement, and work product from one case would have no value in future unrelated cases.
c) No, because it violates the Model Rules to keep a file under seal.
d) No because forfeiting the attorney's own work product in the case could restrict her future practice of law in similar cases.

N.M. Ethics Op. 1985-5 (1985)

379. An attorney represents a large corporate defendant in a tort action over a defective product line. The current action is the first of what may be many such lawsuits, but the problems with its product line have not received any media attention yet, so the company decides to settle the matter quietly. Recognizing that he has a duty to protect the legal interests of his client, the attorney asks for three conditions in the settlement. First, the plaintiff agrees to a waiver and release of this and any other

claims arising out of the use of this product, at least up to that time. Second, the plaintiff and the attorney must agree not to disclose the settlement amount to anyone. Third, the plaintiff's lawyer must agree not to use any information learned in the current representation in any future representation against the corporate defendant, whether in litigation or transactional matters. The attorney recognizes that there can be no restrictions placed on the lawyers right to practice law, so he does not ask the lawyer to refrain from representing other plaintiffs against the corporation, but only that the information from this case not carry over into other unrelated cases. The attorney also points out to opposing counsel that the conflict of interest rules would already prohibit the attorney from using any information learned in a representation against the client. Similarly, the confidentiality rule forbids the disclosure (without the client's consent) of confidential information learned from any source during the representation. Thus, the condition in the settlement overlaps with other disclosure restraints that the Model Rules impose on the other lawyer. Opposing counsel is a notorious plaintiff's lawyer in that region, receiving frequent reprimanded for ethical violations from the state bar. The lawyer has a reputation for bringing up irrelevant but inflammatory evidence from other cases in his trials, telling the jury, "You wouldn't believe what this same company did to my other client!" It seemed appropriate, therefore, to the attorney for this defendant to ask for settlement conditions that recognize this lawyer's previous bad behavior. Is the attorney correct?

a) Yes, given the other lawyer's history, it is proper to ask for a settlement condition in which he agrees not to use information from this case in other cases.

b) Yes, assuming the client also agrees to this condition, and the condition is not adverse to any legal or financial interest of either party in the case.

c) No, prohibiting the disclosure of the settlement amount functions as an impermissible restriction on the lawyer's right to practice, because he cannot inform other potential plaintiffs about how much they might obtain in their own lawsuits.

d) No, prohibiting the lawyer from using any information learned in the representation is an impermissible restriction on the lawyer's right to practice.

ABA Formal Op. 00-417 (2000);
Chi. Ethics Op. 12-10 (2013)

380. An attorney in a small partnership decided it was time to retire. The partnership agreement had clear provisions for the retirement of partners, in which the partnership would buy out the retirement partner's share, including an hourly prorated amount for work on matters that were still pending and had not yet generated divisible fees. The retirement provisions also provided a substantial pension for the retiring partner, purchase of a single-term life insurance policy, and separate payments from an annuity. A condition of these retirement benefits was that the partner permanently leave the practice of law. Is this condition proper?

a) Yes, because restrictions on the right to practice law are permissible as a condition of retirement benefits.

b) Yes, this condition would be proper even if the attorney was not retiring because partnerships are a special exception to the usual rule against restrictions on the right to practice law.

c) No, because this constitutes an impermissible restriction on the attorney's right to do pro bono cases in his retirement.

d) No, because retirement provisions that force lawyers to leave the practice of law are de facto age discrimination, reducing the number of older, more experienced lawyers from the legal profession.

Model Rule 5.6(a)

381. Conglomerate Corporation has a rule for in its legal department against "side hustles," that is, its lawyers working cases for private clients on the side, even on a pro bono basis. The rule, which it embodied in its employment contract with all the in-house attorneys who work there, became a policy there when General Counsel was targeting a certain employee in the legal department, for purely personal reasons, and needed to create an excuse to fire the lawyer. Is this rule proper?

a) Yes, it is a universally recognized exception to the rule against restrictions on lawyer's right to practice law that corporate legal departments can require that in-house counsel confine their entire practice of law to the organization's legal affairs.

b) Yes, because the employer is not a law firm; it is a regular corporation with a department of in-house counsel.

c) No, because it places an impermissible restriction on the lawyers' right to practice law.

d) No, because it became a policy merely as a pretext for General Counsel to target an individual with whom he had an interpersonal problem.

RESTATEMENT § 13

382. A criminal defendant received a death sentence after his murder conviction. The defendant's attorney, a court-appointed lawyer representing the defendant at state expense, had already been representing the defendant in an earlier manslaughter (noncapital) case, which he was handling on a pro bono basis. In this other manslaughter case, the attorney filed a motion alleging newly discovered evidence of innocence, with a view toward eliminating one of the aggravating factors that was also a justification for the death sentence in the capital case. The state then moved to disqualify the attorney from representing defendant in the capital case, arguing that state-appointed capital counsel could not represent a capital defendant in more than one proceeding at a time. A state statute prohibited state-appointed capital counsel from representing a capital defendant in a noncapital proceeding at state expense. Can the attorney avoid disqualification because he is handling the noncapital case pro bono?

a) Yes, because the state is preparing to execute this individual, so his liability in the other case will soon become moot.

b) Yes, because extending the statute to pro bono representation of the capital defendant in other cases would constitute an impermissible restriction on the right to practice law.

c) No, because the statute clearly applies to what this lawyer is doing.

d) No, because the purpose of the statute is to ensure that capital defendants have their lawyer's undivided attention, so their lawyers should not be working any other cases for any clients.

Melton v. State, 56 So.3d 868, 873 (Fla.App. 2011)

RULE 5.7
RESPONSIBILITIES REGARDING
LAW-RELATED SERVICES

383. An attorney practices corporate securities law in a Wall Street firm. The attorney is also one of three owners of a financial forecasting consulting firm, Trends Tomorrow, which employs several well-known economists and financial analysts. The attorney refers clients to this firm when they need consultants to advise them about the timing of new stock offerings, projections for share price and profit forecasts, and so on. The attorney duly discloses to clients before referring them that she is a part owner of the consulting firm and that they are free to shop around and hire other consultants if they prefer; she also explains that the Trends Tomorrow is not a law firm and provides only financial forecasting services. Trends Tomorrow is in the building next door to the attorney's Wall Street firm, and when clients go there, Trends Tomorrow explains as part of their service contract that they provide no legal services. Eventually, complaints emerge that Trends Tomorrow has been leaking confidential client information to the press, and that the consulting firm has potential conflicts of interest, advising competing clients about strategies to encroach on one another's' market share. The attorney faces disciplinary charges for these violations, but the attorney claims that the complaining clients need to show that the disclosures provided were inadequate to apprise them of the fact that the Rules of Professional Conduct for lawyers would not apply to Trends Tomorrow. Who has the burden of proof on this issue?

a) Clients have the burden of proof to show that the lawyer failed to take reasonable measures to ensure that clients had adequate information about the inapplicability of the Rules of Professional Conduct.

b) Attorney has the burden of proof to show that the lawyer has taken reasonable measures under the circumstances to communicate the desired understanding.

c) The burden is on the disciplinary authority to show that the lawyer failed to take reasonable measures to ensure that clients had adequate information about the inapplicability of the Rules of Professional Conduct.

d) The burden is on the press to show that the lawyer failed to take reasonable measures to ensure that clients had adequate information about the inapplicability of the Rules of Professional Conduct.

384. An attorney developed expertise regarding the area of legal ethics and legal malpractice. Another firm hired the attorney to testify as an expert in an adjudication about the reasonableness of the firm's fees. The attorney has testified as an expert regarding legal fees and legal ethics on several prior occasions. During his cross-examination by the lawyer representing the opposing party, the attorney had to answer questions that forced him to disclose some unfavorable information about the client of the firm that had hired him as an expert. The attorney did not object that the information was confidential or attempt to assert privilege; he answered the questions frankly and objectively. If he had been

representing the client directly, the disclosures would have clearly violated his duty of confidentiality. The answers were a setback to the interests of the party that had hired him, and the lawyers and their client were upset. Could the attorney be subject to discipline for his actions while testifying as an expert witness?

a) Yes, the lawyer had a duty to preserve the confidentiality of the client's information while testifying as an expert, as this is a law-related service.

b) Yes, the lawyer had a client-lawyer relationship with the client while serving as an expert witness, and therefore should have asserted attorney-client privilege.

c) No, a lawyer testifying as an expert is not providing law-related services and does not have a client-lawyer relationship with the party that has hired him.

d) No, a lawyer testifying as an expert is not bound by any of the ethical duties pertaining to the practice of law.

ABA Formal Op. 97-407

385. An attorney works for a firm that handles residential real estate closings. The firm also provides title insurance, as part of the legal representation it offers to clients, but for an additional fee. Nonlawyers also provide title insurance in that state, for comparable prices. A prospective client met with the attorney for an initial consultation about their anticipated purchase of a home. Another client of the attorney's firm had referred the prospective client to the attorney. When the attorney mentioned that the firm would also provide title insurance for an additional fee, the prospective client asked if the person who had referred her to the attorney had obtained title insurance through the firm, and how much they had paid for it. Would it be permissible for the attorney to share this information with the prospective client without first obtaining the other client's consent?

a) Yes, because the duty of confidentiality does not apply to services that a nonlawyer may perform without engaging in the unauthorized practice of law, even if the services relate to legal transactions.

b) Yes, when an existing client of a lawyer or firm refers another prospective client to the same lawyer or firm, the referring client impliedly authorizes the lawyer or firm to disclose confidential information about their representation to the prospective client.

c) No, because it is impermissible in the first place for law firms to provide services that a

nonlawyer could perform without engaging in the unauthorized practice of law.

d) No, because a lawyer is subject to the duty of confidentiality, as well as the other ethical rules, with respect to the provision of law-related services, that are not distinct from the lawyer's provision of legal services to clients.

Rule 5.7(a)(1)

386. An attorney practices commercial real estate law in the state capitol, but also provides legislative lobbying services for some clients, especially for firms seeking lucrative government contracts. For example, working on a retainer, the attorney successfully lobbied his state legislature to privatize most of its prison system, and to give his client the contract to operate the private prisons. His client continues to pay the retainer and the attorney continues to lobby for longer statutory minimum sentences for crimes, so that the private prisons remain full. The attorney uses a separate retainer agreement for lobbying work, which specifies that he is not representing the client as their lawyer, but only as a lobbyist, and is not providing legal advice or legal services under their agreement. Meanwhile, one of the attorney's other clients faces charges of securities fraud and hires the attorney to handle his appeal, which includes arguing that the mandatory minimum sentences are unconstitutional. The criminal defendant signs a written waiver of the potential conflict of interest the attorney has over the mandatory sentencing issue, but the attorney fails to obtain a similar waiver from the private prison client on whose behalf he lobbied for the mandatory sentencing laws. If the attorney is successful in having mandatory sentencing laws declared unconstitutional on behalf of his criminal client, will he be subject to discipline for the conflict of interest with his lobbying client?

a) No, because lobbying is a law-related service that a nonlawyer could do, and is distinct from the lawyer's legal services, according to the retainer, so the conflict of interest rules do not apply.

b) Yes, because he lobbied for people to suffer longer periods of incarceration merely to help his corporate clients earn more profits, which is unconscionable.

c) Yes, because the fact that his legal client signed a waiver of the conflict of interest means that a reciprocal waiver was necessary from the lobbying client.

d) No, because lobbying the legislature receives

special constitutional protection due to its integral part in a functioning democracy.

387. An attorney has expertise in launching new businesses. His undergraduate major was entrepreneurship, and he has numerous connections among investment bankers, and venture capitalists in the area. Entrepreneurs seek him out to incorporate their new businesses and help them find loans and equity investors for startup. The attorney drafts articles of incorporation and bylaws. He handles name registration with the Secretary of State, arranges meetings with local commercial bankers and investors, and helps write business plans and market analysis in anticipation of these meetings. Which of the following is true regarding the attorney's activities?

a) Both the legal services (incorporating) and the law-related related services (writing business plans and arranging investor meetings) would be subject to the requirements of the Rules of Professional Conduct.

b) It is improper for the attorney to provide both the legal services and the law-related services.

c) The legal services (incorporating) would be subject to the requirements of the Rules of Professional Conduct, but the law-related related services (writing business plans and arranging investor meetings) are not subject to the Rules.

d) Only the law-related related services (writing business plans and arranging investor meetings would be subject to the requirements of the Rules of Professional Conduct, and not the legal services (incorporating).

146

RULE 8.1
BAR ADMISSION AND
DISCIPLINARY MATTERS

388. An attorney agreed to write a recommendation letter for admission to the bar on behalf of the law student who had worked for him part-time throughout law school. The student had consistently behaved appropriately during her employment, in compliance with the ethical rules for lawyers and law firms. On one occasion, the student intern had confided in the attorney that she had faced academic discipline for plagiarism on a law school seminar paper, and that she was very ashamed of herself about the incident and had accepted a failing grade in the class. She took an overload of courses the following semester to make up for the lost credits from the course she failed. The attorney did not mention this incident at all in his "character and fitness" recommendation to the state bar, because he felt it was out of character and did not represent the way the student normally behaved at the workplace. He also assumed the student would report it herself or that the bar would inquire about the failing grade on her law school transcript. The bar admissions board eventually learned about the incident only from the law school administration, which turned over the student's disciplinary records. Could the attorney who wrote the favorable recommendation be subject to discipline for filing to mention or address the incident?

a) Yes, because the attorney had a conflict of interest in the situation, as it would be in his best interest for his own employee to gain admission to the bar.

b) Yes, because he did not disclose a fact necessary to correct a misapprehension known by the person to have arisen in the matter in connection with an admission to the state bar.

c) No, because the attorney had no duty to report the incident, given that the bar could easily discover it from another source (as it did), and because the attorney was reasonable in believing the incident did not reflect the true character of the applicant.

d) No, because the student intern had told him about the incident in confidence, and it did not relate to her work at the firm, so the attorney had a duty of confidentiality under Rule 1.6.

389. An attorney faced a grievance over a client complaint regarding his neglect of the client's matter. The attorney knew that he had never formally agreed to represent the client, but instead had met with the client once, determined that he had a conflict of interest, and he had refused to represent the potential client by both oral and written communication. The client failed to hire another lawyer, and mistakenly (unreasonably) believed that the attorney she had met with was, in fact, representing her. Because he knew the case was without merit, he did not respond to the state bar when the disciplinary authorities requested a formal response from him. In the end, the client withdrew her complaint and the disciplinary authorities dismissed the grievance as frivolous. The board then commenced disciplinary proceedings against the attorney for failing to respond to its requests in the case it had dismissed. Was the attorney's refusal to respond permissible in this case?

a) Yes, because he knew the case was without merit as he had never agreed to represent the complainant, and the board's determination vindicated him in this regard.

b) Yes, because it was improper for the board to commence new proceedings that it based on prior proceedings that it had dismissed for being without merit.

c) No, every lawyer has the right to refuse to answer, according to the Fifth Amendment.

d) No, because in connection with a disciplinary matter, a lawyer must not knowingly fail to respond to a lawful demand for information from an admissions or disciplinary authority.

Rule 8.1(b)

390. An attorney agreed to represent an applicant to the state bar – a recent law school graduate – in her hearing before the state bar admissions board, which had tentatively denied her application for making false statements on her bar application. The board formally requests the applicant and her attorney make full disclosures about the events in question to help resolve the matter. The client (bar applicant) explains the entire situation to her attorney, including some self-incriminatory information – it turned out that the applicant's misbehavior had been much more serious than the board was aware. The attorney did not disclose this latest information, which would have made it much clearer to the

board that the applicant lacked the character and fitness to practice law. Could the attorney be subject to discipline for this action?

a) Yes, because a lawyer in connection with a bar admission application or in connection with a disciplinary matter, shall not fail to disclose a fact necessary to correct a misapprehension known by the person to have arisen in the matter, or knowingly fail to respond to a lawful demand for information from an admissions or disciplinary authority.

b) Yes, because the lawyer knows that the applicant indeed lacks the requisite integrity to be a lawyer.

c) No, because a lawyer representing an applicant for admission to the bar, or a subject of a disciplinary action, comes under the rules applicable to the client-lawyer relationship, including the duty of confidentiality.

d) No, because the state bar cannot ask other attorneys to disclose unfavorable information about third party applicants.

Rule 8.1 Cmt. 3

391. An attorney faced a disciplinary action over accusations that she had neglected a client matter and had not communicated enough with the client. The state disciplinary authority requested a written account of her version of what happened, and it asked her ten or twelve probing questions during the hearing. At the conclusion of the hearing, the disciplinary tribunal decided that the client complaint was without merit and cleared the attorney of all charges in that regard. At the same time, it also concluded that the attorney had answered one question during the hearing untruthfully, and that she had made a minor misrepresentation regarding dates in her written statement to the board. The tribunal therefore filed a separate grievance against the attorney for these misrepresentations. Could the attorney be subject to discipline for incidental misrepresentations to the grievance committee if the same committee had decided that the underlying case had no merit and issued a dismissal?

a) Yes, because it is a separate professional offense for a lawyer to knowingly make a misrepresentation or omission in connection with a disciplinary investigation of the lawyer's own conduct.

b) Yes, because her the dismissal of the original complaint may have been in

reliance upon some of her false statements, making it seem that the original complaint was potentially valid as well.

c) No, because the board lacks jurisdiction to commence disciplinary proceedings when there is not a client complaint pending.

d) No, because the misstatements were part of a proceeding that has ended in a complete dismissal.

Rule 8.1 Cmt. 1

392. An attorney faced disciplinary action over a client grievance. The disciplinary tribunal asked the attorney several probing questions about her handling of client funds. The attorney had, in fact, used some client funds to pay off a gambling debt, so she was less worried about a temporary suspension of her law license than about potential criminal charges for embezzlement. The attorney, therefore, invokes her Fifth Amendment privilege against self-incrimination and refuses to answer the questions. The disciplinary tribunal then determines that it lacks substantial evidence that the attorney mishandled client funds, but it commences disciplinary proceedings over the attorney's refusal to answer some of its questions. Could the attorney be subject to discipline for refusing to answer the questions in this scenario?

a) Yes, because a lawyer must not knowingly fail to respond to a lawful demand for information from an admissions or disciplinary authority.

b) Yes, because the board found no evidence that the attorney had mishandled client funds, and the attorney had an affirmative duty to clarify any misunderstanding on the part of the admissions or disciplinary authority of which the person involved becomes aware.

c) No, because the rules requiring attorney candor to disciplinary authorities are subject to the provisions of the Fifth Amendment of the United States Constitution and corresponding provisions of state constitutions.

d) No, because the committee did not read the attorney her Miranda rights, according to this fact scenario.

Rule 8.1 Cmt. 2

393. An attorney faced disciplinary action over a client grievance. The disciplinary tribunal asked the attorney several probing questions about her handling of client funds. The attorney had, in fact, used some client funds to pay off a gambling debt, so she felt less worried about a temporary suspension of her law license than about potential criminal charges for embezzlement. The attorney, therefore, simply refuses to answer the questions, without offering any explanation. The disciplinary tribunal then determines that it lacks substantial evidence that the attorney mishandled client funds, but it commences disciplinary proceedings over the attorney's refusal to answer some of its questions. The attorney now claims she was merely exercising her Fifth Amendment right to refrain from self-incriminating statements. Could the attorney be subject to discipline for refusing to answer the questions in this scenario?

a) Yes, because a lawyer can never refuse to respond to a lawful demand for information from an admissions or disciplinary authority.

b) Yes, a person relying on such constitution protections in response to a question must do so openly and not use the right of nondisclosure as a justification afterward for failure to comply with the rules requiring disclosures to the disciplinary authorities.

c) No, because the rules requiring attorney candor to disciplinary authorities are subject to the provisions of the Fifth Amendment of the United States Constitution and corresponding provisions of state constitutions.

d) No, because the committee did not read the attorney her <u>Miranda</u> rights, according to this fact scenario.

Rule 8.1 Cmt. 2

RULE 8.2
JUDICIAL AND LEGAL OFFICIALS

394. A criminal defense attorney was angry at the local prosecutor for pushing forward with a certain matter against one of the attorney's clients. In a state of frustration, the attorney penned a letter to state officials responsible for overseeing the local prosecutors, in which he accused the prosecutor in his case of specific instances of witness tampering, destruction of evidence, and framing innocent victims for crimes they did not commit. The attorney based these allegations solely on inferences that she had drawn from the unfavorable situation with her own case, and some rumors circulating among inmates in the county jail. Could the attorney be subject to discipline for sending this letter?

a) Yes, a lawyer shall not make a statement that the lawyer knows to be false, or with reckless disregard as to its truth or falsity, concerning the integrity of a public legal officer.

b) Yes, prosecutors have absolute prosecutorial discretion and immunity, so even if the allegations were true, there was no point in raising them in a complaint.

c) No, the attorney was exercising her First Amendment right of free speech, and these were not false statements made to a tribunal during a proceeding.

d) No, the attorney had some basis for inferring these things, so she did not know for certain that the accusations were false.

Iowa Supreme Court Att'y Disciplinary Bd. v. Kennedy, 837 N.W.2d 659 (Iowa 2013);
Rule 8.2(a); In re Wells, 36 So. 3d 198 (La. 2010)

395. A district attorney had a dispute with certain judges in the criminal court in his locale. At one point, the district attorney held a press conference at which he criticized the judges, blaming the large backlog of pending criminal cases on these judges' inefficiency, poor work ethic, and excessive vacations. He went further and mentioned that he would not authorize court funds for DNA testing during police undercover investigations, which hindered the enforcement of vice laws. In conclusion, he said, "All this raises questions about racketeer influences on our lazy judges." The district attorney did not have a reasonable belief that all these statements were true, but at the same time, he was not acting

with reckless disregard with the truth. He believed what he said, but he was not entirely reasonable in his belief. Was it permissible for the district attorney to make these statements?

a) Yes, because prosecutors have wide prosecutorial discretion and immunity.

b) Yes, if indeed the district attorney did not make the statements with reckless disregard for their truth or falsity.

c) No, if indeed the district attorney did not have actual knowledge and reasonable certainty that these statements were true and accurate.

d) No, attorneys much not engage in public criticism of judges or make public statements that undermine the integrity or credibility of the judiciary.

Garrison v. Louisiana, 379 U.S. 64 (1964)(very important decision in this area); Rule 8.2(a)

396. A criminal defense attorney received a court appointment to represent a defendant, and at the end of the representation, she sought compensation for her legal fees from the appropriate courthouse office. Unfortunately, she did not have some of the receipts and documentation to verify some of her fees, so she received only half of the compensation she expected. Angered by this incident, the attorney sent a letter to the judge's secretary, in which he harshly criticized that local court's administrative system for compensating appointed counsel. The letter declared that he would not submit the additional documentation required for compensation, even if that meant he could no longer accept court appointments from the judges in that courthouse. An objective reader would have thought the letter "exhibited unlawyerlike rudeness," as one of the judges at the courthouse put it. Could the attorney be subject to suspension of his law license for sending this letter?

a) Yes, it is impermissible for a lawyer to make statements attacking the integrity or qualifications of a judge or court official.

b) Yes, a lawyer may not decline judicial appointments to represent criminal defendants due merely to compensation grievances.

c) No, even though the bar has a right to place restrictions on lawyer speech, the complaints here would be permissible under the Model Rules and First Amendment jurisprudence.

d) No, it would violate the First Amendment for a state bar or judiciary to punish lawyers for the exercise of their free speech.

In re Snyder, 472 U.S. 634 (1985)); Rule 8.2(a)

397. An attorney was running for judicial office. On her campaign website, she referred to herself as "Madame Justice," and depicted herself in traditional judicial robes, even though she had never held judicial office before. The statement and photo were impermissible under the state judicial code, but she was not yet a judge, and it did not violate the regular attorney advertising rules, as she was not soliciting or appealing to potential clients for her legal practice through the campaign website. Was it permissible for the attorney to include these statements and photos on her campaign website while running for judicial office?

a) Yes, the code of judicial conduct did not yet apply to her if she was not yet a judge.

b) Yes, if indeed attorney advertising rules were inapplicable to this website.

c) No, because her statements undermine the integrity of the judiciary with a reckless disregard for the truth.

d) No, a lawyer who is a candidate for judicial office shall comply with the applicable provisions of the Code of Judicial Conduct.

Rule 8.2(b); N.C. State Bar v. Hunter, 696 S.E.2d 201 (N.C. Ct. App. 2010)

398. An attorney was upset when he lost a high-stakes bench trial. When friends and acquaintances asked him about it in the following weeks, he would bitterly complain that the judge must have received a bribe from the opposing party, because there was no way that a reasonable judge could have ruled against the attorney's own client, given the evidence in the case. The attorney has no reason to think that the judge accepted a bribe except that he was shocked when he lost the case. Could the attorney be subject to discipline for making such comments?

a) Yes, because a lawyer shall not make a statement that the lawyer knows to be false or with reckless disregard as to its truth or falsity concerning the qualifications or integrity of a judge.

b) Yes, but only if the attorney makes the statements in the public media, that is, to a reporter or in a press release.

c) No, because the First Amendment protects the attorney's right to free speech, and these are merely complaints made to friends and acquaintances.

d) No, because such comments implicate slander or libel doctrine in tort law, rather than disciplinary actions by a state bar.

Rule 8.2(a)

399. In Texas, state trial judges are elected by popular vote. A well-known liberal-progressive judge is running for reelection. An attorney who is a staunch conservative is campaigning for the opposing candidate from the other party. At a campaign rally, the attorney declares that the liberal judge (seeking reelection) is completely unqualified and incompetent to serve in the judiciary, and that he is an activist judge who uses his court to push a certain political and social agenda. The judge graduated from a prestigious law school, was formerly a partner at a large law firm, and is active in the state bar. He does, however, give consistently lenient sentences to criminal defendants who are black or Hispanic, and has always ruled in favor of unions when adjudicating cases involving collective bargaining agreements. The judge learns of these remarks by the attorney and files a grievance. Could the attorney be subject to discipline?

a) Yes, because the judge is doing the right thing and conservatives like the attorney in this case are criticizing officials merely for upholding civil liberties and seeking justice and equality.

b) Yes, because a lawyer shall not make a statement that the lawyer knows to be false or with reckless disregard as to its truth or falsity concerning the qualifications or integrity of a judge.

c) No, because the comments occurred in the context of a political campaign, where speakers regularly resort to overstatement and soaring rhetoric.

d) No, because the claims are obviously true.

Rule 8.2(a)

400. A would-be judge asked his former law school classmate, a practicing lawyer, to write a recommendation letter for him as part of his application and vetting process for a judicial appointment. The attorney obliged and wrote a glowing recommendation, entirely favorable, even though he personally knew that his friend (the one seeking to be a judge) was an alcoholic. Was is proper for the attorney to write such a letter?

a) Yes, assuming the attorney believes his friend will be a fair judge.

b) Yes, because the attorney has no duty to disclose confidential information he knows about a friend.

c) No, because assessments by lawyers are relied on in evaluating the professional or personal fitness of persons under consideration for appointment to judicial office, so expressing honest and candid opinions on such matters contributes to improving the administration of justice.

d) No, because an attorney should not write a recommendation letter for a prospective judge if there is any chance that the attorney will someday appear in that judge's court representing a client.

Rule 8.2 Cmt. 1

401. Which of the following is true regarding Model Rule 8.2?

a) Unlike defamation cases, which use a subjective test for intent, disciplinary cases for violations of Rule 8.2 use an objective test to assess the lawyer's mental state as to whether the lawyer knew the statement was false or recklessly disregarded its falsity.

b) Reckless disregard as to falsity therefore means essentially the same thing in discipline as it does in public-official libel and slander cases.

c) A lawyer's subjective belief that the statements are true could be a defense in the context of disciplinary proceedings for violations of Rule 8.2.

d) "Reckless disregard as to falsity or truthfulness" does not mean the lawyer has a duty to verify suspicions before making allegations against a judge.

402. An attorney was running for a judicial office, a seat on the county court. She drafted, signed, and mailed a fundraising letter in her own name to local voters announcing her candidacy and asking for campaign contributions. The fundraising letter was typical, would normally have been legal if the attorney were running for the legislature or an executive branch office. The state's code of judicial conduct, however, forbid judges from engaging in direct fundraising. The state bar disciplinary authority brought a grievance against the attorney for violating the judicial code. The attorney objected that she was not yet a judge, but was merely seeking judicial office, and the code itself purports only to regulate the conduct of judges. In other words, she contends the judicial code does not apply to lawyers. Is the attorney correct?

a) Yes, judicial codes hold judges to a much higher standard than would apply to practicing lawyers.

b) Yes; moreover, the judicial code restraint on fundraising by judges violates the First Amendment guarantees of free speech.

c) No, if some of the voters receiving the letter are the attorney's clients or prospective clients, this would constitute solicitation of a substantial gift from a client, in violation of Rule 1.8.

d) No, a lawyer who is a candidate for judicial office shall comply with the applicable provisions of the Code of Judicial Conduct.

> Williams-Yulee v. Florida Bar, 135 S. Ct. 1656 (2015); Rule 8.2(b)

403. Which of the following statements, made publicly by an attorney, would violate Model Rule 8.2?

a) A lawyer accused a judge of anti-Semitism, for which the lawyer had adequate factual support and documentation.[5]

b) A lawyer speculated to a reporter that a judge was "not being honest about the reasons why he committed [a defendant] to the Department of Corrections"[6]

c) A lawyer referred to a judge as "dishonorable" and a "brainless coward"[7]

d) A lawyer criticized a judge's ruling by saying it was "incoherent" and "wrongly decided."[8]

404. Which of the following statements, made publicly by an attorney, would be impermissible under Model Rule 8.2?

a) A lawyer's motion for new trial claiming judge's gestures and expressions demonstrated bias[9]

b) A lawyer's statements that judges in his state were "not learned in the law" and were "laughed at" throughout country[10]

c) A lawyer's statement implying the judge must have been thinking primarily about the political ramifications of his ruling[11]

d) A lawyer's letter stating that the way in which the legislative ethics commission conducted its proceedings "gave cause for some to speculate that the deck was stacked," when the lawyer had factual evidence to support the accusation. [12]

RULE 8.3
REPORTING PROFESSIONAL MISCONDUCT

405. An attorney worked with a partner who developed a chronic debilitating medical condition. Eventually, the condition materially impaired the partner's ability to practice law, but the partner could not cope with giving up on her career, and she kept practicing. She began to miss court deadlines, to forget to make certain filings to complete transactions, and not to follow through to perform agreed-upon tasks. Under Model Rule 1.16, the partner had a duty to decline or withdraw from representation for clients, at least for the more challenging tasks. On the other hand, up to now no clients had suffered serious prejudice to their legal interests or claims because of these mistakes. Does the attorney who observes these developments have

[5] Standing Comm. on Discipline v. Yagman, 55 F.3d 1430 (9th Cir. 1995).

[6] Iowa Supreme Court Att'y Disciplinary Bd. v. Weaver, 750 N.W.2d 71 (Iowa 2008).

[7] In re Oladiran, 2010 WL 3775074, 2010 BL 223466 (D. Ariz. Sept. 21, 2010)

[8] In re Green, 11 P.3d 1078 (Colo. 2000).

[9] United States v. Brown, 72 F.3d 25 (5th Cir. 1995)

[10] Grievance Adm'r v. Fieger, No. 94-186-GA, Mich. Att'y Disciplinary Bd. (Sept. 2, 1997)

[11] State Bar v. Topp, 925 P.2d 1113 (Idaho 1996)

[12] Berry v. Schmitt, 688 F.3d 290 (6th Cir. 2012)

a duty to report her partner for misconduct under Rule 8.3?
a) Yes, all violations of the Model Rules are reportable events under Rule 8.3.
b) Yes, the partner's lack of fitness has evidenced itself through a pattern of conduct that makes clear the lawyer is not meeting her obligations under the Model Rules.
c) No, mandatory reporting under Rule 8.3 pertains to the attorney's honesty, trustworthiness, and character in other respects.
d) No, Rule 8.3 makes reporting on one's partners only advisory, not mandatory.

ABA Formal Op. 03-431

406. An attorney practiced as in-house counsel within Conglomerate Corporation. She learned of serious ethical misconduct there by a fellow employee who was also a licensed lawyer, but who was employed by the Conglomerate in a nonlegal position as a technical writer. Conglomerate does not have any liability or legal responsibility for the employee's misconduct, so the attorney is not approaching it as a liability concern for her corporate client. Would it be permissible for the attorney to refrain from reporting the employee's misconduct to the bar?
a) Yes, because the fellow employee is not working as a lawyer or practicing law.
b) Yes, these facts suggest that the misconduct took place outside the scope of the employee's duties at Conglomerate, and the attorney's duty is to her client, the corporation.
c) No, if a lawyer knows of professional misconduct of another licensed lawyer, even a non-practicing lawyer, must report it where it raises a substantial question as to that lawyer's honesty, trustworthiness, or fitness as a lawyer.
d) No, all violations of the Model Rules are reportable events under Rule 8.3.

ABA Formal Op. 04-433; Rule 8.3

407. A law professor has a tenured faculty position at her institution. She learns of serious ethical misconduct by another law professor on her faculty who is a licensed lawyer in that state, but who engages exclusively in law teaching. The professor who learned of the problem believes she has no duty to report her colleague to the bar, as neither of them are practicing law, though both have law licenses. Is she correct?

a) Yes, the duty to report misconduct does not apply to academic settings, which have their own disciplinary procedures.
b) Yes, the fact that neither the wrongdoer nor the potential reporter are practicing law makes the mandatory reporting rule inapplicable.
c) No, all violations of the Model Rules are reportable events under Rule 8.3.
d) No, if a lawyer knows of professional misconduct of another licensed lawyer, even a non-practicing lawyer, must report it where it raises a substantial question as to that lawyer's honesty, trustworthiness, or fitness as a lawyer.

ABA Formal Op. 04-433; Rule 8.3

408. An attorney discovers that a partner at his own firm has violated the Rules of Professional Conduct by failing to disclose adverse binding precedent to a tribunal, and by depositing client funds into his own bank account instead of a client trust account. Does the attorney have a duty to report the partner from his own firm to the state bar disciplinary authority?
a) Yes, but he must make an anonymous complaint to the state bar.
b) Yes, because a lawyer who knows of a violation of the Rules that raises serious questions about the other attorney's honesty must report it to the state disciplinary authority.
c) No, because lawyers do not have to report violations or misconduct by their own superiors, as this would put the reporting attorney in a difficult position at his workplace.
d) No, because a lawyer does not have to report violations, but instead is merely permitted to do so.

Rule 8.3

409. An attorney discovers that another lawyer has been stealing clients' funds, but he cannot prove it, as he learned about it from another party who was involved and who has since disappeared. He has some evidence, but not enough to prove that the other lawyer stole the clients' funds. When he confronted the other lawyer, the other lawyer admitted it privately but said he would deny it if there was any attempt to expose the matter. Does the attorney who knows about the violation, but was unlikely to be able to prove it, have a duty to report the violation to the state disciplinary authority?

a) No, because if the lawyer cannot prove the misconduct with a preponderance of evidence, he does not have "knowledge" of the misconduct for purposes of the Rules of Professional Conduct.

b) No, because the duty to report depends on the quantum of proof of which the lawyer is aware, not the seriousness of the potential offense.

c) Yes, because it does not matter how serious the misconduct is, it merely matters that there is some evidence of misconduct.

d) Yes, because the duty to report misconduct depends upon the seriousness of the potential offense and not the quantum of evidence of which the lawyer is aware.

Rule 8.3 Cmt. 3

RULE 8.4   MISCONDUCT

410. An attorney represented criminal defendants, and he received court appointments for indigent defendants. Some of the court appointments he received were female clients. The attorney had a crude sense of humor and progressive views about sexuality, and he often made crude sexual jokes to his female clients, complimented them on their bodies, and half-jokingly made sexual advances or requested sexual favors. The clients normally brushed off these comments, even though they later reported that they felt uncomfortable. None of the clients complained to the court or filed charges with the police for harassment. Could the attorney be subject to disciple and face suspension for these comments and jokes?

a) Yes, because indigent defendants who receive a court-appointed lawyer are likely to resent inappropriate humor from their lawyer.

b) Yes, because these comments can constitute sexual harassment and could be prejudicial to the administration of justice.

c) No, because the Model Rules forbid actual sexual relationships with clients, but not sexual joking or suggestive comments.

d) No, because the clients were not upset enough to complain to the court or the police about the comments.

In re Moothart, 860 N.W.2d 598 (2015)

411. A prosecutor was bringing charges against a defendant charged with serious domestic violence. When he met the defendant's victim-girlfriend at the courthouse, she volunteered personal information to the prosecutor in addition to recounting the details of the incident – she explained that she had now had no boyfriend, that she was a struggling single mother, and that she had moved back in with her own parents. The prosecutor and the victim exchanged phone numbers, and he subsequently sent the victim several text messages, the first saying he wished the victim was not a "client" of his office, because "she would be a cool person to know." The next day, he texted her asking, "Are you the kind of girl that likes secret contact with an older married elected DA ... the riskier the better? Or do you want to stop right now before we have issues?" Two days later, he texted again, telling her that she was "pretty" and "beautiful." Then he added: "I'm the attorney. I have the $350,000 house. I have the 6-figure career. You may be the tall, young, hot nymph, but I am the prize! Start convincing! I would not expect you to be the other woman. I would want you to be so hot and treat me so well that you'd be THE woman. R U that good?" Could the prosecutor be subject to suspension of his license for these texts?

a) No, because the woman was not his client, as prosecutors represent the state, but merely a witness in a case.

b) No, because these were merely expressions of romantic interest, not coercion or physical contact.

c) Yes, because prosecutors have special duties to avoid the appearance of bad intentions.

d) Yes, because the texts constitute sexual harassment of the victim.

In re Kratz, 851 N.W.2d 219 (Wis. 2014)

412. An attorney represented a small business owner in litigation against a former employee, who was a Canadian immigrant. During the bench trial, the attorney cross-examined the former employee on the witness stand, and after two of her answers turned to the judge and asked, "Are you going to believe an alien or a U.S. Citizen?" Could the attorney be subject to suspension for these comments?

a) No, because this is a bench trial, and there is less risk of the attorney's inflammatory rhetoric being prejudicial to the outcome of the trial.

b) No, because citizenship is a valid, though not dispositive, consideration when evaluating a witness's reliability and truthfulness.

c) Yes, because the attorney questioned the credibility of a witness during her cross-examination, rather than during closing argument.

d) Yes, because this is discrimination based on national origin.

In re McGrath, 280 P.3d 1091 (Wash. 2012)

413. An attorney represented a father at a child support modification hearing before a judge. During the hearing, the attorney made repeated disparaging references to the facts that the mother was indigent and was receiving legal services at no charge. Could the attorney be subject to a public reprimand for these comments?

a) Yes, because discrimination against persons based on their source of income or acceptance of free or low-cost legal services would be examples of discrimination based on socioeconomic status.

b) Yes, because the attorney should know that these comments are immaterial to the legal issues in the case.

c) No, because child support modifications depend largely on the court's findings about the relative incomes and living expenses of the parties, and if the opposing party has access to a free lawyer, that is a valid consideration in the court's decision.

d) No, because discrimination requires actual harm, such as termination of employment, exclusion from public places, and so on.

In re Campiti, 937 N.E.2d 340 (Ind. 2009)

414. An attorney settled a legal malpractice claim by agreeing to make monthly payments to the former client for five years, which would add up to the full settlement amount. The attorney put forth his car as security for the obligation. After making a few of the monthly payments, the attorney left the jurisdiction with his car, leaving no forwarding address, so the former client (who was now a holder of the security interest in the car) could not locate the attorney or the car for more than one year. The state criminal code provides that it is a class 5 felony to conceal property in which there is a security interest. The attorney never faced criminal charges or arrest, but the state bar received a complaint about the matter and commenced disbarment proceedings against the attorney. Can the attorney face disbarment over a crime for which there were never any charges filed?

a) Yes, the fact that the respondent has not been criminally charged or convicted of this offense is not important for purposes of lawyer discipline.

b) Yes, because the state bar has inherent authority to revoke a lawyer's license at any time, for any reason.

c) No, because the lawyer has a presumption of innocence until proven guilty if the ethical complaint pertains to criminal activity.

d) No, because the courts are a more appropriate forum for addressing this kind of conduct, rather than a state bar administrative hearing.

People v. Odom, 941 P.2d 919 (Colo. 1997)

415. Big Firm engages in aggressive affirmative action in its hiring. It runs ads soliciting applications from minorities and women, and even though they sometimes interview non-minority applicants, they have decided internally to hire only women and minorities for the next five years. Currently, anti-discrimination laws would not require such a practice. Has the firm violated the MRPC?

a) Yes, the firm is practicing discrimination in its hiring by favoring minorities and women over others

b) Yes, substantive law of antidiscrimination absolutely forbids interviewing candidates and then not hiring them based on race or gender.

c) No, the Model Rules do not apply to hiring practices or other law firm management matters.

d) No, lawyers may implement initiatives aimed at recruiting, hiring, retaining, and advancing diverse employees without violating the Model Rules.

Rule 8.4 Cmt. 4

416. An attorney owns his own law practice, and he represents clients if he believes in their cause. He regularly defends racists and hate groups against criminal charges and lawsuits, because he shares their philosophy and identifies with their racist views. Is it permissible for the attorney to advocate on behalf of racists and hate groups in litigation, if he supports their cause on a personal level?

a) Yes, the rules prohibiting discrimination and harassment by lawyers not preclude legitimate advice or advocacy the lawyer

provides to clients who are openly engaging in such conduct.
b) Yes, the lawyer has a First Amendment right to express racist or discriminatory views in public.
c) No, a lawyer must not engage in conduct that is harassment or discrimination based on race in conduct related to the practice of law.
d) No, the rules prohibiting discrimination and harassment by lawyers apply to the advice or advocacy the lawyer provides to clients who are openly engaging in such conduct, if the lawyer supports the client's views.

Rule 8.4(g)

417. An attorney faced prosecution for failing to file tax returns over a five-year period. The attorney worked for a legal aid clinic and never charged clients any legal fees, as the clinic provided free representation to the indigent. The attorney received a modest salary from the legal aid clinic, the funds for which came from the state's IOLTA program and from a federal Legal Services Corporation (LSC) grant. Could the attorney face suspension of his license to practice law?
a) Yes, because the attorney's salary comes from a commingling of state IOLTA funds and federal LSC funds.
b) Yes, because it is professional misconduct for a lawyer to commit a criminal act that reflects adversely on the lawyer's honesty.
c) No, because the attorney's illegal conduct did not pertain to his representation of any of his clients.
d) No, because none of the attorney's income derived from legal fees collected from clients.

Rule 8.4(b) & Cmt. 2

418. An attorney was an immigrant from a country that permits polygamy – men can have up to four wives. The attorney had two wives, which his religion permitted, as did the laws of his homeland. Nevertheless, his multiple marriages constituted bigamy in the American jurisdiction where he practiced law, and eventually a court convicted him of bigamy and imposed a fine. Could the attorney be subject to professional discipline for committing this illegal act?

a) Yes, because it is professional misconduct for a lawyer to commit a criminal act that reflects adversely on the lawyer's honesty.
b) Yes, because having multiple wives significantly increases the opportunities to have conflicts of interest with various clients.
c) No, because offenses concerning personal morality, such as bigamy and comparable offenses, have no specific connection to fitness for the practice of law.
d) No, because his bigamy does not reflect negatively on his character or morality if his religion permits it.

Rule 8.4 Cmt. 2

419. After practicing for two years, an attorney enrolled in an LL.M. program at a local law school, taking night classes. During his second semester, the attorney faced academic discipline for plagiarism in a seminar paper; the school permitted him to graduate, but he received a failing grade in the class and had to make up the credits with another course. As the attorney already has a license to practice law in the jurisdiction, could he be subject to discipline if the state disciplinary authorities learned of the plagiarism?
a) Yes, because it is professional misconduct for a lawyer to commit a criminal act that reflects adversely on the lawyer's honesty.
b) Yes, because it is professional misconduct for an attorney to engage in conduct involving dishonesty, fraud, deceit, or misrepresentation.
c) No, because the attorney already obtained admission to the bar, so his courses now have no bearing on his application for admission to the bar.
d) No, because the incident does not pertain to his representation of a client, so the disciplinary rules do not apply.

Rule 8.4(c)

420. While cross-examining a Hispanic witness during a trial, a defense attorney grew frustrated at the witnesses' evasive answers, and finally asked the witness if "his people" or others "in his community" regularly lie under oath on the witness stand. The prosecutor immediately objected, and the judge sustained the objection, so the attorney withdrew the question. The witness then stated that he did not feel offended by the question because he understood that the

lawyer was simply ignorant and relying on stereotypes. Three of the jurors were also Hispanic. Could the attorney be subject to discipline for this question?

a) Yes, because it is professional misconduct for a lawyer in the course of representing a client to say things that manifest bias or prejudice based upon race or national origin.
b) Yes, because the judge sustained the objection and there were Hispanics serving on the jury.
c) No, because the witness claimed that he did not feel offended.
d) No, because the lawyer immediately withdrew the question.

Rule 8.4(d) Cmt. 3

421. Big Firm handles employee litigation, including workplace harassment suits. Nevertheless, the managing partners at Big Firm have decided they will not take on clients with claims based on same-sex harassment, because they believe the law is still developing and juries return unpredictable verdicts in such cases. Has the firm violated the MRPC?

a) Yes, the rules that prohibit harassment and discrimination by lawyers also limit the ability of a lawyer to accept, decline or withdraw from a representation.
b) Yes, by refusing to represent such clients, they are perpetuating the problem of workplace harassment and discrimination.
c) No, advocating in cases where the results would be unpredictable, or the law is still developing, would constitute a frivolous claim or contention.
d) No, the rules that prohibit harassment and discrimination by lawyers do not limit the ability of a lawyer to accept, decline or withdraw from a representation.

Rule 8.4(g)

422. A judge asks the two lawyers in a case to help him conduct some first-hand investigation of the facts. At the judge's request, the plaintiff's lawyer and the defendant's lawyer together drive the judge to the location where the accident occurred that became the subject of the litigation and allowed the judge to take measurements and photographs of the scene from different angles. They also accompanied the judge to interview several witnesses at their homes, off the record. Both lawyers felt awkward about this, but they were afraid to contradict or confront the judge, out of respect for the judicial office. Could the lawyers be subject to discipline for this conduct?

a) Yes, because it constitutes ex parte communication with the judge.
b) Yes, because it is professional misconduct for a lawyer to assist a judge or judicial officer in conduct that is a violation of applicable rules of judicial conduct or other law.
c) No, because the lawyers did this activity at the judge's behest, and possible under orders from the judge.
d) No, because it furthers the ends of justice and accurate case outcomes for judges to have more complete understanding of the facts of a case.

Rule 8.4(f)

RULE 8.5
DISCIPLINARY AUTHORITY; CHOICE OF LAW

423. An attorney had a license to practice law in two jurisdictions – his home state where he lived and had his primary office, and a neighboring state where he represented several clients each year. The attorney committed serious professional misconduct in his home state and received a public reprimand from the state disciplinary authorities. All the conduct took place in his home state, the client resided in the state, and the representation took place entirely within his home state. The lawyer's conduct would have violated the rules in either of the jurisdictions where he had a license to practice law, because it involved commingling client funds with his own money, and the states mostly had identical rules concerning this activity. After the attorney received a public reprimand in his home state, where the misconduct occurred, the state bar disciplinary authority in the neighboring state (where he also practiced) then commenced disciplinary proceedings against him as well. In the end, the neighboring state bar suspended his license for six months in that state, a much more severe sanction than the public reprimand he received in his home state, where

the misconduct in fact occurred. The attorney claims that the neighboring state bar has no jurisdiction over conduct that occurred entirely outside of the state. He also objects that the second punishment raises double jeopardy concerns. Is the attorney correct?

a) Yes, because even in cases where a second state can administer discipline over the same conduct, double jeopardy rules prevent the second tribunal from imposing a more severe sanction than the first tribunal already imposed on the lawyer.

b) Yes, because a lawyer cannot be subject to the disciplinary authority of two jurisdictions for the same conduct if it occurred entirely within one state.

c) No, because a lawyer may be subject to the disciplinary authority of two jurisdictions for the same conduct and may receive different sanctions in each state.

d) No, because choice of law rules require that each state impose the same sanction.

Rule 8.5(a)

424. An attorney practices law in two adjacent states, as he has a license to practice in each. He lives near the border and can easily serve clients in each jurisdiction. The two states have different rules about attorney disclosures of confidential client information - one state requires disclosures of client confidences whenever necessary to save a third party from death or serious bodily injury, while the other state forbids disclosures even under these circumstances. The attorney did indeed disclose confidential client information to save someone's life (the client was planning a murder and the attorney notified the authorities and warned the potential victim), but this occurred in the state that forbids such disclosures under these circumstances. The client files a grievance against the attorney in both states, and both state bars commence disciplinary proceedings over the same incident. The state bar of the other state, which would have required disclosure in this situation under its own rules, nevertheless reprimands the attorney for making the disclosure in violation of the rules in the state where the incident occurred. The attorney objects that the state cannot impose a sanction on him for conduct that the state's rules would have required. Is the state bar correct?

a) Yes, the state bar should apply the rules of the jurisdiction in which the lawyer's conduct occurred.

b) Yes, because a state disciplinary authority does not have to consider the rules of professional conduct from its own state in making disciplinary determinations, regardless of where the misconduct occurs.

c) No, because each state bar should apply its own rules, otherwise we could have the absurd result of a state bar punishing a lawyer for an action that the rules of that state require.

d) No, because a lawyer can face discipline for professional misconduct only in the state where the misconduct occurred.

Rule 8.5(b)(2)

425. An attorney was representing a client in a probate matter. The representation mostly occurred within the attorney's home state, where the client also lived. One asset of the probated estate, however, was an account receivable from a debtor in a neighboring state; the matter was already the subject of pending contract litigation in that state. The attorney filed a pro hac vice appearance in the neighboring state, and he traveled there to represent his client in the contract matter, which was ancillary to the probate matter in his home state. During the proceedings, the lawyer committed an act that constituted a violation of the ethical rules in his home state, but not in the neighboring state where he was appearing in a proceeding; the states had different rules in this regard. Could the attorney be subject to discipline in his home state for violating its rules before a tribunal in the neighboring state?

a) Yes, because when an attorney takes an oath to uphold the rules of a jurisdiction to obtain admission to the bar, he or she does so without regard to the lawyer's future geographic location when a violation of the rules occurs.

b) Yes, because otherwise, lawyers could simply drive across state lines and violate all the rules of professional conduct without repercussions from the state bar where the lawyer practices.

c) No, because whenever a lawyer's conduct relates to a proceeding pending before a tribunal, the lawyer shall be subject only to the rules of the jurisdiction in which the tribunal sits.

d) No, because a lawyer cannot be subject to discipline in more than one jurisdiction for the same act or incident.

Rule 8.5(b)(1)

426. After graduation from law school, an attorney had taken and passed the bar exam in two neighboring states, and she then had a license to practice law in each state. Her primary office was in her home state where he lived, but she also represented a few clients every year in the neighboring state. Seven years into her career, the attorney committed serious professional misconduct in her home state, and she received a public reprimand from the state disciplinary authorities. The actions that led to her disciplinary reprimand occurred entirely in her home state. The lawyer's conduct would have violated the rules in either of the jurisdictions where she had a license to practice law, because it involved commingling client funds with her own money, and the states mostly had identical rules concerning this activity. Several months after she received her reprimand in her home state, the disciplinary authority in the neighboring state commenced disciplinary proceedings against her as well. In the end, the neighboring state bar suspended her from the practice of law for one year in that state, a much more severe sanction than the public reprimand she had received in her home state, where the misconduct in fact occurred. The attorney appealed this suspension, claiming that the neighboring state bar had no jurisdiction over conduct that occurred entirely outside of its own borders. She also contends that the second punishment raises double jeopardy concerns. Did the state bar in the neighboring state indeed have the legal authority to suspend her license there, if the alleged misconduct occurred entirely in the attorney's home state, and she had already received a punishment for it?

a) Yes, except that choice of law rules require that each state impose the same sanction, so the neighboring state must either impose a reprimand or petition her home state to suspend her license for a year.

b) Yes, attorneys may be subject to the disciplinary authority of two jurisdictions for the same conduct and may receive different sanctions in each state.

c) No, the constitutional prohibition on double jeopardy prevent the second tribunal from imposing a more severe sanction than the first tribunal has already imposed on the lawyer.

d) No, the attorney would not be subject to the disciplinary authority of two jurisdictions for the same conduct if it occurred entirely within one state.

COMMUNICATIONS ABOUT LEGAL SERVICES

RULE 7.1
COMMUNICATION

427. Three attorneys open a new firm (a partnership) together. They drafted the partnership agreement themselves, without hiring another lawyer to represent them, and none of them gave informed consent, confirmed in writing, to the conflicts of interest that might arise as a result of drafting their own partnership agreement and trying to represent their own interests at the same time. The partners decided to call the firm "City of Houston Litigation Center," named after the city where they practice. Their advertising, brochures, and signage contain no disclaimers disavowing any connection with the Houston municipal government or with the Houston City Attorney's Office, which is a department of the municipal government. Are the actions of the attorneys described here proper, according to the Model Rules of Professional Conduct?

a) Yes, because lawyers may practice in an association in the form of a corporation, a partnership, a limited liability corporation, or even a limited-liability partnership, pursuant to the requirements of state statutes.

b) Yes, because there is nothing untruthful or misleading about the name, assuming they have headquarters in Houston.

c) No, because their trade name includes a geographical name without express statements that they are not a public agency or subdivision of government.

d) No, because they did not provide each other with written consent to the conflict of interest when they drafted the partnership agreement themselves, without third-party representation.

Rule 7.1 Cmt. 5

428. An attorney outsources complicated legal research to a firm that exclusively provides background legal research for lawyers. Her newest corporate client is a nationwide business with branches operating in all fifty states, so the corporate client needs information about its legal responsibilities regarding a certain issue in every state – a state-by-state survey. The attorney calls herself a sole practitioner. Could the attorney be subject to discipline for failing to inform the corporate client that she plans to outsource the 50-state survey to a research firm?

a) Yes, because the client may prefer to hire fifty separate research firms to investigate the issue in each state.

b) Yes, because lawyers must not misrepresent their partnership with others or other organizations.

c) No, because this is no different than delegating research tasks to an in-house associate attorney.

d) No, assuming the lawyer does not affirmatively deny that he will outsource the legal work.

ABA Formal Op. 08-451

429. An attorney recently earned her Juris Doctor degree from a prestigious law school and easily passed the state bar exam, gaining admission to the bar in her home state. She worked for three years for a legal aid clinic that provided free legal services for indigent clients. At the end of her third year at the clinic, the attorney decided to start her own firm, representing primarily low-income clients who were ineligible for free services at the legal aid clinic, but who also rarely could afford the fees of most attorneys. As soon as she ended her employment at the legal aid clinic, she sent a certified letter to most of the lawyers in her geographic area describing her experience and explaining that she was starting her own firm and intended to specialize in low-dollar consumer protection cases, simple divorces, adoptions, name changes, and landlord-tenant disputes. The letter concluded by offering to handle such cases for other lawyers if the other lawyers did not want to invest their time on such low-dollar matters. Were the attorney's actions proper?

a) Yes, because the attorney's statements were not false or misleading and the letter was an appropriate announcement of the opening of her new firm and her intent to specialize in certain areas of law.

b) Yes, because the attorney sent the letter only to other lawyers, so there was negligible risk of manipulation or abuse of unsophisticated clients.

c) No, because the attorney failed to disclose that up to that time she had been working for a legal aid clinic, that provides legal services only to indigent clients.

d) No, because the attorney has never handled such fee-generating cases before, if her only work experience is at a legal aid clinic that provides services without charge to indigent clients.

430. Attorney McLemore grew up in a family that spoke the Witchita language in the home. Her law practice advertisements prominently stated that she spoke Witchita, and that she can represent Witchita-speaking clients. Unfortunately, Attorney McLemore was the last known native speaker of the Witchita language. Was it improper for Attorney McLemore to include this language ability in her advertisements?

a) Yes, because it creates a misperception that the attorney is more knowledgeable than other lawyers in the area.

b) Yes, because linguists who have studied the Witchita language, but who live in other states, might misunderstand, and believe that the attorney is admitted in their jurisdiction as well.

c) No, because the statement is true.

d) No, because the attorney has Free Speech rights to make any claim she wants in her public advertisements.

Rule 7.1

431. Attorney Stevenson's law firm is simply "The Law Offices of Attorney Stevenson, Esq." Attorney Stevenson specializes in courtroom litigation. His website address is www.mytrialattorney.com. He selected this domain name and registered it so that he could use it for his law firm's website. Is this website address/domain name proper for Attorney Stevenson's law firm?

a) Yes, because "internet neutrality" requires that anyone can use any domain name they want.

b) Yes, because it is not misleading, and a lawyer or law firm may also use a distinctive website address or comparable professional designation.

c) No, because the ABA Model Rules require that law firm domain names include the names of the partners.

d) No, because the ABA Model Rules forbid lawyers from designating themselves with a distinctive website address.

Rule 7.1 Cmt.5

RULE 7.2
ADVERTISING

432. A certain attorney made an informal agreement with Physician that they would refer clients to each other when the situation seemed appropriate. They did not pay each other any money for referrals, but the relationship was explicitly reciprocal – the attorney referred patients who needed medical examinations to Physician, and when Physician had patients needing legal representation, he referred them to the attorney. The relationship was not explicitly exclusive – each was free to refer clients to others – but it happened that neither had similar reciprocal relationships with anyone else. They always inform their clients when making such referrals that they have a reciprocal relationship. Is such an arrangement proper?

a) Yes, a lawyer may agree to refer clients to another lawyer or a nonlawyer professional, in return for the undertaking of that person to refer clients or customers to the lawyer, assuming clients are aware, and the relationship is not exclusive.

b) Yes, because the agreement is informal, not a written contract.

c) No, because a lawyer may not agree to refer clients to another lawyer or a nonlawyer professional, in return for the undertaking of that person to refer clients or customers to the lawyer.

d) No, because the relationship described here is de facto exclusive, even if they have not agreed specifically to keep the relationship exclusive.

Rule 7.2(b)(4)

433. An attorney received a client referral by email from a friend who worked as a nurse in a nearby emergency room. The client called the attorney's office the same day that the attorney received her friend's email about this potential client. The representation of this new client yielded a favorable outcome, with a generous damages award for the client and substantial fees for the attorney. In appreciation for the referral, the attorney sent her friend a fancy fruit basket that cost around $150, with a card thanking the friend for the lucrative referral. Was it proper for the attorney to give such a gift to a nonlawyer for referring a client to her?

a) Yes, the Model Rules permit a lawyer to give nominal gifts, such as an item that might be a holiday gift item, in appreciation to a person for referring a prospective client.

b) Yes, the Model Rules permit a lawyer to give gifts in consideration for an understanding that referrals would be forthcoming in the future.

c) No, under the Model Rules, a lawyer may not compensate, give or promise anything of value to a person for recommending the lawyer's services.

d) No, the Model Rules permit lawyers to give only small tokens of appreciation for client referrals, such as ballpoint pens or keychains, but not items that might be given for holidays, such as a fruit basket.

Rule 7.2 Cmt. 4 (rev. Aug 2018)

434. An attorney received a client referral by email from a friend who worked as a nurse in a nearby emergency room. The client called the attorney's office the same day that the attorney received her friend's email about this potential client. The representation of this new client yielded a favorable outcome, with a generous damages award for the client and substantial fees for the attorney. In appreciation for the referral, the attorney sent her friend a collectible Star Wars statue (plastic figurine) worth about $20, knowing that the friend avidly collected Star Wars statues. Accompanying the figurine was a thank you card expressing appreciation and promising to send Star Wars collectible figurines every time the friend referred a client to the attorney. Did the attorney act improperly in this instance?

a) No, the Model Rules permit a lawyer to give nominal gifts, such as a small collectible item, in appreciation to a person for referring a prospective client.

b) Yes, the Model Rules prohibit gifts offered or given in consideration of any promise, agreement or understanding that such a gift would be forthcoming or that referrals would be made or encouraged in the future.

c) No, the Model Rules permit a lawyer to give gifts in consideration for an understanding that referrals would be forthcoming in the future.

d) Yes, under the Model Rules, a lawyer may never give any gifts in response to the person recommending the lawyer's services.

Rule 7.2 Cmt. 4 (rev. Aug 2018)

435. An attorney made and distributed bumper stickers advertising for his firm that simply provided a catchy phone number: 1-800-LAWYER-1. The phone number rolled over to the attorney's office phone. The bumper stickers included no other information. Could the attorney be subject to discipline for such an advertisement?

a) Yes, because bumper sticker advertising undermines the dignity of the legal profession.

b) Yes, because it does not include the name and office address of at least one lawyer or law firm responsible for its content.

c) No, because bumper stickers do not constitute advertising under the Model Rules of Professional Conduct.

d) No, because the information on the bumper stickers was truthful and accurate.

436. An attorney identified himself on his letterhead as a "Certified Trial Specialist by the National Board of Trial Advocacy." The attorney's state has no lawyer certification program of its own, besides admission to the bar. Is it inherently misleading, and therefore improper, for the attorney to list a certification if it did not come from an organization that an appropriate state authority has authorized?

a) Yes, because the traditional rule is that lawyers may state areas in which they practice, but they may not claim to be certified specialists in anything.

b) Yes, because consumers are likely to think that the state bar indeed certified the attorney as a Trial Specialist.

c) No, because the Supreme Court has held that such statements are merely "potentially misleading" and that it would violate the First Amendment for states to prohibit such statements completely.

d) No, because the Model Rules place no restrictions on lawyers making claims about certifications, expertise, or specialization.

Peel v. Attorney Registration & Disciplinary Comm'n, 496 U.S. 91 (1990)

437. An attorney made an informal agreement with Physician that they would refer clients to each other when the situation seemed appropriate. They did not pay each other any money for referrals, but the relationship was explicitly reciprocal – the attorney referred

162

patients who needed medical examinations to Physician, and when Physician had patients needing legal representation, he referred them to the attorney. The relationship was explicitly exclusive – each agreed not to refer clients to others – but it happened that neither had similar reciprocal relationships with anyone else anyway. They always inform their clients when making such referrals that they have a reciprocal relationship. Is such an arrangement proper?

a) Yes, a lawyer may agree to refer clients to another lawyer or a nonlawyer professional, in return for the undertaking of that person to refer clients or customers to the lawyer, assuming clients are aware of the existence and nature of the arrangement.

b) Yes, because the agreement is informal, not a written contract.

c) No, because a lawyer may not agree to refer clients to another lawyer or a nonlawyer professional, in return for the undertaking of that person to refer clients or customers to the lawyer, if the relationship is exclusive.

d) No, because the relationship described here is de facto exclusive, even if they have not agreed specifically to keep the relationship exclusive.

438. A certain attorney is a friend of Blogger, who operates a successful local blog about events, news, and gossip about their city. Blogger includes posts about local judges and well-known lawyers. The attorney has a secret agreement with Blogger. The attorney passes along tips to Blogger in the form of courthouse gossip regarding local lawyers and judges, or even about big cases. Blogger, in turn, covers the attorney's successful cases in glowing terms and recommends the attorney to his readers. Blogger's website is so successful that he earns $50,000 or so in advertising revenue from the site. The attorney occasionally purchases a small, inexpensive advertisement on the site, which merely gives the attorney's name, address, phone number, and areas of practice. Could the attorney be subject to discipline?

a) Yes, because the attorney provides gossip that undermines the dignity of the profession

b) Yes, because the attorney provides something of value to Blogger in exchange for recommending his services.

c) No, because the attorney pays a reasonable sum for his advertisements on the blog

d) No, because it is impossible to quantify the value of the information that the attorney provides to Blogger in exchange for favorable reviews of the attorney's legal victories.

439. In his advertisements, an attorney, who practices in California, states, "CERTIFIED SPECIALIST IN CALIFORNIA LAW." The attorney is referring to the fact that he passed the California Bar Exam, not to any other official certification beyond admission to the California bar. According to the Model Rules of Professional Conduct, is such a statement proper in a lawyer's advertisement?

a) Yes, because a lawyer may communicate the fact that the lawyer does or does not practice in specific fields of law.

b) Yes, because passing a state's bar exam demonstrates enough expertise in the laws of that state to practice there as a lawyer.

c) No, because a lawyer shall not state or imply that a lawyer is a certified specialist in a specific field of law without being a certified specialist by an official certifying organization in that state, and without including the name of the certifying organization in the advertisement.

d) No, because under the Model Rules, lawyers should not claim to be "certified specialists" in anything.

440. An attorney describes his areas of practice in his advertisements as "real estate" and "personal injury," but his state bar requires that lawyers use the less descriptive terms "property law" and "tort law" instead. Could the attorney be subject to discipline for using these more descriptive terms instead of the verbiage prescribed by the state bar?

a) Yes, because states have an absolute right to place reasonable requirements on lawyers pertaining to the verbiage used in their advertisements.

b) Yes, because "real estate" and "personal injury" are inherently misleading terms, whereas "property law" and "tort law" are very precise.

c) No, because states may not regulate lawyer advertising in any way.

d) No, because lawyers have a First Amendment right to use verbiage that is accurate and descriptive in their advertisements, assuming the statements are not misleading.

In re R.M.J., 455 U.S. 191 (1982)

441. In his advertisements and firm brochures, an attorney describes his many years of experience litigating in a specific area of commercial real estate litigation, without claiming to be a specialist or an expert. He does not mention any official certification. Is it permissible for the attorney to boast of his years of experience practicing in a specific area, even though some readers might infer from this that he is an expert or a certified specialist?

a) Yes, the Supreme Court has held that state bars may not pass any rules that limit or sanction communications by lawyers to potential clients.

b) Yes, the Supreme Court has held that state bars cannot prohibit lawyers form describing their years of experience with certain types of cases, assuming the information is truthful.

c) No, the Supreme Court has held that describing one's years of experience is too misleading, because readers could incorrectly infer that the lawyer will obtain successful results in their case.

d) No, because the lawyer cannot predict what types of cases he will handle in the future, when new clients hire him.

Zauderer v. Office of Disciplinary Counsel, 471 U.S. 626 (1985)

RULE 7.3
SOLICITATION OF CLIENTS

442. An attorney sends a solicitation letter to a prospective client. The recipient of the letter opens it and reads it, but the person does not respond. The attorney then sends a follow-up letter to the prospective client. Could the attorney be subject to discipline for sending the second letter?

a) No, because the lawyer clearly indicated that it was advertising material on the outside of the envelope.

b) No, because the lawyer had no way to know whether the prospective client received the first letter.

c) Yes, because a lawyer may not solicit individual prospective clients with direct mail unless the prospective client has requested the information.

d) Yes, if after sending a letter or other communication as permitted by the Rules, the lawyer receives no response, any further effort to communicate with the recipient of the communication may violate the provisions of Rules.

Rule 7.3 Cmt. 6

443. After a bizarre accident that received heavy media coverage, the victims took the unusual step of sending written notices to every plaintiff's firm in the area stating that the victims did not want to hear from any lawyers about the matter. The attorney received the notice and promptly forgot about it, because he had not yet seen any of the media coverage about the accident. Two weeks later, the attorney decided to catch up on the latest news, and he read an article online about the bizarre incident. He sent a letter to the victims expressing condolences for their suffering and offering to provide legal services if they decided to file a claim over the incident. The victims read the letter, changed their minds, and agreed to have the attorney represent them. A lawyer at another plaintiff's firm, who had also received the notice from the victims, learned that the attorney was representing the victims. He made some inquiries and discovered how the attorney had found his new clients. The lawyer filed a grievance against the attorney with the state disciplinary authorities. Should the attorney be subject to discipline for the way in which he offered to represent the victims?

a) Yes, because the target of the solicitation has made known to the lawyer a desire not to receive such solicitations.

b) Yes, because it was unfair for the attorney to have the opportunity to represent these clients when other lawyers had diligently avoided soliciting them.

c) No, because the victims decided that they wanted the attorney to represent them.

d) No, because the grievance came from a rival lawyer and the motivation was petty envy.

444. An attorney specializes in criminal defense work. His advertising, signage, and firm brochures offer a service that other lawyers in his

city do not provide – the attorney promises to post bail or bond for any client who cannot afford the amount of his bail or bond. Could the attorney be subject to discipline for such an advertisement offer?

a) Yes, because the advertisement is inherently misleading.
b) Yes, given the coercion and duress inherent in the client's incarceration, using the promise of securing the client's release from custody as an inducement to engage the lawyer would be improper.
c) No, assuming he indeed posts bail or bond for every client who claims to be unable to afford it themselves.
d) No, because lawyers can post bail for clients under certain circumstances, assuming it does not generate a conflict of interest that the client is unwilling to waive.

ABA Formal Op. 04-432

445. An attorney spends about one hour per week, on Monday mornings, calling local small business proprietors who routinely hire lawyers for lease and contract issues, and offers over the phone to provide legal services to them for a competitive (that is, low) fee. Does this activity by the attorney violate the Model Rules?

a) Yes, because the attorney is soliciting professional employment by live person-to-person contact via telephone.
b) Yes, because the attorney is offering to represent prospective clients at a lower fee than some of the other lawyers in the area.
c) No, because the attorney spends only one hour per week on this activity, which falls under the de minimis exception.
d) No, because the attorney is calling individuals who routinely use for business purposes the type of legal services offered by the lawyer.

446. Attorney Stevenson's sister is a dentist. Attorney Stevenson telephones his sister and explains that his firm is not doing well, that he needs more cases, and asks his sister to use him as her lawyer for any malpractice actions she faces or any collection actions against patients who do not pay their bills. Attorney Stevenson's sister finds this request annoying and makes no promises, but she agrees to keep it in mind. Was it proper for Attorney Stevenson attorney to make such a telephone solicitation?

a) Yes, because the recipient of the solicitation has a family relationship with the lawyer.
b) Yes, because he merely asked his sister to use his services whenever a case should arise, without offering to represent him in a specific matter or for a specific fee.
c) No, because the sister found the call annoying and the appropriateness of the solicitation is from the perspective of the recipient.
d) No, because a lawyer shall not by in-person, live telephone or real-time electronic contact solicit professional employment when a significant motive for the lawyer's doing so is the lawyer's pecuniary gain.

RULE 7.6
POLITICAL CONTRIBUTIONS TO OBTAIN LEGAL ENGAGEMENTS OR APPOINTMENTS BY JUDGES

447. An attorney solicits campaign contributions on behalf of an elected judge who is running for reelection. The judge wins reelection and shows his gratitude to the attorney by frequently appointing him to represent indigent defendants at the state's expense. The attorney engaged in the solicitation of contributions for the judge's reelection campaign because he hoped to receive such appointments. The fees from the appointments are disappointing, though, and the attorney later realizes that the fees earned from these appointments were not equal to the time the attorney spent soliciting the contributions. Could the attorney be subject to discipline for accepting these appointments?

a) Yes, because a lawyer shall not accept a government legal engagement or an appointment by a judge if the lawyer makes a political contribution or solicits political contributions for the purpose of obtaining that type of legal engagement or appointment.

b) Yes, because this type of quid-pro-quo arrangement constitutes a bribe.

c) No, because the fees earned from the appointments did not match the time the attorney spent soliciting contributions, so at least some of the solicitation was merely volunteer activity.

d) No, because all constituents who donate or solicit donations for election campaigns are hoping to receive some direct or indirect benefits as a result.

448. An attorney made substantial financial contributions to the reelection campaign of an elected judge. The judge won reelection and showed his gratitude to the attorney by frequently appointing him to represent indigent defendants at the state's expense. The attorney made the donations not because he hoped to receive such appointments, but because he honestly believed that the judge was the best candidate for the position. The attorney especially admired the fact that the judge had attended Harvard Law School and that the judge was an active member of the Federalist Society.

Could the attorney be subject to discipline for accepting these appointments?

a) Yes, because a lawyer shall not accept a government legal engagement or an appointment by a judge if the lawyer makes a political contribution or solicits political contributions.

b) Yes, because attending Harvard Law School is not a valid reason to believe that a candidate would make a good judge.

c) No, because all constituents who donate or solicit donations for election campaigns are hoping to receive some direct or indirect benefits as a result.

d) No, because the lawyer's motivation was a sincere political or personal support for the judge's candidacy, not a design to receive court appointments.

449. An attorney made substantial financial contributions to the reelection campaign of an elected judge. The judge won reelection and showed his gratitude to the attorney by frequently appointing him to represent indigent defendants at the state's expense. The attorney claims that he made the donations not because he hoped to receive such appointments, but because he honestly believed that the judge was the best candidate for the position, though he could not explain why. In addition, it turned out that taken together, the attorney gave more than every other lawyer or law firm in the judge's district. Could the attorney be subject to discipline for accepting these appointments?

a) Yes, because a lawyer or law firm shall not accept a government legal engagement or an appointment by a judge if the lawyer or law firm makes a political contribution or solicits political contributions for the purpose of obtaining that type of legal engagement or appointment.

b) Yes, because contributions that in the aggregate are substantial in relation to other contributions by lawyers or law firms, made for the benefit of an official in a position to influence award of a government legal engagement, and followed by an award of the legal engagement to the contributing or soliciting lawyer or the lawyer's firm would support an inference that the purpose of the contributions was to obtain the engagement

c) No, because all constituents who donate or solicit donations for election campaigns are hoping to receive some direct or indirect benefits as a result.

d) No, because the lawyer's motivation was a sincere political or personal support for the judge's candidacy, not a design to receive court appointments.

Rule 7.6 Cmt 5

450. An attorney made substantial financial contributions to the reelection campaign of an elected judge. The judge won reelection, and he showed his gratitude to the attorney by frequently appointing him to serve as referee or mediator in situations where the attorney received no compensation except reimbursement for travel expenses. The attorney made the donations because he hoped to receive such appointments, but he received no fees as a result. Could the attorney be subject to discipline for accepting these appointments?

a) Yes, because a lawyer or law firm shall not accept a government legal engagement or an appointment by a judge if the lawyer or law firm makes a political contribution or solicits political contributions for the purpose of obtaining that type of legal engagement or appointment, regardless of the amount of the fees earned.

b) Yes, because this type of quid-pro-quo arrangement constitutes a bribe.

c) No, because all constituents who donate or solicit donations for election campaigns are hoping to receive some direct or indirect benefits as a result.

d) No, because the term "government legal engagement" does not include mostly uncompensated services.

Rule 7.6 Cmt 3

DIFFERENT ROLES OF THE LAWYER

RULE 2.1 ADVISOR

451. An insurance company retained an attorney to represent one of its policyholders (i.e., an insured) against a lawsuit. The insurance company that hired the attorney requires its retained counsel to follow its own litigation management guidelines, designed to monitor the fees and costs of the lawyers the insurer retains. The litigation management guidelines include the requirement of a third-party audit of legal bills. Although the guidelines usually serve the interests of both the insured and the insurer by keeping litigation costs low and expediting the resolution of the case, in this instance the attorney finds that the guidelines require tactical moves that are adverse to the insured's interests. The insurer claims that the insured impliedly consented to the guidelines by agreeing contractually in the insurance policy to "cooperate" during litigation. The insurance company hired the attorney for the case. Should the attorney comply with the insurer's litigation management guidelines?

a) Yes, because the insured impliedly consented to the arrangement by accepting the insurance company's choice of legal counsel in defending the claim.

b) Yes, because the insurer retained the attorney to handle the case.

c) No, because a lawyer shall exercise independent professional judgment, and the insurer's litigation management guidelines in this instance materially impair the lawyer's professional judgment.

d) No, because a lawyer hired by an insurance company to represent an insured should always represent the interests of the insured rather than the insurer.

Rule 2.1; ABA Formal Op. 01-421

452. An attorney represented a criminal defendant charged with murder. During their consultations, the client informed the attorney that he had committed another murder, but that someone else – an innocent bystander – was standing trial for that crime. The attorney was aware of this other case, as it had received media coverage, and realized that an innocent person would potentially go to jail for many years, or even face the death penalty, for the crime his own client had committed. Which of the following is true, regarding the attorney's ethical obligations in this situation?

a) The attorney must immediately withdraw from representing this client, even if his trial is already underway, without offering the tribunal a reason for the withdrawal.

b) It would be improper for the attorney to urge his own client to come forward and confess to this other murder to save the innocent person accused of it, because such advice would be contrary to his own client's legal interests.

c) It would be permissible for the attorney to urge his own client to come forward and confess to this other murder to save the innocent person accused of it, even though such advice would be contrary to his own client's legal interests.

d) The attorney may not lecture or give moral advice to the client, but he may offer to refer the client to a mentor, a professional ethicist, or a member of the clergy.

Rule 2.1

453. An attorney represented a client who had an explosive temper. The representation concerned multimillion-dollar litigation, and the attorney received notice that the judge in the case had refused to qualify the attorney's expert witness to testify at trial. Without the expert, the client's case was unlikely to prevail. Faced with the daunting prospect of delivering this unwelcome news to the client, the attorney emailed the client and explained the setback in highly technical terms, citing the relevant sections of the Federal Rules of Civil Procedure, local court rules, precedential cases, and the Code of Judicial Conduct. He also used archaic legal terms in several places. A nonlawyer would have been unlikely to understand the conclusion – that the disqualification of the expert meant the client would lose the case and should withdraw or settle immediately. Based on the Model Rules, which of the following is true?

a) It was proper for the attorney to make this disclosure to the client, because it impacted the client's legal interests, and the report was truthful.

b) The attorney had an ethical duty to spare the client's feelings, and therefore acted properly.

c) The attorney did not have a duty to inform the client about a preliminary ruling regarding the qualification of experts.

d) The attorney violated his ethical duty to the client by providing purely technical legal advice that would be unhelpful to a nonlawyer.

Rule 2.1 Cmt. 2

RULE 2.3
REPORTS FOR THIRD PERSONS

454. A certain client applied to for a loan from a Big Bank based on a security interest in farm machinery that the client claims to own. Big Bank required that all borrowers provide an opinion letter at the time of closing from the borrower's lawyer. The legal opinion letter was to verify, based on a check of courthouse records, that the borrower's title to the machinery carried no encumbrances, such as recorded liens. The client asked his attorney to provide the required opinion, and the attorney produced the letter addressed to Big Bank. Unfortunately, the attorney had in fact made no effort to verify the facts stated by checking courthouse records, instead relying entirely on his client's statements concerning the state of title of the property. If the attorney had conducted the investigation described in the opinion letter, he would have seen that the public records indicated several liens superior to Big Bank's security interest. Which of the following is correct, given these facts?

a) The attorney failed to conduct the investigation described in the opinion letter and therefore violated his duty of care.

b) The attorney-client did not form in this case, so the attorney had no duty of care to the lender.

c) The attorney violated client confidentiality without authorization from the client or the lender.

d) The attorney failed to communicate with the client as required by the Model Rules.

RESTATEMENT § 95

455. A certain client applied for a bank loan from Big Bank based on a security interest in farm land and farm machinery. Big Bank required an opinion letter at the time of closing from the client's attorney, vouching for the deed of trust executed by the client that would give Big Bank a mortgage lien on the property, prior to any other recorded liens. The client's attorney provided the opinion letter. It states that the attorney has neither physically inspected the property nor investigated the state of the record title with respect to the mortgaged property, relying instead on the preliminary title report of a title-insurance company that there are no other liens on the property and that the client has clear title to the property. Unknown to the attorney, a third party had already acquired adverse possession rights in the property. The third party has also incurred unpaid bills that resulted in mechanics' liens on the property. All this occurred after the date of the preliminary title report. Which of the following is correct, based on these facts?

a) The attorney-client relationship never formed in this case, so there is no conflict of interest here that would require informed consent.

b) The attorney had a conflict of interest in the representation described here, because he worked for the client at the behest of the lender.

c) The attorney did not violate a duty of care to Big Bank by relying as stated in the opinion letter solely on the preliminary title report and not conducting any other investigation.

d) Attorney-client privilege still covers the contents of the report to the lender, if the lender kept the report confidential.

RESTATEMENT § 95

169

RULE 1.13
ORGANIZATION AS CLIENT

456. A recent law school graduate obtained her law license and spent several months searching for a job. Eventually, she went to work for a medium-sized corporation as in-house counsel. The company had only recently grown to the size that it could afford to keep legal counsel on staff, as opposed to hiring outside firms to handle le 457. gal matters when they arose. This meant the newly-licensed attorney was the first lawyer to work as in-house counsel at this corporation. After seven months, the attorney discovered that the Chief Financial Officer had falsified the corporation's quarterly earnings report to help boost the firm's share price. Both the attorney and the CFO received stock options every quarter as part of their compensation plan. Realizing that these misrepresented earnings appeared in the filings to the Securities and Exchange Commission, and the attorney feared that the corporation would eventually face severe regulatory fines or civil liability for false earning reports. What should the attorney do in this situation?

a) The attorney should withdraw immediately because she has a conflict of interest, given that she herself receives stock options as part of her compensation.
b) The attorney should start with the Chief Financial Officer, then take the matter to up the chain of command in the organization if necessary, eventually bringing the matter to the board of directors if nobody in management will address the problem.
c) The attorney should immediately report the matter to the appropriate government authorities without warning the Chief Financial Officer or his friends within the corporation, lest they have an opportunity to destroy evidence.
d) The attorney should confront the Chief Financial Officer, but if the CFO remains recalcitrant, the attorney must drop the matter.

457. An attorney served as general counsel for a municipal auditing and enforcement bureau, which monitored the internal affairs and expenditures of the municipal government. The attorney discovered that the head of the bureau engaged in selective enforcement and self-dealing, and he suspected that bribery had occurred in a few instances. The attorney's confrontation of the bureau head proved futile, so the attorney then needed to proceed up the chain of command. Can the attorney, now serving as general counsel for a government bureau, report wrongdoing to anyone higher within that municipality?

a) Yes, but only by testifying under subpoena at a city council hearing or the legislative equivalent for that municipality (town aldermen, board of county commissioners, etc.).
b) Yes, because if the action or failure to act involves the head of a bureau, either the department of which the bureau is a part, or the relevant branch of government may be the client for purposes of the Rules of Professional Conduct.
c) No, because the head of the bureau is the general counsel's client.
d) No, because governmental lawyers do not have a "client" organization in the same sense as attorneys in the private sector, because civil servants must act in the public interest.

Rule 1.13 Cmt. 9

458. An attorney worked for a corporation as in-house counsel. The attorney discovered that the Chief Financial Officer falsified the corporation's quarterly earnings report to prop up the firm's share price, as the CFO's compensation is partly in stock options. The attorney knows that these misrepresented earnings appeared in the filings to the Securities and Exchange Commission, and the misrepresentations will eventually result in severe regulatory fines or civil liability for the corporation. The attorney believes, with good reason, that the violation will result in substantial injury to the organization. The Chief Financial Officer hired the attorney, and he directly supervises the attorney in the organizational chain of command. The attorney confronted the Chief Financial Officer, but this proved unfruitful, and then the Chief Financial Officer discharged the attorney. What should the attorney do in this situation?

a) The attorney should immediately report the matter to the relevant government regulatory authority.
b) The attorney should proceed as the lawyer deems necessary to assure that the organization's highest authority knows about the circumstances of the lawyer's discharge.

c) The attorney should keep the information confidential, because the person who hired him has not authorized him to disclose the information.

d) The attorney should notify the manager directly above the Chief Financial Officer in the corporation and then drop the matter.

Rule 1.13(c)

459. The chief financial officer of Investors' Club, a private investment trust, is under suspicion for converting $100,000 of Investors' Club's assets for personal use. The other responsible corporate officers of Investors' Club, acting on the trust's behalf, retain an attorney to recover the money from the chief financial officer. At the same time, they direct the attorney not to reveal the loss, or file a lawsuit, until she has first exhausted other collection efforts. Given these restrictions, would it be a conflict of interest for the attorney to proceed with the representation?

a) Yes, it would be improper for the attorney to represent Investors' Club, because it would not be in the interest of the organization to proceed in the manner directed.

b) Yes, if she first obtains informed consent to the conflict, with written confirmation, from the chief financial officer and the other responsible corporate officers.

c) No, it would certainly be proper for the attorney to represent Investors' Club, and in doing so she must proceed in the manner directed.

d) No, because attorneys representing organizations are not subject to disqualification for theoretical conflicts of interest.

RESTATEMENT § 131

460. The chief financial officer of Investors' Club, a private investment trust, is under suspicion for converting $100,000 of Investors' Club's assets for personal use. The other responsible corporate officers of Investors' Club, acting on the trust's behalf, retain an attorney to recover the money from the chief financial officer. At the same time, they direct the attorney not to reveal the loss, or file a lawsuit, until she has first exhausted other collection efforts. Although the matter is not yet in litigation, would it be improper for the attorney to proceed with dual representation, of both the organization and the chief financial officer in this matter, if both consent?

a) Yes, the interests of Investors' Club and the chief financial officer are so adverse that even informed consent of both would not permit their common representation by Lawyer in the matter.

b) Yes, because the restrictions placed on the attorney about disclosures create a conflict of interest between the responsible officers and the best interests of the organization.

c) No, even though the interests of Investors' Club and the chief financial officer are technically adverse, informed consent of both would permit their common representation by the same lawyer in the matter.

d) No, because if the officers of a corporation have adverse interests to each other, no individual can provide informed consent to a potential conflict on behalf of the organization.

RESTATEMENT § 131

TRANSACTIONS AND COMMUNICATIONS WITH PERSONS OTHER THAN CLIENTS

RULE 4.1
TRUTHFULNESS IN STATEMENTS TO OTHERS

461. An attorney had struggled all through law school with the volume of reading and memorization, and then she had struggled to establish a successful law practice because everything took so much time and acumen. She complained constantly about her workload and maintained a blog where she espoused strong views about foreign policy, national security, wine, and exercise. Conglomerate Corporation hired the attorney to represent it in a lawsuit in which it was the defendant. During early settlement negotiations, the attorney told the plaintiff that the Board of Directors for her client, Conglomerate, had formally disapproved any settlement for more than fifty thousand dollars, even though Conglomerate's Board of Directors had in fact authorized a much higher settlement amount. Was it improper for the attorney to make such untruthful statements during settlement negotiations?

a) Yes, a lawyer must take care not to convey communications regarding the client's position, which otherwise would not count as statements of fact, in language that converts them, even inadvertently, into false factual representations.

b) Yes, during negotiations, a lawyer may not make any inaccurate or evasive statement of fact or law, regardless of materiality, if the statement could influence the other party's decisions in the matter.

c) No, a lawyer may downplay a client's willingness to compromise, or present a client's bargaining position without disclosing the client's "bottom line" position, in hopes of reaching a more favorable resolution.

d) No, during negotiations, a lawyer may permissibly make a false statement of material fact or law to a third person or the opposing party in the matter.

Rule 4.1; ABA Formal Op. 06-439

462. An attorney represented Conglomerate Corporation in negotiating with an office supplies company for a bulk discount on regular monthly purchases. When the supplier refused to go any lower, the attorney said threateningly that he could pick up the phone at any time and get three of their competitors to beat the supplier's current price. The attorney had no reason to think this – he was just bluffing, hoping to leverage the supplier into a lower price. Under the Model Rules, was it impermissible for the attorney to make this false statement to a third party?

a) Yes, a lawyer shall not knowingly make a false statement of material fact or law to a third person.

b) Yes, misrepresentations can occur by partially true but misleading statements or omissions that are the equivalent of affirmative false statements.

c) No, such remarks are merely posturing or puffing, and are not statements upon which parties would justifiably rely, so they are not false statements of material fact.

d) No, because the rules covering false statements to an opposing party or counsel apply only in the litigation context.

Rule 4.1; ABA Formal Op. 06-439

463. A litigation attorney from Big Firm was representing Conglomerate Corporation as the defendant in a civil matter. The attorney learned that the opposing party had hired an expert witness to support their claims, so she decided to initiate an ex parte contact with the expert witness retained to testify for the opposing party, without first obtaining permission from the opposing counsel. The expert witness was hesitant at first to talk to the attorney, because opposing counsel had asked the expert not to discuss the case with the inquiring lawyer. Nevertheless, the attorney persisted and eventually persuaded the witness to tell him some of his ideas and conclusions so far about the case. Was it proper for the attorney to convey to the opposing party's expert witness that he must speak to her?

a) Yes, because the opposing party or its lawyer may not properly ask the expert not to discuss the case with the inquiring lawyer.

b) Yes, because the Model Rules do not establish an automatic bar to lawyers initiating contact with the opposing parties' experts.

c) No, because the lawyer must communicate with the opposing party's expert witness only through his own side's expert witness, when the two experts collaborate on their findings.

d) No, because the Model Rules establish an automatic bar to lawyers initiating contact with the opposing party's experts without first obtaining permission from the opposing counsel.

ABA Formal Op. 93-378; Rule 4.1

464. A litigation attorney worked for several years for the Office of the Attorney General in his state, but then left to work for Big Firm. At Big Firm, the attorney exclusively handled litigation for Conglomerate Corporation, one of Big Firm's most important clients. Conglomerate Corporation had no litigation with the state government, so Big Firm made no effort to screen the attorney from any cases, though it would conduct customary conflict checks. In one case, the attorney was defending Conglomerate Corporation in a personal injury lawsuit over an accident with one of its delivery truck drivers. The parties agreed to use caucused mediation. In caucused mediation, the mediator meets privately with the parties and their counsel. These meetings or caucuses are confidential, and the mediator controls the flow of information among the parties and their counsel, as agreed by the parties. The attorney customarily starts negotiations or regular mediations by downplaying Conglomerate's willingness to compromise. In the alternative, the attorney might overstate, or sometimes strategically understate, the strengths or weaknesses of Conglomerate's litigation position. Are such statements, which might otherwise be permissible in regular mediation or direct negotiations, improper during a caucused mediation?

a) Yes, there is less concern in the Model Rules about the accuracy of information that lawyers communicate in a caucused mediation, because consensual deception is intrinsic to the process.

b) Yes, the accuracy of communication deteriorates on successive transmissions between individuals, and those distortions tend escalate on continued retransmission and reframing by mediators, so caucused mediation requires greater accuracy from the parties and their counsel than customary in face-to-face negotiations.

c) No, the same standards that apply to lawyers engaged in negotiations also apply to them in the context of caucused mediation, because parties cannot waive, even by mutual consent, the protections against false statements of material fact during negotiations.

d) No, in a caucused mediation, lawyers make statements in confidence to the mediator, who controls the flow of information between the parties in terms of the content of the communications as well as the timing of its transmission, and this agreed-upon environment of imperfect information helps the mediator assist the parties in resolving their disputes.

Rule 4.1; ABA Formal Op. 06-439

465. An attorney was representing Conglomerate Corporation, a large employer, in labor negotiations with the employee's union. The union had demanded, among other things, better coverage for birth control and abortions under the employee health insurance plan. The attorney told the union's lawyers that adding this benefit would cost the company an additional $142.37 per employee per quarter, but the attorney knew that it would in fact cost only $30 per employee. The attorney had learned over the years that using overly specific numbers instead of round numbers was a more effective strategy for bluffing. Under the Model Rules, was it permissible for the attorney to make this false statement to a third party?

a) Yes, such remarks are merely posturing or puffing, and are not statements upon which parties would justifiably rely, so they are not false statements of material fact.

b) Yes, because the rules covering false statements to an opposing party or counsel apply only in the litigation context.

c) No, bluffing by using hyper-specific fictitious numbers is too tricky, especially when round numbers are more accurate.

d) No, a lawyer shall not knowingly make a false statement of material fact to a third person.

Rule 4.1; ABA Formal Op. 06-439

466. A prosecutor was conducting a plea negotiation with a defendant and his lawyer.

During the plea negotiation, the prosecutor told the defendant and his counsel that there was an eyewitness to the alleged crime, who could identify the defendant as the perpetrator. This was not the case – the prosecutor was just bluffing, and the defense counsel suspected it was not true and decided to wait on deciding anything until he could depose or interview the witness himself. Was it permissible for the prosecutor to bluff like this during a plea negotiation, if no harm resulted?

a) Yes, under accepted conventions in negotiation, certain types of statements ordinarily do not count as statements of material fact.

b) Yes, such remarks are merely posturing or puffing, and are not statements upon which parties would justifiably rely, so they are not false statements of material fact.

c) No, a lawyer shall not knowingly make a false statement of material fact or law to a third person.

d) No, because an eyewitness might in fact come forward later, the prosecutor's earlier bluffing about this would undermine the true eyewitness' credibility.

Rule 4.1; ABA Formal Op. 06-439

467. An attorney had struggled all through law school with the sheer amount of reading and memorization, and then she had struggled to establish a successful law practice because everything took so much time and acumen. She advertised heavily as a personal injury plaintiff's lawyer, and she attracted new clients through deal-of-the-day promotions that she ran through a service called PleaseTryThis. Her advertising was so prevalent that when police stopped her vehicle for speeding violations, the officers would immediately recognize her as the lawyer from the advertisements, and sometimes this helped her avoid receiving a ticket. One personal injury client presented an unusually complicated problem. After filing pleadings in the case, while the proceedings were still in the discovery phase, the client died in a car accident, unrelated to the previous injuries that were the basis of the lawsuit. During subsequent settlement negotiations with a corporate defendant, Giant Company, the attorney did not disclose that her client had already died, but continued negotiations as if the client was still alive and had authorized her to accept or reject certain offers. Was it permissible for the attorney to delay disclosure of the client's death during the initial stages of settlement negotiations?

a) Yes, a lawyer engaged in settlement negotiations of a pending personal injury lawsuit in which the client was the plaintiff may temporarily conceal the client's death from the opposing party and their counsel.

b) Yes, because the case could continue as a wrongful death action, the client's death is not a material fact necessitating immediate disclosure.

c) No, because the client's death is a matter of public record.

d) No, a lawyer engaged in settlement negotiations of a pending personal injury lawsuit in which the client was the plaintiff cannot conceal the client's death; she must promptly notify opposing counsel and the court of that material fact.

ABA Formal Opinion 95-397; Rule 4.1

468. A litigation attorney from Big Firm was representing Conglomerate Corporation as the defendant in a civil matter. The attorney learned that the opposing party had hired an expert witness to support their claims, so she decided to initiate an ex parte contact with the expert witness retained to testify for the opposing party, without first obtaining permission from the opposing counsel. The expert witness was hesitant at first to talk to the attorney, because opposing counsel had asked the expert not to discuss the case with the inquiring lawyer. Frustrated, the attorney told the witness that he had to speak to the attorney, under the requirement of law, and that the witness would otherwise face contempt of court charges. She was just bluffing; as with any other witness not under subpoena, an expert witness may choose not to discuss the case with the lawyer. Was it improper for the attorney to convey to the opposing party's expert witness that he must speak to her?

a) Yes, the Model Rules establish an automatic bar to lawyers initiating contact with the opposing party's experts without first obtaining permission from the opposing counsel.

b) Yes, during an ex parte contact, a lawyer may not convey the message, directly or indirectly, that the witness must speak to the lawyer.

c) No, the Model Rules do not establish an automatic bar to lawyers initiating contact with the opposing parties' experts.

d) No, because the opposing party or its lawyer may not properly ask the expert not to discuss the case with the inquiring lawyer.

ABA Formal Op. 93-378; Rule 4.1

469. An attorney surreptitiously recorded a conversation with a potential witness without the other person's knowledge or consent. State law permits recording of conversations when at least one of the participants consents, which would include the attorney in this case. The potential witness learned about the recording later and was upset, because she would not have consented to the recording of the conversation, or at least would have been more judicious about her comments. Even if the attorney did not violate state or federal laws by recording this conversation, could the attorney be subject to discipline for failing to disclose a material fact to a third person?

a) Yes, because a lawyer who electronically records a conversation without the knowledge of the other party or parties to the conversation is violating the Model Rules.

b) Yes, because a lawyer must to be truthful when dealing with others on a client's behalf, and omissions can be the equivalent of affirmative false statements.

c) No, because a lawyer may electronically record a conversation without the knowledge of the other party to the conversation without violating the Model Rules, if the recording is not otherwise illegal.

d) No, if there is no client-lawyer relationship with the other person, the lawyer has no duties to them at all.

ABA Formal Op. 01-422; Rule 4.1

470. An attorney surreptitiously recorded a conversation with a potential witness without the other person's knowledge or consent. The potential witness asked the attorney at the beginning of the conversation if the attorney was recording it, and the attorney assured her that he was not, even though he was in fact recording it. State law permits recording of conversations when at least one of the participants consents, which would include the attorney in this case. The potential witness learned about the recording later and was upset, because she would not have consented to the recording of the conversation, or at least would have been more judicious about

her comments. Assuming the attorney did not violate state or federal laws by recording this conversation, were the attorney's actions proper, given these facts?

a) Yes, if there is no client-lawyer relationship with the other person, the lawyer has no duties to them at all.

b) Yes, because a lawyer may electronically record a conversation without the knowledge of the other party to the conversation without violating the Model Rules, if the recording is not otherwise illegal.

c) No, because a lawyer who electronically records a conversation without the knowledge of the other party or parties to the conversation is violating the Model Rules.

d) No, lawyer who records a conversation without the consent of a party to that conversation may not represent that he is not recording the conversation.

ABA Formal Op. 01-422; Rule 4.1

RULE 4.2 COMMUNICATION WITH PERSON REPRESENTED BY COUNSEL

471. An attorney knows that his opposing counsel has a reputation for refusing to settle cases and forcing lawsuits to go to trial, to impose the full costs of litigation on the opposing party. Cultivating this reputation serves as a deterrent to other would-be litigants against opposing counsel's clients. To avoid a rebuff by opposing counsel, the attorney finds a close friend of the opposing party, and he asks the close friend to communicate an informal settlement offer to the opposing party directly, bypassing the other lawyer. The opposing party is delighted to hear the offer and readily agrees to settle the case. Opposing counsel is furious and reports the attorney for misconduct. The attorney claims that he did not communicate with opposing counsels' client. Instead, the friend did, so the prohibitions on contact with other parties would not apply. Is the attorney correct?

a) Yes, the friend's willingness to be an informal intermediary serves as an independent intervening actor that breaks the line of causation to the attorney.

b) Yes, the opposing party's eagerness to settle the case shows that the attorney did what the other party wanted; such an endorsement after the fact negates any potential violation of the Rules.

c) No, a lawyer may not make a communication prohibited by the Rules through the acts of another, such as the friend in this case.

d) No, lawyers may never speak directly to an opposing party under any circumstances; even if the opposing counsel had consented to the communication, the attorney would be subject to discipline.

Rule 4.2

472. In anticipation of a trial over workplace discrimination, a plaintiff's attorney contacts several current managers of the defendant corporation and interviews them about the day-to-day operations of the company and the chain of command for addressing personnel complaints. These managers supervise employees, address interpersonal problems between workers, filed complaints, and consult with the firm's in-house counsel about personnel matters that seem serious. The attorney does this without permission from the defendant's attorney. Was this proper?

a) Yes, given that these managers are likely to be witnesses at trial and subject to cross-examination anyway, it is reasonable for the attorney to have a chance to speak with them informally before trial.

b) Yes, because 95% of such cases settle before trial, meaning most discrimination cases do not really constitute "litigation" for purposes of the ethical rules.

c) No, because even the identity of the managers at a defendant corporation is confidential information that should not be available to a lawyer in discrimination litigation.

d) No, consent of the company's attorney is always necessary for communication with a present constituent of the organization who supervises, directs, or regularly consults with the organization's attorney concerning the matter.

Rule 4.2

473. An attorney lived in State A, but she had a license to practice in adjacent State B, where she worked for a law firm. Some of her clients also lived in State A, but they had sought legal representation in State B because that is where they worked or owned property. A business owner who lived and worked in State B hired the attorney to help enforce a non-compete agreement against a former employee at their technology firm. According to the client, a rumor started going around just this past week that the former employee had either started his own business nearby or was working for a nearby competitor, either of which, if true, could violate the non-compete agreement. The employee left the client's company on bad terms ten days ago. The former employee lived in State A. The client provided a copy of the non-compete agreement, which the former employee had signed many years before on his first day of work. The human resources director at the client's business told the attorney that she assumed the former employee would have forgotten about the agreement, or that he was unlikely to be aware that he was violating it. The attorney decided that the first step would be to call the former employee and ask whether he has found another job yet or has started his own business. The attorney assumed that the former employee would not have retained counsel yet to challenge the non-compete agreement, given the HR director's comments about him, and how recently the events unfolded. The former employee answered the phone, explained that he was starting his own rival company, and that the non-compete agreement was invalid under state law. When the attorney asked why he thought it would be invalid, the former employee answered that his own lawyer assured him that recent changes in state law made the previous agreement void. They were, in fact, ready to challenge the agreement in court. The attorney asked him to have his own lawyer contact him, so that they could discuss settlement options for the dispute, and then ended the call. Did the attorney act properly?

a) Yes, if the non-compete agreement has a binding arbitration clause, as matters covered under alternative dispute resolution (arbitration, mediation, or a non-judicial referee) do not implicate the prohibition on communication with opposing parties.

b) Yes, as the prohibition on communications with a represented person only applies in circumstances where the attorney knows that

176

the person is in fact represented in the matter under discussion.
c) No, the prohibition on communications with a represented person applies regardless of the attorney's knowledge, because the burden is on every attorney to determine whether an opposing party has representation before making contact.
d) No, because one can easily infer from these facts and circumstances that the attorney indeed knew the former employee had representation.

Rule 4.2

474. An attorney was renting law-office space from an individual property owner. At one point, the attorney was late with his rent, and he soon received a letter from another lawyer, who was representing the property owner. The letter directed the attorney to vacate by a certain date. The attorney visited his property owner in person, without the prior consent of the property owner's lawyer. During the visit, the attorney insisted to the property owner that the lease prohibits the eviction without a one-month grace period. This argument was entirely plausible. Was it proper for the attorney to do this?
a) Yes, because he was visiting the property owner as a tenant, not as the representative of another party.
b) Yes, because he visited the property owner in person, rather than trying to contact him without the other attorney's knowledge.
c) No, because he approached the opposing party in a legal dispute without opposing counsel present to press for his own position in the matter.
d) No, because he approached the property owner in person, instead of sending a letter, email, or text, which opposing counsel could have reviewed before the property owner replied.

Rule 4.2

475. A business owner hires an attorney to enforce a non-compete agreement against a former executive at the client's technology firm. According to the client, a rumor started going around just this past week that the former executive had either started his own business nearby or was consulting for a nearby competitor; if true, either scenario could violate the non-compete agreement. The client explains that the former executive has already asserted that the non-compete agreement is invalid under

a recent decision from the state Supreme Court and is filing an action for a declaratory judgment to challenge the non-compete agreement preemptively, though the client is unsure whether his company received proper service yet about the lawsuit. The attorney decides that the first step is to call the former employee and ask him whether he has found another job yet or has started his own business. The former employee answers the phone, explains that he has started his own rival company, and that he believes the non-compete agreement is invalid under state law. The attorney asks him to have his own lawyer contact him so that they can discuss potential settlement for the dispute. Has the attorney acted properly?
a) Yes, as the prohibition on communications with a represented person only applies in circumstances where the attorney knows that the person is in fact represented in the matter, and this means that the attorney has actual knowledge of the fact of the representation.
b) Yes, if the non-compete agreement has a binding arbitration clause, as matters covered under alternative dispute resolution (arbitration, mediation, or a non-judicial referee) do not implicate the prohibition on communication with opposing parties.
c) No, because one can easily infer from these facts and circumstances that the attorney indeed knew the former employee had representation.
d) No, because this is an action for declaratory judgment rather than money damages, so the usual exceptions to the prohibition on communication do not apply.

Rule 4.2

476. An attorney represents a plaintiff in a civil suit. The defendant also has representation, but he contacts the attorney to negotiate a settlement agreement. The attorney advises the defendant that he cannot discuss the case with the defendant because the defendant has representation by counsel. Defendant faxes the attorney a letter stating that he waives the rule restricting the attorney from communicating with the defendant while the defendant has representation. Upon receipt of the fax, the attorney contacts the defendant and discusses a settlement agreement. Are the attorney's actions proper?
a) Yes, because an attorney may communicate with represented persons assuming the

represented person provides a written waiver to that attorney.

b) Yes, because an attorney may communicate with represented persons assuming the represented person initiates the communication.

c) No, because attorneys may not communicate with represented persons at all unless the attorney representing that person is also present.

d) No, because attorneys may not communicate with represented persons unless the attorney representing that person permits the attorney to communicate with the represented person.

Rule 4.2

477. A state bar pro bono program arranges for lawyers to volunteer at police stations and county lockups to give limited-scope representation to arrestees who plan to proceed pro se, advising them mostly on their pre-trial rights (the right to remain silent, to have court-appointed counsel at trial, and so on). Sometimes these volunteer attorneys accompany arrestees to their arraignments or bond hearings, but then their assistance ends, and the defendant proceeds pro se (without counsel, either by choice or because they are ineligible for court-appointed counsel). The lawyer volunteer program has been going on for a few years, and it has expanded significantly. A local prosecutor receives a case assignment involving a pro se defendant. At the outset of the plea negotiation session, must the prosecutor ask the defendant if he has already received legal advice on a limited basis from a volunteer lawyer, and if so, refrain from further discussions until he has conferred with the other lawyer?

a) Yes, because any prosecutor in that situation has reason to believe that the unrepresented defendant received limited-scope legal services on some portions of the case.

b) Yes, because prosecutors must safeguard the pre-trial rights of pro se defendants.

c) No, assuming the defendant is clearly unrepresented at the time the prosecutor begins the conversation, there is no reason for the prosecutor to inquire about previous limited-scope legal advice.

d) No, because the volunteers provide only limited-scope legal assistance, not full representation in the matter as it proceeds to trial.

Rule 4.2; ABA Formal Op. 15-472

RULES 4.3
UNREPRESENTED PERSONS

478. An attorney sees a friend at a high school reunion. The friend asks the attorney for advice about a potential civil lawsuit that the friend is considering hiring an attorney to file. The attorney gives the friend general information about the area of law and about the specific kind of lawsuit an attorney might potentially file for the friend. The friend lives too far away from the attorney for the attorney to handle the case, and the friend is planning to hire another lawyer near his residence to handle the lawsuit. The attorney later talks to his own wife about the friend's lawsuit. Wife discusses the suit with her own friend. The friend discovers that several people know about his potential suit and is upset, as he believed that the attorney should not have spoken about his potential case to others. Is the attorney subject to discipline?

a) Yes, attorneys shall not disclose information about potential lawsuits they discuss with others unless authorized by that person, whether the person is or is not a potential or current client.

b) Yes, persons with whom an attorney discusses potential litigation, even if only in a general manner, are prospective clients and have the same protection as if they were, in fact, clients themselves.

c) No, an attorney owes no duties or protections, including protections against disclosing information about potential lawsuits, to persons who communicate with attorneys without any expectation of forming a client-attorney relationship.

d) No, an attorney may discuss potential client cases with others assuming the potential client did not retain the attorney to handle the matter that potential client discussed with the attorney.

Rule 4.3

479. A litigation attorney from Big Firm was representing Conglomerate Corporation as the defendant in a civil matter. The attorney learned that the opposing party had hired an expert witness to support their claims, so she decided to initiate an ex parte contact with the expert witness retained to testify for the opposing party, without first obtaining permission from the opposing counsel. In fact, opposing counsel had asked the expert not to discuss the case with the inquiring lawyer. The attorney introduced herself by name, but she did not mention that she was a lawyer or that she had any relationship with the case. Instead, she said she was "researching an issue" and that the expert was a well-known specialist on the topic, which was true. The expert was willing to answer her questions because he was unaware that she was opposing counsel in the case. The attorney pressed the expert for specific examples of the issue they were discussing, which led the expert to mention his research related to the current litigation. The expert revealed information to the attorney that was useful for her representation of her client. Could the attorney be subject to discipline for discussing the matter with the expert without discussing her relationship to the case?

a) Yes, when a lawyer contacts any witness, lay or expert, actual or potential, the lawyer must not knowingly leave the witness in ignorance of the lawyer's relationship to the case that gives occasion to the contact.

b) Yes, because the Model Rules establish an automatic bar to lawyers initiating contact with the opposing party's experts without first obtaining permission from the opposing counsel.

c) No, because the opposing party or its lawyer may not properly ask the expert not to discuss the case with the inquiring lawyer.

d) No, because the Model Rules do not establish an automatic bar to lawyers initiating contact with the opposing parties' experts.

ABA Formal Op. 93-378; Rule 4.3

480. An inexperienced attorney represented an insurance company in a wrongful-death lawsuit. The plaintiff was the widow of the deceased, acting as the personal representative of the deceased. The widow was a pro se litigant, as she did not have legal representation in the matter. The lawsuit was over the death of her husband. The pro se widow asserted that one of the insurance company's policyholders had negligently caused the husband's death. State law required that settlements of a wrongful death claim by a personal representative must have approval from a tribunal. The widow and the insurance company's claims manager eventually agreed on a settlement amount. The attorney, representing the insurance company, prepared the necessary documents and presented them to the widow for her signature. The widow, knowing that the attorney represented the interests of the insurance company, asked the attorney why the documents were necessary. The attorney responded that to effectuate the settlement, they needed to execute the documents and file them for court approval. This was true. Was the attorney's conduct improper, under the Model Rules?

a) Yes, when the lawyer knows or should know that the unrepresented person misunderstands the lawyer's role in the matter, the lawyer shall make reasonable efforts to correct the misunderstanding.

b) Yes, a lawyer shall not give legal advice to an unrepresented person, other than the advice to secure counsel, if the lawyer knows or should know that the interests of such a person are or potentially conflict with the interests of the client.

c) No, a lawyer may give legal advice to an unrepresented person, even if the interests of such a person in conflict with the interests of the client.

d) No, so long as the unrepresented person understands that the lawyer represents an adverse party and is not representing the person, the lawyer may prepare documents that require the person's signature and explain the lawyer's own view of the meaning of the document or the underlying legal obligations.

RESTATEMENT § 103; Rule 4.3 Cmt 3

481. A highly experienced attorney represented Big Bank as the financer in a home sale. The buyer, that is, the borrower, did not have legal representation in the transaction. Under the terms of the transaction, the buyer was to pay the legal fees of the attorney. The buyer wrote an email to the attorney stating, "I have several questions about legal issues in the house purchase on which you are representing me." The buyer also had several phone conversations

with the attorney in which the buyer made similar statements. What is the attorney's ethical duty in this situation, regarding the buyer?

a) The attorney must withdraw from the representation unless both the buyer and Big Bank give informed consent, confirmed in writing, to the attorney's continued representation of Big Bank.

b) The attorney must inform the buyer that the attorney represents only Big Bank, and that the buyer should not rely on the attorney to protect the buyer's interests in the transaction.

c) The attorney must refer the buyer to another lawyer in his firm to answer the buyer's questions about the transaction.

d) The attorney has no ethical duties to the buyer because there is no client-lawyer relationship between them.

RESTATEMENT § 103; Rule 4.3

RULE 4.4
RESPECT FOR RIGHTS OF THIRD PERSONS

482. An experienced attorney regularly represented Conglomerate Corporation as its outside litigation counsel. One of Conglomerate's employees filed a lawsuit against the company as her employer. Conglomerate instructed its information technologies staff to copy the contents of her workplace computer for useful information in defending the lawsuit, and then Conglomerate's management provided copies to its outside counsel. Upon review, the attorney for Conglomerate saw that some of the employee's e-mails have the heading "Attorney-Client Confidential Communication." Under the Model Rules of Professional Conduct, does the attorney for Conglomerate have an ethical duty to notify the employee's lawyer that the employer has accessed this correspondence?

a) Notwithstanding a local court order to the contrary, the Model Rules do not independently impose an ethical duty to notify opposing counsel of the receipt of private, potentially privileged e-mail communications between the opposing party and his or her counsel.

b) The attorney must notify the opposing party, because a lawyer who receives a document relating to the representation of the lawyer's client that the sender obviously sent inadvertently should promptly notify the sender.

c) The attorney should first read the emails thoroughly to see if the contents seem like privileged, confidential communications between a client and her lawyer, and if so, notify opposing counsel.

d) The attorney has an ethical duty to report the matter to the tribunal and let the tribunal decide whether to notify the other party's counsel.

ABA Formal Op. 11-460; Rule 4.4

483. An attorney represented a powerful but controversial politician. A prosecutor was seeking an indictment of the attorney's client, so the attorney located a young woman who volunteered to befriend the prosecutor at a social event and exchange phone numbers. Then, at the attorney's request, the young woman would call the prosecutor and engage in lurid sexual conversations over the phone, while the attorney was recording the conversations. The prosecutor was unaware that the attorney and the young woman were recording the conversations, but the laws of that state required the knowledge and consent of only one participant to record a conversation. The attorney then sent the prosecutor a copy of the recordings of the phone conversations, which were very embarrassing to the prosecutor. The attorney did not include any communication with the recordings, such as threats or extortionary demands. Nevertheless, the prosecutor did not want the recording to become public, so he stopped pursuing the indictment of the attorney's client. Was it permissible for the attorney to record these phone conversations, under these circumstances?

a) Yes, a lawyer has a duty to engage in zealous advocacy on behalf of the client, and to use every legal means available to achieve the client's legal objectives.

b) Yes, because a lawyer may electronically record a conversation without the knowledge of the other party to the conversation without violating the Model Rules, if the recording is not otherwise illegal.

180

c) No, because a lawyer who electronically records a conversation without the knowledge of the other party or parties to the conversation is violating the Model Rules.

d) No, if a lawyer records a conversation with no substantial purpose other than to embarrass or burden a third person, the lawyer has violated Rule 4.4.

Rule 4.4; ABA Formal Op. 01-422

484. Local police obtained photographs from partygoers, and the photographs showed minors from the local high school consuming beer and engaging in sexual activity at a recent drinking party. The police forwarded the photographs to the local prosecutor, who decided not to pursue criminal charges in the matter for several legal and evidentiary reasons. Instead, in hopes of shocking the minors' parents into dealing with underage drinking, the prosecutor showed them photos of their children drinking and engaging in sexual activity at the party. All the parents saw all the photos, including those of other parents' children drinking, some unclothed and others partially clothed, at the party. Could the prosecutor be subject to discipline for his zealous advocacy against underage drinking?

a) Yes, a prosecutor must refrain from making extrajudicial disclosures that have a substantial likelihood of heightening public condemnation of the accused.

b) Yes, a lawyer shall not use means that have no substantial purpose other than to embarrass or burden a third person.

c) No, responsibility to a client requires a lawyer to subordinate the interests of others to those of the client.

d) No, a prosecutor may make disclosures that are necessary to inform the public of the nature and extent of the prosecutor's action and that serve a legitimate law enforcement purpose.

In re Campbell, 199 P.3d 776 (Kan. 2009); Rule 4.4(a)

SAFEKEEPING CLIENT FUNDS AND OTHER PROPERTY

RULE 1.15

485. An attorney had included false statements on his application for admission to the bar, but the lies went undetected, so the attorney obtained his license and began to practice law. The nonlawyer employees he hired to work at his firm were aware that he had lied on his bar application, but they did not report this to the state disciplinary authorities. The firm had no legal malpractice insurance, but the attorney neglected to disclose this to some of the firm's prospective clients. At one point, the attorney represented a seller in a business transaction involving industrial equipment. To complete the transaction, the purchaser sent the attorney a check for the agreed-upon purchase price, with a letter directing the attorney to forward the money to the seller, whom the attorney represented in the matter. The attorney notified his client immediately that the money had come in. The client was traveling at the time and asked the attorney to hold the funds until he returned from his trip. The attorney had only recently launched the firm and did not yet have a client trust account at any banks in the area, so he deposited the check in his own bank account temporarily. As soon as the check cleared, the attorney wrote a check to the client for the full amount, which the client picked up in person. Did the attorney act properly regarding the funds?

a) Yes, because the amount was less than the amount that would trigger the ethical rules pertaining to separate client accounts.
b) Yes, because the client asked the attorney to hold the funds temporarily, and the attorney faithfully delivered the entire sum to the client with his own check.
c) No, the attorney had an obligation to hold the funds in a separate account from the attorney's own property.
d) No, because the attorney should have refused the check and instructed the purchaser instead to write a check directly to the client.

Rule 1.15(a)

486. An attorney has a busy transactional practice and frequently must handle client funds, either for making commercial purchases, sales, leases, dispute settlements, or other transfers. The attorney faithfully deposits client money in a separate trust account and does not commingle the funds with his own, except that he deposits enough of his own money in the account to cover the monthly bank service charges. The attorney keeps complete, accurate records of all deposits and withdrawals for a full year, after which he destroys the records to preserve client confidentiality. Is the attorney acting improperly?

a) Yes, because the attorney did not keep records for a long enough period.
b) Yes, because the attorney should not have deposited any of his own funds in the account together with client funds.
c) No, because the lawyer may deposit the lawyer's own funds in a client trust account for the sole purpose of paying bank service charges on that account.
d) No, because the attorney keeps property of clients or third persons that is in a lawyer's possession in connection with a representation separate from the lawyer's own property, in a separate account maintained in the state where the lawyer's office is situated.

Rule 1.15(a)

487. A natural disaster struck a certain attorney's city and destroyed his office, including many documents of intrinsic value belonging to clients. Which of the following would be one of the attorney's ethical duties as a result?

a) The attorney must self-report the loss to the state disciplinary authority and accept whatever sanction it imposes.
b) The attorney must compensate the clients for the documents, including the return of a portion of the legal fees that the attorney received from the client.
c) The attorney must make reasonable efforts to reconstruct documents of intrinsic value for both current and former clients, or to obtain copies of the documents that come from an external source.
d) The attorney must promptly notify the opposing party in each clients' matter about the loss of important documents that might be relevant or material to the other party.

Rule 1.15; ABA Formal Op. 18-482

488. A natural disaster struck a certain attorney's city and destroyed his office, including many documents of that had no intrinsic value belonging to clients, that serve no useful purpose to the client or former client, or for which there are electronic copies. Which of the following would be one of the attorney's ethical duties as a result?

a) The attorney must self-report the loss to the state disciplinary authority and accept whatever sanction it imposes.

b) The attorney need not notify either current or former clients about lost documents that have no intrinsic value.

c) The attorney must compensate the clients for the documents.

d) The attorney must make reasonable efforts to reconstruct documents of intrinsic value for both current and former clients, or to obtain copies of the documents that come from an external source.

Rule 1.15; ABA Formal Op. 18-482

489. A natural disaster struck a certain attorney's city and destroyed his office, including his records of his client trust accounts. What must the attorney do in response, to satisfy his ethical obligations to keep records of such accounts?

a) The attorney must attempt to reconstruct the records from available sources.

b) The attorney must self-report the loss to the state disciplinary authority and accept whatever sanction it imposes.

c) The attorney must notify current and former clients about the loss of the records, even if the attorney can fully reconstruct the records from available sources.

d) The attorney must compensate the clients by returning a portion of the fees that the clients have paid.

Rule 1.15; ABA Formal Op. 18-482

490. An attorney worked for Big Firm for three years, and thereafter he took several of Big Firm's clients with him to start his own firm. Big Firm had an official unwritten policy that its lawyers should not take Big Firm clients with them when the lawyers left the firm, but the attorney in this case simply ignored this policy.

Big Firm threatened litigation over the attorney's actions, but it did not follow through on the threats. The attorney then advertised on local billboards that he was a former Big Firm lawyer who would provide affordable legal services to working-class clients. A certain new client hired an attorney to represent him in a divorce proceeding and gave the attorney several thousand dollars to cover all legal fees and expenses in the case. The attorney deposited the money in his client trust account, and he explained to the client that he would withdraw money periodically as he earned fees or incurred expenses. Was this arrangement proper?

a) Yes, a lawyer may deposit funds from the client into a trust account and withdraw funds only as billable fees or expenses accrue.

b) Yes, because $10,000 is a reasonable amount for the legal fees and expenses in a typical divorce case, and the lawyer did not charge a contingent fee.

c) No, because the fees are for the lawyer, and therefore the lawyer has commingled his own legal fees in the client trust account, in violation of the Model Rules.

d) No, because withdrawing the fees gradually throughout the course of the representation constitutes a contingent fee arrangement, which is impermissible in representation for a divorce proceeding.

Rule 1.15(c)

491. An attorney represented a female client, the wife in a marriage-dissolution action. The husband had retained a lawyer at Boutique Firm to represent him. Meeting without either lawyer present, the wife and husband negotiated the outlines of an agreement providing for property division and child support. The wife then brought the husband to the attorney's office to have the agreement reduced to writing. The attorney welcomed both the wife and the husband and engaged in a discussion of provisions of the agreement with both the husband and wife. Has the attorney violated the Model Rules?

a) Yes, because he met with a represented opposing party without opposing counsel being present.

b) Yes, because he permitted his client to meet with the opposing party without either lawyer being present.

c) No, because the parties themselves may talk

to each other, and even resolve a dispute, without involving or notifying their lawyers.

d) No, because even though the parties should not have met to discuss the matter without their lawyers being present, they promptly went to the attorney's office to discuss their tentative agreement with the attorney and reduce it to writing.

492. Attorney Stevenson, from Tiny Firm, brings in a lawyer from Giant Firm to work on a complex litigation matter, and they agree to share fees. The client receives a single billing covering the fees of both lawyers, even though they work for separate firms. To comply with the Rules of Professional Conduct, the fee division between Attorney Stevenson and the other lawyer is proportionate to the services performed by each lawyer, and the client agreed in writing beforehand to the arrangement, including the share each lawyer would receive. The total fee is reasonable. At the end of the representation, Attorney Stevenson receives the earned fee from the client, including the share that he owes to the other lawyer at Giant Firm. He promptly notifies the other lawyer. Attorney Stevenson deposits the total sum in his firm bank account (its operating account, not a client trust account), and after confirming that the funds are available from the bank, he sends a check to the other lawyer with his share of the fees. Are Attorney Stevenson's actions proper, as described here?

a) Yes, because the fees were proportionate to the work done by each lawyer, and the client assented to the arrangement in writing beforehand.

b) Yes, because the representation has ended, and the fees belong to the lawyers, not the client, and therefore Attorney Stevenson cannot place them in a separate trust account.

c) No, the client should have received separate billing from each lawyer, because they work for separate firms.

d) No, because Attorney Stevenson should have deposited the other lawyer's share of the fees in a trust account, separate from his own funds.

CODE OF JUDICIAL CONDUCT

493. An experienced litigator became a judge. In her previous litigation practice, she would regularly search online to learn more about the opposing party, opposing counsel, and even jurors. She sometimes found useful information on opposing parties' websites or on social media. Now serving as a judge, she visits the website of the corporate defendant in one of her cases, to learn more background about the company and its products and pricing. In this instance, the judge did not find any information on the company's website that seemed useful in understanding the issues in the pending case. The judge did not do any online research about the other party (the plaintiff) in the case. Was the judge's research proper?

a) No, because the Code of Judicial Conduct prohibits judges from conducting online research to gather information about a party or juror in a pending case, even if the research yields no useful information.

b) No, because if a judge researches one party, fairness requires that the judge should do the same research about the other party.

c) Yes, because the judge is merely learning information that is available to the public through the company's official website.

d) Yes, because the Code of Judicial Conduct encourages judges to use modern research tools, such as the Internet, to reach more accurate or well-informed decisions in their cases.

494. A judicial clerk researched alternative methods of toxic mold remediation in homes having mold problems and wrote a memo about her findings for the judge to consider in a case. The defendant alleged, among other things, that the plaintiff in a toxic mold case before that judge had failed to mitigate damages. Has the judge violated the CJC?

a) No, because the clerk did the research, not the judge.

b) No, because this type of research on background material does not constitute an adjudicative fact for purposes of the rules pertaining to independent research by judges.

c) Yes, because the judge must do research for relevant facts that might be in dispute in a pending case, rather than entrusting this research to an inexperienced judicial clerk.

d) Yes, this violates Rule 2.9(c) of the Code of Judicial Conduct, because the clerk is conducting the research on behalf of the judge.

495. A trial judge is going through a divorce, and he hired an attorney to represent him. The attorney's law firm partner is representing another client who is appearing before the same judge in his personal injury lawsuit. The judge and the litigation client both give written informed consent to the representation despite the potential conflicts of interest. Even so, the judge is trying to keep the divorce quiet until after the upcoming elections, because this occurs in a state with elected judges. The judge therefore refuses to disclose to the parties in the personal injury case that counsel for one side is from the same firm as the lawyer representing the judge in his pending divorce. Neither the attorney nor his partner can reveal to opposing counsel in the personal injury case that their firm represents the judge, due to their duty of confidentiality. The judge believes he will be unbiased in the personal injury case, even though he is the client of a partner of one of the lawyers in the case, so the judge does not need to disqualify himself from the case. The Code of Judicial Ethics does require, however, that the judge disclose the representation to the litigants appearing before him, which the judge has refused to do at this time. Can the attorney continue representing the judge in his divorce?

a) Yes, if the judge and the litigation client both provided written, informed consent, then Attorney can continue with the representation.

b) Yes, because in a case where the judge does not need to disqualify himself, the lawyers would not need to withdraw merely because the judge refuses to disclose the representation to the other litigants appearing before the judge in the tort case.

c) No, because the lawyer must withdraw from the representation of the judge under these circumstances.

d) No, because the lawyer would need the judge's permission to withdraw from representing him in the divorce case, and the judge is unlikely to agree to that.

ABA Formal Op. 07-449

496. A President appointed an experienced circuit court judge to fill a vacancy on the U.S. Supreme Court. During the Senate confirmation hearings, a committee member asked the candidate if he supported a textualist or originalist approach to interpreting statutes and the Constitution. How should the candidate respond?

a) The candidate must refuse to discuss his jurisprudence or views on statutory or Constitutional interpretation, and he should not indicate how he would rule on a specific upcoming case.

b) The candidate may discuss his jurisprudence or views on statutory or Constitutional interpretation, but he should not indicate how he would rule on a specific upcoming case.

c) The candidate may declare his intention to decide specific upcoming cases on textualist or originalist grounds, as these positions merely reveal his judicial philosophy, and do not relate to the facts of a specific case.

d) The candidate must indicate a willingness to set aside his own views on textualism or originalism to decide each case based on justice and fairness.

497. A President appointed an experienced circuit court judge to fill a vacancy on the U.S. Supreme Court. During the Senate confirmation hearings, a committee member asked the candidate if he would overturn Roe v. Wade if he had an opportunity to do so, or if he would uphold Roe v. Wade due to stare decisis. How should the candidate respond?

a) The candidate should refuse to commit beforehand to ruling a specific way on any given case.

b) The candidate may answer that he would side with whatever most of the other justices on the Court decided.

c) The candidate may not promise to overturn a specific case but may promise to uphold stare decisis in any case.

d) The candidate should promise to ask the committee member himself how to decide the case whenever the situation arises.

498. A President appointed an experienced circuit court judge to fill a vacancy on the U.S. Supreme Court. During the Senate confirmation hearings, a committee member asked the candidate about his personal beliefs about abortion. The candidate explained that he thought women had a right to make decisions about their own bodies, and that a fetus is not a person under the law. Was it proper for the candidate to give this answer to the committee?

a) Yes, because the candidate has in effect promised to uphold stare decisis in a specific case that might come before the Court.

b) Yes, if he does not say how he would rule in any specific case, the candidate can discuss his views on legal and political issues.

c) No, judicial candidates must not announce their political or legal views on controversial subjects before taking the bench.

d) No, because the candidate should indicate a willingness to set aside his own views if the facts of a specific case merited a new exception to the doctrine announced in Roe v. Wade.

Republican Party of Minnesota v. White, 536 U.S. 765 (2002)

499. An attorney practices personal injury law in a small town. One of the judges who regularly presides over the attorney's cases is celebrating his twenty-fifth year on the bench, and the judge's friends and family have planned a banquet honoring the judge for reaching this milestone in his career. The organizers of the event invited many of the lawyers and judges in the area to the event. Many of the invitees are planning to bring a congratulations card or small congratulatory gift to the banquet. The personal injury attorney purchased a $250 silver-encased commemorative watch as a gift for the judge. The attorney presented it at the banquet, and the next day the judge made a public report of the gift. Was it improper for the attorney to give this watch to the judge?

a) No, because the judge is receiving many small gifts celebrating his twenty-fifth year on the bench, and this specific watch is unlikely to influence how the judge rules in future cases.

b) No, because the judge publicly reported the gift the very next day.

c) Yes, because lawyers cannot give any gift of significant value to a judge.

d) Yes, because watch cost more than $200.

CJC 3.13(c)(3)

500. An experienced litigator became a judge. In her previous litigation practice, she would regularly search online to learn more about the opposing party, opposing counsel, and even jurors. She sometimes found useful information on opposing parties' websites or on social media. Now serving as a judge, she visits the website of the corporate defendant in one of her cases, to learn more background about the company and its products and pricing. In this instance, the judge did not find any information on the company's website that seemed useful in understanding the issues in the pending case. The judge did not do any online research about the other party (the plaintiff) in the case. Was the judge's research proper?

a) Yes, because the judge is merely learning information that is available to the public through the company's official website.

b) Yes, because the Code of Judicial Conduct encourages judges to use modern research tools, such as the Internet, to reach more accurate or well-informed decisions in their cases.

c) No, because if a judge researches one party, fairness requires that the judge should do the same research about the other party.

d) No, because the Code of Judicial Conduct prohibits judges from conducting online research to gather information about a party or juror in a pending case, even if the research yields no useful information.

ANSWER KEY

Rule 1.7	Conflict of Interest

1. a
2. b
3. d
4. b
5. d
6. d
7. c
8. a
9. c
10. b
11. a
12. c
13. c
14. b
15. a
16. a
17. a
18. a
19. c
20. d
21. c
22. b
23. a
24. c
25. d
26. a
27. d
28. b
29. d

Rule 1.8	Conflicts - Specific Rules

30. a
31. b
32. c
33. b
34. d
35. d
36. a
37. d
38. d
39. a
40. b
41. d
42. c
43. b
44. b
45. b
46. a
47. b
48. b
49. d
50. d

Rule 1.9	Duties to Former Clients

51. b
52. d
53. b
54. a
55. c
56. d
57. c
58. d
59. a
60. d
61. c

Rule 1.10	Imputation of Conflicts

62. b
63. c
64. c
65. a
66. c
67. d
68. a
69. b
70. d
71. c
72. d
73. b
74. b
75. a
76. c
77. d
78. d

287. d
288. c
289. d
290. c
291. b
292. d
293. c
294. a
295. b
296. a
297. d
298. b
299. d
300. d
301. a
302. c
303. c
304. d
305. c
306. d
307. a
308. b
309. b
310. a
311. a
312. c
313. d
314. d
315. a
316. b
317. c
318. b
319. d

Work Product Doctrine

320. a
321. c
322. a
323. c
324. d
325. d
326. a
327. d

328. a
329. a
330. d
331. d
332. d
333. d

Rule 5.1   Responsibility of Partners
            & Supervisors

334. c
335. b
336. b
337. c
338. c
339. b

Rules 5.2   Responsibilities of a
             Subordinate Lawyer

340. c
341. b
342. c
343. b

Rule 5.3   Responsibilities
            Regarding Nonlawyer
            Assistants

344. b
345. a
346. b
347. b

Rule 5.4   Professional
            Independence

348. b
349. c
350. a
351. a
352. c
353. c
354. c

Rule 5.5   Unauthorized Practice &

Rule 4.4   Rights of Third Persons

        482. a
        483. d
        484. b

Rule 1.15   Safekeeping Property

        485. c
        486. a
        487. c
        488. b
        489. a
        490. a
        491. a
        492. d

Code of Judicial Conduct

        493. a
        494. d
        495. c
        496. b
        497. a
        498. b
        499. b
        500. d

Made in the USA
Coppell, TX
12 January 2020